Pragmatics in the History of English

How were *you* and *thou* used in Early Modern England? What were the typical ways of ordering others in Early Medieval England? How was the speech of others represented in the nineteenth-century novel? This volume answers these questions and more by providing an overview of the field of English historical pragmatics. Following introductory chapters which set out the scope of the field and address methods and challenges, core chapters focus on a range of topics, including pragmatic markers, speech and thought representation, politeness, speech acts, address terms, and register, genre, and style. Each chapter describes the object of study, defines essential terms and concepts, and discusses the methodologies used. Succinct and clear summaries of studies in the field are presented and are richly illustrated with corpus data. Presenting a comprehensive and accessible yet state-of-the-art introduction to the field, it is essential reading for both students and academic researchers.

LAUREL J. BRINTON is Professor Emerita of English Language at the University of British Columbia. Recent publications include *English Historical Linguistics* (2017) and *The Evolution of Pragmatic Markers in English* (2017). She serves as co-editor of *English Language and Linguistics*.

T0382140

Pragmatics in the History of English

Laurel J. Brinton

University of British Columbia

CAMBRIDGE
UNIVERSITY PRESS

Shaftesbury Road, Cambridge CB2 8EA, United Kingdom

One Liberty Plaza, 20th Floor, New York, NY 10006, USA

477 Williamstown Road, Port Melbourne, VIC 3207, Australia

314–321, 3rd Floor, Plot 3, Splendor Forum, Jasola District Centre,
New Delhi – 110025, India

103 Penang Road, #05–06/07, Visioncrest Commercial, Singapore 238467

Cambridge University Press is part of Cambridge University Press & Assessment,
a department of the University of Cambridge.

We share the University's mission to contribute to society through the pursuit of
education, learning and research at the highest international levels of excellence.

www.cambridge.org
Information on this title: www.cambridge.org/9781009322928

DOI: 10.1017/9781009322904

First published 2023

A catalogue record for this publication is available from the British Library.

*A Cataloging-in-Publication data record for this book is available from the
Library of Congress*

ISBN 978-1-009-32292-8 Hardback
ISBN 978-1-009-32287-4 Paperback

Contents

Figures

Tables

Preface

This volume is intended as an accessible and comprehensive overview of developments in one field of English historical linguistics, historical pragmatics. It presents the "state of the art" in the first quarter of the twenty-first century, describing the scope and nature of the field and bringing together a wide range of research in the area.

The text consists of two introductory chapters, six core chapters, and a concluding chapter. Each core chapter sets out to define the object of study (e.g., "What is a speech act?", "What is a pragmatic marker?" "What is an address term?", "What constitutes (im)politeness?", etc.). It then discusses methodologies used to study these phenomena and presents an overview of current studies in the field, providing a summary of existing scholarship, along with rich corpus data for illustration. Chapters end with a section on "Further Reading" and a series of self-testing "Exercises."

Chapter 1 introduces the field of historical pragmatics as an intersection between pragmatics and historical linguistics. Chapter 2 focuses on the subfields of historical pragmatics, on approaches within the field, on the levels studied, and on the challenges posed by the "bad data" problem. Chapter 3 examines the pathways of the development of pragmatic markers and processes of language change responsible for their development. Chapter 4 traces changes in the categories of speech and thought representation over time. Chapter 5 examines changes in politeness systems in English, such as the rise of deference politeness in Middle English and non-imposition politeness in Modern English. Chapter 6 discusses the difficulties of studying speech acts and presents a number of case studies of speech acts in the history of English. Chapter 7 is concerned with both pronominal and nominal terms of address, focusing on the honorific system of second-person pronouns in Medieval and Early Modern English. Chapter 8 provides a selective introduction to registers (news and religious discourse), genre (sermons, prayers, recipes, letters), and style (the shift from "oral" to "literate"). Chapter 9 summarizes the core chapters, focusing on challenges that have arisen in historical pragmatic study and successes that have been achieved. Present and future directions of future research in historical pragmatics are explored.

The volume is addressed to advanced level students (and teachers) who wish to gain an understanding of the concepts and topics of historical pragmatics and the nature of research undertaken in the field, including both methodology and data. But it will also prove useful to established scholars in allied areas who wish to have a comprehensive introduction to the field. For students, while general linguistic knowledge is assumed, no specialized knowledge of pragmatics is required.

I would like to express my gratitude to the reviewers of the book proposal and especially to the reviewer of the book manuscript for Cambridge University Press, whose meticulous reading of the text, with extensive, helpful, and insightful comments, led to improvements in both content and presentation. At Cambridge University Press, I would like to thank Andrew Winnard, who initially solicited the book, and Helen Barton, who carried though with the project; Isabel Collins provided invaluable assistance as did Laheba Alam. Sue Browning's expert eye in copy-editing caught many an inconsistency. Without the sabbatical year (2020–21) and pre-retirement research year (2022–23) provided by the University of British Columbia – not to mention forty-two years of a rich and rewarding work environment – this book could not have been completed. Thank you too to my graduate students in the fall of 2021, who read many chapters in draft form. I am grateful to Andreas H. Jucker, who supplied the data for Figures 6.3 and 6.4. Ralph Brands helped with many of the figures, and gave general computer and life support, as always.

Solutions to the self-testing exercises in Chapters 3–8 can be found online at www.cambridge.org/BrintonPragmatics.

Abbreviations

CED	*A Corpus of English Dialogues 1560–1760*
CEN	*The Corpus of English Novels*
CLMET3.0	*The Corpus of Late Modern English Texts, version 3.0*
CMEPV	*Corpus of Middle English Prose and Verse*
COCA	*The Corpus of Contemporary American English*
CoER	*Corpus of Early English Recipes*
COERP	*Corpus of English Religious Prose*
COHA	*The Corpus of Historical American English*
DOEC	*Dictionary of Old English Web Corpus*
ED	*English Drama*
EEBO	*Early English Books Online*
EModE	Early Modern English
(F)DS	(free) direct speech
(F)DT	(free) direct thought
FID	free indirect discourse
FTA	face-threatening act
HC	*The Helsinki Corpus of English Texts*
IFID	illocutionary-force-indicating device
IS	indirect speech
IT	indirect thought
LModE	Late Modern English
ME	Middle English
MED	*Middle English Dictionary*
Movies	*The Movie Corpus*
NI	internal narration
NRSA	narrative representation of speech act
NRTA	narrative representation of thought act
NT	narrative representation of thought
NV	narrative representation of voice

OE	Old English
OED	*Oxford English Dictionary*
OSS	*Open Source Shakespeare*
PDE	Present-day English
T/V	*tu/vos*

1   The Field of Historical Pragmatics

1.1   Introduction

This book focuses on the ways in which the study of pragmatics has been incorporated into the study of the history of language, resulting in a new field of study, "historical pragmatics." While any language can be studied using the methodology of historical pragmatics, this book focuses on its application to the English language.

The field of English historical linguistics has a long history, becoming institutionalized as an academic field in the nineteenth century in northern Europe and Britain and arising out of philology and comparative linguistics, though the study of the history of English obviously has a much longer history. The field of pragmatics became a proper subdiscipline within linguistics only in the 1970s and 1980s, growing out of "ordinary language" philosophy – such as the work of the Anglo-American philosophers J. L. Austin and John Searle, among others (Jucker 2012b). Various changes within both historical linguistics and pragmatics set the stage for the rise of historical pragmatics, the youngest of the three disciplines. Of course, like all such developments, there are precursors and earlier work, but the field itself did not take coherent shape until the mid-1990s with the publication of the edited volume, *Historical Pragmatics: Pragmatics in the developments in the history of English* (Jucker 1995) and my own book, *Pragmatic markers in English: Grammaticalization and discourse functions* (Brinton 1996). The *Journal of Historical Pragmatics* was founded in 2000, and by 2010, the field had reached such a state of maturity that it was possible to bring out a comprehensive (700+-page) handbook of *Historical pragmatics* (Jucker and Taavitsainen 2010), involving a range of international scholars working in areas as diverse as pragmatic markers, politeness, speech acts, and religious discourse. At this point, more descriptive work began to give way to "considerations of the underlying principles in the search for explanations to better understand language use in the past" (Taavitsainen 2012: 1458). Interestingly, scholars did not initially agree upon what to call the developing field. Suggested names included "New Philology" (Fleischman 1990), "pragmatic stylistics" (Sell 1985), "post-/interdisciplinary philology"

(Sell 1994), "historical discourse analysis" or "historical text linguistics" (Enkvist and Wårvik 1987: 222), and "diachronic textlinguistics" (Fries 1983). Yet it is one of the earliest names, "historical pragmatics" (Stein 1985) which ultimately gained acceptance.

This chapter introduces you to the field of historical pragmatics. After defining historical pragmatics, the chapter explores the two sides of the name – "historical" and "pragmatics," reviewing how changes in both historical linguistics and pragmatics enabled the development of historical pragmatics. A case study from historical pragmatics (pragmatic markers) is presented in order to illustrate the nature of the field. A final section compares historical pragmatics to related fields, including historical sociolinguistics and historical sociopragmatics.

1.2   Definition(s) of Historical Pragmatics

As a combination of pragmatics (the study of language in use) and historical linguistics (the study of language variation and change), historical pragmatics can be defined as the study of language in use as it varies within historical periods and over time. Historical pragmatics thus has a dual focus: it is the study of pragmatic phenomena in earlier stages of the language (its synchronic dimension) and well as the ways in which these phenomena develop and change over time (its diachronic dimension). This dual focus is clearly captured in Jucker and Taavitsainen's definition: for them, historical pragmatics is "the study of patterns of language use in the past and how such patterns developed in the course of time" (2013: 2). Other definitions likewise capture this dual perspective:

[T]he aim of historical pragmatics is to discover and describe patterns of past language use, how the patterns developed and how meaning was made, and what factors underlie both synchronic variation in past periods and changes in a diachronic perspective. (Jucker and Taavitsainen 2013: 32)

[A] field of study that wants to understand the patterns of intentional human interaction (as determined by the conditions of society) of earlier periods, the historical developments of these patterns, and the general principles underlying such developments. (Jucker 2008: 895)

In Chapter 2, §2.2 "The Scope of Historical Pragmatics" we look in more detail at these complementary sides of the field of historical pragmatics.

1.3   The Intersection of Historical Linguistics and Pragmatics

Existing at the intersection between historical linguistics and pragmatics, historical pragmatics takes from both fields: "Historical pragmatics inherits the interest in language change from historical linguistics, and the overarching concern in meaning-making practices derives from pragmatics" (Taavitsainen 2012: 1460). But the fields of linguistics and pragmatics were not obviously a good match, with differing views of fundamental matters such as the nature of language or the types of data relevant for study. Certain paradigmatic shifts in linguistics as well as adaptations in pragmatics had to occur before a union became possible: historical pragmatics is "the direct result both of the paradigm shifts in linguistics in general and the shifts within pragmatics" (Jucker 2012b: 510).

Within the generative paradigm dominant in the field of linguistics in the latter half of the twentieth century, historical studies did not hold a central place. But important changes occurred in linguistics in the last quarter of the century which brought the study of language variation and change to the forefront (see Traugott 2008: 207–210). As discussed by Taavitsainen and Jucker (2015; also Jucker 2012b; Jucker and Taavitsainen 2013: 6–9), these changes, or "turns," as summarized in Table 1.1, facilitated the rise of historical pragmatics.

First, the "pragmatic turn" represents the change from an understanding of language as an internalized system of "competence" to the view that we would better focus on "performance," language as it is used, often variably and imperfectly. This change moved pragmatics into the mainstream. According to Taavitsainen and Jucker (2015:4), "The pragmatic turn was the most important precondition for historical pragmatics to take off as an independent field of study." Second, in the "dispersive turn," the attention of linguists began to shift from "core" areas such as phonology, morphology, and syntax to more "peripheral" or colloquial phenomena such as idioms, pragmatic markers,

Table 1.1 *Changes in the field of linguistics underlying the rise of historical pragmatics (based on Taavitsainen and Jucker 2015)*

The "pragmatic turn"	from language as internalized competence to language as externalized performance
The "dispersive turn"	from a focus on core features to a focus on peripheral features of language
The "discursive turn"	from language as a stable, homogeneous system to language as a heterogeneous system, negotiated through usage
The "sociocultural turn"	from language as an autonomous system to language as a system embedded in the sociocultural context
The "diachronic turn"	from an emphasis on synchrony to an emphasis on diachrony
The "empirical turn"	from findings about language based on native speaker intuition to findings based on empirical investigation
The "digital turn"	from qualitative analysis to quantitative analysis based on corpus findings

hesitation markers, discourse planners, turn-takers, and so on. Third, the change in understanding from language as a fixed and homogeneous system to language as a more heterogeneous system, with meanings not inherent but agreed upon through usage, is the "discursive turn." This changing view also recognizes the fuzziness of categories (e.g., between interjection, conversational routine, hesitation marker, and pragmatic marker; see Chapter 3, §3.2). Fourth, rather than viewing language as an independent system of systematic rules and conventions, language is understood as a product of the societal and cultural context and is hence dynamic and changing, often shaped by sociolinguistic factors such as age, gender, and class. This is the "sociocultural turn." Fifth, the "diachronic turn" led from an exclusive focus on the contemporary state of the language to a renewed interest in historical stages of the language and to processes of language variation and change. Sixth, the "empirical turn" represents a change in methodology: research into language rests on the empirical investigation of actual language use rather than on the intuitions of native speakers about invented examples. We see the empirical emphasis in fields such as sociolinguistics and conversation and discourse analysis, which involve the analysis of natural data. Historical linguistics, which has no access to native speaker intuition, has, of course, always relied upon textual data, but increasingly there has been an interest in "speech-related" data, as is discussed in Chapter 2, §2.5 "The 'Bad Data' Problem." Finally, the "digital turn" is the direct result of the development of computer corpora, which have facilitated the collection of large quantities of data and allowed linguists to undertake increasingly more sophisticated quantitative studies. However, as we will see (Chapter 2, §2.6 "Diachronic Corpus Pragmatics"), not all aspects of pragmatics, such as speech acts or politeness, are easily studied using corpora. The changes in linguistics detailed here go hand-in-hand with developments in the field of pragmatics, which we turn to next.

Pragmatics is the study of the contextualized use of language, focusing on how language is shaped by the situation of the verbal interaction, the interlocutors, and/or the specific communicative purposes at play: "Pragmatics studies the use of language in human communication as determined by the conditions of society" (Mey 2001: 6; italics removed). There are two main approaches to pragmatics, designated by the locations of their practitioners, namely, the "Anglo-American" approach and the "European Continental" approach (see Huang 2010, 2017a). We will see these reflected in the subfields of historical pragmatics.

The Anglo-American (or cognitive-philosophical) tradition arises out of philosophy of language and is quite narrowly circumscribed. It focuses on implicature, presupposition, deixis, reference, speech acts, and conversation analysis, often depending on invented data and native speaker intuition. It is the "systematic study of meaning by virtue of, or dependent on, the use of language" (Huang 2017a: 2). In this approach, pragmatics is a core component of language, like phonology, morphology, or syntax. It is seen as "micro-pragmatics" because of its focus on linguistic forms. "Diachronic pragmatics," a subfield of historical pragmatics which we discuss in Chapter 2, embodies this micro focus, in that it concentrates "on the interface between a linguistic structure and its communicative use across different historical stages of the same language" (Huang 2017a: 11).

The European Continental (or sociocultural-interactional) tradition takes a much broader cultural and social perspective. It embodies a functional (cognitive, social, cultural) perspective on the core linguistic components and broader areas of linguistics and beyond, such as sociolinguistics, psycholinguistics, or discourse analysis and other social sciences (Huang 2017a: 3). For this reason, it is dubbed the "perspective approach." The European Continental tradition focuses on the cognitive or social and/or cultural contexts in which pragmatic meanings originate. While this type of pragmatics is perhaps truer to the origins of the discipline, it may seem so broad as to appear to be a "study of 'everything'" (Huang 2010: 14–15). With this expansive scope, the European Continental approach is "macro-pragmatics." We will see in Chapter 2, §2.2 that the subfield of historical pragmatics known as "historical pragmatics (proper)," understood as the study of the contextual features of historical texts at a particular time, takes a macro perspective, as does "historical socio-pragmatics" (see below, §1.5).

These delineations within the field of pragmatics remain discernible today, though increasingly there are studies which bridge the divide. But both approaches have merit: "Whereas the strength of the Anglo-American branch lies mainly in theory, and philosophical, cognitive, and formal pragmatics, the Continental tradition has much to offer in empirical work, and socio- (or societal), (cross- or inter-) cultural, and interlanguage pragmatics, to mention just a few examples" (Huang 2010: 15; bolding removed).

The rise of historical pragmatics as a discipline depended on two developments within the field of pragmatics. The first was the expansion of pragmatics to include an ever increasing variety of pragmatic phenomena as legitimate sources of study; these include pragmatic forms (pragmatic markers, address terms); interactional pragmatics (speech acts, (im)politeness, speech representation); and domains of discourse (scientific and medical discourse, newspapers, religious discourse, courtroom discourse, literary discourse, public and private correspondence). A second development was a change in the types of language data serving as the source for pragmatic study. Traditionally, pragmatics had relied either on invented or collected data; the collected data consisted primarily of (transcribed) oral conversations. Obviously, neither type of data is available for historical study. Conversational data do not exist for historical periods of the language, though it is possible to find "speech-related" data, such as witness depositions, trial transcripts, or fictional dialogue, and written colloquial data, such as personal letters, from at least Early Modern English onwards. In order for historical pragmatics to take root, it is necessary to recognize not just speech or speech-related data as a legitimate subject of investigation, but also purely written data, which constitute the majority of surviving historical documents: Written data are not simply imperfect approximations of the "real thing" (oral data), but "can be understood as communicative manifestations in their own right, and as such they are amenable to pragmatic analysis" (Jacobs and Jucker 1995: 9). The "communicative view," as Jucker and Taavitsainen designate it, "holds that both spoken and written language are forms of communication produced by speakers/writers for target audiences with communicative intentions, and language is always produced with situational constraints" (2013: 25). Hand-in-hand with this acceptance of written data as a source of pragmatic study comes a more nuanced view in which a clear-cut dichotomy between spoken and written language breaks down. Using the concepts of "language of immediacy" and "language of distance," Jucker and Taavitsainen show that these categories cut across the oral/written divide. Language of immediacy contains written documents, such as diaries, private letters, and emails as well as spoken data (i.e., face-to-face conversation). Dramatic discourse, fictional dialogue, model conversations in language-learning texts are representations of oral discourse, but they exist only in written form. Language of distance likewise contains written documents, such as academic prose or legal writing, as well as spoken data, such as public lectures or sermons, which, though written, are intended for oral delivery, and trial transcripts, depositions, and parliamentary proceedings, which are transcriptions of spoken (often rather formal) discourse (see Jucker and Taavitsainen 2013: 20–25). Thus, we see that discourse exists on a continuum from written to oral, all of which – given that we acknowledge their complexities – may serve as a sources for pragmatic study. We come back to the question of the data sources of historical pragmatics in Chapter 2, §2.5 "The 'Bad Data' Problem."

1.4   A Case Study: Pragmatic Markers

The case study presented here is intended to illustrate how historical pragmatics is practiced. The study of pragmatic markers, a well-known pragmatic phenomenon, has constituted a significant part of historical pragmatics since its inception. The methodology used in the study of pragmatic markers also exemplifies important approaches (form-to-function, diachronic corpus pragmatics) which we take up in Chapter 2. As is often the direction of study, we begin by looking at pragmatic markers in modern English and then turn our attention to the past. Pragmatic markers are treated in detail in Chapter 3.

In Present-day English (PDE), especially in informal oral conversation, one frequently encounters words and fixed phrases or clauses that appear to be semantically rather empty. They are syntactically independent of the sentence to which they are attached, and hence are moveable and appear to be omissible. Studies of contemporary spoken discourse have shown these forms to be pragmatically rich, providing information about the nature of the surrounding discourse, the speaker's subjective opinions, and/or the relation between the speaker and the hearer. They are known as "discourse markers," or "pragmatic markers." Table 1.2 provides some examples from the *Corpus of Contemporary American English* (COCA) of single-word (*like, well, so, now*), phrasal (*and stuff, all right, of course, kind of, by the way*), and reduced clausal (*you know, you see, I mean, let's see, I guess*) pragmatic markers.

The forms shown in Table 1.2 meet the definition of pragmatic markers. They are:

(a) invariable expressions which are (b) semantically and syntactically independent from their environment, (c) set off prosodically from the rest of the utterance in some way, and (d) their function is metatextual, relating a text to the situation of discourse and serving the organization of texts, the attitudes of the speaker, and/ or speaker–hearer interaction. (Heine et al. 2021: 6)

Pragmatic markers are marginal in word class, though in their independence, they show an affinity to interjections (and are often described as such in dictionaries). They may be identical in form to adverbs, conjunctions, or prepositions (from which they are assumed to derive historically), as in the case of *now, so,* and *like* in Table 1.2, though they differ in position and function. Typically, pragmatic markers exist outside the syntactic structure, in a separate intonation group, and as a consequence are moveable. While most often occurring in sentence-initial position, they are less often found sentence-medial or final. They are typically fixed in form; thus, only *I mean*, but not *I am*

Table 1.2 *Examples of pragmatic markers from COCA*

but I could never **like** memorize all those words.	(1998 COCA: FIC)
Well, you know, it's also one of the things I love about, **you know**, where I'm at in my life and my career.	(2010 COCA: SPOK)
Like his grandparents get to take him to the zoo **and stuff.**	(2011 COCA: SPOK)
All right. **Now, you see**, you mix that together.	(2007 COCA: SPOK)
Anyway, by the way, we have that extra feature on our Web site now	(2008 COCA: SPOK)
Oh, let's see. So, of course, my father wanted me to go to college,	(2019 COCA: SPOK)
So, I mean, who knows, **you know**, he's putting words in his mouth.	(2019 COCA: SPOK)
I guess, kind of, I've been married since I was 21	(2006 COCA: SPOK)

meaning or *I really mean* or *I meant*, can function as a pragmatic marker. However, especially the phrasal and clausal forms may allow some degree of variability, such as *and stuff / and other stuff / and all that stuff / and all this stuff / and lots of stuff.* Significantly, they lack semantic content, with their original literal meaning bleached or absent. Thus, *you know* usually has little to do with what the addressee has cognition of, and may not even be directed at a specific addressee. The presence of pragmatic markers in a discourse is syntactically optional, but may be pragmatically necessary in order to produce natural, fully communicatively comprehensible oral discourse.

Pragmatic markers do not contribute to the syntax or semantics of the sentence to which they are attached but rather function at a more global scope, contributing on the level of the text or on the level of the speaker–hearer. "Textual" functions are related to how the discourse or exchange is organized. Thus, introducing, shifting, or resuming a topic, denoting what is new and old information, marking a new episode, distinguishing between foregrounded and backgrounded information, and so on, can all be achieved by the use of pragmatic markers. In a conversational exchange, pragmatic markers can also initiate or close a discourse, claim the attention of the hearer, and acquire, hold, or relinquish the floor. On the "interpersonal" level, pragmatic markers may be used by the speaker subjectively to express a response or reaction to the preceding or following discourse, denote an attitude, signal understanding or continued attention, or hedge an opinion. They may also function intersubjectively to effect cooperation or sharing, show intimacy, confirm shared assumptions, check on understanding, request confirmation, express deference, or save face (politeness). The range of pragmatic functions is vast, and individual pragmatic markers are often multifunctional.

For the historical pragmaticist, the question is whether pragmatic markers existed (or can be found) in earlier stages of the language, where records of naturally occurring oral discourse are absent or rare and fictional representations of speech may be highly stylized. Even with historical trial transcripts and depositions, which might be thought to approximate real oral discourse, there is the added possibility that pragmatic forms might be edited out by scribes, transcribers, or copyists. This is the "bad data" problem of historical pragmatics that we discuss in greater detail in Chapter 2.

Scholars have often noted the existence of what Longacre (1976) calls "mystery particles" in earlier English; these are semantically empty and grammatically unnecessary forms. Traditionally they are seen as defects of style, or evidence of a more paratactic, primitive, or simply clumsy style. In a more positive light, they may be seen as

(a) metrical expedients used to add syllables to a line of verse;
(b) markers of emphasis, intensity, or vividness; or
(c) residues from an earlier period of transmission in which information was structured as it is in oral discourse.

The presence of "mystery particles" in earlier texts, forms which resemble pragmatic markers in important ways, raises a series of questions: Do these forms function like pragmatic markers in Present-day English? More generally, have language users always expressed pragmatic functions? If so, what forms have they used, what factors influence their use, and how has the inventory of such forms changed over time? How do such forms develop? Why are some forms lost and others preserved?

In examples, (1) to (3), I provide some examples of "mystery particles" in Old English (OE), Middle English (ME), and Early Modern English (EModE), respectively. Because they are semantically bleached or empty, they are often difficult to translate into PDE, but approached from a historical pragmatic perspective, we can see that these forms serve important pragmatic functions. *Ða* (and lower-case *þa*) 'then' is a ubiquitous form in OE prose, often as in example (1a) beginning sequential sentences. The 'then ... then ... then ... ' structure, traditionally dismissed as a sign of a primitive paratactic style, has undergone significant reassessment. Enkvist (1986) was the first to observe that *þa* "does its main job or jobs at text and discourse level" (301). He argues that *þa* is a marker of foregrounded action, that is, actions which advance the plot of the story. It may also act as a foreground "dramatizer," allowing the narrator to bring to the fore a stative (and otherwise backgrounded) element. Enkvist identifies a number of other discourse functions, such as sequencer of events, peak marker, and narrative segmenter. Lenker (2000) shows that OE *witodlice*, an adverb meaning 'certainly', occurs in initial position outside the syntactic structure; here its literal meaning is bleached, as in (1b). Like *þa*, *witodlice* does discourse work, serving to introduce new episodes, at points where there is a change in time, location, participants, action sequence, and so on; that is, it serves as a boundary marker. OE *hwæt þa*, literally meaning 'what then', has caused translators difficulties, being rendered as 'so then', 'lo then', 'well then', 'moreover', 'thereupon', 'whereupon', 'behold', an so on. In Brinton (1996: 193–197, 2017c: 57–60), I argue that *hwæt þa* indicates a causal relation between the preceding event and the following event, or as in the case of (1c), signals that the following event is understood as a conclusion from the preceding event. Thus, like *so* in Present-day English, it may denote 'result' (*John is sick, so he is at home*) or function like "inferential *so*" (*John's lights are on, so he is at home*; that is, 'so I infer that he is at home', not *'as a result he is at home').

(1)   a.   **Þa** for he norþryhte be þæm lande; let him ealne weg þæt weste land on
             ðæt steorbord 7 þa widsæ on ðæt bæcbord þrie dages. **Ða** wæs he swa feor
             norþ swa þa hwælhuntan firrest faraþ. **Ða** for he þa giet norþryhte swa feor
             swa he meahte on þæm oþrum þrim dagum gesiglan. (Or 1 81–83;
             DOEC[1])

---

[1] Quotations from Old English in this book follow the *Dictionary of Old English Web Corpus* (DOEC) and the textual abbreviations used there.

'Then he travelled northwards along the coast; keeping all the way the waste land on the starboard and the open sea on the portside for three days. Then he was as far north as the whale hunters go furthest. Then he travelled still northwards as far as he could sail in another three days' (translation of Enkvist and Wårvik 1987: 234)

b. **Witodlice** betwux þæs heortes hornum glitenode gelicnys þære halgan Cristes rode breohtre þonne sunnan leoma, (LS 8 [Eust] 41; DOEC; Lenker 2000: 240)

'Behold, between the hart's horn glittered the likeness of Christ's holy rood, brighter than the sun's beam' (Walter Skeat's translation)

c. Ða sende Eugenia þa twægen halgan, Protum and Iacinctum to ðam hæðenen mædene. **Hwæt þa** Basilla mid blysse hi underfæng, and … (ÆLS [Eugenia] 102–3; DOEC; Brinton 2017b: 59)

'Then Eugenia sent the two saints, Protus and Jacinctus, to the heathen maid. What then Basilla received them with joy and … '

In (2a), ME *gan*, related to PDE *began* (from OE *biginnan*), cannot be translated literally. As punctual actions, awaking and noticing do not allow a breakdown into stages: one can 'awake' and 'notice' but not *'begin to awake' or *'begin to notice'. The occurrence of *gan* in these semantically incompatible contexts and its frequency in ME verse have led scholars to suggest that it is a meaningless tense carrier often employed as a metrical expedient, allowing the infinitive to appear in end position. An analysis of the position of *gan* in the narrative structure of Chaucer's *Troilus and Criseyde*, however, points to a discourse-structuring function as well as an evaluative function: it marks significant transitions or junctures in the narrative plot and denotes structurally significant transitions, or "pivotal events," in the plot sequence (Brinton 1996: 75–78). ME *anon* literally means 'at once, immediately, instantly', but its repetition in sequential sentences in (2b) suggests that it no longer denotes a sense of urgency. Rather, it marks more foregrounded or plot-advancing actions that are causally, thematically, or humanly important in the context of the narrative; it emphasizes the sequence of events (Brinton 1996: 97–101). Sentence-final *than* in (2c) does not seem to be functioning as an adverb of time meaning 'then'. Instead, it seems to be a signal for the hearer to interpret the preceding clause as a conditional *if*-clause ('if you are clean') and the clause to which it attaches as the conclusion ('then God will make you holy') (Haselow 2012).

(2)   a. And **gan** awake, and wente hire out to pisse,/ And cam agayn, and **gan** hir cradel mysse (1387 Chaucer, *Canterbury Tales*, A.Rv. 4215–16; Brinton 1996: 68)[2]

---

[2]   Quotations from Chaucer in this book follow Benson (1986). The dating of the *Canterbury Tales* is difficult to determine (see Benson 1986: xxix); I will use the approximate date of 1387.

'And she awoke and went out to piss and came inside again and noticed her cradle missing'

b. And **anone** he harde a grete noyse and a grete cry as all the fyndys of helle had been aboute hym . . . And than he toke hys armys and hys horse and set hym on hys way. And **anone** he herde a clocke smyte on hys ryght honde, and thydir he cam to an abbay which was closed with hyghe wallis, and there was he lette in. And **anone** they supposed that he was one of the knyghtes of the Rounde Table that was in the queste of the Sankgreall, so they led hym into a chambir and unarmed hym. (1469 Malory, *Morte d'Arthur* 16, 12, 966, 9–10, 15–21; Brinton 1996: 100)

'And at once he heard a great noise and a great cry as if all the fiends of hell had been about him . . . And then he took his arms and his horse and went on his way. And at once he heard a clock strike on his right side and thither came to an abbey that was enclosed by high walls, and he let himself in. And at once they supposed that he was one of the knights of the Round Table that was in quest of the Sangreal, so they led him into a chamber and unarmed him'

c. Therfore be clene, bothe wife and man,/ This is my reed; God will make in yow haly **than** (1463–1477 *York Plays* 21; Haselow 2012: 164)

'Therefore be clean, both wife and man, this is my advice; God will make you holy then'

In (3) you will find EModE examples, which, like the OE and ME examples given above, cannot be understood literally. *Why* in (3a) is not functioning as an interrogative adverb of cause. It is set off from the sentence and serves as an expression of the attorney's feelings of impatience or perhaps annoyance at the less than accurate testimony given by the witness. In (3b) parenthetical *it seems* functions as it does in Present-day English as a subjective marker of the speaker's doubt or uncertainty. It may also serve as a means of softening the opinion expressed and thus respecting the perhaps differing views of the addressee; in this regard, it functions as a politeness marker. Parenthetical *if you will* in (3c) does not literally ask for the speaker's permission 'if you are disposed or willing to consent to'. While it still expresses concern for the addressee's opinion, its meaning is pragmatic or metalinguistic, 'if you are willing to call it that' (i.e., an honorable murder).

(3)   a. Mr. Cambridge: His neck was dislocated, Sir.
        Mr. Att[orney] G[eneral]: **Why,** that is broken. (1678 The Tryals of Robert Green, Henry Berry and Lawrence Hill; Lutzky 2012a: 197)
        b. In our Protestant Almanacks, **it seems**, we give another Bishop place (1685 Trial of Titus Oates; López-Couso and Méndez-Naya 2014: 196)
        c. Why any thing:/ An honourable murderer, **if you will**;/ For nought I did in hate but all in honour. (1603–4 *Othello* V.ii; *Open Source Shakespeare* [OSS]; Brinton 2008: 170)[3]

---

[3] Quotations from Shakespeare in this book are taken from *Open Source Shakespeare* (OSS), which follows the Globe Shakespeare text: www.opensourceshakespeare.org.

How do the forms exemplified in (1) to (3) come to acquire their pragmatic functions (and lose their semantic content)? This question represents the diachronic focus of historical pragmatics and will be examined in detail in Chapter 3.

What these examples do show us is that pragmatic markers are intrinsically quite transitory; many have been lost, such as OE *þa*, *witodlice*, *hwæt þa*, or ME *anon*, *gan*. There may be many reasons for the loss of pragmatic markers. Although not originally a metrical expedient, ME *gan* may have been coopted as such and thus gradually have lost its discourse-structuring meaning. ME *anon* seems to have become stylistically stigmatized – as is common for pragmatic markers in general – and been relegated to playful use: you could jokingly say to your friend "until me meet anon." (We might, for example, predict the same fate for a frequent, but highly stigmatized pragmatic marker in Present-day English, *like*.) Other pragmatic markers which once had general use seem to have become confined to specialized registers, such as *to wit*, now primarily used in legal writing. *What*, which was a common pragmatic marker in Old English (we will look at this in more detail in Chapter 3, §3.4), became functionally overextended (as an interrogative adjective, adverb, conjunction, and noun) and thus was lost as a pragmatic marker. The form of some pragmatic markers may have led to their demise; thus, *as it were*, is now relatively infrequent, possibly because of the subjunctive verb form *were* (again described in more detail in Chapter 3, §3.4). Finally, I have also argued (see Brinton 1996) that the change from an oral to a literate narrative structure led to the loss of some pragmatic markers, as when the ME episode boundary marker *then it bifel that* 'then it happened that' was replaced by backgrounded *when*-clauses. (You are probably familiar with *then it happened that* from biblical language.)

At the same time, some pragmatic markers have been preserved over long periods of time. The EModE pragmatic markers exemplified in (3), namely *why*, *it seems*, and *if you will*, have survived to the present day. Even forms that can be traced back to Old English, such as appositional *(that is) to say*, or to Middle English, such as *I guess*, *I think*, and *you know*, are still found as pragmatic markers in Present-day English. What seems important is that despite sometimes significant changes in form, there is a continuity of pragmatic functions over time. Speakers will always have the need to organize their discourse, to express their subjective opinions, to hedge their opinions, to express common ground with their interlocutors, to be (im)polite to their addressees, and all of the many functions that seem most conveniently expressed by the short, formalized, and fixed expressions we know of as pragmatic markers.

1.5 Related Fields

Related to, and overlapping in part with, historical pragmatics are two other fields of study: historical sociolinguistics (or sociohistorical linguistics) and historical sociopragmatics.

Historical sociolinguistics has grown out of contemporary work in sociolinguistics, which studies the extralinguistic determinants of language use, including socioeconomic class, age, gender, group membership (social networks), register, and style. Pioneering work in this field began in the 1970s, with recorded (and transcribed) interviews with informants used as the primary source of naturally occurring (oral) data (often complemented by other techniques of data collection such as questionnaires or discourse completion tasks).

The starting point of sociolinguistic studies is the "linguistic variable," a set of different ways of saying the same thing. For example, in telling a friend about your departure from a party, you can say *I must leave now*, *I have to leave now*, *I've got to leave now*, *I gotta leave now*, or *I need to leave now*, but which variant you use is likely determined by the context of use, your age and gender, your relationship to your interlocutor, and so on. Variables exist on all linguistic levels – phonological, morphological, syntactic, semantic, and discoursal. The use of a particular variant by an individual is usually not categorical but varies in degree. Studies have attempted to determine the extent to which the choice among variants and their relative frequency are determined by extralinguistic factors or perhaps by purely linguistic factors. The choice of variant can be either a matter of deliberate choice ("from above" the level of consciousness) or not ("from below" the level of consciousness). It can also be influenced by prestige forms, where lower-middle-class speakers, for example, adopt the more formal speech forms of upper-middle-class speakers (again, change from above), or it can be a case of speakers adopting the speech forms of lower or working-class speakers, usually as a matter of in-group identity (again, change from below).

Sociolinguistic studies often find that one variable seems to be displacing another variable, thus indicative of a "change in progress," a change that we can actually witness taking place. This is determined by a process called an "apparent-time" study, where age is used as a proxy for change over time as the use of variables exists in different proportions in different age groups. New/incoming linguistic forms are found to be more common with younger speakers and older/outgoing forms with older speakers. As younger speakers age, the forms they use will ultimately displace the forms that their parents used. (This assumes that one's language does not change over one's lifetime, which may not be entirely correct.) An important finding of these sociolinguistic studies has been that change from above is more common in women than in men and that (young) females are often the prime agents of change. Thus, contemporary sociolinguists are studying "change," but in a very circumscribed time frame, the present (sometimes extended backward from the present into the nineteenth century using archives of oral recordings).

In contrast, historical sociolinguists attempt to study change over long stretches of time and in periods divorced from the present. Historical socio-linguistics assumes the "Uniformitarian Principle" – that is, the principle that if linguistic forces are known to operate today, then they must have operated in the past. Therefore, if variables exist today, they must have existed in the past, and language change in the past must have been influenced by a set of social factors similar to those found in Present-Day English. In contrast to apparent-time studies, historical sociolinguistics undertakes "real-time stud-ies" involving change over time and considers how change is influenced by a range of extralinguistic factors: "those related to individual language users (e.g., gender, age, class/rank/status), those related to communities (e.g., social networks, discourse communities, communities of practice), and those that pertain to specific social contexts and situations)" (Grund 2017b: 226). Studies of this sort pose considerable difficulties. In addition to the lack of relevant conversational data from the past (the "bad data" problem, see Chapter 2, §2.5), information on the social characteristics of speakers is often fragmentary or nonexistent, and the social conditions of the past may have been considerably different from those of the present. For example, the concept of "socioeconomic class" is inappropriate before the present age, and it is necessary to use available social and historical information to reconstruct concepts of rank or status that shaped social stratification in historical contexts. Even the concept of gender, as Grund points out (2017b: 227–228), is not entirely straightforward as we must take into consideration the social standing, education, and expectations of men and women in the past, which differ significantly from the present.

Historical sociolinguistic study in Old English and Middle English is restricted, due to limited data and knowledge of the extralinguistic, social, and situational factors at work, but it is not impossible if a less strict view of sociolinguistics is adopted. Opportunities and data for sociohistorical study open up in the Early Modern period. Increased literacy, the existence of private correspondence (especially letters), and a much wider range of other "speech-related" texts (such as trial transcripts, witness depositions, wills, business records, newspapers, and dramatic and fictional dialogue) allow for more accurate information about the social factors underlying language use and change. Historical sociolinguistics has revealed a rich and rewarding area of study. Many of the findings of modern sociolinguistics have been confirmed in the historical context. For example, the replacement of nominative *ye* by objective *you* between the first half of the sixteenth century and the beginning of the seventeenth century, proceeding outwards from London, was promoted by upper-class usage and hence a change from above (Nevalainen and Raumolin-Brunberg 2003). More broadly, woman were the leaders in eleven out of the fourteen changes investigated. Women tended to favor new, standard, and "supralocal" forms, while men tended to prefer nonstandard and "local" forms (Nevalainen 2006b: 360–361).

In the course of this book, you will see that it is not possible to disentangle historical sociolinguistics and historical pragmatics. Since historical pragmatics focuses on language use (including the speaker and addressee and relation between them), it is inevitable that social factors may play a role in pragmatic variation and change.

Historical sociopragmatics is closely aligned to historical pragmatics. The concept of "sociopragmatics" was first introduced by Leech (1983: 10–11), who divided general pragmatics into "pragmalinguistics," the "more linguistic end of pragmatics," closely related to grammar, and "sociopragmatics," which is concerned with "the more 'local' conditions on language use" and closely related to sociology. Sociopragmatics evolves from the European Continental approach to pragmatics, as discussed above, and from macro- and sociologically oriented perspectives. Historical sociopragmatics is concerned with how language use is determined by the sociohistorical context of a period in the past (its synchronic aspect), and it is also concerned with how changes in the sociohistorical context over time lead to differences in language use (its diachronic aspect). Any aspect of the context can shape the functions and forms of language used. Historical sociopragmatics is defined by Culpeper (2009: 182) as follows: it "concerns itself with any interaction between specific aspects of social context and particular historical language use that leads to pragmatic meaning." Hence, its focus is not on individual linguistic forms but more on the social, cultural, and historical contexts that determine language use. It thus requires extensive study of primary sources on the social and cultural conditions of historical periods. While a typical historical pragmatics study might trace how the forms expressing a particular speech act (e.g., apologizing) have changed over time, a typical historical sociopragmatic study would focus on how a speech act function has changed over time in response to changing social and historical conditions, with resulting changes in the forms employed. A recent sociopragmatic study is Grund's (2021b) examination of stance in the records of the Salem witch trials. Here he is interested not only in how stance is expressed in the records but how stance is embedded in a particular historical community, revealing members' identities, relations, aspirations, and so on. That is, a study of stance in these documents tells us about the "connections between language use and community construction and community roles" (3).

1.6   Chapter Summary

This chapter covered the following topics:
- the definition of historical pragmatics, with its dual focus on the study of pragmatic phenomena in earlier stages of a language (its synchronic dimension) and the study of ways in which pragmatic phenomena change and develop over time (its diachronic dimension);
- the intersection of historical linguistic and pragmatics, as a result of both paradigmatic changes in the field of historical linguistics (the pragmatic, dispersive, discursive, sociocultural, diachronic, and empirical turns) and a convergence of the "micro" and "macro" fields of pragmatics (i.e., of the cognitive-philosophical and the sociocultural-interactional traditions):
  - with recognition of an increasing variety of pragmatic features as legitimate sources of study; and
  - with adoption of a "communicative view" recognizing not just speech and speech-related texts as sources of pragmatic study but also written texts.
- a case study of pragmatic markers, exemplifying the methodology of historical pragmatics (see further Chapter 3):
  - starting from the characteristics of pragmatic markers in Present-day English; and
  - turning to "mystery particles" in Old English (*þa*, *witodlice*, *hwæt þa*), Middle English (*gan*, *anon*, *than*), and Early Modern English (*why*, *it seems*, *if you will*), all of which can be shown to have pragmatic (subjective, text-structuring, metalinguistic) functions.
- a description of two related fields:
  - historical sociolinguistics, which studies historical variation and change (including pragmatic change) as motivated by extralinguistic factors (e.g., age, gender, rank, or social class); and
  - historical sociopragmatics, which studies how language use is determined by the sociohistorical context of a period in the past (its synchronic aspect) and how changes in the sociohistorical context over time lead to differences in language use (its diachronic aspect).

1.7   Further Reading

For a short history of English historical linguistics, see Section XI "History of English historical linguistics" in Bergs and Brinton (2012b). Jucker (2012b) provides a brief history of pragmatics.

Numerous textbooks of historical linguistics exist; a good one is Campbell (2021). Likewise, there is a large number of introductory textbooks of pragmatics. For the Anglo-American perspective, see, for example, Cummins (2019); Mey (2001) provides the broader Continental European perspective.

The pragmatics encyclopedia (Cummings 2010) and *The Oxford handbook of pragmatics* (Huang 2017b) provide good overviews of the field. On scholarship in the field of pragmatics, see the *Bibliography of pragmatics online*,[4] an open access, wiki-style resource, as well as the curated *Handbook of pragmatics online*, edited by Jan-Ola Östman and Jef Verschueren.[5] For a good introduction to historical sociolinguistics, see Grund (2017b). *The handbook of historical sociolinguistics* (Hernández-Campoy and Conde-Silvestre 2012) contains a collection of papers illustrating the scope of the field. See also the *Journal of Historical Sociolinguistics*, published since 2015, and the Historical Sociolinguistics Network.[6] A ground-breaking work in the field of historical sociolinguistics is Nevalainen and Raumolin-Brunberg (2003). On sociopragmatics, see Culpeper's introduction (2009); his edited collection of articles (2011a) illustrates the range of the field. Archer (2005) is a book-length sociopragmatic study.

On pragmatic markers, see Chapter 3 and further reading suggested there. On OE *þa*, one of the earliest and most extensively studied pragmatic markers in the history of English, see Wårvik's comprehensive account (2013).

---

[4] www.benjamins.com/online/bop   [5] www.benjamins/online/hop   [6] HiSoN; https://hison.org

2   Historical Pragmatics
Scope, Methods, Challenges

2.1   Introduction

The field of historical pragmatics is quite wide-ranging, with a number of subfields. After discussing the scope of historical pragmatics and its three traditionally recognized subfields, this chapter moves on to a description of the two common approaches to historical pragmatics, form-to-function and function-to-form. These approaches may be applied to a range of pragmatic units, including expressions, utterances, and genres/domains of discourse. A serious challenge for the discipline of historical pragmatics – what has been called the "bad data" problem – is described. We will see that in large part this challenge has been met through the "digital turn" in pragmatics, or, more specifically, diachronic corpus pragmatics and corpus annotation.

2.2   The Scope of Historical Pragmatics

The field of historical pragmatics was initially divided into three subfields by Jacobs and Jucker in 1995 in the introduction to their ground-breaking volume. While these subfields have been differently named and differently understood over the years, I retain their three-way distinction as it is still useful today. I recognize, however, that the dividing lines among the subfields may be difficult to delimit. As we will see, the first two involve adding a historical or diachronic dimension to pragmatics, while the third involves adding a pragmatic dimension to historical linguistics.

The first subfield is what Jacobs and Jucker call "pragmaphilology"; this is similar to the name "New Philology" originally applied to the entire field. I will call it "historical pragmatics (proper)." It describes the pragmatic aspects of a historical text or period. According to Jacobs and Jucker (1995: 11), these aspects include, among other things, the addressee/addresser and their social and personal relationships, the physical/sociohistorical setting of the text, the aims or communicative intentions of the addresser, and the goals of the text. Studying these aspects requires a thorough knowledge of the (socio)historical contexts in which the text is produced. For this reason, it has been seen as the "macro" aspect of historical pragmatics (Arnovick 1999: 8; Culpeper 2010: 189).

Understood somewhat more narrowly, historical pragmatics proper focuses on discourse-pragmatic features at a particular period of time. It is thus "historical" but not "diachronic," and essentially synchronic in its approach. Discourse-pragmatic features which might be studied here include words, phrases, and clauses of high frequency but low semantic content (i.e., pragmatic markers, interjections, address forms, comment clauses, deictics, topic and focus markers), tense and aspect forms used in "non-grammatical" ways (the "historical present" used for narrative segmentation and internal evaluation, the perfective used for foregrounding, the imperfective used for backgrounding), or distinctive word-order patterns used to mark topic/comment, new information/old information, or background/foreground (see Brinton 2015). Functional categories, such as polite-ness, speech acts, or speech representation, might also be subject to examination in a particular period, as might genre or register conventions. Specific examples falling under this rubric might be the following:
- address terms (*thou/you*) used by Chaucer or Shakespeare;
- speech representation in Old English;
- conventions of medical writing in Middle English;
- (im)politeness in the Early Modern courtroom; or
- apologies in Late Modern English (LModE).

An early study by Brown and Gilman (1989) of the speech act of "directives" (commands) in Shakespeare's plays takes an approach which could be classified as historical pragmatics proper. They show that Shakespeare utilizes a range of directive strategies. In addition to direct imperatives (which are more polite when accompanied by a second-person pronoun, e.g., *Take thou, Retire thee*) and verbless forms (e.g., *Peace*), which are rude and brusque, Brown and Gilman find directives that express the speaker's sincere wish that the hearer do something (e.g., *I pray you, prithee, I entreat you, I beseech you, I would that, I require that*) and directives querying whether the hearer is willing, sees fit, or is pleased to do something (e.g., *so/if it please you, by your leave*). Despite imposing on the hearer to do something, *I beseech* can also be deferential since it occurs almost always with the formal *you* rather than the informal *thou* and is accompanied by an honorific term of address (e.g., *sir, madam, lord*) 40 percent of the time. This makes it much more deferential than *I pray*, which occurs only 10 percent of the time with an honorific. *Prithee* (from *pray thee*), in contrast, occurs mainly with in-group markers such as *good friend* or *my daughter*. Thus, there is evidence of two types of politeness that will be discussed in detail in Chapter 5: politeness recognizing "negative face" (the desire not be imposed upon) and politeness recognizing "positive face" (the desire to be approved of).

The second subfield of "diachronic pragmatics" "focuses on the linguistic [pragmatic] inventory and its communicative use across different historical stages of the language" (Jacobs and Jucker 1995: 13). It involves tracing the development of discourse-pragmatic features, functions, and genre conventions over time. This approach is truly diachronic. It has been seen as "micro." Examples of studies belonging to this tradition might be the following:

• the history of directive speech acts;
• the history of compliment speech acts;
• changes in the inventory of interjections over time;
• the development of the pragmatic marker *well*; or
• the origin of the comment clause *I think*.

Because there may be change in a form within a particular period or even within one writer's usage, Culpeper (2010: 190) suggests that we may need to propose a field called "diachronic pragmaphilology," but such fine-grained distinctions are probably unnecessary.

> The form and function of speech representation over time in the news register is the subject of Jucker and Berger's (2014) study, representing an example of the diachronic pragmatic approach. They focus on changes in speech representation in one broadsheet newspaper, *The Times*, from 1833 to 1988. As a way to authenticate the news, earlier editions of *The Times* use indirect speech and sometimes narrative reports to convey the words of reliable sources and important newsmakers. In more recent editions, speech representation becomes an important means of giving a faithful account of official meetings, conferences, reports of rail accidents, or any events in which the words of speakers are important. Jucker and Berger find a number categories of speech representation in their corpus, with considerable fluctuation over time. However, they demonstrate a trend toward more direct means of representation, that is, direct speech, at the expense of less direct means such as indirect speech. Long passages of indirect speech and free indirect speech are replaced with more selective quotations in mixed forms; these serve to summarize or characterize events. In this regard, Jucker and Berger find that the broadsheet is moving in the direction of the tabloid, where direct speech is "especially pervasive" (83). Their results thus point to changes in the representation of speech over time as well as changing genre conventions in newspapers (both are discussed in more detail in Chapters 4 and 8).

The third subfield is "pragmahistorical linguistics." It is the study of the discourse-pragmatic factors motivating language change, and thus also a "micro" approach. Increasingly, historical linguistics has turned to pragmatic factors as a means of explaining linguistic (phonological, morphological, syntactic, semantic) change. We see this especially in the concept of inferencing used to explain semantic change (Traugott and Dasher 2002), and its importance to grammaticalization, which we explore in Chapter 3. Word-order change is also often pragmatically motivated, related to pragmatic concepts such as topic and focus marking as well as foregrounding and backgrounding.

An example of a pragmahistorical linguistics study is Los and van Kemenade (2012). This article explains aspects of OE word order and changes in this word order by evoking pragmatic notions such as given and new information. Old English allows for two positions for the subject, before or after *þa/þonne* 'then'; the position to the left is "earmarked for discourse-linking" (1481) and is correlated with given information (definite, specific noun phrases with a discourse antecedent). Likewise, the variable position of the object in respect to the verb (object-verb or verb-object order) depends on givenness: typically, given objects precede and new objects follow the verb. However, "[w]hen the syntactic SVO pattern became more and more canonical (as the result of the loss of OV orders in Early Middle English and the decline of verb-second in Late Middle English), the subject appears to have become increasingly reserved for Given information and the object for New information" (1486). At the same time, the needs of information structuring remain and lead to the development of, or increased use of, certain less common syntactic structures, including left dislocation, topicalization, *there*-insertion, passive, and clefts.

2.3 Form-to-Function and Function-to-Form Approaches

In their early delineation of the subfields of historical pragmatics, Jacobs and Jucker suggest that there are two possible approaches in diachronic pragmatics: form-to-function and function-to-form (1995: 13–25). In fact, these two approaches are possible whether one's study falls under the historical pragmatics proper, diachronic pragmatics, or pragmahistorical linguistics rubric.

In the form-to-function approach, one begins with the linguistic form (e.g., a pragmatic marker, address terms, performative verb, reporting verb, vocative, conversational formula, interjection, exclamation, topic changer) and studies how it functions (either at a point of time or over time). This is a "semasiological" approach, focusing on the discourse-pragmatic function of a form (see Lewis 2012: 903). Synchronically, one explores the pragmatic functioning of a form in a particular period of English. Diachronically, assuming the form remains the same, or undergoes only minor changes, one traces the way in which the pragmatic meaning has arisen and/or changed, what pathways of development the form has followed, and what mechanisms of change have been at work. The case studies of pragmatic markers presented in Chapter 1, §1.4 are prototypical examples of the form-to-function approach. The origin of the forms, the emergence of pragmatic meaning in context, and ongoing changes in their use (including their obsolescence) are all part of such a study. It must be recognized, of course, that establishing the pragmatic meanings of forms in earlier periods can be difficult; one can make use of studies of the form or of comparable forms in Present-day English, but one must recognize that the pragmatic meaning of the form may have changed over time. Thus, careful examination of the contexts in which the form is used is necessary.

An example of a form-to-function approach is Moore's (2015) study of the history of the reporting verbs *quethen*, *quoth*, and *quote*. These verbs have the pragmatic function of marking a change in speaker and dialogic turns in the narrative, thus contributing to textual organization. *Quoth* (OE *cweþan*, ME *quethen*) is the most common verb introducing direct and indirect speech in Old English. In Middle English it is displaced by *seien* 'to say'. *Quethen* becomes more and more specialized, so that by Early Modern English it is a kind of "invariant quotative marker," restricted to marking direct speech; it occurs in the past-tense form and with verb–subject order, invariably in a parenthetical reporting clause (*quod he/she*). It may be abbreviated qd. or qð. The verb declines in the eighteenth century and becomes archaic by the nineteenth; it is now used only for jocular or ironic purposes. Moore believes that the loss of *quoth* coincides roughly with the spread of quotation marks: "As written language settled on the convention of using punctuation to mark reported speech, the grammaticalized verbs of speaking became a redundant strategy for indicating the shifts in speaker" (2015: 265). *Quote*, a later addition to this set of speech communication verbs, arises in the eighteenth century, serving a different function. It defers authority of the spoken words to another, insisting that the reported words are a precise copy. Moore calls it a "credentializing pragmatic element." Moore associates it with a more text-based and literate society in which indicating sources and faithfulness in presentation become important (on reporting verbs, see further Chapter 4).

Other examples of form-to-function studies are Brinton (2014) and Biber (2004) summarized below.

In the function-to-form approach, one begins with the pragmatic function (speech act, speech representation, (im)politeness, genre) and studies how that function is expressed formally (either at a point in time or over time). This is an "onomasiological" approach, focusing on how a discourse-pragmatic function is expressed (Lewis 2012: 903). Synchronically, it involves a search for the inventory of terms that are used to express a functional category. Diachronically, modifications in this inventory of terms as well as changes in the nature of the category itself are both important. Thus, for example, if you are trying to understand the speech act of complimenting in the eighteenth century, you would need to determine how compliments are expressed formally and how they function in this century; both may be very different from what we know about compliments in Present-day English. The function-to-form approach poses considerable challenges, especially for a corpus-based approach (see below, §2.6). We discuss these challenges in more detail in Chapter 6, §6.3.

An example of a function-to-form approach is Landert's (2019) study of stance. A pilot study reveals that markers of stance (i.e., "speaker's or writer's attitude toward the certainty, reliability and source of information of their statements" [173]) are not evenly distributed but cluster in certain passages. She uses twenty lexical items commonly known to express stance: verbs (e.g., *believe, seem, think, suppose*), adjectives (*evident, (un)likely, (im)possible, (im)probable*), and adverbs (e.g., *certainly, perhaps, surely, truly*). She then automatically extracts these items from a corpus of Early Modern English dated from 1460 to 1760 containing speech-related texts, medical writing, pamphlets, and letters. The function-to-form part of her study involves the qualitative analysis of 300-word extracts, all containing a relatively high density of stance markers (9–12 markers) to determine how stance actually works. She finds some previously unidentified stance markers, such as *I collect* 'I conclude' and *I credit* 'I believe' – what have been called "hidden manifestations" (see Chapter 6, §6.3). She also finds that simple quantitative studies may be misleading as multiple stance markers may combine elaboratively in a single stance marking, or markers which individually do not mark stance may combine to mark stance. Her finding that stance is marked in a wide range of contexts but particularly seems to collocate with rhetorical questions and direct discourse suggests that Biber's (2004) purely quantitative (form-to-function) findings about the overall lower marking of stance in Early Modern English compared to Present-day English (see below) may not be correct.

Other examples of function-to-form approaches are the studies by Brown and Gilman (1989) and Jucker and Berger (2014) summarized above.

2.4   Pragmatic Units

Another way to conceptualize the scope of historical pragmatics is to focus on the size of the linguistic unit studied. While any level of linguistic structure can carry pragmatic meaning, even intonation, spelling, or punctuation (see, for example, Claridge and Kytö 2020), Jucker (2008: 898–902) identifies the levels of expression, utterance, and genre or domain of discourse.

Expressions encompass words, phrases, and clauses serving pragmatic functions. Pragmatic expressions range from single-word pragmatic markers (*well*, *why*) and address terms (*you, thou, madam, sir*) to phrasal conversational formulas (*thank you, no problem*) and pragmatic markers (*by the way, in fact*) to (elliptical) clausal reporting structures (*he said, she's like*) and comment clauses (*you know, I think*). You will see detailed examples of pragmatic expressions in this book, especially the chapters on pragmatic markers (Chapter 3), speech representation (Chapter 4), and address terms (Chapter 7). Corpora are often used to identify frequencies and distributions of these expressions, following a form-to-function approach.

An example from fairly recent history of the rise of a pragmatic expression is exclamatory *as if!* (as in *He thinks you'll be impressed. As if!*). Pragmatically, *as if* is a dismissive or derisive response to some expressed or implied state of affairs. It expresses disbelief that this state of affairs does or will occur (*Oxford English Dictionary* [OED], s.v. *as*, adv., and conj., def. P1(c)). In Brinton (2014), I explore the source of this form and its pathway of development. The earliest example cited in the OED dates from 1903, but corpus examples are not frequent until the 1990s. Monoclausal *as if* and *if only* clauses (e.g., *As if he cared, If only he'd stop drinking*), occurring as independent sentences, bear a strong affinity to exclamatory *as if* and would appear to be a likely source. The earliest examples of *as if* monoclauses can be dated to the mid- to late sixteenth century, but they are rare. They have a denial sense and are used as part of rhetorical strategy in a developing argument. In work on what is called "insubordination," it has been argued these monoclauses (which look like subordinate clauses but function as independent clauses) arise from full sentences in which the main clauses have been ellipted (e.g., *If only he'd stop drinking, I'd be happy*) (see Evans 2007). But in this case reconstruction of the ellipted main clause remains elusive. A more plausible source is the construction *it be/appear/look/seem* with a complement *as if*-clause (e.g., *it seems as if he cared*), which appear early; these express negative epistemic stance, a plausible source for the 'denial/refutation' meaning. Independence of the *as if*-clause involves deletion of the semantically depleted main clause (*it seems*). The final step in the development of exclamatory *as if* is deletion of the content of the *as if*-clause, which can typically be inferred from context.

The level of utterances refers to speech acts (e.g., compliments, apologies, insults, promises, greetings, thanks), but can be more broadly understood to encompass conversational routines, (im)politeness, verbal aggression, and speech representation, which denote pragmatic functions typically expressed on the utterance level. Studying these calls for a function-to-form approach.

A study focused on the utterance level is Jucker's (2011b) study of changes in politeness in the history of English. In contemporary Anglo-American society, we emphasize "negative politeness" by trying not to impose upon others, by offering options and asking indirectly, and we are concerned about "saving face." In Early Medieval society, however, we do not find evidence of these strategies. Jucker hypothesizes that neither positive nor negative politeness played a role then, since one's place in the social hierarchy was fixed and relations were based on kin loyalty and mutual obligations. Commands, for example, tended to be expressed directly, in (what looks to us) a face-threatening way. This is what Jucker calls "discernment politeness." The ME period, as a result of French influence, is a period marked by *curteisie* 'courtesy'. This evolves into a system of "deference" or "negative politeness," where *you* and *thou* mark status and distance between speaker and addressee but are not used as a way of saving face. Studies of Shakespeare suggest that by Early Modern English, positive politeness (in-group identity markers, hedges to avoid disagreement, naming of admirable qualities) has come to predominate. The subsequent change to contemporary negative politeness is marked by a number of formal changes, as shown in Table 2.1. The topic of politeness is taken up in detail in Chapter 5 and the question of commands (directives) is treated in Chapter 6, §6.5.

The third level is the level of discourse or text; this is the level above the sentence, or a "self-contained linguistic unit consisting of utterances" (Jucker 2008: 901). While it is possible to differentiate between spoken "discourse" and written "text," many do not make this distinction. The terminology here is somewhat confusing, with overlapping terms. But I will consider "register" to be a type of language use that is socially determined, that is, defined by the social use made of the discourse and by a set of contextual and situational features, such as subject matter, nature and role of the participants, and function. Registers may be shaped in important ways by extralinguistic forces. Examples of registers include the discourse of sports, the discourse of science, the discourse of medicine, the discourse of religion, the discourse of literature,

Table 2.1 *Some formal correlates to the change from positive to negative (non-imposition) politeness (based on Jucker 2011b)*

formal change	positive > negative politeness
thou > you	*thou* is intimate and marks in-group membership *you* is deferential
pray, prithee (beseech, exhort, beg, etc.) > please, can/could/would you	*pray/prithee* asserts the speaker's sincere wish for the hearer to do X
	please (< if it please you), can/could/would you questions the willingness of the hearer to do X
excuse me/ pardon me/ forgive me > sorry	the older forms impose upon the hearer to forgive the speaker the new form expresses regret and is deferential
must > should, need to	*must* expresses an obligation imposed from outside; *should* expresses either an internal or an external obligation; *need to* expresses an internal or subjective obligation

the discourse of news, or the discourse of law. Jucker (2008: 901) calls these "discourse domains."

Within any register there are a variety of "genres." These are texts that share a conventional structure, a set of stylistic features, and a specific communicative purpose. Within the religious register, for example, we find biblical texts, sermons, prayers, biblical exegesis (commentary), and saints' lives, all of which are differently structured and serve different purposes. Newspapers encompass genres such as news reports, editorials, opinion pieces, sports reports, business reports, obituaries, movie and book reviews, classified advertisements, recipes, and so on, all of which are shaped by very different textual conventions. Historical pragmaticists seek to determine the genres which constitute each register, focusing on the characteristic features of a genre at a particular historical period or tracing the development of those features over time. Change may involve the rise of new genres and the death of others. Some genres may undergo little change while others change in significant ways. Prayers, for example, are remarkably stable and highly conservative (see Kohnen 2012b). The form of prayers, as we know them, was established in the EModE period. Because they are interactive (between the supplicant and their god) and performative, prayers are characterized by frequent "oral" features, such as first- and second-person pronouns, terms of address, and a small set of speech act types (ordering, thanking, confessing, praising). In contrast, the genre of news reporting, as we know it today, is almost unrecognizable in the earliest newspapers. (Both religious texts and newspapers are discussed in more detail in Chapter 8.)

One example of a historical discourse study is Biber's (2004) examination of markers of stance in the genres of drama, personal letters, newspaper reportage, and medical prose from 1600 to 1990. Stance – or the marking of personal attitude – may be expressed by a wide variety of forms, including modal auxiliaries (*might, should*) and semi-modals (*ought to*), stance adverbials (*obviously, wisely, mainly, undoubtedly*), *that-* or *to*-complement clauses introduced by verbs (*prefer, urge*), adjectives (*it is advisable/convenient*), or nouns (*opinion, intention*). Looking first at contemporary registers, he finds that stance is more frequently expressed in conversation than in the written registers (fiction, news, or academic). The most common forms are (semi-)modals and complement clauses, though the relative frequencies of different types varies in the four registers. Over time, all markers of stance have increased, except for modals, which have declined in frequency, especially in the last fifty years (cf. Leech et al. 2009: Ch. 4). The "popular" genres (i.e., personal letters and drama) have led the way with increased stance marking; newspapers show only modest increases, medical prose has shown a decline (see Figure 2.1). Different types of stance marking predominate in different genres. Biber concludes that it is not the case that one grammatical system is being replaced by another. Rather, he suggests that there is a change in cultural norms, with speakers being more willing to express stance, whether as a result of deliberate stylistic policies or popular attitudes, especially in the current century.

2.5   The "Bad Data" Problem

It was famously pointed out by the sociolinguist William Labov (1972: 100, 1994: 11) that the data available for historical linguistic study is "impoverished": it survives by accident, may not resemble the vernacular of the time, and was perhaps never anyone's native language. We have no phonetic records before the early part of the twentieth century. For this reason, he sees it as "bad" – "'bad' in the sense that it may be fragmentary, corrupted or many times removed from the actual production of native speakers." For Labov, "[h]istorical linguistics can then be thought of as the art of making the best use of bad data." Furthermore, "[w]e usually know very little about the social positions of the writers, and not much more about the social structure of the community . . . we know nothing about what was understood, and we are in no position to perform controlled experiments . . . we cannot use the knowledge

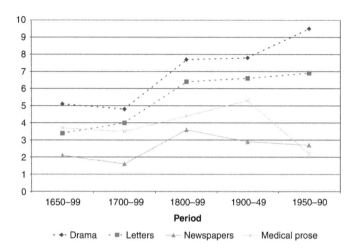

Figure 2.1 Changes in stance marking from 1650 to 1900 in four genres
(frequency per 1,000 words) (adapted from Biber 2004: 122)

(Douglas Biber. 2004. Historical patterns for the grammatical marking of stance.
Journal of Historical Pragmatics 5(1). 122. https://jan.ucc.nau.edu/
biber/Biber/Biber_2004.pdf. Reprinted with permission.)

of native speakers" (1994: 11). This problem is especially exacerbated for
historical pragmatics, since pragmatics has typically used as its source of
data naturally occurring oral conversation or narrative. In some sociolinguistic
corpora, there are archival oral narratives where, using the age of the speaker as
a proxy for distance in time (the "apparent-time" approach), we can perhaps
extend our time frame to the mid-nineteenth century when we assume the
speech of the speakers became fixed. But "real-time" approaches, if based on
oral data, can only extend back to the advent of speech recording. As
Taavitsainen and Fitzmaurice observe, "data problems grow more conspicuous
the further back in time we go" (2007: 11).

How can the "bad data" problem be addressed in historical pragmatics? One
avenue is to observe that there is never an absolute dichotomy between
"written" and "spoken" and that as we go back in time the gap between written
and spoken narrows (Culpeper 2010: 191). Medieval texts are widely acknowledged to contain an "oral residue." As Fleischman notes (1990: 23), "many of
the disconcerting properties of medieval vernacular texts – their extraordinary
parataxis, mystery particles [i.e., pragmatic markers] ... and jarring alterna-
tions of tenses, to cite but a few – can find more satisfying explanations if we
first of all acknowledge the extent to which our texts structure information the
way a spoken language does."

Another avenue is to recognize that there are a number of types of written texts from the past that are "speech-related" and we can thus assume them to be close to the spoken English of the time. Culpeper and Kytö (2010: 17–18) distinguish three categories of speech-related texts, all of which come down to us in written form, of course:

- speech-based: for example, trial transcripts, witness depositions, and parliamentary records; these are based on actual speech events;
- speech-purposed: for example, sermons, prayers, dramatic dialogue, dialogue in handbooks, and proclamations; these are read or performed and may be mimetic of actual speech; and
- speech-like: for example, personal letters and diaries; these are produced as written texts but contain speech-like (oral, colloquial) features.

In the speech-based category, transcripts of trials and of witness depositions primarily date from Early Modern English, and a record of British parliamentary proceedings dates from the early nineteenth century. For these we cannot, of course, know the degree to which the scribe or recorder has interceded and edited or redacted the text, nor can we know the extent to which the formality of the settings has transposed the language used out of the realm of "real conversation." Studies have shown that we must take a cautious view of the veracity of the speech in these documents. It is agreed that the transcriber, whether a professional scribe or lay recorder, plays a crucial role in shaping the language in such records. For example, Grund (2007) looks at depositions from the Salem witch trials (see Rosenthal 2013) that have come down to us in multiple copies (i.e., with different recorders). He finds significant variation in the language and sometimes in the content of the different records, and suggests that the records represent reconstructions of the actual speech based on notes. He admits that the records "do seem to approximate spoken language," albeit not necessarily the language of the speakers of these documents "but rather what constituted spoken language in the eyes of the recorder" (145). One example he cites is the appearance of pragmatic markers, a well-known feature of oral discourse (see Chapter 3). While frequently edited out of written transcripts of oral speech, some do appear in the Salem records, especially *well*, *why*, and *oh*. (See Lutzky's discussion of the pragmatic marker *why* in Early Modern English in Chapter 3, §3.3). But as the markers used vary in the parallel records, he postulates that they might have been added by the recorders in order to make the records more speech-like. Moore (2002), looking at slander depositions in Early Modern English (mixed language texts in Latin and English), where one would assume that the exact reproduction of the slanderous statement would be crucial, finds that rather than verbatim speech representation, the language is often made to conform to a template of defamatory speeches. Moore still believes that these can be used as speech-based texts for linguistic research "as long as they are used with deference to their limitations" (412). Kytö and Walker (2003) look at the trial transcripts and witness depositions in the *Corpus of English Dialogues* to determine the extent to which they are reliable written representations of past speech. Trial transcripts are presented in dialogue form and witness depositions in the scribe's third-person narration with passages of indirect speech; both may have explicit scribal interventions. Kytö and Walker find some evidence of these as indeed speech-like. While we expect false starts, hesitations, pauses, and slips of the tongue to be edited out, these do sometimes occur in the records. Further evidence of them as faithful transcripts of speech include the glossing of dialect terms, the occurrence of identical phrasing in different documents, admissions by the scribe that he has not heard a passage clearly, references by the scribe to his notes, and endorsements of transcripts as "correct" or "official" copies. But there is also evidence of scribal or editorial inference that is either inadvertent or purposeful. Direct speech may be "reconstructed" or speech may be presented in indirect form (which places it within the viewpoint of the recorder; see Chapter 4), texts may be tidied up or corrections introduced to make the text more readable (rather than more faithful), additions and amendments may be made after the fact, sometimes for religious or political reasons. Many of these records exist in one or more forms (contemporaneous manuscripts or printed texts), later printed copies, and more recent editions, with the contemporaneous forms obviously being closer to the original speech. Given all this, Kytö and Walker conclude: "In all, we can never claim that the available early speech-related texts are equivalent to actual speech. However ... there is evidence to suggest that certain texts may be relatively faithful written records of spoken interaction of the past" (2003: 230).

In the speech-purposed category, sermons and prayers date back to Old English (see Chapter 8, §8.5). We have dramatic dialogue from Middle English; this reflects the authors' conception of contemporary speech. Its verisimilitude is always a question, since the dialogue is shaped in part by conventions of genre but also in part by the individual author's talents in capturing real speech. Speech-purposed data also occur in instructional handbooks, such as conversation and language-learning manuals. While all speech-related data only approximate speech, the consensus is that dramatic dialogue comes closest to real speech (Culpeper and Kytö 2000); furthermore, drama has the advantage of supplying motivation, characterization, and action sequences.

Texts in the speech-like category were not produced orally nor typically intended to be performed aloud, but they lie toward the colloquial rather than literate end of the style spectrum. These include, above all, personal letters. Letters are a rich source of sociopragmatic data since we often know who wrote the letter and to whom and in what context. They thus include a rich array of address terms, for example (see Chapter 7, §7.8). Language use in personal letters resisted standardization and remained more speech-like well into the nineteenth century. We also have letters of uneducated speakers unfamiliar with the conventions of writing. Personal letters date back to the late ME period, with the collections of the letters of the Paston and Cely families (see Davis 2009; Hanham 1975). Today, we can see the descendants of letters, namely emails and instant messages, as clearly incorporating oral features. Personal diaries and journals, shaped by the exigencies of time or space and often recorded for one's own private use, are also a source of colloquial language. Newspapers, in their early form, consisted of "letters" from correspondents abroad, while later newspapers include considerable amounts of quoted speech. Early pamphlets, often addressing a controversial topic, could be framed as a dialogue between contesting viewpoints (see Chapter 8, §8.3). The speech-like category also includes represented speech in narrative fiction and non-fiction (in prose and verse) extending back to Old English (see Chapter 4). But we must always be aware that within any of these genres there is a range from more colloquial (more speech-like) to less colloquial (less speech-like), as in the difference, for example, between private and personal letters. We will see in the next section that the development of genre-specific corpora has facilitated the study of speech-based and speech-like genres.

Perhaps the best avenue to approach the "bad data" problem, however, is to recognize that *all* texts, either spoken or written, are communicative acts shaped and constrained by pragmatic principles and including pragmatic forms and thus amenable to pragmatic analysis. For example, we find that some pragmatic markers – which are typically associated with oral discourse (see Chapter 3) – are much more common in, and characteristic of, written discourse; these include forms such as *notwithstanding*, *parenthetically*, or *accordingly*. All texts are legitimate objects of study. As Jucker and Taavitsainen conclude, "[B]oth spoken and written language are forms of communication produced by speakers/writers for target audiences with communicative intentions, and language is always produced within situational constraints. Therefore all forms of language that have survived and provide enough information to contextualise the use, are considered potential data for historical pragmatics" (2013: 25).

2.6   Diachronic Corpus Pragmatics

Diachronic (or historical) corpus pragmatics is the use of corpus-linguistic methods in research in pragmatics involving historical data. As Taavitsainen notes (2015: 252), "it is no exaggeration to say that corpus linguistics using large computer-readable language data has established itself as the main methodology in historical pragmatics." This is the case whether one is undertaking a diachronic pragmatics study (looking at change in a pragmatic phenomenon over time) or a historical pragmatics (proper) study (looking at a pragmatic phenomenon in a historical stage of the language). This has not always been the case. In the three areas that come together here – historical linguistics, historical pragmatics, and pragmatics – historical linguistics was the first to embrace corpus-linguistic methods, with access to large collections of data that were electronically searchable and providing statistically verifiable and replicable quantitative results. Historical pragmatics in its infancy made use of the qualitative methods of philology, dependent upon close readings of texts to extract pragmatic forms, with careful analysis of these forms in context. But very early on, corpus methodology began to be used in historical pragmatics; for example, Brinton (1996) and many of the articles in the early collection by Jucker (1995) make use of corpus analytic techniques. Pragmatics proper has been slowest to incorporate corpus methodology. Neither Anglo-American pragmaticists with their foundation in philosophy and the use of a small set of invented examples, implicit meaning, and intuitive linguistic judgments nor pragmaticists working with small sets of conversational data immediately welcomed the "digital turn" in linguistics. But as is evidenced, for example, by the handbook on corpus pragmatics by Aijmer and Rühlemann (2015), pragmatics too has changed, perhaps following the lead of historical pragmatics.

The use of corpus methods in historical pragmatics is not without its critics. As Jucker notes, this methodology runs "the risk of losing the philological sophistication of earlier research" (2008: 903). The focus on large sets of quantitative data might lead to "decontextualization," or the loss of focus on context, which is crucial to pragmatic analysis. Moreover, while one can achieve more objective and empirical results with corpus methodology, it is not clear that the results will be replicable, as pragmatics depends on the interpretation of forms in context and is thus to some degree subjective and variable. Furthermore, corpora tend to use normalized spelling and edited editions that distance the researcher from the original data, often important for pragmatic analysis. This creates a dilemma: "On one hand, scholars want to make use of even larger corpora in order to achieve more solid and statistically valid generalizations, and on the other hand, they realize that they need rich contextualizations in order to grasp the subtleties of language use in all the extracts retrieved from the corpora" (Jucker and Taavitsainen 2014: 12).

These concerns have been met foremostly by retaining qualitative analysis as an essential part of diachronic historical pragmatics, to serve as a complement to, or sometimes a corrective of, the quantitative results obtained by corpus analysis. The compilation of more sophisticated corpora is also a step in addressing these concerns; these provide access to original spellings and images of original texts (as well as means to search the corpus despite original spellings) (see §2.7 below on corpus annotation).

For the most part, the approach taken in diachronic corpus pragmatics has been what is called "corpus-based" (or "corpus-aided"). This is a deductive or top-down approach where researchers begin with a feature or set of features about which they have formulated a hypothesis and then extract the relevant data from the corpus. The collected data serve to validate, refute, or refine the initial hypothesis. For example, examples of *well* might be collected from a corpus of Early Modern English to determine when, or if, it functioned as a pragmatic marker during this period and to attempt to trace its development from an adverb/adjective to a pragmatic marker over time. In contrast, a "corpus-driven" approach, which is bottom-up and inductive, consists of approaching a corpus without prior assumptions and seeing what emerges from the corpus investigation. This approach is less often used in diachronic corpus pragmatics. Here, for example, one might search a corpus of Old English to reveal the resources used for issuing commands (but it would be impossible to be entirely inductive since one would likely have to have some preconceived notion of what forms one is looking for).

Corpus searches are not equally suitable for studying all types of pragmatic phenomena, since such searches require an identifiable and precise search string. Thus, corpus methods are best suited to the form-to-function approach (see above), where one begins with linguistic forms and queries how they function pragmatically. For example, beginning with the pragmatic marker *you know* (in its variant spellings) one could collect all examples of it in a historical corpus of English. Of course, the collected data would need to be manually examined (qualitatively) in order to rule out cases of *you know* that are not pragmatic markers (this is dependent on how finely tuned one's search string is). Corpus methods are less well suited to the function-to-form approach (see above). Studying a pragmatic function, such as a speech act, in a corpus would require determining all the formal exponents of that function; this is not an easy task, especially for earlier periods of the language, where formal marking may differ from that in Present-day English, where the speech act may be performed indirectly, or where the speech act function may itself be different. Scholars have devised a number of "work-arounds" for studying functional pragmatic categories such as speech acts and politeness. We will look at these in detail in Chapters 5 and 6.

Despite some difficulties posed for historical pragmatic work, corpus linguistics has overall made an important advancement in the field: "we feel able to make claims about earlier generations' or communities' discourse practices because we base those claims upon real language use and the quantitative analysis of large databases representing authentic language use make these claims valid" (Taavitsainen and Fitzmaurice 2007: 27).

The development of electronic corpora of English, beginning with the pioneering but (by modern standards) small *Helsinki Corpus of English Texts* (HC), issued in 1991, has both facilitated the incorporation of corpus linguistics into historical pragmatics and served to address the "bad data" problem. While the "communicative view" (introduced in Chapter 1, §1.3) argues that written texts are as suitable for pragmatic study as spoken texts (since both represent intentional communicative acts involving an addresser and addressee) and that the dichotomy between spoken and written is not at all clear, there may be reasons for a historical pragmatist to prefer spoken or speech-related genres as a source of data. For example, a much more diverse set of pragmatic markers is found in spoken texts at a higher frequency than in written texts (see Chapter 3). Second-person address terms and vocatives are rare in written texts but used frequently in spoken or speech-related texts, such as letters (see Chapter 7), politeness phenomena may be much more extensive in spoken texts (see Chapter 5), and certain kinds of speech acts, such as directives, commissives, and expressives, are much more likely to occur in a spoken interaction than in a written text (see Chapter 6).

Thus, inclusion of speech or speech-related data in available corpora may be important for the pragmaticist. Some of the large multi-genre ("first-generation") historical corpora contain a substantial proportion of fiction (and thus significant amounts of constructed dialogue). For example, the 475-million-word *Corpus of Historical American English* (COHA; Davies 2010) (1820–present) contains 47 percent fiction; the size of this corpus provides an unparalleled source for the study of the history of American English. The smaller *Corpus of Late Modern English 3.0* (CLMET3.0; 1710–1920), containing historical British English, includes about 46 percent fiction, 4 percent drama, and 7 percent letters out of a total of approximately 34 million words. In the 13.5-million-word large *Corpus of Early American Literature* (CEAL; 1690–1920), 42 percent in the second period and 93 percent in the third period consist of fiction (fiction is less readily available for the first period, 1690–1780). Fiction constitutes the entire contents of the 26-million-word *Corpus of English Novels* (CEN), covering a later period, 1881–1922, and including examples of British, American, and Canadian English. The 3.3-million-word *ARCHER 3.2: A Representative Corpus of Historical English Registers* (including British texts from 1600 to 1999 and American texts from 1750 to 1999) includes two speech-related genres (drama, sermons) as well as a number of written genres falling on the colloquial end of the spectrum (fiction, personal letters, journals/diaries, news reportage). Drama constitutes 14 percent of the corpus and fiction 17 percent.

In addition to linguistic corpora, which allow for searches of various kinds (lexical, grammatical), text collections may – with various degrees of ease and success – be used for linguistic study. The massive text collections, *Early*

English Books Online (EBBO), containing 146,000 titles published between 1475 and 1700 in England, *Eighteenth Century Collections Online* (ECCO), containing over 180,000 titles published during this century, and *Evans Early American Imprints, Series I* (Evans), containing virtually all books, pamphlets, and broadsides published in America between 1639 and 1800, likely include a significant amount of fiction and drama, though the exact amount is difficult to determine. All of EEBO and Evans and part of ECCO are available in formats usable for linguistic searches (through the Text Creation Partnership). Smaller text collections, such as the Chadwyck-Healey *Eighteenth Century Fiction* (ECF; 1700–1780), are valuable collections, but difficult to use for linguistic searches. They allow lexical searches but there is no way to easily calculate the frequency of items; moreover, because the collections are image-based, search results are not provided in a readily useable list (a KWIK concordance [key word in context]); each result must be individually checked in the original image of the text. Nonetheless, the Chadwyck-Healey *English Drama* (ED) collection, containing 3,900 dramatic works from the late thirteenth to early twentieth century, is important for pragmaticists because of the wealth of historical constructed dialogue it contains. Finally, online, fully searchable collections of dramatists, such as the online Shakespeare collections, are an invaluable resource, though typically only lexical choices are possible.

It is the development of typically smaller and more focused genre-specific ("second-generation") corpora that has provided the richest source of data for historical pragmatics, especially those corpora including speech or speech-related data of the past. Table 2.2 gives a partial listing of such corpora, including corpora devoted to personal letters, witness depositions, trial transcripts, tracts, religious writing, and newspapers. Several of the corpora contain so-called "ego documents" such as letters, diaries, travelogues, and memoirs, which are autobiographical in nature; these are a particularly important source of speech-like data, especially as they tend to be colloquial in nature and record nonstandard varieties.

- The *Corpus of English Dialogues* (Table 2.2a) is a compilation of a variety of speech-based and speech-purposed data for the EModE period, including what is called "authentic" dialogue (trial transcripts, witness depositions) and "constructed" dialogue (prose fiction, drama comedy, didactic works).
- There are several corpora of letters (Table 2.2b). The *Corpus of Early English Correspondence* exists in several forms covering the period c.1410–1800, a full version, a parsed version, and an extended version. All of the letters are sociolinguistically annotated with available information about the writer and

Table 2.2 *Some genre-specific English corpora*

	Text types	Dates	Corpus	Corpus size
a.	Authentic and constructed dialogues	1560–1760	*A Corpus of English Dialogues* (CED)	1.2 million words
b.	Personal letters	1410?–1680	*Corpus of Early English Correspondence Sampler* (CEECS)	450,000 words
	Personal letters (Scottish)	1540–1750	*Corpus of Scottish Correspondence* (CSC)	417,000 words
	Personal letters (Richard Orford)	1761–1790	*A Corpus of late 18c Prose*	300,000 words
	Personal letters (selected 19th c. figures)	1861–1919	*A Corpus of late Modern English Prose*	100,000 words
c.	Witness depositions	1560–1760	*An Electronic Text Edition of Depositions* (on CD-ROM)	270,000 words
d.	Trial transcripts	1720–1913	*The Old Bailey Corpus, version 2.0* (a subset from *The Old Bailey Proceedings Online, 1674–1913*)	24.4 million words
e.	Tracts (on religion, politics, economy, science, law, and miscellaneous)	1640–1740	*The Lampeter Corpus of Early Modern English Tracts*	1.1 million words
f.	Religious prose	1150–1800	*Corpus of English Religious Prose* (COERP)	1 million words (EModE sampler)
g.	Medical writing, ranging from more academic texts to more popularized and utilitarian texts	1375–1800	*Corpus of Early English Medical Writing* (CEEM) (on CD-ROMs)	ME: c. 500,000 words EModE: c. 2 million words LModE: c. 2 million words
h.	Newspapers	1661–1791	*Zurich English Newspaper Corpus* (ZEN) (on CD-ROM or online)	1.6 million words
	Newspapers	1653–1654	*Newsbooks at Lancaster*	800,000 words
i.	Parliamentary proceedings (British)	1803–2005	*The Hansard Corpus*	1.6 billion words
j.	Television	1950s–present	*The TV Corpus* (TV)	325 million words
k.	Movies	1930s–present	*The Movie Corpus* (Movie)	200 million words

recipient. There are also several more specialized letter corpora containing Scottish letters, letters written to Richard Orford (steward to Peter Legh the Younger, Lyme Hall, Cheshire), and letters written by a selection of important nineteenth-century figures (e.g., Gertrude Bell, Lord and Lady Amberley).

- A collection of witness depositions from across Britain is included in *An Electronic Text Edition of Depositions* (Table 2.2c). It includes the texts with their original spelling, but makes corpus searches possible by providing a word list giving the variant spellings of all words.
- *The Old Bailey Corpus* (Table 2.2d) is an ongoing project of converting *The Old Bailey Proceedings Online, 1674–1913*, a record of London's criminal court (including trial transcripts, indictments, interrogations, witness statements, verdicts, etc.), into a linguistic corpus which is annotated sociolinguistically (age, gender, social class of speaker), pragmatically (role of speaker), and textually. The offense, verdict, and punishment for each trial is also tagged. In Figure 2.2 you will see an example search using this corpus.
- Tracts on religion, politics, economy, science, law, and miscellaneous topics are included in the *Lampeter Corpus* (Table 2.2e). As we will see in Chapter 8 §8.3, tracts are an important precursor to newspapers.
- The *Corpus of English Religious Prose* (Table 2.2f) contains a variety of religious writings, including sermons, catechisms, prayers, religious biographies, prefaces, treatises, and pamphlets (see Chapter 8, §8.5).
- In the *Corpus of Early Medical Writing* (Table 2.2g) one will find a range from more academic to more popular and utilitarian medical texts. They are given in both original and normalized spelling, which greatly aids corpus searches. The EModE part supplies links to the original (non-normalized spelling) version in the EEBO database. Early medical writings are an important source of recipes, as we will discuss in Chapter 8 §8.6.
- There are two corpora of newspapers of different sizes and covering different periods (Table 2.2h). In addition to specialized newspaper corpora, we have available to us historical archives of most of the world's major newspapers, such as of *The New York Times* (1851–2017) (Chadwyck-Healey "Historical Newspapers") or *The Times* (London) (1785–2019) (Gage Cengage "The Times Digital Archive"). For linguistic study these can prove difficult to use as they are usually image-based. (Newspapers are briefly discussed in Chapter 8 §8.3.)
- *The Hansard Corpus* (Table 2.2i) contains a record of nearly every speech given in the British Parliament over a 200-year period. These data represent more scripted, formal speech but are nonetheless a valuable resource.
- Two corpora containing transcripts of British, American, Canadian, Australian, and New Zealand television and movies are *The TV Corpus* and *The Movie Corpus* (Table 2.2j). Rather than naturally occurring speech, these

contain informal spoken language as conceived of by writers of television programs and movies (i.e., constructed dialogue) and are an important source of data on recent (twentieth-century) language history.

As an example of a search using one of these more specialized corpora, let's search for *well* in *The Old Bailey Corpus*. While we cannot search by part of speech, the search returns many examples of *well* as a pragmatic marker (but also, of course, the adjective and adverb *well*). One example of the pragmatic marker is found in the trial of Vincent Davis for the murder of his wife in 1725, in the deposition of Mary Jeffery, a neighbor of the accused. She quotes the accused using *well* (see Figure 2.2). Here, the speaker is a woman, though she is quoting a man. The landlady, Mary Tindall, who is also deposed, is described in the corpus metadata as a "working proprietor (catering, lodging or leisure services)." The corpus also connects us to the transcribed text in *The Old Bailey Proceedings* (Figure 2.3) with a link there to the original page image (Figure 2.4). We can deduce quite a bit here about who uses the pragmatic marker and in what way. The speakers all seem to be of middling rank, though the accused, Vincent Davis, is likely a more lowly ranked worker as he and his wife lodge with Mrs. Tindall. Importantly, we see him using *well* in much the same way that it is used in Present-day English, as a qualifier that indicates that what follows is not exactly what the hearer expects to hear or is not optimally coherent (see Chapter 3, Exercise 2).

2.7   Corpus Annotation

It is possible to automatically tag corpora for word class and to parse the syntax, but annotating corpora for pragmatic elements is considerably more difficult and appears to have to be done manually. Because manual tagging is time-consuming, expensive, and in some cases subjective, progress in this area has been slow and incomplete. As Weisser notes, "Any type of linguistic annotation is a highly complex and interpretive process, but none more so than pragmatic annotation" (2015: 84). Archer et al. (2008: 637) conclude, somewhat pessimistically, that "[u]nlike grammatical annotation, pragmatic annotation cannot be fully realized." If individual words or phrases are associated with particular pragmatic meanings, as in the use of *please* with commands, *thanks/ thank you* with thanking, or BE *sorry* with apologies, for example, we obviously have inherent meaning that can easily be tagged pragmatically, but such convention-alized phrases are only a small part of pragmatics.

A number of different (semi-)automatic systems have been developed to annotate speech acts (or what is often called dialogue structure) in corpora of Present-Day English. The corpora used are often quite constrained and task-oriented. For example, one such tagging schema uses telephone calls to and from British Rail customer service and tags for forty-one different speech acts

Figure 2.2 Sample search result for *well* in *The Old Bailey Corpus* (https://obc-client.de)

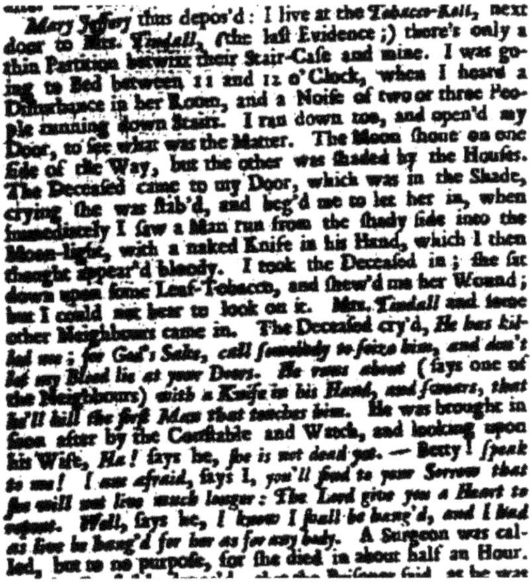

Mary Jeffery this depos'd: I live at the Tobacco-Roll, next door to Mrs. Tindall, (the last Evidence;) there's only a thin Partition betwixt their Stair-Case and mine. I was going to Bed between 11 and 12 o'Clock, when I heard a Disturbance in her Room, and a Noise of two or three People running down Stairs. I ran down too, and open'd my Door, to see what was the Matter. The Moon shone on one side of the Way, but the other was shaded by the Houses. The Deceased came to my Door, which was in the Shade, crying she was stab'd, and beg'd me to let her in, when Immediately I saw a Man run from the shady side into the Moon-light, with a naked Knife in his Hand, which I then thought appear'd bloody. I took the Deceased in; she sat down upon some Leaf Tobacco, and show'd me her Wound; but I could not bear to look on it. Mrs. Tindall and some other Neighbours came in. The Deceased cry'd, He has killed me; for God's Sake, call somebody to seize him, and don't let my Blood lie at your Doors. He runs about (says one of the Neighbours) with a Knife in his Hand, and swears, that he'll kill the first Man that touches him. He was brought in soon after by the Comfortable and Watch, and looking upon his Wife, Ha! says he, she is not dead yet. - Betty! speak to me! I am afraid, says I, you'll find to your Sorrow that she will not live much longer: The Lord give you a Heart to repent. Well, says he, I know I shall be hang'd, and I had as live be hang'd for her as for any body. A Surgeon was called, but to no purpose, for she died in about half an hour.

Figure 2.3 Text excerpt from *The Old Bailey Proceedings Online*, April 1725, Vincent Davis (t17250407-9)

(Tim Hitchcock, Robert Showmaker, Clive Emsley, Sharon Hoard, Jamie McLauglin et al., *The Old Bailey Proceedings Online, 1674–1913*. www.oldbaileyonline.org, version 8.0, 2018. Reprinted under Creative Commons Attribution NonCommercial 4.0 International (CC-BY-NC 4.0) license.)

Figure 2.4 Original page image from *The Old Bailey Proceedings Online*

(Harvard Law School Library, Historical & Special Collections. Reprinted with permission.)

(e.g., inform, direct, refuse, suggest, thank, correct, answer) as well as for turn, syntactic form, topic, mode (i.e., semantic categories such as deixis, probability), and polarity (see Leech and Weisser 2003).

But, again, there is much more to pragmatics than speech acts, and the question arises as to how, or whether, this information – including speaker characteristics (age, gender, social class), physical context of the interaction, social context (personal relations of interactants [power, social distance, role]), background or shared knowledge, cultural or societal values – can be tagged in a corpus. While some of this information may be included in the metadata attached to a corpus file, there have been attempts to embed this information in the file itself and attach it to each utterance, thus accounting for the sometimes shifting interactions between interlocutors. For example, *The Old Bailey Corpus 2.0* includes sociobiographical information on the speaker (gender, age, occupation, social class) and pragmatic information (speaker role in the courtroom [defendant, judge, victim, witness, lawyer, interpreter]) as well as textual information about the scribe, printer, and publisher, which can be accessed for each text. Using a selection from the *Corpus of English Dialogues*, Archer and Culpeper (2003) tag each utterance for the identity, sex, role, status, and age of both the speaker and the addressee; role includes activity role, kinship role, social role, and dramatic role. For this reason, they call this a "sociopragmatic corpus." (see Chapter 1, §1.5 on "Related Fields"). This type of tagging accounts not only for static features but also for changing features based on the nature of the interaction. Using the trial transcripts from this corpus and focusing specifically on questions, Archer (2005: 109–134) tags for three additional fields. The first is the interactional field consisting of "initiation" (typically questions, requests, requirements), "response" (typically answers, replies, acceptances, refusals), "response-initiation" (response– request), "report" (typically statements, explanations), "follow up" (typically comments, evaluations), and "follow up-initiation" (comment–question). This is combined with the force field, which overlaps with traditional speech act categories: counsel, question, and request (i.e., directive), sentence (i.e., declarative), express (i.e., expressive), and inform (i.e., representative). The third field is a grammatical form field (e.g., *wh*-interrogative, tag question, and so on). Obviously, this sort of manual tagging, which requires nuanced judgments about speaker intent and linguistic form, is very time-consuming and laborious, but it yields substantive results.

Archer (2014) reports on an attempt to use an automatic semantic tagger designed for modern English to study verbal aggression in a ten-year period of *The Old Bailey Proceedings* (1783–1793), a period associated with William Garrow, a barrister known for his aggressive style. The tagger relied on semantic fields such as good/bad, true/false, angry/violent, calm, polite/ impolite, respect/lack of respect; it also tagged for speech acts. The tagging found a relatively low number of aggression tags, suggesting to Archer that impoliteness was indirect, as it is in the modern courtroom, relying on what she calls "metapragmatic framing strategies," where, for example, requests for information, clarification, or confirmation could actually function as accusations and insinuations. Archer notes, however, that while the tagging produces interesting leads, each case requires manual inspection. For example, the term *politely* is in one case used to describe the act of pick-pocketing, and several other instances of the term are used metalinguistically. For historical study such a tagger would also have to take into consideration semantic change; for example, in the eighteenth century *politely* meant 'smoothly, in a polished manner'. She suggests that connecting the tagger to the *Historical Thesaurus of English* might be a means to address this problem.

Archer and Culpeper (2009) is a study using the sociopragmatically annotated comedy and trial proceedings of the *Corpus of English Dialogues* combined with "keyness" analysis (key words, key parts of speech, and key semantic fields). Deploying keyness analysis, they identify the statistically based correlations in two dyads (examiner–examinee, master/mistress–servant). Like sociopragmatics (see Chapter 1, §1.5 on "Related Fields"), this approach allows them to study how local contexts (e.g., age, gender, status, role) motivate the use of linguistic forms, but keyness analysis allows context to be approached in a theoretically informed way. They thus propose a third-way approach complementing the form-to-function and function-to-form approaches discussed above, namely a context-to-form and/or -function approach, which they call "sociophilology," "describing or tracing how historical contexts, including the co-text, genre, social situation and/ or culture, shape the functions and forms of language taking place with them" (2009: 287).

2.8   Chapter Summary

This chapter covered the following topics:
- the scope of historical pragmatics, covering:
  - "historical pragmatics (proper)," a macro approach looking at the pragmatics of a historical text or period (e.g., directives in Shakespeare);
  - "diachronic pragmatics," a micro approach tracing a discourse-pragmatic form or function as it changes over time (e.g., changing speech representation in the news register over time); and
  - "pragmahistorical linguistics," a micro approach examining pragmatic factors which influence linguistic forms (e.g., changes in word order from Old to Middle English brought about by the givenness or newness of information).

- two approaches to historical pragmatics:
  - form-to-function, an approach that begins with the linguistic form and studies its function in a historical period or over time (e.g., the changing form and function of *quoth* as a reporting verb);
  - function-to-form, an approach that works from discourse-pragmatic functions and examines their formal exponents (e.g., stance in Early Modern English).
- the pragmatic units studied, including expressions (e.g., exclamatory *as if!*), utterances (e.g., forms of politeness), and discourse or text (e.g., expression of stance in different genres);
- the "bad data" problem, resulting from the lack of naturally occurring oral conversation from the past, now addressed in part by different types of "speech-related" data (e.g., trial records, sermons, dramatic dialogue), which – with significant caveats – can be understood as close to spoken data;
- diachronic corpus pragmatics, the primary methodology used today in historical pragmatics, utilizing large, multi-genre corpora, smaller and genre-specific corpora as well as text collections; and
- corpus annotations, or attempts to pragmatically annotate corpora, which remain in their infancy.

2.9   Further Reading

For good overviews of the field historical pragmatics, start with Jacobs and Jucker (1995) and Jucker (1998), but for more recent descriptions, see Brinton (2015, 2017c), Culpeper (2010), Jucker (2006a, 2008), Jucker and Taavitsainen (2013: Chs. 1–3), Taavitsainen (2012), Taavitsainen and Jucker (2010b, 2015), Taavitsainen and Fitzmaurice (2007). And for a rather different view, see Traugott (2006).

A good introduction to corpus linguistics is Hundt and Gardner (2017). Lists of corpora suitable for use in historical pragmatic work are given in Kytö (2010), now somewhat dated, and Taavitsainen (2015). For a good overview of corpus annotation, see Archer, Culpeper, and Davies (2008); Weisser (2015) compares several speech-act annotations that have been developed for Present-day English (this is quite a technical article). On diachronic corpus pragmatics, see Jucker (2013), Jucker and Taavitsainen (2014b), Taavitsainen (2015), and Taavitsainen and Jucker (2020). Aijmer and Rühlemann (2013) is a good handbook on corpus pragmatics, while Taavitsainen, Jucker, and Tuominen (2014) is a collection of articles on English diachronic corpus pragmatics.

While a number of the corpora mentioned in this chapter are freely available online (such as COHA, TV, Movies, Hansard, *The Old Bailey Corpus*, EEBO, ECCO), others require that you contact the developer in order to acquire access to the corpus (such as CLMET3.0, CEAL, CEN). Signing up for the CQPweb

(Corpus Query Processor) at the University of Lancaster[1] provides access to a number of important corpora, such as *The Helsinki Corpus*, *A Corpus of English Dialogues*, ARCHER-3.2, Shakespeare's First Folio, *Newspapers at Lancaster*. Some corpora require subscriptions, often provided by university libraries. A quite complete listing of English corpora can be found at the Corpus Resource Database (CoRD) provided by the Research Unit for Variation, Contacts and Change in English of the University of Helsinki.[2] For full details on individual corpora, see "Sources (dictionaries, corpora, primary texts)" in the References.

[1] https://cqpweb.lancs.ac.uk/   [2] https://varieng.helsinki.fi/CoRD/corpora/index.html

3   Pragmatic Markers

3.1   Introduction

The study of pragmatic markers was presented as a case study in historical pragmatics in Chapter 1. This chapter takes up the topic in more detail. We first provide a nuanced definition of pragmatic markers and their characteristics, examining how they compare with or differ from related "short" forms. We then examine how pragmatic markers are studied historically. In the sections that follow, we explore the origins of pragmatic markers, using representative examples of one-word, phrasal, and clausal pragmatic markers in the history of English, and the pathways that they follow in their development. The question of what processes of change explain the rise of pragmatic markers – a topic that has been hotly debated – is explored in the last section of the chapter.

3.2   Characteristics of Pragmatic Markers

As you saw in Chapter 1, pragmatic markers – often called discourse markers – are forms that are set off syntactically from their clause (their "host") and lack clear lexical or propositional content, such as *well, now, you see, after all, I mean, so, in fact,* and *you say* in the following examples:

(1)   a.   Ah, **well, now, you see**, they're me best customers. (2000 *Fantasy & Science Fiction*; COHA)
       b.   **After all, I mean**, a thing can be just so lousy. (1942 Hale, *Prodigal Women*; COHA)
       c.   **So, in fact, you say**, let us forget that war we started, and the defeat, ... (1961 *The Atlantic Monthly*; COHA)

As the names suggest, however, these forms are understood as serving textual ("discourse") and interpersonal ("pragmatic") functions: "they situate their host unit with respect to the surrounding discourse and with respect to the speaker–hearer relationship" (Waltereit 2006: 64). Rather than propositional or referential meaning, they have what is called "procedural" meaning. That is, they guide the hearer/reader to the correct interpretation of the surrounding discourse. Pragmatic markers have a wide range of functions and often serve multiple functions at the same time. Textually, they may initiate or end discourse, mark a boundary in discourse, introduce, resume, or shift the topic of discourse, acquire, hold, or relinquish the floor in conversations, or denote new or old information. Subjectively, they may express a response or attitude to the preceding or following discourse, signal understanding or continued attendance to what is being said, or hedge an opinion. Interpersonally, they may confirm shared knowledge, effect cooperation or sharing, request confirmation, evoke politeness by expressing deference or showing intimacy. Pragmatic markers thus form a functional class rather than a clear morphosyntactic class. As a result, membership in the category of pragmatic marker is rather fluid, and scholars do not agree upon a definitive set of forms belonging to the category.

Pragmatic markers can be identified by a number of characteristics that are summarized in Table 3.1. While often "short" one-word items (*well, now, so, like*), they may also be phrases (*of course, indeed, by the way*) and (reduced) clauses (*I guess, you know, it seems*). They are often identical in form to fully lexical and compositional forms (e.g., *like* as a preposition or conjunction as well as a pragmatic marker). They occur preferentially at the clause boundaries (right or left) outside the core syntactic structure ("parenthetically"), often in a separate intonation group. At the same time, they may be moveable and also occur in sentence-medial position. They lack semantic content; that is, they are non-propositional or non-referential in meaning. For this reason, they are not easily glossed or translated. Because they are syntactically and semantically optional: their absence "does not render a sentence ungrammatical and/or unintelligible" (Fraser 1988: 22). But it can be argued that they are communicatively and pragmatically necessary, contributing in critical ways to the interpretation of the discourse. Pragmatic markers are frequent and salient in oral discourse and hence colloquial and frequently stigmatized, though a different set of pragmatic markers may also be found in written discourse.

Pragmatic markers overlap with a number of classes of other short, independent forms, such as interjections, conversational routines, hesitation and backchannelling markers, and general extenders. Interjections (e.g., *ouch, oops, gee*), like many pragmatic markers, are invariable and typically a single morpheme. Some interjections – most notably *oh* and *hwæt* (see below, §3.4) – have been analyzed as both interjections and pragmatic markers. However, there are differences between the two categories. Some interjections express the speaker's wishes (e.g., *shh, psst*) while others establish contact between speaker and hearer (*yeah, mhm*), but most are essentially emotive, uttered by the speaker as a spontaneous emotional reaction to a situation (*ugh, ouch, gosh*). Unlike pragmatic markers, which must be adjoined to a phrase or clause, interjections form a complete utterance on their own. The majority of interjections – the so-called "primary interjections" such as *wow, oho, oops* – are not identical with any other part of speech; however, some interjections – the "secondary interjections" such as *Goddammit, my goodness, thank God* – have

Table 3.1 *Characteristics of pragmatic markers (adapted from Brinton 2017b: 9)*

Phonological and lexical characteristics

(a) Pragmatic markers are often "small" items, although they may also be phrasal or clausal; they are sometimes phonologically reduced.

(b) Pragmatic markers may form a separate tone group, but they may also form a prosodic unit with preceding or following material.

(c) Pragmatic markers do not constitute a traditional word class, but are most closely aligned to adverbs, conjunctions, or interjections.

Syntactic characteristics

(d) Pragmatic markers occur either outside the syntactic structure or loosely attached to it.

(e) Pragmatic markers occur preferentially at clause boundaries (initial/final) but are generally moveable and may occur in sentence-medial position as well.

(f) Pragmatic markers are grammatically optional but at the same time serve essential pragmatic functions (and are, in a sense, pragmatically non-optional).

Semantic characteristics

(g) Pragmatic markers have little or no propositional/conceptual meaning, but are procedural and non-compositional.

Functional characteristics

(h) Pragmatic markers are often multifunctional, having a range of pragmatic functions.

Sociolinguistic and stylistic characteristics

(i) Pragmatic markers are predominantly a feature of oral rather than written discourse; spoken and written pragmatic markers may differ in form and function.

(j) Pragmatic markers are frequent and salient in oral discourse.

(k) Pragmatic markers are stylistically stigmatized and negatively evaluated, especially in written or formal discourse.

(l) Pragmatic markers may be used in different ways and at different frequencies by men and women or native and non-native speakers.

both independent uses and conventional uses as interjections (see Ameka 1992). For the most part, primary interjections cannot be traced back to full-content forms, though there are a few exceptions: *gee* < *Jesus* (Gehweiler 2008), *marry* < *by Mary* (Lutzky 2012a), *pardie* < *par Deu* 'by God', *alas* < *ha/a las* 'miserable'. The inventory of interjections in English has changed in significant ways over time. OE interjections such *eala, la/ lo, efne, wa* and ME interjections such as *a(h), alas, fie, hei, tush, parde, weilawei* look very foreign to us today. Many of the most common interjections of Present-day English arise only in the modern period (*oops, wow, ouch, yuck*). Despite their intrinsic interest, interjections will be omitted from the discussion in this chapter for the sake of space.

Conversational routines, "formulaic speech acts such as thanking, apologizing, requesting, offering, greetings, complimenting" (Aijmer 1996: 2), such as *thank you, I'm sorry, how are you?, excuse me,* while they bear some resemblance to pragmatic markers in their fixed form and interpersonal meaning, retain their content meaning to a much greater extent than do pragmatic markers, can stand alone as independent utterances, and serve primarily illocutionary functions. A number of these forms are thus treated in Chapter 6 on speech acts (i.e., greetings, thanks) and in Chapter 5 on politeness (i.e., responses to thanks). Backchannel devices and hesitation markers (*mhm, uh, um, er*) are similarly short, fixed, and syntactically free forms used in oral discourse, but they have strictly defined functions and do not necessarily occupy the clause boundaries. Like primary interjections, they do not derive from content forms and thus do not overlap with other more lexical forms. Forms such as *mhm,* as you can see, are variously interpreted as either interjections or back channels – thus pointing to the fuzzy boundaries between categories and definition. Finally, "general extenders" such as *and stuff, or something (like that),* and *and so forth,* like pragmatic markers, have interpersonal and other discourse-pragmatic functions, occupy the right sentence periphery, and have high frequency in speech, but they are more syntactically and prosodically incorporated than pragmatic markers and form a fairly homogeneous set of forms generally following a fixed pattern (see Overstreet and Yule 2021). See Table 3.2 for a summary of the differences between pragmatic markers and other "short" forms.

3.3   Studying Pragmatic Markers

Once identified, pragmatic markers lend themselves most readily to the form-to-function approach discussed in Chapter 2. But identification can be a challenge. Pragmatic markers may be transitory, and over time the set of pragmatic markers in English has undergone considerable change. For instance, we have lost pragmatic markers such as *hwæt, witodlice, anon, iwis, for the nones, what ho, whilom, pray/prithee, faith, marry, I thee bihote, trusteth me wel, forsooth, peradventure, God woot,* and *I warrant,* though at the same time, some pragmatic markers are of long standing, for instance *that is to say* (from Old English), and *I think/guess/ believe, you know, you see/say* (all from Middle English). It is also necessary to recognize that pragmatic markers may be highly multifunctional, and distinguishing between content uses and pragmatic uses of a particular form is an ongoing challenge.

Pragmatic markers may be studied using a historical pragmatics (proper) or diachronic pragmatics approach, as was discussed in Chapter 2. That is, the use and function of a pragmatic marker in a particular period (or text, or genre, or author) can be the focus of study, or the origin and development of a pragmatic marker over time, from its lexical source, can be explored.

Table 3.2 *Pragmatic markers vs. other "short" forms*

	like pragmatic markers	**unlike pragmatic markers**
Interjections	– are typically invariable in form and monomorphemic	– serve primarily an emotive function – stand as a complete utterance – are not identical to other parts of speech[*] – cannot be traced back to full-content forms[*]
Conversational routines	– are fixed in form – are interpersonal in meaning	– retain semantic content to a great extent – serve an illocutionary function – can stand as a complete utterance
Backchannel devices and hesitation markers	– are short and fixed in form – are syntactically free	– have a single, clearly defined function – are not limited to clause boundaries – do not derive from content forms
General extenders	– are discourse-pragmatic in function	– occur only at the right periphery – are syntactically and prosodically incorporated – constitute a fairly homogeneous group – follow a fixed syntactic pattern

[*] These features do not apply to secondary interjections.

An example of the historical pragmatic approach is Lutzky's (2012b) study of *why* and *what* in EModE drama. These are markers that in Present-day English seem to be restricted to American English. Within the EModE period, Lutzky also considers change over time, from 1500 to 1760, thus incorporating a diachronic pragmatic approach. She finds that while both have continuing uses as interrogatives in this period, *why* functions as a pragmatic marker 70 percent of the time and *what* 12 percent of the time, with *why* increasing in this use over time, as shown in Figure 3.1

In their pragmatic use, when introducing interrogatives, both *what* and *why* express speaker surprise, irritation, or even contempt; *why* can also have the implication of disbelief and serve to challenge what the interlocutor has said (2a–b) (see Culpeper and Kytö 2010: 383). When introducing declaratives, *why* is more common and has an explanatory or hedging function (2c), while *what* displays impatience. When used in conjunction with a vocative, they can also serve to attract the attention of the interlocutor.

(2)   a. *Medley* Get thee gone for the prettiest Hero that ever was shown on any Stage.
        Exit Pistol
        Sowrwit Short and sweet, faith, **what**, are we to have no more of him?
        (1737 Fielding, *The Historical Register* 22–3; CED; Lutzky 2012b: 182)

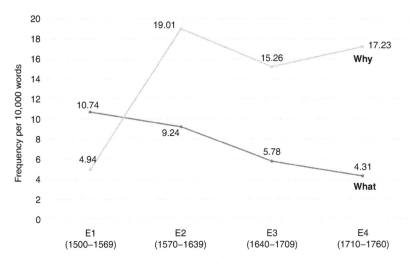

Figure 3.1 Distribution of the pragmatic markers *what* and *why* in Early Modern English by period (adapted from Lutzky 2012b: 181)

(Ursula Lutzky. 2012. *Why* and *what* in Early Modern English drama. In Manfred Markus, Yoko Iyeiri, and Reinhard Heuberger (eds.), *Middle and Modern English corpus linguistics: A multi-dimensional approach*. Amsterdam: John Benjamins, 181. https://benjamins.com/catalog/scl.50.16lut. Reprinted with permission.)

    b. *Ranger* ... Here have I been at it these three Hours – but the Wenches will never let me alone –
    Bellamy Three Hours! – **Why**, do you usually study in such Shoes and Stockings? (1747 Hoadley, *The Suspicious Husband* 4; CED; Lutzky 2012b: 186)
    c. *Countesse* ... vnlesse you will sweare to me, you will neither court nor kisse a dame in any sort, till you come home againe.
    Moren **Why** I sweare I will not. (1599 Chapman, *An Humerous Dayes Myrth* D3V–D4 R; CED; Lutzky 2012b: 185)

In sum, both are primarily interpersonal markers, expressing the speaker's attitude toward the interlocutor's utterances (Jucker 2002: 221).

An example of the more obviously diachronic pragmatic approach is Davidse et al.'s (2015) study of the development of *no doubt/I have no doubt*. The original epistemic meaning (of certainty and predictability) of this form has eroded, and as a pragmatic marker, it has come to express interactional relations and interpersonal stance, sometimes with irony and ridicule, as in these examples:

(3)   a.   "Well, I'm sorry for it," replied he, with more of sulkiness than contrition:
            "what more would you have?"
            "You are sorry that I saw you, **no doubt**," I answered, coldly.
            "If you had not seen me," he muttered, fixing his eyes on the carpet, "it
            would have done no harm." (1848 A. Brontë, *The Tenant of Wildfell Hall*;
            The Corpus of Late Modern English Texts (extended version) [CLMETEV];
            Davidse et al. 2015: 49)
       b.   "My father is a man who seldom gives way to any elation of mind."
            "Ah, indeed! A philosopher, **I have no doubt**, like his son."
            "I have no claims to the title of philosopher, . . . " (1826 Disraeli, *Vivian
            Grey*; CLMETEV; Davidse et al. 2015: 45)

The pragmatic marker "can be used to invite a response from the addressee ... or to express agreement to the preceding utterance" (2015: 55). Davidse et al. argue that a set of structures predated the pragmatic marker use, including existential *there/it/∅ be (no) doubt*, personal *I have/ make (no) doubt*, and adverbial *no doubt* (perhaps modeled on *without doubt/out of doubt*), all of which developed epistemic meaning from the original lexical meaning. The pragmatic marker use arose in Late Modern English in the case of the latter two structures, the adverbial form with its greater positional flexibility leading the way. But the existential form did not develop into a pragmatic marker.

The assumption behind diachronic pragmatic studies is that pragmatic markers derive from fully compositional, lexical structures that undergo processes of change in the evolution toward pragmatic marker status. As Traugott and Dasher (2002: 156) argue, pragmatic markers "typically arise out of conceptual meanings and uses ... Over time, they not only acquire pragmatic meanings (which typically coexist for some time with earlier, less pragmatic meanings) but also come to have scope over propositions." The semantic development of pragmatic markers is fairly well understood and follows general principles of semantic change (see Traugott and Dasher 2002: Ch. 4):

- Content meaning evolves into procedural meanings through invited inferences that arise in the context of use. Invited inferencing occurs in many types of semantic change. For example, hearing a sentence such as *I have been unhappy since they left*, you might infer a causal meaning ("because they left") from a meaning that is originally temporal ("after they left"). The causal meaning can (and in this case does) then become part of the conventional meaning of the word.

- Meanings which are neutral and objective develop into meanings expressing speaker attitude or subjective belief ("subjectification") as well as meanings focused on the speaker–hearer interaction ("intersubjectification"). For example, the change in *while* from its temporal meaning (*I listen to podcasts while I cook*) to a concessive meaning (*While the book is well written, I didn't like the plot*) shows a change from an objective meaning of temporal simultaneity to one which expresses my subjective opinion of contrast, or subjectivity. We can see a change to intersubjective meaning in *surely*: from the subjective meaning (*We surely wouldn't be paid for that day* – i.e., 'I am confident/I believe we wouldn't be paid') to intersubjective meaning (*Surely, she of all people understands* – i.e., 'I believe she understands and I believe you do too').

- Meanings within the scope of the sentence come to have meanings related to the sentence as a whole or to larger chunks of discourse (Traugott and Dasher 2002: 40, 281).

In contrast, the syntactic pathways that pragmatic markers follow may be quite varied. Pragmatic markers have been found to originate in a wide variety of sources, including adverbials, conjunctions, prepositions, nouns, reduced main clauses, adverbial and relative clauses, nonfinite clauses, imperative clauses, pseudo-cleft clauses, and other structures (see Heine et al. 2021: 245). The syntactic pathways followed by pragmatic markers are examined in the next three sections.

3.4   Single-Word Pragmatic Markers

An early hypothesis concerning the development of pragmatic markers was that they develop from adverbs via conjunctive uses: adverb > conjunction > pragmatic marker (Traugott 1982). This pathway might explain the origin of the OE pragmatic marker *hwæt*. *Hwæt* functions as an interrogative adverb meaning 'what, why' introducing direct questions (4a) and as a conjunction introducing indirect questions (4b). It can also be syntactically independent from the sentence that it is adjoined to and serve as an introductory particle with vague or indeterminate meaning (4c). This last usage appears at the beginning of *Beowulf* as well as a number of other OE poems and often introduces important sections within the poems. Translators have struggled to gloss this form, suggesting a range possibilities, including 'indeed', 'certainly', 'lo', 'listen', 'hear me', and 'what ho'.

(4)   a. **Hwæt** sceal ic ma riman yfel endeleas? (Jul 505; DOEC; Brinton 2017b:14)

            'why must I recount more endless evil'

        b. God ana wat **hwæt** him weaxendum winter bringað. (Fort 8; DOEC; Brinton 2017b:14)

            'God alone knows what the winter brings for the growing one'

        c. **Hwæt**, we for dryhtene iu dreamas hefdon,/ song on swegle selrum tidum, (Sat 44–5; DOEC; Brinton 2017b: 48)

            'Why, we before had joys in front of the lord, song in the heavens in better times'

Because of its syntactic independence and apparently expressive or exclamatory force, the usage in (4c) has traditionally been treated as an "interjection," though this view has been contested (Walkden 2013). If we carefully examine the contexts in which this form occurs, we see that *hwæt* almost always occurs in the context of first- or second-person pronouns (i.e., an interpersonal context) in which the poet or character in the poem indicates how information has been acquired, reminds the hearer of what has been said or narrated, recalls past events (as in 4c), or points out what is evident or visible. What follows *hwæt* is common knowledge because it is part of the cultural or historical tradition, it is part of the immediate past of the hearer, or it has been given in the text. That is, *hwæt* serves to call attention to the following discourse and to establish common ground or knowledge between speaker or hearer. It may also serve to bring information to consciousness by renewing interest in it and making it salient. Thus, OE *hwæt* serves the same functions that have been identified for the pragmatic marker *you know/y'know* in Present-day English. This pragmatic use of *hwæt* declines and falls out of use in Middle English. A common pragmatic marker in Middle English is *what ho*, used as an attention-getting device. The PDE use of *y'know what?* and *guess what?* as an attention-getting device and narrative opening, especially in children's language, may show remnants of both the OE and ME uses. The EModE use of *what* to express surprise (discussed above) can also be traced back to Middle English.

The question of whether the pragmatic marker develops out of the conjunctive use, following the pattern adverb > conjunction > pragmatic marker must be answered in the negative, however. While the conjunctive use develops from the use of *hwæt* as an interrogative adjective/adverb, it is not clear that the pragmatic use derives from the conjunctive use. In fact, the pragmatic use is contemporary with, or predates, the conjunctive use.

Addressing problems of this sort, Traugott (1995/97: 13) proposes a different sequence of development: clause-internal adverb > sentential adverb > pragmatic marker. That is, an adverb such as a manner adverb moves from its position in the predicate of the sentence where it has narrow scope to the position of a sentential adverb (typically clause-initial position) where it has scope over the entire proposition. In this position it then acquires pragmatic meanings (such as those relating to the upcoming discourse or to speaker–hearer relations) and ceases to evaluate the proposition. Lenker (2010) discusses such a development for the ME adverb *truly*. It begins as a manner adverbial meaning 'faithfully, loyally, with steadfast allegiance', as in (5a). It then acquires epistemic meaning and begins to function as a sentence adverbial, expressing a subjective perspective 'I am being truthful when I say', 'it is true (in my opinion) that', as in (5b). Finally, it loses its epistemic meaning and acquires procedural meaning, serving as a pragmatic marker, or what Lenker calls a "transition marker"; it highlights the connective function of *and* and links to the following discourse (5c).

(5)   a. He was also a lerned man, a clerk,/ That Cristes gospel **trewely** wolde preche; (1387 Chaucer, *Canterbury Tales* A.Prol. 480–1; Lenker 2010: 124)

'He was also a learned man, a clerk who would loyally preach Christ's gospel . . .'

b. For **trewli**, fader I love oon (1393 Gower, *Confessio Amantis* 5.2536; Lenker 2010: 125)

'For indeed, father, I love one'

c. The which a long were to devyse./ And **trewely**, as to my juggement,/ Me thynketh it a thyng impertinent, (1387 Chaucer, *Canterbury Tales* E.Cl 52–4; Lenker 2010: 126)

' . . . it would take a long time to describe this thing to you and [TRANSITION marker], in my mind it is an irrelevant thing'

Another pragmatic marker that seems to follow this pattern is ME *whilom* (see Brinton 2017b: Ch. 3). This form is the dative plural of OE *hwīl* 'a while, space of time'. In Old English it is a sentence-internal adverb meaning 'at times, for a time, sometimes', as in (6a); this usage becomes rare in Middle English and obsolete by Early Modern English. *Whilom* begins to function as a sentence adverbial with the meaning 'formerly, at some past time'; this is its usual meaning from Middle English through Early Modern English (6b). In (6c) we see *whilom* functioning as a pragmatic marker with global scope marking textual structure. Specifically, it serves to introduce an episode or story and, as Jucker and Taavitsainen note (2013: 61), it also has genre-specific functions, setting up the expectation that a romance or fabliau will follow.

(6)   a. Þinceð him on mode þæt he his mondryhten clyppe ond cysse, . . . swa he **hwilum** ær in geardagum giefstolas breac. (Wan 41; DOEC)

'he thinks in his mind that he embraces and kisses his lord, . . . just as sometimes before in days gone by he enjoyed the throne'

b. & he answered þus:/ **Whilen** hit wes iseid; inne soð spelle,/ þat moni mon deð muchel vuel (a1225 Layamon, *Brut* 4129–31; *Corpus of Middle English Prose and Verse* [CMEPV]; Brinton 2017b: 81)

'and he answered thus: formerly it was said, in a true story, that many men did much evil'

c. **Whilom** ther was dwellynge in my contree/ An erchedeken, a man of heigh degree, . . . (1387 Chaucer, *Canterbury Tales* D.Fri 1301–2; CMEPV)

'Once upon a time there was dwelling in my country, an archdeacon, a man of high degree . . . '

While these two examples, *truly* and *whilom*, seem to show the progression from clause-internal adverb to sentential adverb to pragmatic marker, the historical data are often messy and sometimes scant. We see in the case of *truly*, for example, that all of the uses cited in (5) are roughly contemporaneous (fourteenth century). For *whilom*, the sentence adverbial and pragmatic marker uses (6b–c) seem to overlap in time; the *Middle English Dictionary* (MED) (s.v. *whīlom*, adv.) does not distinguish clearly between the two uses: "At one time, formerly, once; also, in narrative contexts: once upon a time" (def. a). Moreover, the examples of *hwilom* in the DOEC are already overwhelmingly clause-initial, suggesting that the sentence adverbial use is already possible. Thus, while the progressions look plausible, it is difficult to establish firm dating in these and similar cases.

3.5   Phrasal Pragmatic Markers

A number of pragmatic markers derive from prepositional phrases that are "univerbated" (coalesced) and "lexicalized" (comprehended as a single word, though not always written as such). These include forms such as ME *forsooth*, *peradventure*, EModE *perchance*, *perhaps*, *indeed*, and LModE *in fact*, *in truth*, *instead*, *after all*, *anyway*, and *of course*.

Traugott and Dasher (2002: 159–165) trace the development of *indeed* from sentence-internal adverb to sentential adverb to pragmatic marker. In Middle English, it serves as an adverbial meaning 'in action, practice' (7a). By the sixteenth century, it appears in initial position as a sentential epistemic adverb meaning 'in truth' (7b). Finally, it is recruited as a pragmatic marker meaning something like 'what's more' (7c) where it "signals that what follows is not only in agreement with what precedes, but is additional evidence being brought to bear on the argument" (2002: 164).

(7)   a.   Fals witnesse is in word and eek **in dede**. (1387 Chaucer, *Canterbury Tales* I.Pars 795; CMEPV).

'false witness is in word and also in deed'

b.   *Dan.*: . . . I pray you tell me. I thinke you take me for your friend.
Sam.: **In deede** I haue always found you my very good friend . . . (1593 Witches, p. A4V; Traugott and Dasher 2002: 163)

c.   last of all came in his youngest sonne, riding in a chariot, that it was drawne with buffeles ['buffalos'], which me thought was very vnseemly: **in deed** they haue but few horses, the which are smal nags, i neuer saw any of them put to draw, but only to ride on, (1606 Scott, *An Exact Discourse* . . . ; EEBO)

As in the case of *truly* and *whilom* above, the matter of timing here casts some doubt on the proposed sequence. The sentence adverbial use and the pragmatic marker use are almost contemporaneous. Moreover, distinguishing semantically between the sentence adverbial and pragmatic marker use is often very difficult.

In more recent work, Traugott (2020, 2022) does not argue for this simple linear progression, though she still traces a pathway from sentence-internal adverbial to pragmatic marker. The "digressive" pragmatic marker *by the way* originates in an adverbial in Middle English with the literal meaning 'along the way', in either a static or dynamic sense, as in (8a). Frequent use of this form with verbs of speaking (e.g., *talkynge by the way, told him by the way*) contributed to acquisition of figurative meaning (based on the schema that an argument is a journey). We see an example of this in (8b), where *by the way* means 'in passing'. Traugott notes that this meaning is related to discourse organization but its scope is still local, not global, and hence it is not a fully formed pragmatic marker. Structures such as those in (8c), where the form occurs with a relative clause that the speaker marks as an unimportant elaboration, express a high degree of subjectivity and represent an important step toward pragmatic marker status. The form achieves this status in examples such as (8d), where *by the w*ay occurs in clause-initial position, makes no mention of a path, either literal or textual, and expresses a high degree of subjectivity; that is, the upcoming discourse is only partially relevant in the speaker's opinion.

(8)   a. And **by the weye** his wif Creusa he les. (c. 1430 (c.1386) Chaucer, LGW 945; MED; Traugott 2020: 123)

            'And along the way his wife Creusa he lost'

        b. plato in his dialogue ... maketh mention **by the way** of a wonderfull earthquake, (1563 Fulke, *A Goodly Gallery*; EEBO; Traugott 2020: 124)
        c. it may be also, that within these two or three hundred yeares one of their great Auncestors, whom **by the way** they repeat in their genealogies from their demigorgons, i would say demigods, might come in at the window indirectly. (1630 Vaughn, *The Arraignment of Slander*; EEBO; Traugott 2020: 125)
        d. bees turn not droanes, nor courages ever abate or degenerate: **by the way**, I observe that none have ever arrived to an eminent grandeur, but who began very young. (1661 Argyll, *Instruction to a Son*; EEBO; Traugott 2020: 126)

What seems clear is that strict pathways do not capture the many and varied ways in which sentence-internal adverbs develop into pragmatic markers and each form follows its own unique path.

3.6   Clausal Pragmatic Markers

In English, there exist a wide variety of clausal pragmatic markers, also known as "comment clauses." In form, they represent a number of different structures, as shown in Table 3.3.

Declarative main clause pragmatic markers have received the most attention. In an important article Thompson and Mulac (1991), using synchronic data, propose a sequence of development for parenthetical *I think* and *I guess*, forms which they call "epistemic parentheticals." They observe that *guess* and *think* together constitute 65 percent of all complement-taking verbs, occur

Table 3.3 *Some clausal pragmatic markers in English*

Type	Examples
Declarative main clauses	*I believe/think/guess/ suppose/reckon, you know, I mean, I see, I say, I promise, I pray (you/thee), I find, I gather, it seems, I'm afraid, I'm sorry, I/you admit, I'm just saying*
Imperative main clauses	*look (you), lookee, say, see, listen, hark/harkee, mind you*
Adverbial clauses	*if you will/choose/want/prefer/like/want/wish, if you ask me, if I may say so, as you say, as you see, as it were, as you know, as it seems*
Absolute or free relative clauses	*(that is) to wit, (that is) to say, this is not to say, what's more, that said (being said, having been said), all/what I'm saying*

overwhelmingly with first-person subjects, and are the most common verbs in epistemic parentheticals in their corpus of conversational English. They argue that epistemic parentheticals originate as main clauses followed by *that* complements, as in (9a).

(9)   a.   **I think that** we can do it this time. (2002 LaBute, *The Mercy Seat*; COHA)
       b.   **I think** ∅ the neighbors complained. (2001 Glancy, *American Gypsy*; COHA)
       c.   It's too late for that, **I think**. (2000 Cruz, *Yellow Eyes*; COHA)
             We've spoken only two or three times, **I think**, in all our years of school. (2002 *Fantasy & Science Fiction*; COHA)

In Thompson and Mulac's data, *I think* and *I guess* occur over 90 percent of the time without the complementizer *that*, as in (9b). Here the status of *I think* is indeterminate, allowing for its reanalysis as a parenthetical. This results in the reversal of the main clause/complement clause structure: the original main clause (*I think*) assumes parenthetical status and the complement clause (*the neighbors complained*) takes on main clause status. Once *I think* assumes parenthetical status, it becomes moveable, as in (9c). I have termed this the "matrix clause hypothesis" (Brinton 2008: 36).

Boye and Harder (2007) propose a development pathway incorporating both structure and usage which is compatible with Thompson and Mulac's. They argue that the source construction consists of a main lexical clause, *I think*, with "primary discourse status" (it is the main point of the utterance and is inherently addressable – one could ask *really?*) followed by a complement clause. This undergoes usage reanalysis in which the main clause assumes secondary status. It is no longer the main point of the utterance but rather has a "modifying status." *I think* has been reanalyzed at the level of usage but not of structure. Finally, *I think* is structurally reanalyzed as "grammatical" (inherently non-addressable) and secondary to the point of the utterance (non-addressable, and moveable).

The matrix clause hypothesis has intuitive appeal. But does the synchronic progression proposed by Thompson and Mulac (1991) account for the diachronic development of main clause pragmatic markers? Do they all originate as complement-taking main clauses? Extensive studies of these forms in English suggest that in some cases, the matrix clause hypothesis is borne out and in other cases it is not. I provide an example of each case.

Methinks/methinketh 'it seems to me' is a pragmatic marker formed from univerbation of the dative personal pronoun *me* and impersonal uses of the verb *thinken*. (ME *thinken* is a conflation of two verbs in Old English, one personal and one impersonal.) This form can be followed by a *that* clause (10a) or a *that*-less clause (10b), and it may also function parenthetically, in either the present or past tense (10c–d).

(10)   a.   **Me þincð þæt** hit hæbbe geboht sume swiðe leaslice mærðe. (King Alfred tr. Boethius *De Consol. Philos.* (Otho) xxiv.54; OED)

'it seems to me that it has bought some very false fame'

b.   With such gladnesse I daunce and skippe, **Me thenkth** I touche noght the flor. (a1393 J. Gower, *Confessio Amantis* (Fairf.) iv.2785; MED)

'with such gladness I dance and skip, it seems I do not touch the floor'

c.   'Twere good, **me thinks**, to steal our marriage (1590–1 Shakespeare, *Taming of the Shrew* III.ii; OSS)

d.   Nay, by the mass that he did not; he beat him most unpitifully, **me thought**. (1597 Shakespeare, *Merry Wives of Windsor* IV.ii; OSS)

Wischer (2000) argues that in Old English and Middle English *me thinks* was a free syntactic construction that could occur with other pronouns, in a full range of tenses and moods, and with variant word orders. However, over time it came to have a more fixed order (with the pronoun immediately preceding the verb) and to be followed by a *that*-less complement. Impersonal uses of the verb declined in the fifteenth century, with the exception of those with the first-person pronoun. The impersonal use was reserved for expressing 'opinion', while the personal use could express 'have in mind' as well as 'opinion' (Palander-Collin 1997). These changes allowed for the complement clause to be reinterpreted as the main clause, and *me thinketh* to be reanalyzed as an epistemic or evidential parenthetical, a change that began in the fifteenth century. Parenthetical *methinks* continued to be used until the eighteenth century but is now archaic, poetic, or regional (OED, s.v. *methinks*, v.). The progression outlined in Wischer thus conforms to the "matrix clause hypothesis." Palander-Collin's (1997: 387) statistical data also shows a progression from *that* clause to ∅-clause to parenthetical for impersonal *thinken*, but she notes that the earliest parentheticals in her data are second person, not first person.

Diachronic evidence suggests that the very forms that Thompson and Mulac (1991) use to illustrate the matrix clause hypothesis, *I think* and other epistemic parentheticals, arise historically in a different way. As I have argued (Brinton 2017b: Ch. 5), first-person epistemic parentheticals are well established in Middle English, formed with a variety of verbs. They may occur in final position (11a), in medial position (11b), and ambiguously in initial position (11c).

(11) a. "And that ye weten wel yourself, **I leve**." (1380–86 Chaucer, *Troilus and Criseyde* II 238; Brinton 2017b: 142)

'And that you know well yourself, I believe'

   b. "I nas, ne nevere mo to ben, **I thynke**,/ Ayeins a thing that myghte the forthynke." (1380–86 Chaucer, *Troilus and Criseyde* II 1413–14; Brinton 2017b: 142)

'I wasn't, nor never more to be, I think, against a thing that might displease you'

   c. "**I woot right wel**, thou darst it nat withseyn." (1387 Chaucer, *Canterbury Tales* A.Kn. 1140; Brinton 2017b: 148)

'I know quite well, you dare not deny it'

Thompson and Mulac's matrix clause hypothesis rests on the frequency of ambiguous *that*-less clauses as well as the predominance of first-person subjects. Middle English data on *that*-deletion and the use of cognitive verbs with first-person subjects are not, however, persuasive (see Brinton 2017b: 158–159). Moreover, if we look back to Old English, we find that although it has a large set of cognitive verbs that occur frequently with an adjoined *þæt*-clause, the omission of the complementizer is rare. A much more likely OE source for epistemic parentheticals is an adverbial clause with *þæs þe*, as shown in (12a). The complementizer *þæs þe* functions as an adverbial connective meaning 'the measure in/the extent to which' (Fischer 2007). This construction is continued by ME adverbial clauses with *as* or *so* (12b).

(12) a. se hæfde ænne sunu nu for þrym gærum, & se wæs, **þæs þe ic wene**, V wintre, (GDPi and 4(C) 19.289.3–4; Brinton 2017b: 156)

'he had one son now for three years, and he was, so I know, five winters old'

   b. "For thrittene is a covent, **as I gesse**." (1387 Chaucer, *Canterbury Tales* D. Sum. 2259; Brinton 2017b: 160)

'For thirteen is a convent, as I guess'

The development of epistemic parentheticals from these adverbial clauses is straightforward. As adverbial clauses they are by nature more or less loosely adjoined to the main clause. Deletion of the complementizer leads to greater independence and parenthetical status and allows for movement to clause-medial and initial position. Unlike the matrix clause hypothesis, there is no reorganization of the syntactic hierarchy. Another type of epistemic parenthetical, the impersonal *it seems (to me)* seems to arise in the same way. López-Couso and Méndez-Naya (2014) find that adverbial *as/so it seems/thinks* clauses predate and give rise to "bare" parentheticals. Furthermore, they find that *that*-deletion with *it seems* becomes frequent only well after the development of parenthetical forms, concluding that it is the parentheticals which motivate the deletion of *that*, not the reverse.

Adverbial clauses are a frequent source of clausal pragmatic markers (see Table 3.3). An example of an adverbial clause development is *as it were*, which functions exclusively as a metalinguistic PDE pragmatic marker meaning that "a word or statement is perhaps not formally exact though practically right" (OED, s.v. *as*, adv. and conj., def. P2a); it hedges the linguistic adequacy of the expression (Claridge 2013: 162). Unlike other pragmatic markers, this marker is equally common in speech and in some types of writing. The remnant subjunctive *were* undoubtedly contributes to its more "literary" quality and its use in academic writing as well as fiction. Also, unlike other pragmatic markers, *as it were* has a more local scope, often qualifying the adjacent word or phrase. For example, it may accompany figures of speech, clichés, words set off by quotation marks, foreign words or phrases, unusual native formations, or a word that is unexpected in context. The development of this form has been studied by Brinton (2008: 171–177, 180–182) and Claridge (2013), who arrive at similar if not identical conclusions. The form *swa/swilc hit wære* is rare in Old English; here and in Middle English it is followed by a subjective complement and forms a complete clause. It is a clause of hypothetical comparison meaning 'as if it were X'. *It* refers back to a noun in context (13a). This usage dies out after the sixteenth century. By the first half of the fourteenth century, *as it were* occurs without a complement and has metalinguistic meaning; *it* is no longer referential (13b). In Early Modern English, pragmatic *as it were* is the majority form, becoming the only possible use by c. 1700 (Claridge 2013: 166). *As it were* occurs in EModE contexts similar to those in modern English, for example with figurative language (13c).

(13)   a.   His comb was redder than the fyn coral,/ And batailled **as it were** a castel wal; (1387 Chaucer, *Canterbury Tales* B.NP 2859–60; Brinton 2008: 172)

'His comb was redder than fine coral and notched with crenellations as if it were a castle wall'

   b.   Hi seye an aungel ... a ffayr ȝong man **as hit were**, Ycloþed in white cloþes. (a1325 (c1280) *South English Legendary: Temporale (Passion of Christ)* (Pep2344) 1824; MED; Brinton 2008: 173)

'They saw an angel ... a fair young man as it were clothed in white clothes'

   c.   Sir, he hath never fed of the dainties that are bred in a book; he hath not eat paper, **as it were**; he hath not drunk ink. (1594–95 Shakespeare, *Love's Labours Lost* IV.ii; OSS)

Pragmatic *as it were* is a native construction, though its frequency in Middle English is likely influenced by Latin *quasi*, adopted through French, which is often translated *as it were*. The development postulated for *as it were* again (unlike the matrix clause hypothesis) does not involve any change in syntactic hierarchy, since the adverbial clause is intrinsically semi-independent and subordinate to the main clause. The adverbial complementizer is preserved in this case but the clause is truncated. How is the complement lost? One scenario sees the complement being reanalyzed as an appositive (e.g., (13a) could be read "his comb was redder than fine coral and crenelated (as it were), a castle wall"). Another scenario sees change as occurring in ambiguous contexts such as (14), where *as it were* can be read as a comparative clause with the complement belonging to the *as it were* clause ("which is to God as if it were an enemy"), or it can be read as parenthetical with the complement belonging to the main clause and hence omissible ("which is to God an enemy") (Claridge 2013: 164).

(14)   þe whiche is to God **as it were** an enmye … (1350–1420 cmcloud; HC; Claridge 2013: 164)

'which is to God as (if) it were an enemy'

The metalinguistic meaning preserves the comparative 'similar to' sense of the source construction but the form also acquires subjective meaning since it expresses the speaker's assessment of the state of affairs (Claridge 2013: 167). There is general fossilization of the form:
- *as* expresses comparison, whereas in other contexts this meaning becomes obsolete (OED, s.v. *as*, adv. and conj., def. BI1b), replaced by *as if* or *as though*;
- the subjunctive is preserved; and
- *it* becomes non-referential and non-anaphoric.

As a result of clausal truncation and ossification, *as it were* loses its clausal qualities and becomes particle-like – a "fossilized formula" in Claridge's terminology. It becomes fully independent or parenthetical (often set off by commas in contemporary texts) and becomes moveable.

Imperative and free relative clauses/absolutes are much less common as sources of pragmatic markers (see Table 3.3). Like declarative Subject Verb constructions such as *I think*, imperatives such as *look*, *say*, and *see* are frequently followed by complement clauses (including both *that* clauses and *wh*-clauses). In their development as pragmatic markers, the imperative forms undergo the same reversal of syntactic hierarchy we see in the matrix clause hypothesis, as in:

main[Look] subordinate[that you love your wife] > parenthetical[Look (you)] main[love your wife]

A free relative clause such as *what I'm saying* also undergoes a reversal in syntactic hierarchy. It begins as the subject of a pseudo-cleft clause (as in 15a) and is "demoted" to a parenthetical pragmatic marker attached to the original complement (as in 15b). Interestingly, we see a case of syntactic misanalysis (in 15c) where the free relative in its parenthetic use is accompanied by the original main verb *is*.

(15)   a. **What I'm saying** is that there should be a diversity of dollars spent. (2017 Fox: Ingraham Angle; COCA)

        b. **What I'm saying**, I think it's something genetic. (1997 *The Massachusetts Review*; COCA)

        c. **All I'm saying is**, you looked with me and it took them about five minutes. (2005 CNN_Dolans; COCA)

3.7   Processes of Change

The preceding sections have looked at the different historical sources of pragmatic markers. While scholars are generally agreed on the sources of many pragmatic markers and the pathways they follow in their (often complex) development, there is one area which is still much disputed: the process of change which best explains the changes. A number of well-known processes of change have been suggested, including lexicalization, grammaticalization, pragmaticalization, and, most recently, cooptation. We will examine this controversy below.

Lexicalization: Lexicalization refers to the creation of new lexemes, or content words. This may involve the following:

- the univerbation of a syntactic phrase into a single word (e.g., *nuts-and-bolts* 'practical details', *wherewithal* 'necessary means');
- the change of a complex form into an unanalyzable or simple form (e.g., *nightmare* < *night* + OE *mære* 'incubus, spirit'), often known as *folk etymology*;
- the change of a morpheme into an indivisible part of a word's phonology (e.g., *handiwork* < OE *hand* + *ge-* + *weorc* 'hand + prefix + work'), sometimes known as *phonogenesis*; and
- the shift of a grammatical to a lexical form (e.g., *up* [adverb/preposition] > *up* [verb])

The univerbation that we see in some pragmatic markers has suggested to scholars that pragmatic markers may undergo lexicalization. For example, Wischer (2000) argues that *methinks* changes from a free syntactic phrase into a fossilized and fused form; it thus becomes an entry in the lexicon. Fischer (2007) likewise argues that *I think* forms a single lexical unit, at the same time retaining much of its lexical meaning. Krug (1998) sees lexicalization in the development of the phrase *is it not* > *in't it* > *innit*, a common pragmatic marker in British English. The form becomes invariant, inseparable, and morphologically opaque. It loses phonological substance and is desemanticized, serving pragmatic functions such as turn-taking.

An immediate difficulty with this suggestion is that it could account for changes undergone by phrasal and clausal pragmatic markers, but not single-word pragmatic markers. More significantly, pragmatic markers cannot be understood as (fully) lexical items. They do not express content (referential) meaning, they do not belong to a major lexical category, and, unlike lexical items, they are syntactically and prosodically constrained. Lexicalization often involves loss of compositionality, that is, the meaning of the whole is not a sum of the meaning of the parts (e.g., the meaning of *nuts-and-bolts* is not a sum of the meaning of 'nuts' and 'bolts' and the meaning of *innit* is not a sum of the meaning of 'is', 'not', and 'it'). But it does not involve the loss of semantic content which we see in the case of many pragmatic markers. For these reasons, this view has not been widely accepted.

Grammaticalization: The majority of scholars studying pragmatic markers have suggested that they undergo grammaticalization.

Grammaticalization is a process by which an independent lexical item becomes a grammatical marker (such as a function word, clitic, or inflection). An oft-cited example of grammaticalization is the development of the French future tense inflection, as in *chanterai* 'I will sing'. Historically we know that the ending *-erai* develops from the Latin independent verb *habere* 'have', which joins with the preceding verb *cantare* 'sing'; in the process, *habere* becomes a (lexically depleted) grammatical marker of 'future'; it is phonologically reduced, coalesced and bonded with the preceding verb, losing its status as a verb and becoming an inflection. It is also desemanticized as it loses the meaning of 'possession' that it carried as a verb.

In the history of English, grammaticalized forms do not typically become inflections but remain at the less fully grammaticalized stage of function words. For example, *will* and *shall*, which were full verbs in Old English (taking direct objects) with the meaning of 'intention' and 'obligation', grammaticalized as markers of the future tense, supplying the language with overt markers of the future. The preposition *to*, which was followed by an "inflected infinitive" (a verb with a noun case ending) in Old English, has come to be an "empty" marker of the infinitive followed by the bare form of the verb (e.g., *tō singenne > to sing*). *To* does not retain directional meaning or prepositional status but is simply a grammatical marker. Closest to the French example given above is the adverbial ending *-ly* (as in *quickly*), which grammaticalizes from the full OE word *līc* meaning 'body'. In the process it loses semantic content and becomes a bound form. The words discussed above, *whilom* and *indeed*, involve grammaticalization in their early stages, though in separate developments. *While* as a conjunction (e.g., *He cooked, while I walked the dog*) grammaticalizes from a noun, *hwīl* 'a space/period of time', in the OE phrase *þa hwīle þa* 'at the time that'. It reduces to *while that* and ultimately to *while*. The adverb *indeed* develops from the full noun *deed* 'that which is done, acted, performed' in the prepositional phrase *in deed* 'in action'. In both cases, the nouns are demoted to a more grammatical category (conjunction/ adverb), with their content meaning (referring either to time or action) bleached.

Grammaticalization is a unidirectional and gradual change from lexical (source) to grammatical (target), involving a change from more major to more minor part of speech. Grammaticalized items undergo "decategorialization," or loss of the morphosyntactic characteristics of the source category. For example, a noun grammaticalizing to an adverb loses the ability to pluralize, to be modified by adjectives or specified by determiners, and to function as subject, object, or complement. It becomes fixed or "frozen" in form. Grammaticalizing items typically undergo some amount of phonetic loss and fusion. They also undergo desemanticization, losing semantic content, though the grammaticalized item usually retains some of the original lexical content (what is called "persistence"). As was discussed above, this loss of meaning is accompanied by the acquisition of subjective and intersubjective meanings, or (inter)subjectification, and a change from propositional to procedural meaning. In typical cases of grammaticalization, there is reduction in the scope of the grammaticalized item (e.g., an inflection has scope only over the word to which it attaches while an independent word may have scope over a larger construction). A grammaticalized item also becomes fixed in position (e.g., an inflection does not have the positional flexibility of an independent word), as in the case of -*ly*, which must attach to the end of the word it modifies, or *to* and *will/shall*, which must precede the verb they modify. Moreover, unlike an independent word, a grammaticalized form may become an obligatory element in a grammatical paradigm ("paradigmaticization"; e.g., one of a set of future markers. When a word grammaticalizes, it is often also retained in its non-grammaticalized form (what is called "divergence"). Finally, there may be "layering" of earlier and later grammaticalized forms, as when the newer future *be going to* coexists with the older *will/shall* futures.

Let's see whether the pragmatic marker *I mean* exhibits signs of grammaticalization (see Brinton 2008: Ch. 5). The original content meanings of *mean* are 'to intend (to do something)' and 'to signify, to intend to convey a certain sense'. Here *mean* is a full verb taking a complement (a noun, a phrase, or a clause), as in (16a). *I mean* begins to occur parenthetically and pragmatically in a metalinguistic sense, to make a formulation more precise, correct, or explicit (16b–c). Later we see uses in which the speaker is expressing attitude (16d–e) in the context of an evaluative adjective/adverb, and finally, *I mean* is used in formulas such as "do you see what I mean," which function as a check on understanding (16f).

(16)   a.   excepte there be any aunciente hystorye, **I mean** before the tyme of geffraye of monemouthe or beda, (1542 Elyot, *Bibliotheca Eliotæ Eliotis Librarie*; EEBO)
       b.   Take Saffron . . . then tease it, **I mean**, pull the parts thereof asunder. (1617 Woodall, *Surgeons Mate* [1653] 344; OED; Brinton 2008: 120)

    c. Let us now take a Prospect of their Governours, **I mean**, consider the Manners and Maxims of their Nobility. (1677 de la Houssaie, *Government of Venice* 266; OED; Brinton 2008: 122).

    d. Tell him also that he is properly appreciated – his honesty, **I mean**, and good intention, in his note to poor Lucia. (1823 Neal, *Seventy-Six*, volume 1; COHA)

    e. Can we make the inference that he has acted virtuously? virtuously, **I mean**, in the highest and best sense of the term? (1846 Richards, *Lectures on Mental Philosophy and Theology*; COHA)

    f. I have seemed to take the place in your household that – pray, forgive me, Mrs. Greyfield – only a husband, in fact or in expectancy, could be expected or permitted to occupy. **Do you see what I mean**? (1877 Victor, *The New Penelope*; COHA)

The development of *I mean* resembles grammaticalization in important ways. The process begins with a verb of general meaning, which is usual for grammaticalization. As *I mean* changes from a fully formed clause governing a complement to a reduced clause functioning as a parenthetical, it undergoes decategorialization. *I mean* becomes frozen in the first person and present tense and coalesced; that is, it does not allow adverbial modification to intercede between *I* and *mean* (e.g., *I truly/only/really mean*). It thus assumes a particle-like quality. Phonological attrition can occur, with pronunciations such as [əmiːn] or [miːn]. Semantically, the original meaning of 'to intend to do something' or 'to intend to convey something' becomes weakened as the parenthetical acquires metalinguistic meaning (as in 16b–c). But there is not complete desemanticization: the metalinguistic meaning retains vestiges of the original 'to intend to convey' meaning. In the parenthetical contexts, the speaker infers that the information is being rephrased for some reason, namely for the purposes of repair, reformulation, explicitness, or exemplification. *I mean* in these contexts has procedural rather than content meaning because it serves as an instruction on how to interpret the following discourse. Subjectification occurs in examples such as (16d–e), where the speaker expresses an attitude about honesty and virtue, and intersubjectification in examples such as (16f), where the speaker appeals to the hearer's understanding. In Present-day English, *I mean* may continue to function as a fully formed and variable matrix clause with its original meaning (e.g., *I was meaning to answer you earlier*), thus exhibiting divergence. Finally, *I mean* is also layered with older pragmatic forms with similar functions, such as *to wit*, *that is to say*, and *namely*.

    There are three respects in which the development of pragmatic markers is inconsistent with grammaticalization. We see two of these in the case of *I mean*. First, pragmatic markers generally *expand* in scope rather than retract because they change from having scope over a proposition to having scope over discourse. *I mean* exhibits this expansion in scope. Second, pragmatic markers do not become an obligatory part of a grammatical paradigm as it is conventionally understood. This is true of *I mean*. Third, while grammaticalization involves syntactic fixation, most pragmatic markers become *less* fixed in position and more mobile than their sources. *I mean* is atypical for pragmatic markers in being fairly restricted in position, typically occurring after the word or phrase it is reformulating.

The differences just noted have led some to question whether pragmatic markers can be said to undergo grammaticalization. However, on the question of scope, it could be argued that there are two types of scope, morphosyntactic scope and semantic-pragmatic scope. Standard cases of grammaticalization refer to the former, whereas in the case of the grammaticalization of pragmatic markers we must refer to the latter and understand there to be scope expansion. On the question of "paradigmaticization," one might argue that pragmatic markers, while they do not become an obligatory part of a grammatical paradigm (as might, for example, a future inflection), they are communicatively and pragmatically "obligatory." Moreover, like grammatical paradigms, pragmatic markers belong to a set of forms with common (pragmatic) functions and each marker stands in contrast to the other, much like a grammatical paradigm.

Pragmaticalization: Because pragmatic markers are in a sense "agrammatical" (they stand outside the core syntactic structure and do not belong to any recognized grammatical class), some scholars have been uncomfortable in explaining their development as grammaticalization. For this reason, an alternative process called "pragmaticalization" was proposed (Erman and Kotsinas 1993). This refers to the rise of a pragmatic marker either directly from a lexical source or via an intermediate grammatical stage. Pragmaticalization differs from grammaticalization by the optionality of pragmaticalized forms and their non-truth-conditionality (i.e., they do not denote something of which it can be said that it is "true" or "false"). The two processes as described, however, are "virtually indistinguishable" (Diewald 2011: 376). Both include decategorialization, loss of phonetic content, bleaching of the original propositional meaning, persistence of some degree of lexico-grammatical meaning, conventionalization of pragmatic inferences, subjectification, and scope expansion (over the whole proposition or utterance), layering of older and newer forms, and divergence between pragmaticalized and non-pragmaticalized variants. As Diewald notes, "The only difference lies in the perceived results of the diachronic process" (2011: 376). That is, pragmaticalization leads to the development of discourse-pragmatic forms.

Pragmaticalization can be subsumed within grammaticalization if one adopts a more encompassing view of "grammar." On the one hand, many aspects of grammar as it is traditionally defined (e.g., tense, aspect, mood, and deixis) rest upon pragmatic principles, and on the other hand, many aspects of pragmatics, such as information structuring, have a "grammatical" (or syntactic) dimension.

It is even possible to incorporate discourse-pragmatic elements into a formal theory of syntax (Wiltschko 2021). Thus, there seem to be good reasons for viewing grammar more broadly to encompass discourse functions. Hence, pragmaticalization can either be seen as a subtype of grammaticalization or dispensed with altogether.

Cooptation: The most recent suggestion concerning the development of pragmatic markers is that they undergo a process of "cooptation" followed by grammaticalization (Heine et al. 2021). This approach rests upon the view of grammar as containing two dimensions, sentence grammar and discourse or "thetical" grammar. The latter contains all extra-clausal elements, such as comment clauses, reporting clauses, tag questions, appositive relative clauses, left and right dislocations, and so on. Theticals are syntactically and prosodically independent, separate from the meaning of the sentence, "metatextual" in function (i.e., procedural), flexible in position, and with semantic-pragmatic scope beyond the sentence. Cooptation is a cognitive process which lifts an element out of sentence grammar into thetical grammar. Once this happens, the element may undergo grammaticalization (including decategorialization, desemanticization, phonetic erosion). Cooptation postulates an instantaneous change involving acquisition of the characteristics of theticals, followed by gradual grammaticalization.

I would argue that what cooptation explains is the rise of syntactically and prosodically less integrated and positionally mobile forms (i.e., the rise of parentheticals) but not the other characteristics (i.e., meaning independent of the sentence, procedural function, semantic-pragmatic scope beyond the sentence) that are central to the function of pragmatic markers. Furthermore, only a gradual change can motivate the change from the original lexical meaning to the type of procedural meaning that develops in a specific pragmatic marker, involving the conventionalization of invited inferences and dependent on contexts which permit both older and newer interpretations. That is, cooptation cannot account for why particular lexical items develop into expressions of certain kinds of pragmatic meaning, nor can it account for the persistence of aspects of the original lexical meaning in the pragmatic marker. Finally, cooptation does not explain decategorialization, which is considered a defining characteristic of the pragmatic marker.

3.8   Chapter Summary

This chapter covered the following topics:
- the characteristics of pragmatic markers as syntactically independent, grammatically optional words, clauses, and phrases with little or no conceptual meaning that are frequent in oral discourse;

- the relation of pragmatic markers to other "short" items such as interjections, conversational routines, backchannel devices, and general extenders;
- the study of pragmatic markers from a form-to-function approach either in a historical pragmatics (proper) or diachronic pragmatics perspective;
- the assumption that pragmatic markers derive diachronically from fully compositional, lexical constructions;
- the semantic development of pragmatic markers by general principles of semantic change, including invited inferencing, (inter)subjectification, and extension of scope;
- the syntactic pathways followed by single-word pragmatic markers, phrasal pragmatic markers, and clausal pragmatic markers (including declarative main clauses, adverbial clauses, imperatives and free relatives);
- the viability of the "matrix clause hypothesis," especially in relation to epistemic parentheticals; and
- the choice of processes of change responsible for the development of pragmatic markers, with grammaticalization favored over lexicalization, pragmaticalization, and cooptation, if an expanded definition of grammar is accepted.

3.9   Further Reading

An overview discussion of pragmatic markers is Brinton (2010). Brinton (1996) is an early treatment of pragmatic markers in English, Brinton (2008) focuses on clausal pragmatic markers, and Brinton (2017b) is a compilation of work on pragmatic markers over twenty years, containing fuller discussions of *hwæt* (Ch. 2), of *whilom* (Ch. 3), and of epistemic parentheticals (Ch. 5).

A treatment of pragmatic markers in British English, both synchronic and diachronic, is Beeching (2016); it has a semantic and sociolinguistic focus. Heine et al. (2021) is a comprehensive treatment of the development of pragmatic markers, with a focus on cooptation. Both contain useful definitions of pragmatic markers. There are numerous collections of essays on pragmatic markers. An early volume, Jucker (1995), contains a section on pragmatic markers in English; an excellent more recent collection is Fischer (2006).

The literature on grammaticalization is vast. Classic treatments are Hopper and Traugott (2003) and Lehmann (2015[1995]); for a recent and comprehensive treatment, see Narrog and Heine (2021). Principles such as "decategorialization," "persistence," and "layering" are introduced by Hopper (1991). On lexicalization, see Brinton and Traugott (2005), and on pragmaticalization, see Claridge and Arnovick (2010).

3.10   Exercises

1. Below is a passage from "The Knight's Tale" in Geoffrey Chaucer's *Canterbury Tales*. In this passage Arcite is praying to Mars (god of war) to give him success in the tournament with his cousin Palamon, a battle which will decide who gains the hand of the beautiful Emilie.

> I am yong and unkonnynge [ignorant], as thow woost
> And, as I trowe, with love offended [injured] moost
> That evere was any lyves creature,
> For she that dooth [makes] me al this wo endure
> Ne recceth [cares] nevere wher I synke or fleete [float].
> And wel I woot, er she me mercy heete [promises],
> I moot with strengthe wynne hir in the place,
> And wel I woot, withouten help or grace
> Of thee ne may my strengthe noght availle.
> Thanne help me, lord, tomorwe in my bataille,
> For thilke [that same] fyr that whilom brente [burnt] thee,
> As wel as thilke fyr now brenneth me,
> And do [make] that I tomorwe have victorie.
> (ll. 2393–2405)

   (a) Locate the epistemic parentheticals in the passage and discuss their function. In general, the function of epistemic parentheticals is to express evidentiality (the source of knowledge), epistemicity (the degree of reliability claimed by the speaker), and evaluation.

   (b) Is *whilom* used as a discourse marker here (l. 2403)? Explain.

2. The discourse marker *well* is one of the most ubiquitous and well-studied discourse markers in English. A wide variety of functions have been identified. Jucker (1997) sorts these into four types in Present-day English:

   (i) frame marker: *well* marks a change in topic, introduces direct speech, or otherwise indicates a textual boundary;

   (ii) fact-threat mitigator: *well* signals and mitigates some confrontation (e.g., a disagreement, a refused request, a rejected offer);

   (iii) qualifier: *well* indicates that what follows is not exactly what the hearer wants to hear, is not optimally coherent, or is insufficient in some way;

   (iv) pause filler: *well* bridges an interactional silence.

   Function (i) works on the textual level, serving to organize the discourse. Function (ii) is intersubjective, as is function (iv). Function (iii) is subjective.

   Which (if any) of these functions can you identify in the historical examples of *well* given below (all examples from Jucker 1997)? During which period do you find the different uses?

   Old English (*wel* + *la* [interjection]; *wella* falls out of use after Old English)

(a)   and cwæð þa on his geðance; **Wella** min drihten . hwaet ic her nu hreowlice
        haebbe gefaren (*Old English Legend of the Seven Sleepers* 1.23.574–6)

        'and said then in his thought, Alas, my Lord, what! how pitiably have I now
        fared here!'

[This represents internal speech on the part of the speaker.]
Middle English

(b)   "A wyf axeth ful many an observaunce./ I prey yow that ye be nat yvele
        apayd."/ "**Wel**," quod this Januarie, "and hastow ysayd? Straw for thy Senek,
        and for thy proverbes!" (1387 Chaucer, *Canterbury Tales* E.Mch 1563–7)

        "'A wife asks for much attention. I pray you that you be not ill pleased."
        "Well," said this January, "and have you spoken? Straw for your Seneca and
        for your proverbs!'"

[Here, January (the Merchant) is receiving advice from his friend about
marriage, which he rejects.]

(c)   "Aske what ye woll and ye shall have hit and hit lye in my power to gyff
        hit." "**Well**," seyde thys lady, "than I aske the head of thys knyght that hath
        wonne the swerde, . . ." (1469 Malory, *Morte d'Arthur*)

        "'Ask what you will and you shall have it if it lies in my power to give it."
        "Well," said this lady, "then I ask for the head of this knight that has won the
        sword . . . '"

[In this conversation, a knight says that he will provide his lady with anything
that is within his power to provide; she need only ask. The lady then says what
she wants.]
Early Modern English

(d)   CHOLMELY: Why what do I, I pray you, M. Throckmorton? I did nothing,
            I am sure you do picke Quarrels to me.
        THROCKMORTON: Well Maister Cholmely, if you do well, it is better for you,
            God help you. (1554 Trial of Sir Nicholas Throckmorton)

[In this trial transcript, Cholmely denies doing what Throckmorton has
accused him of doing. Throckmorton seems to (grudgingly) accept
Cholmely's protestations of innocence.]

(e)   Hee taught her how she might bring her to confesse. **Well**, she followed his
        counsell, went home, caused her to be apprehended and caried before
        a Iustice of peace. (1593 Gifford, *A Handbook on Witches and Witchcraft*)

[This passage occurs in a handbook and describes an event.]

(f)   LORD CHIEF JUSTICE: Did you lie with them?
        DUNNE: No, my Lord, I did not.
        LORD CHIEF JUSTICE: **Well**, I see thou wilt answer nothing ingenuously,
            therefore I will trouble my self no more with thee:. . . (1685 The Trial
            of Lady Alice Lisle)

[In this trial transcript, the Lord Chief Justice reacts to the witness Dunne's denial.]

(g)   KING LEAR: Vengeance! plague! death! confusion! Fiery? what quality? Why, Gloucester, Gloucester, I'ld speak with the Duke of Cornwall and his wife
GLOUCESTER: **Well**, my good lord, I have inform'd them so. (1605–6 Shakespeare, *King Lear* II.iv)

[Incensed at seeing his servant, the Earl of Kent, in stocks, King Lear demands to speak to his daughter Regan and her husband (the Duke of Cornwall). Gloucester says that he has already told them that the King wishes to speak with them.]

3. The pragmatic marker *(you) see* exists in a number of forms in Present-day English, with a range of functions. *You see* frequently prefaces an explanation or justification for a previous claim. *As you see* is frequently literal, but both *as you see* and *so you see* may express result; both are rare in Present-day English. *See (here/now)* can be used to ascertain the hearer's comprehension or agreement. And both *you see* and *see* can be used to express triumph:

(i)   They're just too weak, **you see**, to stand up for the Constitution and their own belief (2012 dissenter.firedoglake.com; COCA)
(ii)   So, **as you see**, the reason the bills have that phrase is because they were created by politicians (2012 patheos.com; COCA)
(iii) and I have a trust, **so you see**, money isn't my problem (1995 *Homicide: Life on the Street*; COCA)
(iv)   There was this thing, **see**, and we didn't like this Stamp Act. (2012 mediaite. com; COCA)
(v)   **You see**, I told you it wasn't anything. (1995 *How to Make an American Quilt*; COCA)

Fitzmaurice (2004) argues that the matrix clause hypothesis accounts for the development, as follows:
You see that/ Ø S > you see (parenthetical) > see
(She also argues that *you see* derives from *I see*, but there seems little evidence of this.)
(a)   The most frequent form historically is *you see* followed by a noun phrase. Figure 3.2 shows the frequencies of other forms of *you see* over time (note: CLMET here refers to *The Corpus of Late Modern English Texts*, an earlier version of CLMET3.0). Parenthetical *you see* takes off in Early Modern English. Is there evidence, in the frequencies shown, that parenthetical *you see* derives from main clause *you see*?
(b)   Pragmatic uses of *see (here/now)* appear in the nineteenth century. Does it seem likely that this form derives from truncation of parenthetical *you see*? If not, what could be a possible source for this form?

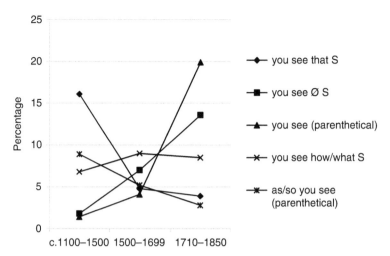

Figure 3.2 Occurrences of *you see* constructions. Based on the MED quotation database, the OED quotation database for Early Modern English, and CLMET for Late Modern English (from Brinton 2017c: 265)

(Laurel J. Brinton. 2017. Historical pragmatic approaches. In English historical linguistics: Approaches and perspectives. Cambridge: Cambridge University Press, 265. Reprinted with permission.)

4. *Whatever* can function as a pragmatic marker used to suggest "the speaker's reluctance to engage or argue, and hence often implying passive acceptance …; also used more pointedly to express indifference, indecision, impatience, skepticism" (OED, s.v. *whatever*, pron. and adj., def. E), as in

   (i) It's not that big a deal, **whatever**." (2006 *Chicago Tribune*; COHA)
   (ii) "You be good now, hear?" # Yeah, right. **Whatever**. (2009 Levine, *Killer Cruise*; COHA)

Looking at *whatever* in COHA, set off in final position (search string:, whatever .) and independently (search string: . whatever .), can you identify the earliest use of *whatever* in this sense? Might it be possible to reconstruct a grammaticalization path?

4 Speech Representation

4.1 Introduction

Languages provide speakers with a variety of means for inserting the speech of others into their own discourse, ranging from verbatim recitation of the other's words (1a), to a recording of the content of what the other said (1b), to brief reports of the other's speech act, with or without the content of what was said (1c–d):

(1) a. My friend John said, "I can meet you tomorrow at noon if I can find a ride."
   b. John told me that he could probably meet me the next day at noon.
   c. He agreed to meet me.
   d. He provisionally agreed.

"At its root, speech presentation is a pragmatic issue" (Moore 2016: 482). As Collins (2001: xiv) observes:

> One of the reasons why [reported speech] is of significance for pragmatics is that the differences between its formal varieties cannot be understood in any meaningful sense without reference to pragmatic (contextual) factors … the choice of a given strategy is determined by the larger structure of the discourse and by the communicative intentions of the speaker or writer … Speakers and writers choose the form that they perceive as potentially most effective for what they want to communicate and, concomitantly, for how they intend to organize their texts.

According to Bublitz and Bednarek (2006), the central pragmatic function of reported speech is evaluative. The way in which the source of the speech is labeled, described, or evaluated (*my friend John, John, he*) can influence "the hearer's judgment of the reliability of what is reported" (550–551). The reporting expressions used (*said, told me, (provisionally) agreed*) may indicate the degree to which the speaker agrees with what was said or positively or negatively evaluates it. And the category of speech representation chosen (direct speech, indirect speech, report of speech act, etc.) has a range of different expressive functions, as we will discuss in the course of this chapter. Bublitz and Bednarek (2006) also suggest that speech representation can have a social function in establishing and maintaining social relationships and a textual function in foregrounding or backgrounding elements in the narrative. Representation of the thoughts of others can take similar forms and serve many of the same functions.

The historical study of speech and thought representation has focused on three questions as they have changed over time (cf. Grund and Walker 2021a on speech representation):

1. The mechanics of representing speech and thought, such as the reporting verbs used, the placement of reporting clauses, or even the use of quotation marks. As Grund and Walker note, "the present-day system of marking is not directly reflected in historical materials" (2021a: 7).
2. The categories of speech and thought representation existing in earlier stages of the language compared to those of Present-day English, including the extent to which they are found in different genres.
3. The textual, discursive, and sociopragmatic roles served by the different types of speech and thought representation. Grund and Walker point to a number of functions, such as the expression of evidentiality, credibility, authority, detachment or distancing, dramatization, negotiation of relationships, or characterization and theme; they argue that the same effects existed historically as do today.

In this chapter, we begin with the framework of speech and thought representation identified for Present-day English. We then take a diachronic approach to see how speech and thought have been represented over the course of English language history and how pragmatic concerns are central for the use and development of discourse representation resources and functions. You will be introduced to speech representation in Old and Middle English, speech and thought representation in Early Modern English and Late Modern English. The development of quotation marks in early printing provided a dedicated means of representing direct speech. The rise of free indirect speech is often associated with the rise of the novel in the LModE period. Finally, the appearance of new reporting verbs, such as *be like*, is characteristic of Present-day English.

Note that the terms scholars use – speaking of the "report," the "presentation," or the "representation" of speech and thought – imply different views of the relationship between the original speech or thought act and its record. I have chosen "representation" because the recorder is often not just repeating the earlier speech or thought by rote but actively creating or constituting it.

4.2   Categories of Speech and Thought Representation

One of the most widely recognized categorizations of speech and thought in Present-day English is that of Semino and Short (2004), which is an adaptation of the framework originally proposed by Leech and Short (2007[1981]). Apart from pure narration, they propose a set of parallel categories for speech, thought, and writing on a cline from the most narrator-controlled to the most autonomous categories and also ranging from most to least summarizing (see Table 4.1). It is widely acknowledged that these categories are quite porous, with somewhat fuzzy boundaries, leading to mixed or indeterminate forms. However, the schema is a useful starting point for the understanding of speech and thought representation. (For the sake of space, I will leave the parallel categories of writing representation out of the following discussion.)

The most autonomous forms are (free) direct speech ((F)DS) and (free) direct thought ((F)DT). The only difference between the free and non-free form is the absence of a reporting clause in the free form. The structure of the form is biclausal, with two semi-independent clauses: the reporting clause (belonging to the narrator or reporter) and the quoted clause (belonging to the speaker or thinker). The reporting clause – often called the *inquit* (Latin for 'he/she/it says') or quotative clause – may precede, follow, or intervene in the direct speech/thought, and in medial and final position it frequently involves inversion of the subject and verb. In (2), an exchange between Jane Eyre and Mr. Rochester in *Jane Eyre* is presented in free direct speech, ending with direct speech from Mrs. Fairfax, with the reporting clause "remarked Mrs. Fairfax."

(2)   "You are very cool! No! What! A novice not worship her priest! That sounds blasphemous."
       "I disliked Mr. Brocklehurst; and I was not alone in the feeling. He is a harsh man; at once pompous and meddling; he cut off our hair; and for economy's sake bought us bad needles and thread, with which we could hardly sew."
       "That was very false economy," remarked Mrs. Fairfax, who now again caught the drift of the dialogue. (1847 E. Brontë, *Jane Eyre*; B. Busse 2020: 115–116)

Table 4.1 *Cline of speech and thought representation*

		Speech	Thought
Most autonomous	Least summarizing	(Free) direct speech (F)DS (ex. 2)	(Free) direct thought (F)DT (ex. 3)
		Free indirect speech (ex. 7)	Free indirect thought (exx. 6, 8)
		Indirect speech (IS) (ex. 4)	Indirect thought (IT) (ex. 5)
		Narrative representation of speech act (NRSA) (ex. 10)	Narrative representation of thought act (NRTA) (ex. 12)
Least autonomous	Most summarizing	Narrative representation of voice (NV) (ex. 9)	Narrative representation of thought (NT) (ex. 11)

Direct speech is independent of the reporter, presenting a verbatim – or at least faithful – replication of what the speaker said. All of the expressive material within quotation marks is purported to belong to the original speaker. (We know, of course, that much of what is presented as direct quotation, even in real-life situations, is invented or constructed.) Pragmatically, (F)DS may be used for vividness, liveliness, or dramatic effect, is a foregrounding device, and provides a sense of authenticity or credibility. FDS has no overt narrative intervention and may be used to capture the rapid nature of conversational exchanges.

(F)DT presents thought as internal speech. It is suggestive of an omniscient reporter who has inner knowledge of the minds of others. Again, all of the expressive material apart from the reporting clause (when it is present) belongs to the consciousness of the thinker. The thoughts are generally understood as conscious and may represent a sudden realization or revelation on the part of the thinker. (F)DT is typically not set off by quotation marks (3a) but it may be (3b):

(3)   a. Only these, thought I—what an education! (1910 Thackeray, *Book of Snobs*; B. Busse 2020: 127)
        b. "And when," thought Emma, "will there be a beginning of Mr Churchill?" (1815 Austen, *Emma*; www.gutenberg.org/files/158/158-h/158-h.htm)

FDT, especially when it is ungrammatical and is disjunctive or disconnected, is often associated with what is called *interior monologue* or *stream-of-consciousness*.

Indirect speech (IS) and indirect thought (IT) are presented entirely from the point of view of the reporter, as we can see from the shifted pronominal, deictic, and tense forms, which conform to the time and place or "deictic center" of the reporter. They are fully integrated into the discourse. The expressive elements of DS and DT are eliminated, with the indirect form expressing the content or "gist" but not the exact wording of the speech or thought. Indirect discourse consists of a single main clause (the reporting clause), which always assumes initial position, and a subordinate clause (the reported material), expressed in a nominal or infinitival clause. No non-embeddable structures are permitted. The complementizer (*that, if, whether*) may or may not be present, and there is no graphic device distinguishing the two parts, as there is in DS. A constructed comparison is a helpful way of identifying the formal differences between direct and indirect speech most clearly, though there is not a derivational or one-to-one relationship between direct and indirect forms:

Elizabeth asked John, "Oh, will you, my dear friend, write that ridiculous note for me tomorrow?"

Elizabeth asked John whether he would write that ("ridiculous") note for her the next day.

Here we see the shift of the speaker's *you* to the reporter's *he*, of *me* to *her*, of *will* to *would* and of *tomorrow* to *the next day*. The direct question with auxiliary-subject inversion is replaced by an embeddable form, an indirect *whether* clause with subject–auxiliary order. Indirect speech may sometimes contain quoted expressive elements from direct speech ("ridiculous"), but most such elements, for example, interjections ("oh") and vocatives ("my dear friend"), are eliminated. IS is often used for backgrounding, summarizing, or providing factual information.

Here are some literary examples of IS (4) and IT (5).

(4)   He explained, in gentle and convincing tones, that his wife had started at a moment's notice for Brittany to her dying mother; (1907 Conrad, *The Secret Agent*; www.gutenberg.org/files/974/974-h/974-h.htm)

(5)   and this persuasion, joined to all the rest, made her think that she *must* be a little in love with him, in spite of every previous determination against it. (1816 Austen, *Emma*; B. Busse 2020: 135)

Direct speech in (4) would be "My <u>wife</u> has <u>started</u> …", whereas direct thought in (5) would be "<u>I</u> must be a little in love with him." In (5) "a little in love" is ambiguous: it may be attributed to Emma's own verbalized thought or it could be a narrative paraphrase of the content of her thought.

In between direct and indirect speech/thought is free indirect speech and thought. This form has received a wealth of scholarly attention (see Further Reading). It goes by a number of different names: erlebte Rede, style indirect libre, empathetic narrative, narrated monologue, represented speech and thought, and so on. I will refer to it collectively as free indirect discourse (FID). Several controversies surround this form: how and when it developed (discussed below), whether it is "single" or "dual" voiced, that is, whether we are hearing just the voice of the original thinker/speaker or whether we hear both that and the voice of the narrator, whether it may express empathetic identification with the character or ironic distancing, or both, whether it is restricted to literary genres or can be found in other genres, whether the sentences of FID are "unspeakable" (because they lack the *I–you* of communication), and whether all or most of the formal features must be present to qualify as FID. Here is a prototypical example of free indirect thought:

(6)   Never had she imagined she could look like that. Is mother right? she thought.
        And now she hoped her mother was right. (1922 Mansfield, "The Garden
        Party"; Brinton 1980: 366)

In this example, we see many of the characteristic features of the style, including:
- a third-person subject of consciousness (expressed pronominally) to whom
  all of the expressive content belongs (*she*);
- reference to others by means of pronouns, pet names, or familial relationships (*mother*);
- narrative past tense cooccurring with present or future time deictics representing the here and now of the character's act of consciousness (*now she hoped*);
- shifted modals with past time reference (*could*);
- non-embeddable, independent clauses of direct discourse, such as questions,
  imperatives, fragments, sentences with fronting, dislocations, initial conjunctions, and so on (*Is mother right?*); and
- an optional reporting clause, typically appearing final or medial (*she thought*).

Other characteristics include expressive lexical items belonging to the character
(e.g., *dear, miserably, fool*), dialect or pronunciation features, idioms or colloqui-
alisms of the character, the past progressive, (reflexive) pronouns with no antecedent in the preceding discourse, and expressive structures such as interjections,
exclamations, sentence adverbs, repetitions, hesitations, pragmatic markers, or
fillers.

The advantage of FID is that it creates a seamless juncture between narrative
(the external discourse) and speech and thought. It allows the (verbatim) speech
and thoughts of characters – of other consciousnesses – to be presented in the
third-person narration with no narrative break. It leads to an alignment of
character and narrator, thus overcoming the limitations of one narrator/one
point of view and leading to the loss of authorial omniscience. It "erases some
of the impression of clear hierarchy, of an external teller and an observed
character being told about" (Toolan 2006: 705). Inner and outer worlds become
one, giving a sense of immediacy. But it does not completely sacrifice narrative
control (exerted by narrative tenses and pronouns) and thus retains the possibility of distancing. In free indirect speech, speech is presented as it is experienced (interpreted) by others, and thus the form may be used for the purposes of
irony or parody in a way that DS cannot. In free indirect thought, we are given
an illusion of the character's mental state. Thoughts are not assumed to be fully
verbalized but may be unarticulated, partly conscious, or on the threshold of
verbalization. This avoids the artificiality of direct thought. We are inside the
head of the character and hear the inner voice with which consciousness
addresses itself.

In the free indirect speech below, we hear the speech of the conjurer (7a) and
of Lizzie and the Secretary (7b), and in the free indirect thought, we have direct

access to Emma's (8a) and Arthur's (8b) private thoughts. FID is often recognized by some cues in the immediate context which direct the reader to the character's speech or thought:

(7)   a. The object of his discourse was a panegyric of himself and a satire on all other conjurors. **He was the only conjuror, the real one, a worthy descendant of the magicians of old.** (1826 Disraeli, *Vivian Grey*; B. Busse 2020: 111)

b. Lizzie was very desirous to thank her unknown friend who had sent her the written retraction. **Was she, indeed?** observed the Secretary. **Ah!** Bella asked him, **had he any notion who that unknown friend might be? He had no notion whatever.** (1864–5 Dickens, *Our Mutual Friend*; Fludernik 1993:119)

(8)   a. She then took a longer time for consideration. **Should she proceed no farther? – should she let it pass, and seem to suspect nothing? – Perhaps Harriet might think her cold or angry if she did; or perhaps if she was totally silent, it might only drive Harriet into asking her to hear too much** … (1816 Austen, *Emma*; www.gutenberg.org/files/158/1 58-h/158-h.htm)

b. When he [Arthur Clennam] got to his lodging, he sat down before the dying fire … and turned his gaze back upon the gloomy vista by which he had come to that stage in his existence: **So long, so bare, so blank. No childhood; no youth, except for one remembrance; that one remembrance proved, only that day, to be a piece of folly** (1855–7 Dickens, *Little Dorrit*; Fludernik 1993: 237)

FID, especially free indirect thought, when it is lacking many of the grammatical markers, can be difficult to distinguish from pure narration; that is, we cannot know whether we are hearing the thoughts of the character or of the narrator. But it is this uncertainty which often contributes to the literary depth and complexity of the style.

At the most summarizing end of the scale of speech representation are narrative representation of voice (NV), which conveys in the briefest possible way that some communicative act has occurred (9), and narrative representation of speech act (NRSA), which expresses the illocutionary force of the speech act and sometimes the topic (10). In both cases, the wording is that of the narrator, as is the point of view. The effect is distancing or backgrounding, implying that the character's speech and actual words are unimportant. Both forms have a summarizing or encapsulating function which serves to move the narrative forward:

(9)   He then stepped across the pavement to her, and said something; she seemed embarrassed, and desirous of getting away; (1847 E. Brontë, *Wuthering Heights*, CLMET3.0; Grund 2021a: 109)

(10)   The "How d'ye do's" were quiet and constrained on each side. She asked after their mutual friends; (1816 Austen, *Emma*; www.gutenberg.org/files/158/15 8-h/158-h.htm)

In the realm of thought representation, we find narrative representation of thought (NT), which encapsulates a thinking process (11), and narrative representation of thought act (NRTA), which records a thought act (12) but has less content and immediacy than IS:

(11)   He sat really lost in thought for the first few minutes; (1816 Austen, *Emma*; B. Busse 2020: 139)

(12)   She put to herself a series of questions. (1919 Woolf, *Night and Day*; Semino and Short 2004: 45)

Semino and Short (2004) propose an additional category called internal narration (NI), "the presentation of mental states and changes which involve cognitive and affective phenomena but which do not amount to specific thoughts" (132). Internal narration allows access to a character's internal viewpoint but does not explicitly specify that a thought act has occurred. This is similar to what Fludernik (1993) calls "psycho-narration." We see this in (13):

(13)   a. **She was vexed beyond what could have been expressed – almost beyond what she could conceal. Never had she felt so agitated, mortified, grieved at any circumstance in her life**. (1815 Austen, *Emma*; www.gutenberg.org/files/158/158-h/158-h.htm)
         b. and when I could hardly see the dark mountains, I felt still more gloomily. **The picture appeared a vast and dim scene of evil** … (1818 Shelley, *Frankenstein*; B. Busse 2020: 142)

Note that there are various refinements and alternatives to these categories and their labels. For example, Vandelanotte (2009) proposes a new category of "distancing indirect speech and thought" to account for an example such as the following:

(14)   So I suggested we dine. But Priscilla wasn't hungry. She had eaten too much of the smoked salmon at the reception. I proposed we visit a few of the places we had known together … Dancing, she claimed, would exhaust her utterly. Did I want that? (1961 Fuller, *The Father's Comedy*; Vandelanotte 2009: 143)

In (14), we have IS ("So I suggested we dine," "I proposed …"), but the rest, despite appearances, cannot be interpreted as FID, Vandelanotte argues. The proper name *Priscilla* and *I* (in "Did I want that") would be *she* and *he*, respectively, in FID. Here the *I*-narrator takes over, draws the speech representation into his own perspective, structuring an utterance from his or her own deictic perspective, and appropriates the original speaker's expressivity. The discourse is from the point of view of the narrator, or current speaker, much as it would be in IS, not of the represented speaker, as it would be in FID. (On alternative schemas, see Further Readings.)

In a corpus study which looks at these categories of speech and thought (and writing) representation in prose fiction, newspaper reports, and (auto) biography in Present-day English, Semino and Short (2004) find that for the presentation of speech, (F)DS is the norm in all genres, followed by NRSA and IS. This is consistent with Leech and Short's claim that "DS is a norm of baseline for the portrayal of speech" (2007[1981]: 268). Fiction privileges the direct end, (F)DS and free indirect speech, while non-fiction privileges the non-direct end, IS and NRSA. Thought is more often expressed in fiction and (auto) biography, where NI is the norm, followed by free indirect thought. NRTA and (F)DT are the least frequent. Semino and Short's findings are inconsistent with Leech and Short's claim (2007[1981]: 276) that IT is the norm for thought, a claim based on the assumption that the thoughts of others are not directly accessible to others and are not verbally formulated, so cannot be reported verbatim. But news reporting and autobiography do favor IT. News reporting rarely uses FDT or NRTA, and free indirect thought is absent. We will see below that the categories found in earlier genres differ from these.

4.3   Speech Representation in Old English

In Old English, only the representation of speech (and writing) is found. Thought representation is absent (Louviot 2016).

Prior to the advent of printing and the (eventual) adoption of quotation marks to denote direct speech, a multiplicity of strategies were used in medieval manuscripts to set direct speech off from narrative: these include physical aspects of the page (*mise-en-page*), such as rubricated letters, underlining, paragraph marks (¶), special line spacing, marginal notes, and various marks of punctuation (e.g., marks known as the virgule, the punctus, and punctus elevatus), but none of these is used exclusively for the purposes of marking quotation and they are often applied inconsistently even within the same manuscript (see Moore's (2011, 2016) discussion of ME manuscripts). Punctuation of quotation is "sparse and unsystematic" in Old English (Louviot 2016: 59). The same means can be used for quoting the direct speech of characters and, perhaps even more often, for citing the words of authorities (such as scriptural quotations).

Lacking clear graphic devices, medieval manuscripts make use of reporting verbs, or *verba dicendi* 'verbs of speech', to mark direct speech. These appear in reporting clauses, which in Old English typically precede a passage of quoted speech, and in verse may often be quite long and elaborate (15a). A variety of verbs all meaning 'to speak, say' (e.g., *maþelian, cweðan, sprecan, frignan, secgan, reordian*) are used in Old English. Speeches may be followed by a final inquit which echoes the initial one (15b):

(15)   a. **Þa spræc guðcyning**, Sodoma aldor, secgum befylled, to Abrahame him
        wæs ara þearf. "Forgif me …" (Gen A,B 2123; Louviot 2016: 50)

'then spoke the battle king, the prince of Sodom, deprived of his men, to Abraham (he was in need of favours: "Grant me …"

b.   … **Swa hleoðrode halig cempa**, ðeawum geþancul. (And 461; DOEC)

'… thus said the holy warrior, mindful of his servants'

Reporting clauses that interrupt or follow the passage of direct speech, what Cichosz (2018) calls "parenthetical reporting clauses," often show inversion of the subject and the verb, especially with nominal subjects. In Old English, the most common verb here is *cweþan*, the origin of Modern English *quoth* (OED, s.v.v. *queath*, v. and *quoth*, v.):

(16)   Þæt is soð, **cwæð Beotius** (Bo 26.59.10; Cichosz 2018: 189)

'that is true, said Boethius'

In a study of direct speech in Old English verse, Louviot (2016) argues that speeches in Old English are lengthy, formal or public, and often spoken in isolation. There are what she calls "pseudo-exchanges" consisting of a series of speeches by the same character resembling a long speech interrupted by inquits. But in verse there are few examples of the back-and-forth exchanges that we expect in contemporary dialogues (though these may occur more often in other genres, such as saints' lives). Louviot concludes that direct speech is a fundamental part of the narrative, allowing the poet to create salient points in the narrative and to actualize the narrative, but it is not a way to represent conversations ("what characters might have said") or to supply characterization.

Both direct and indirect discourse have been available from the earliest English. IS in earlier English shows the backshifting of tenses, shifting of personal pronouns and of locative/temporal adverbs, and omission of expressive elements characteristic of the form in contemporary English. But Visser (1972: 775–779) points out the existence of a form consisting of an introductory reporting clause and complementizer *that* followed by the actual words spoken. We recognize this form by the lack of backshifting of the verbs *is* (17a) and *purposeth* (17b), though shifting of pronouns does occur (i.e., *I* to *he* in (17b)):

(17)   a. Mid ðæm worde he cyðde **ðæt hit is se hiehsta cræft**, (CP 52.409.19; Visser 1972: 776)

'he said that his is the highest craft'

b. He toke and tolde him his corage, **That he purposeth a viage** (1393 Gower, *Confessio Amantis*; Visser 1972: 780)

'he took and told him his desire, that he plans a journey'

Visser argues that "[t]his is perhaps the oldest form of reporting speech or thought" (1972: 775), citing examples from Old English through the nineteenth century, and thus should not be considered an "exception." Among mixed forms in Old English, a form that apparently shows indirect speech morphing into direct speech was termed "slippage" by Schuelke (1958). The passage in (18) begins indirectly (*sege him þæt* 'tell him that') but the unshifted pronouns *ðe* and *ðu* (*bit ðe þæt ðu cume* 'command you that you come') suggest direct speech:

(18)   Ða cwæð se cyngc: Ga rædlice and **sege him þæt** se cyngc **bit ðe þæt ðu cume** to his gereorde. (*Apollonius of Tyre* 14.11; Visser 1972: 782)

'then said the king "Go quickly and say to him that the king commands you that you come to his feast"'

Slipping was initially thought to be inadvertent, perhaps due to either a misconstrual of the first part as indirect discourse or to the scribe's inability to maintain the shifted tenses and pronouns of indirect speech over longer passages. But more recent thinking (e.g., Richman 1986) is that the switch from indirect to direct speech may be a conscious technique, with direct discourse being used – on account of its increased vividness and drama – to emphasize the most important part of the quoted material.

4.4   Speech Representation in Middle English

In Middle English, reporting clauses continue to be the primary means of marking direct speech. Moore (2011) finds, for example, that in Chaucer's *Troilus and Criseyde*, 92 percent of the instances of direct speech are marked by reporting clauses, 64 percent of which precede the quotation and 28 percent of which are inserted within the quoted speech, typically immediately after its onset, as follows:

(19)   "Noon oother lyf," **seyde he** "is worth a bene;" (1387 Chaucer, *Canterbury Tales* E.Mch 1263)

"'No other life," said he "is worth a bean,"'

(Note here that the quotation marks have been added by the modern editor.) *Seien* 'to say' becomes the primary reporting verb in Middle English, and it frequently shows inversion, as in this example. Cichosz suggests that the sudden popularity of *seien* may be due to the need for a more flexible verb than *quoth*, with inversion occurring by analogy with *quoth* as a means to distinguish the inquit from the comment clause *I say* (2018: 201–202). (In a comment clause, *I say* does not introduce speech but serves other (inter)subjective functions, such as emphasis, as in *This much, I say, is indisputable* [COCA]; see Chapter 3 §3.6.) In the *Corpus of Middle English Prose and Verse*, Moore (2011) finds that 80 percent of the instances of direct speech occur with reporting clauses, with the verb *seien* used over half the time. *Seien* has lost its propositional meaning to a great extent, serving primarily as a textual or boundary marker. Evidence for the reduced meaning is the occurrence of conjoined structures such as *asked and seide* or *answerd & seyd*, where *say* is always the second verb. While the second instance of *say* has been explained as an empty punctuation mark or pragmatic marker, or as a complementizer introducing direct discourse, Herlyn (1999) argues that it serves a cohesive function; it signals the quotedness of the following discourse and ties the material more closely to the narrative frame.

Moore (2011) considers three Middle English genres which have a large proportion of speech representation – defamation depositions, sermons, and histories – and in which we might expect a high degree of faithfulness to the defendant's words, to scriptural passages and the opinions of church fathers, and to the speeches of historical figures, respectively. She argues, however, that the looser and less determined way of marking direct and indirect speech in Middle English suggests a laxity in faithfulness, perhaps because speakers did not feel that exactness was necessary and did not assume that speeches were reported in a verbatim manner. For example, in depositions, witnesses may represent speech, and scribes report it, in a way that makes it conform more with the legal standard of defamation than with what was actually said (which may be imperfectly remembered). In sermons, one finds biblical quotations that are loosely cited, paraphrased, wrongly attributed, or incorrectly sourced: "the levels of fidelity expected were not those of absolute precision that present-day readers expect from quotations of written sources" (112). In general, Moore argues, a strict distinction between the *de dicto* ('about what is said') quality of DS, its fidelity to the actual linguistic expression of speech, and the *de re* ('about the thing') quality of IS, its fidelity to the content or sense of speech, did not hold; direct speech could allow a *de re* interpretation. Moore sees this as closer to modern spoken discourse, in which it is often the case that direct speech is not verbatim but in a sense "constructed" or imagined (see also Moore 2002).

In *Sir Gawain and the Green Knight*, Pons-Sanz (2019) calculates that represented speech constitutes almost half of the lines of the poem. For speech, (F)DS is the norm, as it is in Present-day English. In contrast, the norm for thought is DT, or fully verbalized internal discourse, often accompanied by clauses such as "he said to himself"; thus, Pons-Sanz classifies this as a kind of internal direct speech. Pons-Sanz also groups NRSA together with NV as "narrated speech," as both are expressed in single clauses and serve to summarize relatively unimportant parts. Based on the assumption that the *Gawain*-poet chooses carefully the mode of speech representation used, Pons-Sanz argues that the mode chosen has stylistic and pragmatic effects: it serves to emphasize aspects of the narrative and to shape the audience's interpretation of the text. Moore (2011) also argues that the indeterminacy of modes of speech representation in *Sir Gawain and the Green Knight* as well as in *Pearl* highlights "the homiletic insights, moral dilemmas and narrative frames" (134) of the poem. Likewise, the permeability of speech forms in the *Canterbury Tales* allows for different voices (narrator, character, pilgrim) without clearly disentangling these voices; Chaucer uses this indeterminacy for artistic purposes.

4.5   The Development of Quotation Marks

The rise of quotation marks is associated with the advent of printing, but it took some time for this particular form of punctuation to become regularized and conventionalized. The development of a distinct set of markers for direct speech had not only typographical consequences but pragmatic ones as well, since it allowed authors to clearly distinguish between different voices in the text and to bring direct speech into the foreground of the narrative.

The quotation mark (or inverted comma) arose out of the *diple* 'double', a graphic symbol going back to Greek and Latin manuscripts. As discussed by Parkes (1992: 58–59), the diple, shaped like a semi-circular comma mark (›), was first printed outside the left margin on every relevant line to indicate scriptural quotations or sententiae. This alerted the reader to the presence of the words of an authoritative figure. In the 1570s this mark was extended to indicate direct speech and moved to within the line. It was not until the eighteenth century that printers created out of the diple a new punctuation symbol, the quotation mark, which was gradually accepted by the second half of the century. It was first used to mark the opening of a passage of quoted speech (inverted comma) and only later the closing of the passage (uninverted comma). Crystal (2015) suggests that the quotation mark is associated with the rise of the novel. Single and double quotation marks were originally exploited for different purposes – single for indirect speech and double for direct speech – but they are now differently distinguished, for example, for quotations within quotations or by nationality (the British preferring single quotations, Americans double quotations). As Crystal points out, while direct speech is uniquely marked with quotation marks (though they may be omitted), quotation marks serve a variety of other functions, such as denoting titles of short works, linguistic glosses, scare quotes, citation forms, and so on.

Prior to the conventionalization and acceptance of the quotation mark, printers and writers experimented with a variety of means of displaying quoted material. The quoted material could be set in italics or indented. A common technique, used somewhat unevenly and often inconsistently from the sixteenth to the eighteenth century, was to enclose the reporting clause within parentheses. Reporting clauses could also be set off by commas or dashes. Examples of the use of parentheses begin to appear in the 1520s. For example, an Early

Modern printed edition of Chaucer punctuates the line given above in (19) as follows:

(20)   non other lyfe (said he) is worthe a bean (Thynne, ed. 1532; Moore 2020: 85)

As Moore points out (2020), the marking of the backgrounded reporting clause rather than the foregrounded quoted clause is a pragmatic choice which points to differing organization of discourse. Moore (2020, 2021) studies the use of parentheses with *say* and *quoth* clauses in *Early English Books Online*. Overall, nearly 40 percent of the clauses are set off by parentheses in the seventeenth century. *Quoth* clauses are more likely to appear in parentheses than *say* clauses since they are more restricted as inquits with direct speech. *Say* is a more versatile verb, has wider use, and is more frequent. But despite the fairly high correlation of parentheses with reporting clauses, parentheses never became specialized for the quotative use and were, as Moore observes, only "partially pragmaticalized." We should note also that a variety of typographical means for marking quotation remained in use much longer in private (handwritten) correspondence before the conventionalization of the quotation mark.

4.6   Speech and Thought Representation in Early Modern English

The representation of speech and thought in Early Modern English has been fairly extensively studied, with focus either on the formal marking of direct speech or on the categories of speech and thought representation in different text types.

Reporting clauses, speech-internal markers, and speech descriptors: The formal marking of speech can be either external to the quoted material (i.e., reporting clauses) or internal to the quoted material.

Reporting verbs in the *Corpus of English Dialogues 1560–1760* have been surveyed in two studies, one focusing on the witness depositions (Aijmer 2015) and one on prose fiction (Walker and Grund 2020). Both studies find the neutral verb *say* to be the most common reporting verb, as it is in Present-day English, and both find a decline in *quoth* over time. Aijmer identifies no example of *quoth* after 1639. She also finds no cases where the reporting clause is omitted. Walker and Grund (2020) record an increasing inventory of *verba dicendi* 'verb of speaking' over time, including "structuring" verbs such as *question, answer*, and *reply* and "descriptive" verbs such as *continue* and *cry (out)*. Double quotatives (e.g., *answered and said*) or even longer forms (*did revile and curse and said*), which were observed in Middle English, continue to occur in Early Modern English; Aijmer (2015) argues that *and said* here has lost its propositional meaning and become a highly routinized and grammaticalized quotative marker. Reporting clauses in initial position almost always have subject–verb order, and medial/final inquits invariably have verb–subject word order. Grund and Walker find *quoth* to occur only with verb–subject order in medial/final position; overall, verb–subject order is evenly split between nominal and pronominal subjects. Medial position of the reporting clause increases over time, serving to emphasize the shift between speakers. Moore (2002, 2006) finds that a reporting verb distinctive to Early Modern legal language is *videlicit (viz., vit., vid.)*, Latin for 'namely, that is to say'. This is used in slander depositions to introduce the alleged slanderous utterance in either direct or indirect speech, often marking a shift from Latin to English. Moore see *videlicit* becoming grammaticalized as a quotative marker. Latin *dixit* 'says' or *denonit* 'testifies' can also serve this function.

The absence of quotation marks in EModE direct speech as well as the placement of reporting clauses in medial or final position means that the beginning of direct speech is often not explicitly signaled. Identifying the onset of direct speech may depend, therefore, on the presence of what Moore (2011: 46) calls "speech-internal perspective shifters." These include interjections (*alas, ey*), vocatives (*Sire, Madame*), first- and second-person pronouns (*I/we, thou/you*), deictic pronouns, shifted tenses, conversational routines (*yes/no*), and pragmatic markers (*but, well, why*) as well as non-embeddable structures not found in indirect speech (direct imperatives and questions). All of these signal a change in voice from narrative to DS: they focus on the speaker and the here and now of direct speech, place the discourse within a conversational exchange, and/or evoke the colloquial language of direct speech. Examining two Middle English texts (Chaucer's *Troilus and Criseyde* and Hoccleve's *The Regiment of Princes*), Moore (2011: 46–49) finds that although the vast majority of direct speech instances are marked externally by reporting clauses and inquits, there is also considerable dependence upon vocatives, interjections, deictic and personal pronouns, and pragmatic markers; even in Middle English she finds examples of conversational exchanges which depend exclusively on the presence of vocatives to distinguish the different speakers. Looking at the witness depositions and prose fiction texts of the *Corpus of English Dialogues*, Lutzky (2015, 2021) finds that three-quarters of all instances of direct speech contain speech-internal perspective shifters. Pragmatic markers (*ah, and, but, marry, now, oh, pray, well, what*, and *why*) are the most common form in both genres; they signal a change in speaker but may also show emotional involvement, be interactive, and structure discourse. First- and second-person pronouns predominate in witness depositions, while prose fiction makes use of vocatives. Pragmatic markers are much more common in prose fiction than in witness depositions. Lutzky hypothesizes that pragmatic markers may have been omitted by scribes in witness depositions, perhaps due to the formal nature of the proceedings (on pragmatic markers, see Chapter 3).

Reporting clauses may be accompanied by "speech descriptors," modifiers that evaluate, clarify, or hedge a reporting clause. They provide pragmatic information about "how the reporters view the speech, what characteristics the speech event had beyond what is signaled by the actual representation and the reporting expression, and how faithful a given representation is to the original speech event" (Grund 2017a: 42). Here, "says the Gentleman, very gravely" is a speech descriptor:

(21)   You may call her out, there she is, why Sister, says the Gentleman, very gravely, What do you mean? (1722 Defoe, *Moll Flanders*; CED; Grund 2018: 274)

Studying speech descriptors in EModE witness depositions and prose fiction, Grund (2017a, 2018) argues that they are markers of stance (pragmatic subjectivity) in that they allow the reporters to signal their attitude toward the represented speech (and speaker). They may take the form of a prepositional phrase (*said in a trembling voice*), an adverbial (phrase) (*said sharply*), a participle (*said smiling*), an adjectival (phrase) (*said scurrilous things*), an *or* construction (*said the following or words to this effect*), or a noun phrase (*said several times*). Grund proposes five pragmatic categories of speech descriptors: evaluation, emphasis, frequency/quantity, formulation hedging, and clarification. All the categories are found in witness depositions, though evaluation is the most common. Speech descriptors are less common in prose fiction but he finds that they increase over time, especially in Late Modern English (Grund

Table 4.2 *Evaluation subtypes in speech descriptors in Late Modern English (adapted from Grund 2020: 307, 2021a: 122)*

Subtypes of evaluation	Examples of evaluation
Intent	*scornfully, insistently, disdainfully*
Language variety	*in pretty good English, in the gentlest of accents, in Spanish*
Length	*briefly, very concisely, rather shortly*
Mental state	*pensively, gruffly, impetuously, passionately*
Pitch	*in her deep voice, in a high jocular voice*
Speech character	*recklessly, perversely, repellingly*
Speech quality	*huskily, hoarsely, in a much shaken voice*
Speed	*hurriedly, quickly, slowly, hastily*
Strength	*quietly, faintly, in a lower voice*
Style of speaking	*with emphasis, interrogatively, mechanically*

2020, 2021a); their function is strongly evaluative, falling into a number of subcategories, as set out in Table 4.2. Grund attributes the predominance of evaluation in fiction to the fact that represented speech in fiction is often a means by which the narrator can characterize a person or situation and thus inject a subjective attitude.

Categories of speech and thought representation: A number of studies of the realizations of Semino and Short's (2004) categories in Early Modern English have been undertaken. It is not always easy to compare these studies as they look at different genres (where we might well expect the speech and thought categories to be differently realized). Moreover, incompatibilities in the findings of existing studies may also result from the categorization of examples by different scholars, which may differ rather widely, or at least are not always entirely clear.

Włodarczyk (2007) examines two EModE trial transcripts, adapting the Semino and Short system to a context in which there is no narrator per se. Walker and Grund (2017) look at speech representation in EModE witness depositions. McIntyre and Walker (2011) is a study of the different categories in EModE news journalism and narrative fiction (1511–1736), and Evans (2021) examines categories of speech representation in sixteenth-century letters.

Overall, speech presentation is much more common in Early Modern English than is thought presentation. Unlike in Present-day English, where the "showing" end – (F)DS – is the norm for speech presentation, in Early Modern English, the "telling" end – NRSA, IS, and NV – predominates, as in these examples from Walker and Grund (2017):

- NV (*talking*), which sets the scene for further verbal behavior or evaluates verbal behavior;
- NRSA (*ded confesse the truth wyth lamenting*), which frames speech events; and
- IS (*askyd hym where Mr Doctor Barrett was*), which summarizes and backgrounds, focusing on actions rather than words.

IS and NRSA may contain bits of quoted direct speech (e.g., *he said he did not care a t—d for him, he might kiss is arse*). NRSA and IS are equally common in witness depositions while IS predominates in correspondence. McIntyre and Walker find somewhat different results for fiction and news reporting, but compared to Present-day English, DS is the most underrepresented and NV the most overrepresented in Early Modern English, again pointing to EModE's preference for more "telling" types of speech representation. Thus, McIntyre and Walker see a trend toward less narrator interference over time. Interestingly, Włodarczyk and McIntyre and Walker find a few rare examples of free indirect speech, while Grund and Walker and Evans find none, though Evans does find mixed DS/IS forms.

For the representation of thought, Early Modern English again favors the "telling" end of the spectrum, including NRTA, IT, and NI. (F)DT and free indirect thought are either not found or are extremely rare. In the trial transcripts, Włodarczyk finds that NRTA is most common, but IT is of very low frequency. McIntyre and Walker find that NI is most common in their fiction and newspaper corpus (as it is in Present-day English), with NRTA and IT twice as common as in Present-day English. The frequent use of IT in news reporting is apparently used to speculate about the reactions of others to reported events.

Włodarczyk (2007) finds occasional slipping from indirect to direct speech (which she sees as inadvertent). Walker and Grund (2021) look specifically at the existence of mixed modes in witness depositions. While infrequent (only 5.6 percent), they are identifiable most often by the presence of subjective vocabulary (swearing, insults, glossed words, dialect features, pragmatic markers, idiomatic phrases, evaluative adjectives), by switches in mode (direct to indirect and vice versa), and by pronoun, tense, and deictic switches (first-person ~ third-person pronoun, past ~ present tense, *now* ~ *then*), all of which evoke the voice of the original speaker. In (22a), we see subjective language, "not very wise" and "such beardles boys" in the context of indirect speech ("said that"), while in (22b), also in the context of indirect speech ("Reeve told him") we see a passage of direct speech ("if you goe to Mrs Jennings") followed by indirect speech ("she would give him the Guniea"), indicated by the pronoun shift from *you* to *him*:

(22)   a. said that the Magestrates of Colchester were not very wise to choose such beardles boys to be Constables as Tom Smith the Appoth[e]cary a Constable of S[t] Runwals (1650–75 F_3EC_Colchester_021; ETED; Grund and Walker 2021a: 169)

         b. the s[d] Reeve told him if you goe to M[rs] Jennings in S[t] Peters of Mancroft she would give him the Guniea, (1700–54 F_4EC_Norwich_018; ETED; Grund and Walker 2021a: 170)

Walker and Grund reject an explanation of such passages as FID or "slipping" since here there are switches in both directions, not just from indirect to direct discourse. To see the system of speech representation as one in flux, not yet fully developed and not yet fully distinguishing between direct and indirect discourse, as has been suggested by Moore (2011), while it has appeal, is ultimately rejected by Walker and Grund. They argue that the mixed forms are "artful" and "help in disambiguation, in dramatisation, and in foregrounding or backgrounding a voice" (2021: 180). As we pointed out in the introduction, the way in which speech is represented (the source of speech, the characterization of the speech, the (in)directness of speech) has important pragmatic functions, influencing the reader's judgment concerning reliability or veracity and their ultimate acceptance (or not) of the content of the speech. Moreover, the form of speech representation can also serve a textual function in foregrounding (with DS) or backgrounding (with IS) the content of speech.

4.7   The Rise of Free Indirect Discourse

The existence of FID in pre-modern texts is highly debated. It is typically associated with the rise of the novel and the expression of consciousness and seen as exclusively literary (e.g., Banfield 1982). However, Fludernik (1993: 93–99) argues that free indirect discourse does indeed exist, at least in proto-form and for speech only, as early as Middle English. She cites an example from Chaucer (23), where the expressive element *thanked be God* and the unshifted past-time modals *moste* and *sholde* point to free indirect speech:

(23)   Daun John ... hym told agayn, ful specially,/ How he hadde well yboght and graciously,/ Thanked be God, al hool his merchandise;/ Save that he moste in all maner wise,/ Maken a chevyssaunce, as for his best,/ And thanne he sholde been in joye and reste. (1387 Chaucer, *Canterbury Tales* B.Sh 342–8; Fludernik 1993: 93–94)

'Dan John ... told him again, very specially, how he had bought well and successfully, thanked be God, all of his merchandise; except that he must no matter what arrange for a loan as for his best, and then he should be in joy and rest'

Pons-Sanz (2019) and Moore (2011) agree that Middle English examples such as (24a–b), while they resemble free indirect discourse, are better seen as "mixed speech" in which the boundary between direct and indirect speech is blurred: "Although medieval works do have passages that evoke a blending of voices and some that permit the intrusion of a character's thoughts into the narrative, the result is not the application of consistent conventions of a separate discourse mode, but is rather a mixture of incompletely divided discourse modes" (Moore 2011: 131). These examples lack many of the features of the fully developed free indirect discourse form:

(24)   a. And he nicked hym "Naye!" — he nolde bi no ways' (1390–1400 *Sir Gawain and the Green Knight* 2471; Pons-Sanz 2019: 215)

'And he told him "No!" – he would not on any account'

b. And there he swoor on ale and breed/ How that the geaunt shal be deed,/ Bityde what bityde! (1387 Chaucer, *Canterbury Tales* B.Th 872–4)

'And there he swore on ale and bread that the giant shall be dead, Come what may!'

Likewise, Walker and Grund (2021) point to EModE instances such as (25), which, while it resembles free indirect discourse because of the third-person pronoun, unshifted *wolde*, and subjective language, does not exemplify FID as a "full-fledged, separate mode": it is introduced by a reporting clause ("the said Seaton ... said") and does not create ambiguity of voice (dual voice), which would be expected for FID:

(25)   the said Seaton was in a greate rage and said God damn Him He would have another knock att Him, (1724–58 F_4NC_Northern_004; ETED; Walker and Grund 2021: 166)

Fludernik (1993) sees free indirect discourse as appearing in full form, albeit rarely, in the late seventeenth century, particularly in literary imitations of colloquial language (see also Leech and Short 2007[1981]: 266):

(26)   When Father Worsley came to discourse [with] Don Tomazo in English, heavens, what a refreshing it was him! For he had not spoken to any person whatever in ten weeks before (1680 *Don Tomazo*; Fludernik 1993: 95)

Adamson (1994, 2001) agrees with Fludernik's dating, relating the rise of what she calls "empathetic narrative" to Puritan conversion narratives in the seventeenth century; in (27) one finds *was* cooccurring with *now/at this time*, where the past tense and present-time deictic bridge the gap between the remembering self (who has attained grace) and the remembered self (who is not spiritually reborn):

(27)   And now was I both a burthen and a terror to myself, nor did I ever so know as now, what it was to be weary of my life and yet afraid to die. Oh, how gladly now would I have been anybody but myself (1666 Bunyan, *Grace Abounding*; Adamson 1995: 81, 2001: 88)

For Adamson, the extension of this style from first to third person occurred in the Bildungsroman, the secular equivalent of the conversion narrative, and laid the groundwork for FID. McIntyre and Walker (2011) likewise find rare examples of free indirect speech (28) in their EModE corpus of news journalism and fictional prose:

(28)   the rogues presented each a pistol to them and bid them deliver, or they would blow the brains out of their head (1736 *Country Journal*; McIntyre and Walker 2011: 104)

Vandenalotte (2021) sees the rise of FID as a "drift" away from the norms of indirect speech (144), with gradual conventionalization of the style over the course of the nineteenth century. Authors keep the pronouns and tense of ID but allow for the syntactic freedom of DD. Early examples may even retain the *that* complementizer. In the early part of the century, typographical practices are not yet stable, so quotation marks may be used for DD and FID or even ID, or they may be omitted. This passage from Jane Austen begins with FID (both speech and thought) without quotation marks, followed by free indirect speech with quotation marks, and then FDD and DD using quotation marks.

(29)   She asked after their mutual friends; they were all well. – When had he left them? – Only that morning. He must have had a wet ride. – Yes. – He meant to walk with her, she found. "He had just looked into the dining-room, and as he was not wanted there, preferred being out of doors." …
"You have some news to hear, now you are come back, that will rather surprize you."
"Have I?" said he quietly, and looking at her; "of what nature?" (1815 Austen, *Emma*; www.gutenberg.org/files/158/158-h/158-h.htm)

By the time of Dickens (mid-nineteenth century), non-quotation-marked FID seems to have become established.

The pragmatic challenge posed by the representation of speech is to incorporate it without interrupting the narrative frame (as does (F)DS) and yet to preserve its exact wording, dramatic import, and subjectivity of speech (which are not allowed in IS). Free indirect speech allows the speech of characters to be expressed seamlessly within the narrative frame (in the third person and past tense of narration), with all of the speaker's subjectivity retained; the speech is often portrayed as it is experienced by others. At the same time, because FID is within the narrator's control, the narrator is able to adopt either an empathetic closeness to or ironic distance from the character or their speech. The pragmatic challenge posed by the representation of thought is to present thoughts with immediacy and subjectivity (not allowed in IT) yet not to suggest that the thoughts are "internal speech" and necessarily conscious (as does (F)DT). FID allows the representation of thought in a way which gives an illusion of the character's mental state, often with thoughts below the level of consciousness. FID thus seems to be a literary form highly suited to the expression of consciousness, a phenomenon which we associate with the novel.

4.8   Speech and Thought Representation in Late Modern English

B. Busse (2020) is a study of speech, thought, and writing representation in a selection of nineteenth-century novels (by Austen, Scott, C. Brontë, E. Brontë, Thackeray, Gaskell, Kingsley, Dickens, Eliot, Oliphant, Stevenson, Wilde, and Hardy). She counts both the units of speech, thought, and writing and the number of words within each unit. She compares her numerical results with those of Semino and Short (2004) discussed above. Overall, she finds that units of speech representation and pure narration are equally common in nineteenth-century fiction, but units of speech representation are more common in PDE fiction. In both centuries, however, narration comprises the largest number of words. This means that twentieth-century narrators produce longer passages of pure narration, while nineteenth-century speakers give longer speeches.

In terms of speech representation, (F)DS is the most common in both periods, with slightly more frequent and more verbose passages of (F)DS in the nineteenth century. Free indirect speech is still remarkably uncommon in the nineteenth century, under 1 percent of the words, compared to c.19 percent in PDE. Thought representation occurs less often than does speech representation in both periods. In the nineteenth century, NRTA is the most common and IT the second most common means of presenting thought, whereas NI is the most common in Semino and Short's corpus. (F)DT is much rarer in the nineteenth century than in the twentieth (0.3 percent compared to 28 percent of the words). Free indirect thought is also much rarer (7 percent compared to 26 percent of the words), but the passages are comparatively longer. B. Busse concludes, "In 20th-century thought presentation, the presentation of mental states dominates, whereas in the 19th century it is the summary of a mental act in NRTA" (81). What B. Busse's results seem to show us is that in general in the nineteenth century the direct, character-centered representation of internal thought does not figure prominently and that FID, especially free indirect speech, is not yet fully developed. Thus, we can say that in the nineteenth century, thought is presented indirectly, from the viewpoint of the narrator and in the narrator's words; we do not experience thoughts directly as the unfiltered expressions of the subjective consciousness of the character; pragmatically, this determines the extent to which we accept the statements as accurate representations of the character's thoughts.

4.9   Reporting Verbs in Late Modern English and Present-day English

While the formal marking of direct speech more or less stabilizes by Late Modern English (with the exception of FID), the inventory of reporting verbs continues to grow. *Say* remains the foremost reporting verb, but Cichosz (2018) finds at least thirty-eight other verbs used in inquits in her corpus (e.g., *add*, *reply*, *answer*, *return*, *ask*, *exclaim*, *repeat*, *go on*, *remark*, *resume*). *Quoth* is all but obsolete. The newer and less frequent verbs do not show inversion of the subject and verb, though inversion remains common for *say* and some of the more frequent verbs, as shown in (30a) with a speech descriptor. The forms *says I* and, more rarely, *says you* also appear as reporting clauses in Late Modern English (30b) (OED, s.v. *say* v.1 and int, def. I1c(b)).

(30)   a. "I said so!" **cried Morrice triumphantly**, "I was sure there was no gentleman but would be happy to accommodate two such ladies!" (1782 Burney, *Cecilia*; CLMET3.0)

b. "Ah, Betsey," **says I**, "you are always building castles in the air." (1827 Royall, *The Tennessean*; COHA)

We also see growing specialization of reporting verbs, where some are restricted to DS (*go*, *be like*, *recite*), some to IS (*indicate*, *alert*), some to DS and FID (*cry*, *consider*, *splutter*), some to IS and FID (*notice*, *object*, *gather*), and so on (see Fludernik 1993: 292–293).

For the speaker of Present-day English, what seems most striking is the rise of the new reporting verbs and constructions *go*, *be like*, and *be all*:

(31) a. **I go,** "Dad, why don't we just put it where it belongs?" (1999 *Dr. Katz, Profession ...*; COHA)
      b. And **I was like**, What have they done to my boy over there? (1987 Jakes, *Heaven and Hell*; COHA)
      c. And **I'm all**, "You know, I just made some gingerroot gazpacho, come on over." (1999 Edtv; COHA)

These forms occur in spoken conversation (personal narratives and transcribed interviews) and represented speech (in fiction) but rarely in written English (except in more speech-like written forms such as blogs). They invariably accompany DS, not IS.

Go is the oldest of these three forms. It likely arose out of the use of *go* to record a sound or noise (see OED, s.v. *go*, v., def. 11c(b)), which occurs as early as the nineteenth century (see 32a–b); this was then extended to the quoting of direct speech (see 31a and 32d). This is the source suggested by an early commentator (Butters 1980). The first example of quotative *go* cited in the OED dates from 1967. A related use is to specify the wording of a proverb, saying, song, account, and such (OED, s.v. *go*, def. 14), which dates from the late sixteenth century (32c). Like other reporting verbs, *go* can occur in medial and final position (32a, c, d) as well as initial position (31a, 32b).

(32) a. And then the tapping in his head became louder, more metallic, like a carpenter's mallet. "Toke-toke toke," **it went**. (1935 Green, *The Body the Earth*; COHA)
      b. **He goes**, "Quack, quack, quack. Hello." (1988 *Full House*; COHA)
      c. We convalescents and exinvalids have a theme song. "Until I got sick," **it goes**, "I never dreamed how lovely life could be." (1943 *Good Housekeeping*; COHA)
      d. "China," **she goes**, "your poetry is closer to the surface, just under your skin." (2002 Frank, *Life is Funny*; COHA)

The origin and spread of quotative *be like* has been the source of exhaustive study in the sociolinguistic literature, which notes its appearance in global varieties of English, in the speech of young people, at roughly the same time (e.g., Buchstaller 2014). According to the OED, *be like* appears in the early 1980s (s.v.v. *like*, adj, adv, conj., prep., def. P8 and def. B6c; *be*, v., def. 21), though it can be dated somewhat earlier:

(33)   a. **I'm like**, "Watch out for that!" I said, "Would you like!" (1976 *Saturday Night Live*; COHA)
        b. **It was like** "You're coming. We're driving away." (SCVE/f/1945; D'Arcy 2021: 93)
        c. And **I was all like**, "You want me to do a verse on your album? That's 100 k …" (1976 *Saturday Night Live*; COHA)

While *be like* is often associated with "Valley Girl Speak" (see the OED entry), it clearly did not originate in this variety. In her corpora of oral narratives and interviews (unscripted speech materials), D'Arcy (2021) finds examples of quotative *be like* in speakers born as early as the 1950s (see 33b); *be like* surpasses *say* in 1970/75 and is increasing rapidly in frequency. There are also earlier forms such as *think like*, *say like*, *feel like*, and *go like* (OED, s.v. *like*, def. B6c).

Quotative *be like* is not synonymous with either *say* or *go* (see Table 4.3). *Say* typically introduces the direct speech of the self or of others and is seen as the neutral or unmarked form. Both *say* and *go* imply vocalization and cannot be used for the expression of thought. Like *go*, *be like* may introduce sound, but it is more often used to introduce thought or inner monologue, or one's own speech (i.e., for self-presentation). Thus, it most often occurs in the first person (*I'm like*, *I was like*), while *go* is more common in the third person. *Be like* has an expressive or affective dimension and is used to "indicate aspects of speaker subjectivity" (Romaine and Lange 1991: 242). It does not make strong claims to faithfulness of the quoted speech or thought: the "speaker stands in reduced

Table 4.3 *Quotative uses of* say, go, *and* be like

Form	Function
say	represents the speech of the self or of others involves explicit vocalization
go	represents the speech of others, typically third person can represent non-speech sounds involves explicit vocalization
be like	represents the speech of the self, typically first person can represent non-speech sounds can be used for thought (inner monologue) may not involve explicit vocalization

responsibility and commitment to the truth of the report" (Romaine and Lange 1991: 263). It frequently occurs in the historical present, contributing to the sense of dramatized or enacted thought or speech and expressing evaluation. It must always occur in initial position, preceding the quoted material, never medially or finally. *Be* operates as an auxiliary in subject–auxiliary inversion and negative placement, though questions and negatives with *be like* are uncommon, perhaps because pragmatically we do not question or negate our own thoughts.

In contrast to *be like*, *be all* seems to have had a short span of popularity. But it is not obsolete. The OED gives the first example from 1982 (OED, s.v. *all*, adj., pron., and n., adv. and conj., def. C1d). (34b) looks like an unusually early example.

(34)   a. I'm not so sure. **You were all**, "I'm sure he's heard of styling gel." (1974
        The Life and Times of the Happy Hooker; COHA)
        b. but he looked so stupefied. The way **he was all**, "Great, great, I'm hip. I'm
        cool." (1952 *Something to Live for*; COHA)

Considering the use of reporting verbs exclusively in spoken English, D'Arcy (2017: 16–23, 2021) presents the following scenario. In the late nineteenth century *say* predominates, primarily in the third person and past tense, for the representation of speech. Over this period a range of other reporting verbs arise. In the early twentieth century, *say* remains dominant, but *think* gains ground for the expression of internal monologue, as does first-person quoted speech. The mid- to late twentieth century sees a greater range of content expressed, including speech, thought (real or imagined), writing, sound, and gesture, using a wide range of verbs: *say* for speech in the third-person past tense, *think* for first-person thought, *go* for mimetic content, and *be like* for first-person thought in the historical present.

There is considerable debate about the origin of *be like*. Some scholars relate its development to the rise of the pragmatic marker *like* (e.g., *Do you think we need people to be, like witnesses?* [COCA] or *Like one day I was doing the laundry for example* [COCA]; see D'Arcy 2017 and Chapter 3 on pragmatic markers). But others see them as separate developments. Meehan (1991) sees forms of *like* as grammaticalizing from the OE adjective *gelic* 'similar to'. The development of quotative *be like* is related to both the complementizer and pragmatic marker functions because *like* is a "quasi-complementizer" having scope over an entire clause and it focuses new information. It is related to the original meaning 'similar to', since it denotes that the quoted information need not be exact. Romaine and Lange (1991) see *like* in *be like* as a specialization within the textual domain of the grammaticalized complementizer *like* (as in *you sound like you care*) meaning 'as if', with the addition of a dummy *be* verb. It derives from the meaning of comparison or exemplification of *like*: "the speaker presents the clause created for comparison or exemplification so that it can be construed as a report of speech or thought" (262). While they see *like* in *be like* as deriving from the complementizer, they note that *like* is unlike *that* in *say that* since it does not effect the deictic shift found in indirect speech. Rather, much like FID (see above, §4.2), it retains in the quoted clause the deictic perspective of the represented speaker. They suggest it might be the "natural historical development" of FID in the spoken channel because it allows the speaker to keep the vividness of direct speech without suggesting that the words were actually spoken.

The view of *be like* as a case of grammaticalization has been contested, however. D'Arcy (2017) does not find that *be like* undergoes the contextual expansion found in grammaticalization but is grammatically stable, and Vandelanotte (2012) sees no sense in which *be like* is decategorialized or fossilized. D'Arcy (2017: 16–23, 2021) argues that *be like* develops from resources already available in the system, namely quotative *be*, dating from the late nineteenth century; the pragmatic marker *like* meaning 'in this way' or 'for example' is added by analogy with earlier forms such as *say like, think like, go like,* or *feel like.* The fact that *be* is pragmatically unrestricted makes *be like* suitable for representing all types of content, while the discourse marker *like*'s meaning of exemplification makes it suitable for mimetic representation and implies that the quotation need not be exact. Vandelanotte (2012) argues against the complementizer source, because *like* does not function as a complementizer; that is, it does not take a nominal complement and it does not introduce indirect but rather direct speech. He sees the entire clause (e.g., *I am like*) as undergoing constructionalization, with the meaning of *be like* as deriving transparently from the semantics of *like*: speakers using *I am like* announce "that they are about to give a partial or 'approximative' imitation of thought, emotion states or words" (183).

4.10 Historical Overview

The history of speech and thought presentation in English yields a complex picture of changes in form and type, which are at least in part pragmatically motivated. Over time, we can see increasing frequency of thought presentation over speech presentation, a change from more indirect (narrator-controlled, summarizing) to more direct (autonomous or non-narrator-controlled, verbatim) ways of presenting speech and thought, and an expanding use of specialized reporting verbs and speech evaluators. While the development of quotation marks in the EModE period allows quotation to be clearly delineated from narrative, which was not the case in medieval manuscripts, the development of FID in the modern period again erases the boundary between speech/thought and narrative. Which form of speech and thought a writer chooses can have pragmatic consequences, in influencing, especially, intersubjective relations between the writer, speaker/thinker, and reader: are we to accept the speaker/thinker as credible or authoritative, are we to believe their words/ thoughts to be accurate or verifiable, what attitude is the writer taking toward the speaker/thinker, how are we expected to respond to the speaker/thinker? The form of speech and thought presentation adopted can also have textual functions in distinguishing voices within the text (or blurring such voices). It can serve purposes of foregrounding or backgrounding speech and thought within the text or of dramatizing speech and thought. Finally, of course, it can serve purposes of characterization and thematic development within a text.

4.11   Chapter Summary

This chapter covered the following topics:
- the formal features and pragmatic functions of different categories of speech and thought representation in Present-day English, ranging from least to most summarizing and from most to least autonomous:
  - with (F)DS found to be the norm for speech representation, and NI (and also free indirect thought) the norm for thought representation;
- speech representation in Old English, where medieval manuscripts have no one designated way to mark direct speech but make frequent use of inquits:
  - with direct speech consisting of long, formal speeches spoken in isolation; and
  - with "slippage" from indirect to direct speech;
- speech representation in Middle English, where speech is more loosely represented, and there may be indeterminacy between *de dicto* and *de re* interpretations:
  - with *seien* the most frequent reporting verb; and
  - with thought often presented as internalized speech;
- the gradual conventionalization of quotation marks to denote DS in printed texts;
- speech and thought representation in Early Modern English, where categories of speech and thought fall on the "telling" end of the spectrum (NRSA, IS, NV and NRTA, IT, IN, respectively):
  - with an increase in the inventory of reporting verbs and decline of *quoth*;
  - with the use of speech-internal perspective shifters and speech descriptors for evaluation; and
  - with the frequent use of mixed modes;
- the development of FID, associated with the expression of consciousness and the rise of the novel, resulting in conventionalization of the form in the nineteenth century;

- speech and thought representation in Late Modern English, where speech representation is still more common than thought representation:
  - with longer passages of speech compared to longer passages of narration in Present-day English;
  - with thought on the "telling" end (using NRTA and IT) as opposed to the "showing" end of Present-day English (NI and free indirect thought);
- reporting verbs in Present-day English, including *go*, *be like*, and *be all*.

4.12   Further Reading

For a good overview of speech and thought representation from a historical perspective, see Grund and Walker (2021a). The categories of speech and thought representation discussed here are first presented in Leech and Short (2007[1981]: Ch. 10) and revised by Semino and Short (2004); a very useful overview is Toolan (2006). A somewhat outdated bibliography is Güldemann et al. (2002). B. Busse (2020: Ch. 5) is a thorough discussion of the functions of the different categories of speech and thought representation. Alternative frameworks are presented in, for example, McHale (1978) and Fludernik (1993). The literature on free indirect discourse – in the linguistics, stylistics, and literary critical fields – is vast; important treatments include Cohn (1978), McHale (1978), Banfield (1982), Fludernik (1993), and Vandelanotte (2009). Fludernik (1993: Chs. 3–4) is an exhaustive discussion of the linguistic features of free indirect discourse. For a lively discussion of quotation marks, see Crystal (2015: Ch. 31). Quotative *be like* receives extensive treatment in the sociolinguistic literature; a monograph-length treatment of *be like* and *go* is Buchstaller (2014). A recent collection of articles on speech representation in the history of English is Grund and Walker (2021b), and issue 16(1) (2017) of the *Nordic Journal of English Studies* is a special issue on speech representation in the history of English. On speech and writing representation in Old, Middle, and Early Modern historiography, see Claridge (2017b, 2021). Grund (2020, 2021a) are studies of speech descriptors in Late Modern English, continuing his earlier work in this area.

4.13   Exercises

1. Identify the category of speech and thought representation to which each of the following EModE examples belongs and note the features that are characteristic of that category. Note that some examples may be "mixed" categories. (Examples adapted from Włodarczyk 2007; Evans 2021; McIntyre and Walker 2011.)
   (a) Very well, thought I.

(b) My Ladie Hobby saith Mr Townesend & his wyef shall lye at her house all this wynter.

(c) He aunswered first to the graunting of saufconduites.

(d) and he shou'd have been entirely comforted, but for the Thought that she was possess'd by his Grand-father.

(e) Whan he did com home to his house his wife sayd, where is my Brandiron or trefete.

(f) My lord then made another and a longer speech of the same sort.

(g) A you blynd betel can you not se?

(h) the wynde also began to blow agayne: wherfore we were glad and lauded and thanked god.

(i) Vppon the redyng of Mr. Knyghtis lettre his Grace saied not mych, but that if Bewreyne cum to his Grace he wilbe playne with hym.

(j) Wherto I answerd that I wold not say the contrary.

(k) wherwith your grace was veray moch displeasyd Saying I am not well handelyd.

(l) I remember I am not alienate from you, but that I am your Christian Brother.

(m) As for the Rebels, she would in no wise deliver them, for it was against her Honour: As for the Holds, she should not deliver any; for it were against the Safety of her Friends in Scotland.

(n) he should understand his whole Mind particularly from time to time.

2. In the following passage from Jane Austen's *Emma* (1815), Emma finds herself, after a ball, alone in a carriage with Mr. Elton. She has been attempting to arrange a match between her friend Harriet Smith and Mr. Elton, while Mr. Elton's attentions – unbeknownst to Emma – have actually been directed at Emma.

Identify how speech and thought are represented in this passage. What categories of speech and thought are represented? What purposes do the different categories serve in this extract?

To restrain him as much as might be, by her own manners, she was immediately preparing to speak with exquisite calmness and gravity of the weather and the night; but scarcely had she begun, scarcely had they passed the sweep-gate and joined the other carriage, than she found her subject cut up—her hand seized—her attention demanded, and Mr. Elton actually making violent love to her: availing himself of the precious opportunity, declaring sentiments which must be already well known, hoping—fearing —adoring—ready to die if she refused him; but flattering himself that his ardent attachment and unequalled love and unexampled passion could not fail of having some effect, and in short, very much resolved on being seriously accepted as soon as possible. It really was so. Without scruple—without apology—without much apparent diffidence, Mr. Elton, the lover of Harriet, was professing himself *her* lover. She tried to stop him; but vainly; he would go on, and say it all. Angry as she was, the thought of the moment made her resolve to restrain herself when she did speak. She felt that half this folly must be drunkenness, and therefore could hope that it might belong only to the passing hour. Accordingly, with a mixture of the serious and the playful, which she hoped would best suit his half and half state, she replied,

"I am very much astonished, Mr. Elton. This to *me*! you forget yourself—you take me for my friend—any message to Miss Smith I shall be happy to deliver; but no more of this to *me*, if you please."

"Miss Smith!—message to Miss Smith!—What could she possibly mean!"—And he repeated her words with such assurance of accent, such boastful pretence of amazement, that she could not help replying with quickness,

"Mr. Elton, this is the most extraordinary conduct! and I can account for it only in one way; you are not yourself, or you could not speak either to me, or of Harriet, in such a manner. Command yourself enough to say no more, and I will endeavour to forget it."

But Mr. Elton had only drunk wine enough to elevate his spirits, not at all to confuse his intellects. He perfectly knew his own meaning; and having warmly protested against her suspicion as most injurious, and slightly touched upon his respect for Miss Smith as her friend,—but acknowledging his wonder that Miss Smith should be mentioned at all,—he resumed the subject of his own passion, and was very urgent for a favourable answer. (www.gutenberg.org/files/158/158-h/158-h.htm)

3. The following passage from Jane Austen's *Mansfield Park* (1814) discusses how a contrite letter from the impoverished Mrs. Price to her wealthier sisters, Mrs. Norris and Lady Bertram, has the effect of bringing about a reconciliation among them.

   Identify how speech, thought, and writing are represented in this passage. What categories of speech and thought are represented? What purposes do the different categories serve in this extract?

   The letter was not unproductive. It re-established peace and kindness. Sir Thomas sent friendly advice and professions, Lady Bertram dispatched money and baby-linen, and Mrs. Norris wrote the letters.

   Such were its immediate effects, and within a twelvemonth a more important advantage to Mrs. Price resulted from it. Mrs. Norris was often observing to the others that she could not get her poor sister and her family out of her head, and that, much as they had all done for her, she seemed to be wanting to do more; and at length she could not but own it to be her wish that poor Mrs. Price should be relieved from the charge and expense of one child entirely out of her great number. "What if they were among them to undertake the care of her eldest daughter, a girl now nine years old, of an age to require more attention than her poor mother could possibly give? The trouble and expense of it to them would be nothing, compared with the benevolence of the action." Lady Bertram agreed with her instantly. "I think we cannot do better," said she; "let us send for the child."

   Sir Thomas could not give so instantaneous and unqualified a consent. He debated and hesitated;—it was a serious charge;—a girl so brought up must be adequately provided for, or there would be cruelty instead of kindness in taking her from her family. He thought of his own four children, of his two sons, of cousins in love, etc.; —but no sooner had he deliberately begun to state his objections, than Mrs. Norris interrupted him with a reply to them all, whether stated or not. (www.gutenberg.org/files/141/141-h/141-h.htm)

5   Politeness

5.1   Introduction

Norms of politeness underlie a number of the pragmatic features discussed in this book, especially address terms (Chapter 7) and speech acts (Chapter 6) and, to a lesser extent, pragmatic markers (Chapter 3). This chapter begins by discussing a number of different ways that politeness has been approached from a pragmatic perspective. This is followed by a shorter discussion of its opposite, impoliteness. It is well recognized that conventions of politeness may change over time, and the remainder of the chapter is concerned with these changes in English, focusing on several case studies: compliments (an example of politeness) versus insults (an example of impoliteness) and thanks (again an example of politeness) versus responses to thanks (not an example of impoliteness but an attempt to minimize or deflect politeness). The chapter ends by exploring the norms of politeness most characteristic of Present-day English, including non-imposition politeness and camaraderie politeness. As the studies unfold, you will see that although we can study politeness using a form-to-function approach by looking at conventionalized politeness expressions such as *thank you, please, I'm sorry, excuse me* and so on, politeness is a much more complex phenomenon often requiring a global function-to-form approach (as discussed in Chapter 2).

5.2   Theories of Politeness

Politeness as the avoidance of face-threatening acts: The traditional approach to politeness is based on the work of Brown and Levinson (1987[1978]). They begin with the notion of "face" as understood in the non-technical sense of "reputation, honor, good name," as in *lose face* or *save face* (OED, s.v. *face*, n., defs. III 17, P8 h). Brown and Levinson recognize two types of "face":

> **Negative face**: the desire to not be impeded in one's action, to not be imposed upon;
>
> **Positive face**: the desire to be liked, approved of, or appreciated by others.

When interacting with others, many of our actions (linguistic or otherwise) may violate either negative or positive face. These are what Brown and Levinson call *face-threatening acts* (FTAs). For example, FTAs against the hearer's negative face include the following: requests, suggestions, reminders, or threats (which call upon the hearer to act in some way), offers and promises (which place the hearer under an obligation to accept), or even compliments and expressions of strong negative emotion (which may call on the hearer to act in some way). FTAs against the hearer's positive face include: disapproval, criticism, insults, accusations against the hearer, disagreements with or challenges to the hearer, expressions of violent emotion, mention of inappropriate, divisive, or dangerous topics, bad news affecting the hearer, the speaker's boasting, interruptions, and using status-marked address terms (Brown and Levinson 1987[1978]: 65–67).

In polite behavior, we are aware of these two faces and we try to avoid FTAs, what Brown and Levinson call "redressing" face. "Positive politeness" consists in the ways in which we address our hearer's positive face (redress possible FTAs against positive face). This may involve complimenting the hearer, seeking agreement or avoiding disagreement with the hearer, assuming common ground with the hearer, expressing interest in the hearer, attending to the wants or desires of the hearer, giving reasons, using in-group or affectionate terms of address, joking with the hearer, thanking the hearer, or offering reciprocal kindness in exchange for a favor (Brown and Levinson 1987[1978]: 101–129). "Negative politeness" consists in the ways in which we address our hearer's negative face (redress possible FTAs against negative face). This may involve giving deference to the hearer, minimizing our imposition on the hearer (e.g., by using indirect speech acts), not presuming or assuming about the hearer, questioning or hedging, being pessimistic, apologizing, and impersonalizing (e.g., avoiding *I* and *you*), stating required actions as general rules (Brown and Levinson 1987[1978]: 129–211). See Table 5.1 for some examples of these strategies. We also may redress FTAs "off record." Off-record acts are ones where the communicative intention is not explicit and the hearer must infer the intention. They are prototypically "indirect," such as hints, under- and overstatements, contradictions, tautologies, irony, metaphors, rhetorical questions, and ambiguous or vague utterances. The speaker has an "out" (*That's not what I meant*), as does the hearer, who can ignore the inference (Brown and Levinson 1987[1978]: 211–230).

In addition to paying attention to the face of the hearer, the speaker may also be concerned about their own face. Thus, there may be a careful balancing act occurring in which a speaker is balancing possible FTAs against the hearer's and their own face.

Brown and Levinson's theory of politeness has come in for a fair amount of criticism. In addition to a broad criticism focused on the unfortunate use of

Table 5.1 *Examples of positive and negative politeness strategies*

Positive Politeness	
Complimenting	*Well, first of all, this is so gracious of you to do.* (COCA: SPOK)
Using close terms of address	*Honey, it's the last game of the season.* (COCA: FIC)
Thanking	*I really appreciate your joining us tonight.* (COCA: SPOK)
Offering reciprocal kindness	*I could buy you a cappuccino, in exchange for the cigarette.* (COCA: FIC)
Seeking agreement	*When that moment comes, one's ambition ceases. Don't you agree?* (COCA: MAG)
Negative Politeness	
Being deferential	*If I could just ask you to hold on for one minute, sir.* (COCA: SPOK)
Minimizing imposition	*I know I'm asking a lot, but it doesn't have to be a permanent move.* (COCA: FIC)
	As a courtesy, I was wondering if you could upgrade my room. (COCA: MAG)
Apologizing	*Dad, I wrecked your car, I'm so sorry.* (COCA: SPOK)
Impersonalizing	*Sometimes it's necessary to let your feelings out.* (COCA: FIC)
Stating a general rule	*Parents and students should communicate openly during high school.* (COCA: SPOK)

evaluative terms such as "negative" and "positive" and the association of politeness with insincere behavior, critics have argued that this theory conceptualizes politeness almost exclusively in terms of face. It reduces politeness to the mitigation of FTAs or behavior which is designed to solve problems in social interactions, with an emphasis on non-imposition politeness (which is discussed in detail below). This may not correspond to our everyday notions of politeness, which focuses more on the choice of socially and situationally appropriate behavior. Brown and Levinson assign each politeness form a fixed value, based on a summation of P (power), D (social distance), and R (rank or size of imposition), but forms in actual use seem to have variable values and are not a simple summation of these three factors. Though they may have default meanings, politeness strategies are always negotiated by speakers in use and dependent on context; thus, for example, *You are a fine friend* may be judged as positively polite and affectionate or as impolite and rude depending on context (and intonation) (cf. *A fine friend you are*, which is always impolite). Despite the criticisms, you will see as you read this chapter, that Brown and Levinson's concept of face, FTA, and negative/positive politeness remain very useful notions.

Politeness as "comity": For Leech (2014), politeness is behavior which leads us "to avoid communicative discord or offence, and maintain or enhance communicative concord or comity" (87). In our interactions, we follow a "General Strategy of Politeness" in which we assign favorable value to the hearer and assume unfavorable value ourselves. Leech retains the notion of what he calls "pos-politeness" and "neg-politeness," but defines them some-what differently than Brown and Levinson do. Pos-politeness involves giving a positive value to the hearer and is thus hearer-oriented. Neg-politeness – which Leech sees as the stronger force – involves taking value away from the speaker and is thus speaker-oriented. Its function is to reduce or lessen causes of offense. A test for expressions of pos-politeness is the possibility of adding intensifying expressions (such as *very*); a test for neg-politeness expressions is the possibility of their being hedged. Politeness operates according to a set of Maxims of Politeness, which are constraints that influence a speaker's behavior. He identifies ten maxims, among which six are most important for our purposes. In Table 5.2 the Maxims are set out with examples of speech acts for each.

For example, in a promise (as will be discussed in Chapter 6), such as *I'll pay for your ticket*, the speaker is attending to the hearer by assuming that the hearer wants the promised action. The speaker is valuing the hearer's wants. This is the Maxim of Generosity and it represents a case of pos-politeness. Apologies (also discussed in Chapter 6), such as *I'm sorry that I didn't call*, are also an instance of pos-politeness; here a speaker admits fault and hence assumes a debt to the hearer. While it might also be possible to see apologies as neg-politeness since they are focused on repairing relations with the hearer and redeeming the speaker's lost face (which has

Table 5.2 *Leech's Maxims of Politeness (adapted from Leech 2014: 92, 120)*

Definition of Maxim	Name of Maxim	Examples of speech acts	Type of politeness
M1: give a high value to H's* wants	Generosity	Commissives (promises, invitations, offers)	Pos-politeness H-oriented
M2: give a low value to S's* wants	Tact	Directives (requests, orders, entreaties)	Neg-politeness S-oriented
M3: give a high value to H's qualities	Approbation	Compliments, praise	Pos-politeness H-oriented
M4: give a low value to S's qualities	Modesty	Self-devaluation, responding to compliments	Neg-politeness S-oriented
M5: give a high value to S's obligation to H	Obligation (of S to H)	Apologies, thanks	Pos-politeness H-oriented
M6: give a low value to S's obligation to H	Obligation (of H to S)	Response to thanks, response to apologies	Neg-politeness S-oriented

* S = Speaker, H = Hearer (or other person)

been humbled by the apology), what is important is the effect on the hearer, namely, that their face is enhanced. Apologies are like thanks, which are discussed below. A case of neg-politeness is exemplified by the Maxim of Modesty in the response to compliments. A receiver of a compliment may choose to make a self-deprecating statement, such as *Oh, I was just lucky* (i.e., it had nothing to do with my actions or qualities), thus lessening their own qualities. Too much self-deprecation may, however, be seen as "fishing for compliments."

For Leech, politeness is a matter of degree, which depends on three scales of value:

1. The vertical distance between the speaker and the hearer (in terms of power, role, age, etc.);
2. The horizontal distance between the speaker and the hearer (in terms of intimacy, familiarity, or acquaintance, including in-group vs. out-group relations); and
3. The cost/benefit (indebtedness) of the favor or obligation, including socially defined rights and obligations such as student–teacher or host–guest.

A system of politeness that is dependent on factors (1) and (2) is what Leech calls a "bivalent" system, whereas one that involves all three factors is a "trivalent" or interactional system. A bivalent system is one of honorifics, including both honorific and humiliative forms, chosen on the basis of vertical and social distance between interlocutors. The working of such a system in the history of English will be discussed in Chapter 7. In a bivalent system, honorific usage is required in all situations, even the most neutral (such as giving a weather report). In a trivalent system, politeness applies only in situations where there is a cost/benefit.

5.3   Impoliteness

In theory, impoliteness could be seen as the opposite of politeness, as an attack on face. For example, Culpeper defines impoliteness as cases where "(1) the speaker communicates face-attack intentionally, or (2) the hearer perceives and/or constructs behavior as intentionally face-attacking" (2011b: 23). Rudanko (1993: Ch. VI) sets out rules of impoliteness – or what he calls "nastiness" – by reversing all of Brown and Levinson's positive and negative politeness strategies. Culpeper (1996) envisages a somewhat more streamlined system consisting of five strategies:

- bald on-record impoliteness: aggravating the face of the interlocutor: insult, threaten, command, and the like
- positive impoliteness: attacking the hearer's positive face: ignore, snub, exclude, deny association, be uninterested in the hearer, seek disagreement,

use secretive language, inappropriate terms of address, or taboo words, call the hearer derogatory names;
- negative impoliteness: attacking the hearer's negative face: frighten, condescend, scorn, ridicule, challenge, invade the hearer's space, associate the hearer with a negative aspect, put the hearer's indebtedness on record;
- sarcasm or mock politeness: using obviously insincere politeness strategies; and
- withholding politeness.

Bald on-record FTAs are impolite, though there may be extenuating reasons for their use, which reduces or eliminates their impoliteness, for example, in cases of urgency (e.g., *Watch out, there's a crack*) or efficiency (e.g., *Look, the point is . . .*), where the danger is very small and we use formulaic imperatives (e.g., *Come in, Pardon me*), where there is a vast power differential between speaker and hearer (e.g., *Bring me wine, Jeeves*), or where the FTA is in the hearer's interest (e.g., *Take care*) or is an offer (e.g., *Have another piece of cake*) (Brown and Levinson 1987[1978]: 94–101).

Leech (2014: Ch. 8) also views impoliteness in terms of the reversal of his Maxims. The opposite of M1 (Generosity) is to threaten, curse, refuse a request, of M2 (Tact) is to order or demand, of M3 (Approbation) is to insult, complain, or accuse, of M4 (Modesty) is to boast or be complacent, of M5 (Obligation of S to H) is to withhold thanks or apologies, and of M6 (Obligation of H to S) is to demand thanks or apologies. In addition, Leech notes that there can be impoliteness in aspects of discourse management, such as interrupting, engaging in discussion of "taboo" topics (age, appearance, job, etc.), non-engaging in discussion, using offensive language, shouting, and so on. Leech treats sarcasm/irony as a case of overt politeness which leads to impoliteness.

In more recent work, Culpeper (2011b) has expanded his definition of impoliteness beyond the notion of face attack to include social norms, intentionality, and emotion: "Situated behaviours are viewed negatively – considered 'impolite' – when they conflict with how one expects them to be, how one wants them to be and/or how one thinks they ought to be" (2011b: 23). An expanded notion of face – especially what he calls "quality face" (our desire for people to evaluate us positively in terms of our personal qualities) is important in English – to account for insults, pointed criticisms/complaints, curses, ill wishes, and unpalatable questions. But breaches of social conventions and norms can also be central to impoliteness, just as congruence with these norms is central to polite behavior. He adds "association rights" (our rights to have relationships with others) to account for the impoliteness of excluding others from conversations, and "equity rights" (our rights to personal consideration from others) to account for the impoliteness of dismissals (e.g., *get lost*), silencers (e.g., *shut up*), threats, condescensions (e.g., *that's childish*), and message enforcers (e.g., *you got it?*). Finally, he adds to impoliteness the use of taboo words or the addressing of taboo topics and physical intimidation.

5.4   Politeness over Time in English

Historical studies of politeness can face unique challenges both because conceptions of politeness change over time and because our data for the study of politeness may be limited. Even the way we talk about (im)politeness has changed over time. While the word *polite* has been in English since Middle English, it only began to be used in the sense of 'courteous' in the mid-eighteenth century (OED, s.v. *polite*, adj. and n.). In Middle English, *courtesy* was the preferred term, while *civility* was popular in Early Modern English. *Rude/rudeness* has been the most frequent term used to describe impolite behavior over time (see Jucker and Kopaczyk 2017), with *impolite* appearing for the first time in Early Modern English (OED, s.v. *impolite*, adj.).

Jucker (2011b, 2012a, 2020) presents a reconceptualized set of politeness categories, tailored, in part, to developments over time in English. He proposes the following categories:

- **discernment politeness**: this refers to socially appropriate behavior in a given social situation; it is not a matter of strategic choices to maintain or enhance the speaker's or hearer's face;
- **politeness of humility and gentleness**: associated with Christian virtues, this refers to "God-fearing behaviour of innocence, humility, kind-heartedness, obedience and goodness" (Jucker 2020: 38);
- **deference politeness**: this focuses on the relative power and status of speakers and hearers, typically involving the humbling of the self and raising of the other; its linguistic exponents are honorifics (*sir*, *madam*, *you*) (see Chapter 7) and thanking expressions (see below §5.6). It compares to one aspect of positive politeness and is the continuation of discernment politeness. It is what Leech (2014) calls "bivalent politeness";
- **solidarity politeness**: manifest in the use of "in-group" identity markers and terms of endearment, this type of politeness serves to establish and reinforce good relationships between speaker and hearer; and
- **non-imposition politeness** (discussed below).

We see changing norms of politeness over time in English. As we will discuss in more detail in Chapter 6, Old English had more apparently face-threatening commands (first-person performatives, imperatives) than contemporary English and fewer verbs of the 'suggest' class. The word closest to *politeness* in Old English was *þeawfæstnes*, meaning 'obedience to rule, adherence to right conduct.' Kinship terms referred to fixed rank but were not face-enhancing. The lack of negative or positive politeness in the Brown and Levinsonian sense is attributed to the fact that in Early Medieval society, relations between individuals were based on kin loyalty, a strict social hierarchy, and mutual obligations. Individuals needed only to use the forms appropriate to their place in the social order. This is what Jucker calls *discernment politeness*. Concurrently, Christian texts extolled the virtues of *humilitas* and *caritas*, what Jucker calls *humility and gentleness politeness*. Leech (2014) shows that in the speeches of Beowulf, the Maxims of Generosity, Tact, and Approbation could all be part of discernment politeness, but that the Maxim of Modesty had little place. As Kohnen observes (2017b), boasting is a necessary element in Germanic warrior culture and is positively evaluated, but in a Christian context, it is negatively evaluated and seen as wicked and sinful.

The ME period saw the introduction of the French concept of *curteisie* 'courtesy' and politeness forms (*thou/ye* forms). *Curteisie* represented a courtly form of behavior which was in accordance with certain norms of social decorum. It was associated with the aristocracy and to a lesser extent the clergy, but was also emulated by the lower-ranked members of society. This French-influenced form of behavior accounts for the density of politeness terms in the ME period (Jucker et al. 2012). Because *curteisie* did not involve the strategic use of politeness forms or behavior, however, Jucker (2020) still views it as discernment politeness. In principle, the *thou/ye* pronouns constituted an honorific system marking the social roles of speaker and hearer, an example of Leech's bivalent system of politeness. But Jucker argues that it was a more flexible system dependent upon specific interactions negotiated between interlocutors, with the *ye* forms being a means of showing respect (but not necessarily formality or distance) and the *thou* forms being used where no respect was necessary (we will look at this in more detail in Chapter 7). Thus, in marking social distinctions (roles and relationships), the pronouns served as exponents of what Jucker calls *deference politeness*. In late Middle English this system of deference is apparent in the prologues and epilogues of Caxton, where the writer adopts a pose of extreme humility in respect to his patron and readers (addressed indirectly in the third person), showing Approbation, Modesty, Generosity, and Obligation (Leech 2014).

In the EModE period, politeness terms such as *polite(ness)*, *deference*, *civil(ity)*, and *conduct* came into use, as did *sprezzatura* 'effortless mastery', referring to the courtier who behaves with cultivated ease. A system of face-based politeness is seen as emerging, but whether it was primarily a negative or a positive politeness system has been a matter of scholarly debate. Studying four Shakespearian tragedies and four comedies, Kopytko concludes, "I tentatively assume that the high rate of occurrence of positive politeness strategies in Shakespeare's plays characterizes the interactional 'ethos' of Elizabethan society" (1995: 531). In contrast, as we will see in Chapter 7, §7.8, address terms in EModE correspondence were preponderantly negative politeness forms, though there was a trend toward terms of positive politeness (e.g., endearments) later in the period. However, because the forms used depend on the power and distance between the speaker and hearer but not the weight of the imposition and are thus not used strategically to mitigate a presumed FTA, Jucker (2020: 87) suggests that the system is best described as one of deference. The movement toward endearments represents what Jucker calls *solidarity politeness* and what Leech views as a reduction of bivalent politeness and decreasing importance of vertical distance. Toward the end of the period, the inherited deferential second-person pronoun address system underwent a change to a system more shaped by positive emotions (of closeness, intimacy, or solidarity) and negative emotions (of dislike, resentment, and hatred); this led to the retention of the originally deferential *you* form and loss of the *thou* forms, which could be used for endearment but also insult (the use of *thou/you* in Early Modern English is a complex topic which we will tackle in Chapter 7).

"Polite society" in the eighteenth century in England can be characterized as a culture of positive politeness. Polite behavior, polite manners, and elegant refinement were extolled (in handbooks of etiquette, plays, and novels), were expected of the upper classes, and were strived for by the middle classes. Politeness had attained the status of an ideology. Ceremonious compliments and thanks, expressed in ornate language, were the rule (see below, §5.5). Jucker calls the politeness of the age "compliment culture." At the same time there was a realization that politeness may be "mere conduct" and if not resting on morality and virtue, could be hollow, hypocritical, and even deceptive.

It is widely and almost universally argued that Present-day English is a period of *non-imposition politeness*. This form of politeness is most obviously seen in the indirect strategies used in performing directives, which are discussed in more detail below. Leech (2014: Ch. 11) sees two major trends in the history of English:

1. the decline and virtual obsolescence of honorific terms of address (see Chapter 7); and
2. the growth of indirect forms of requests.

While the latter is associated with non-imposition politeness, the former is associated with what Leech calls "camaraderie politeness," both of which are discussed in §5.7 and §5.8, respectively.

5.5   Compliments and Insults

Perhaps the most obviously (im)polite linguistic behavior is the issuing of compliments and insults. These have been fairly extensively studied in the history of English.

Compliments: Compliments are "speech acts pointing out pleasant and agreeable things about the addressee or something or someone connected with the addressee" (Taavitsainen and Jucker 2008: 198). For Leech, compliments express the Maxim of Approbation, in which the speaker places a high value on the hearer's qualities and enhances the hearer's face. It is thus a case of pospoliteness (2014: 186–191).

A receiver of a compliment is in an awkward position. To accept the compliment is immodest (violating what Leech calls the Modesty Maxim) but to reject the compliment expresses disagreement (violating the Agreement Maxim). Since accepting a compliment may also threaten the receiver's face, they may be compelled to denigrate the object of the compliment (e.g., their appearance or accomplishments) and thus lessen their own positive face. A typical response is to try to deflect or evade the compliment, by, for example, simply thanking the complimenter (which shows appreciation for the act but neither agrees or disagrees), adding some informative remark, questioning the sincerity of the compliment, or downgrading or reducing the power of the compliment (see Leech 2014: 189–191).

Compliments may be either "personal" or "ceremonial" (Taavitsainen and Jucker 2010a), as we see in (1a–b) and (1c), respectively. Ceremonial (or ritual) compliments are conventionalized, often rule-governed, and occur in specific contexts. (Interestingly, the definition of *compliment* in the OED captures only the ceremonial meaning in both the noun and verb entries, but neither entry has been updated since 1891.)

(1)   a. "It keeps you in great shape," Richard says. # She ignores the **compliment** (2019 *The Carolina Quarterly*; COCA)
        b. By the way, **I compliment** you again on the book. (CNN_News; COCA)
        c. "In appreciation of services rendered, **with my compliments**," said President Washington. (2007 Shetter, *Child Life*; COCA)

Note that the explicit performative *I compliment*, as in (1b), is quite rare.

When Taavitsainen and Jucker (2008) approached the study of compliments in historical texts, they searched for the metacommunicative label "compliment" in Renaissance drama and fiction. The use of *compliment* in the ceremonial sense of paying respects or greeting, as in (2a), is common. But personal compliments coexisted with these, as in (2b); here, Mrs. Beauclair uses the label to indicate that she recognizes Sir Francis Wildlove's speech as a compliment:

(2)   a. TOLINS: Colonel Toper, presents his **compliments** to you, Sir, and having no family down with him in the country, he, and Captain Hardbottle, if not inconvenient, will do themselves the honour of taking a family dinner with you. (1697 Macklin, *The Man of the World* II; ED)
        b. SIR FRANCIS WILDLOVE: Faith, Madam, I must speak freely, tho' you are a Woman of Quality, and my Friend's Neice, you talk so prettily, 'tis pity you shou'd not do it often in a Mask: But then agen, you are so pretty, 'tis pity you shou'd ever wear one.
           MRS. BEAUCLAIR: I did not design by railing to beg a **Compliment**; Sir Charles, where's the Musick? (1697 Pix, *The Innocent Mistress* III.ii; ED)

Renaissance findings would seem to be consistent with the modern situation in which women receive and give more compliments than men (Holmes 1988). In the Renaissance, both men and women compliment their interlocutors on appearance, attire, and qualities, but men also compliment a wider range of features, including nationality, patriotism, and manners. Certain topics frequent in modern compliments, such as possessions or food, however, are not complimented. Women use compliments to create solidarity. Men are thought to use them to exert power or to promote themselves, but Taavitsainen and Jucker (2008) found that the primary use of complimenting by men in their texts was for flirting.

In eighteenth-century polite society, ceremonial compliments assume great importance. Handbooks of etiquette give instructions on how to compliment in numerous contexts, such as when paying a visit or issuing or accepting an invitation. In public contexts, compliments form the basis of diplomacy and are used in welcoming or thanking foreign dignitaries on state visits or in recognizing the accession to office, birthdays, weddings, or birth of nobility (Taavitsainen and Jucker 2010a; Jucker 2020: 122–127).

The results of a study of compliments in American English from the 1820s–2000s (in COHA) suggest that men issue compliments more than women (with some decrease over time), and that men and women receive compliments equally frequently (Jucker and Taavitsainen 2014a). The topics of compliments are primarily personality/friendship and ability/performance; appearance, which ranks highly in contemporary English, constitutes less that 20 percent of the total. It is known that Americans have a high rate of acceptance of compliments, but this is a fairly recent phenomenon, with the acceptance rate rising from an average of 60.3 percent in the first four decades of COHA to 72.8 percent in the last decade of the twentieth century.

Insults: Insults occupy the opposite end of the politeness spectrum from compliments. They constitute a face-threatening act against positive face, by demeaning or wounding the self-respect of the addressee. What is important in an insult is its effect on the addressee. An insult may be unintentional or intentional on the part of the speaker and may range from mock to aggressive and from ironic to sincere (Archer 2010). It is also possible that the recipient fails to recognize an utterance as an insult, and we might then question whether it is a successful insult at all. Like compliments, insults are either ritual or personal. Ritualized insults are conventionalized, even rule-governed, and typically elicit a response in kind. They are often *ludic* 'playful' and ironic and always intentional. Personal insults are creative and ad hoc, typically aggressive, and range from sincere to unintentional. They are met with denial, mitigating excuses, counter-insults, silence, or even violence (see Jucker and Taavitsainen 2000). Insults bear a relationship to a number of other speech acts, such as slanders/slurs, swearing, cursing (see Chapter 6, §6.7), and oaths.

Chapman (2008), in a study of personal insults in Old English, finds that in religious contexts and genres (saints' lives, in addresses to sinners, in complaints between the body and the soul at judgment day, and in addresses to the devil), the insults serve a didactic purpose. They consist of "overwhelmingly" formulaic language, such as *earm* 'wretched, poor' or *ungescælig* 'unfortunate', making them immediately recognizable by the target and any other listeners. The semantic categories are typical of insults generally (e.g., low social status, mental deviation, lack of cleanliness, nationality), but sexual and scatological references – common in Present-day English – are missing in Old English. Nonetheless, insults can be quite specific (e.g., devils were evil but not stupid), and the few creative insults to be found (e.g., *maþemete* 'maggot-food', *deofles wulf* 'devil's wolf') seem to have a clear pragmatic function: to ridicule or belittle the target.

Taavitsainen and Jucker (2007) examine verbs containing 'insult' in their definition in five historical corpora. They find descriptive uses, but no performative uses, of the verbs in the OE and ME sections of the *Helsinki Corpus*. Again, insults are primarily restricted to religious texts, often describing God's anger. The one performative example in the EModE section contains the second-person familiar pronoun *thou* used as an insult verb (on *thou*, see Chapter 7):

(3)   ATTORNEY: All that he did was by thy Instigation, thou Viper; for **I thou** thee, thou Traitor (1603 Trial of Sir Walter Raleigh; Taavitsainen and Jucker 2007: 125)

Ritual insults in Old English and the Germanic heroic tradition generally have been extensively studied. These rituals consist of the exchange of boasts and insults about past deeds, and threats, vows, and curses concerning future action. The insults typically focus on cowardice, failure of honor, irresponsible behavior, and crimes of kinship. Pakis (2011) identifies three types of ritual insult in Germanic: *flyting* (the exchange of insults and boasts that leads to combat), *senna* (the exchange of boasts and insults that does not lead to combat), and *hvǫt*, or whetting (insults issued by a woman to her kinsman in order to incite him to action or retribution). Flyting differs from ritualized insults in other cultures because it is not ludic, but often evokes strong feelings and may lead to combat (see Jucker and Taavitsainen 2000; see also Arnovick 1999: Ch. 2). Pakis discusses the Viking leader's 'jeering' (*lytegian*) at Byrhtnoth, the East Saxon leader, in the *Battle of Maldon* as an example of flyting as it leads to combat between the Viking and Saxon forces, with the eventual defeat of the Saxons.

Perhaps the best-known example of ritual insult in Old English is the Unferð episode in *Beowulf* (ll. 499–606); this would qualify as a senna in Pakis's schema. Unferð, envious of Beowulf's fame and annoyed at his boast that he can vanquish Grendel, insults Beowulf by recalling a swimming contest (with Breca) that Beowulf apparently lost. He predicts that Beowulf will not do better in his battle against Grendel. Beowulf counters by accusing Unferð of drunkenness, retelling the Breca episode in a light favorable to himself (i.e., he killed nine sea monsters and fulfilled his boast), and attacking Unferð for his inaction against Grendel. Boasting is an integral part of such an exchange.

A modern form of ritualistic insult is "sounding," or "playing the dozens," a cultural practice among urban black adolescents. As Jucker and Taavitsainen (2000: 89) note, "the purpose . . . is to better one's opponent with caustic and humorous insults that are seen as patently untrue." The insults exchanged have to do with sexuality, cowardice, cleanliness, and personal defects. Overall, the purpose of the exchange of insults is "ludic," or "mock impoliteness." It is a kind of braggadocio. Insults are met with counter-insults, rather than denials or mitigating excuses. Sounding differs from Old English flyting in that flyting is serious, may relate to real events, often evokes strong feelings, and contains a strong element of boasting (see Arnovick 1999: Ch. 2). Sounding, in contrast, is a means to negotiate one's social status or rank. As Leech notes (2014: 239), banter (of which sounding is an extreme type) is "probably one of the main discriminators of camaraderie," a case where overt impoliteness leads to politeness. If people (of equal status) who are exchanging insults treat them as nonserious, "they share a powerful way of signaling their solidarity." He cites the example of the insults exchanged between fans of rival football teams. (On camaraderie, see §5.8).

Personal insults in Middle English, in Chaucer's *Canterbury Tales*, are varied and highly creative, as Jucker (2000a) shows. The insults involve name-calling, sexual innuendo, scatology, and animal imagery. Insults may involve a number of rhetorical strategies, such as similes, generalization, mock praise, ironic disclaimer, subjective disclaimer (*it seems to me*), and so on. Insults are met most often with counter-insults, but sometimes by hurt silence or physical violence. An insulting sequence occurs after the Friar has interrupted the Wife of Bath's lengthy prologue. The Summoner swears at the Friar and then insults him by comparing him to a fly (4). The Friar counterattacks by promising to tell a story that will shed a bad light on summoners. The Summoner responds, "I bishrewe thy face" 'I curse thy face'. The conflict escalates to the point that the Host must intercede: "Pees! And that anon! . . . Lat the womman telle hire tale" (ll. 850–851).

(4)   "Lo," quod the Somonour, "Goddes armes two!/ A frere wol entremette hym everemo./ Lo, goode men, a flye and eek a frere/ Wol falle in every dyssh and eek mateere." (1387 Chaucer, *Canterbury Tales* D.WB 833–6)

"'Lo," said the Summoner, "By God's two arms! A friar will always intrude himself (in others' affairs). Lo, good men, a fly and also a friar will fall in every dish and also every discussion'".

Note that, as is typical for Middle English, the Summoner's swearing is religious ("by Goddes armes two"). Two very common religious oaths in Middle English evolve into pragmatic markers. *Gee (jeeze, jeepers, jebus)* evolved from the proper name *Jesus*, originally used in invocations in religious contexts (see Gehweiler 2008), and the now obsolete *marry* derived from *by Mary*, an oath invoking the name of the Virgin Mary (see Lutzky 2012a).

In Early Modern English, insults are used in a broader range of genres, such as secular comedy. The topics referenced by an insult in this period are consistent with what are found in contemporary insults: impolite actions, family relations, social standing, money, personal skills, breaking commitments, and national insults (Taavitsainen and Jucker 2007). In Shakespeare, name-calling is the most common form of insult, with swearing, taunting, and cursing (all with different effects) intermixed (Jucker and Taavitsainen 2000). Shakespeare's name-calling insults can be highly creative and colorful:

(5) a. A pox o' your throat, you bawling, blasphemous, incharitable dog (1610–11 Shakespeare, *The Tempest* I.i; OSS)
   b. His wit's as thick as Tewkesbury mustard (1597–8 Shakespeare, *Henry IV, Part II* II.iv; OSS)
   c. Why, thou clay-brained guts, thou knotty-pated fool, thou whoreson, obscene, grease tallow-catch,— (1596–7 Shakespeare, *Henry IV, Part I* II.iv; OSS)

Examples of real-life insults in Early Modern English can be found in trial transcripts, where because of the power differential between interrogators and witnesses, impoliteness can be rife. The treason case of Lady Alice Lisle held in the summer of 1685 was presided over by the infamous Lord Chief Justice Jeffreys, known for his intimidating and ruthless manner in court. In (6) he cross-examines Mr. Dunne, a baker, whose testimony he does not believe. Having previously called him a "vile Wretch" and "a strange prevaricating, shuffling, sniveling, lying Rascal," in this passage, laced with invective and insult, he holds Dunne up for all to see as a liar, "a very pretty Tool," below "a Turk," among the "Pretenders to Christianity," and without morality and honesty.

(6) *L. C. J.* It seems the Saints have a certain Charter for Lying; they may lye and cant, and deceive, and rebel, and think God Almighty takes no notice of it, nor will reckon with them for it: You see, Gentlemen, what a precious Fellow this is, a very pretty Tool to be employ'd upon such an Errand, a Knave that no body would trust for half a Crown between Man and Man, but he is the fitter to be employ'd about such Works; what Pains is a Man at to get the Truth out of these Fellows, and it is with a great deal of Labour, that we can squeeze one Drop out of them? A *Turk* has more Title to an Eternity of Bliss than these Pretenders to Christianity, for he has more Morality and Honesty in him. Sirrah, I charge you in the presence of God, tell me true, What other Persons did you see that Night? (1685 Trial of Lady Alice Lisle; Kryk-Kastovsky 2006: 221)

We see, therefore, that both personal and ritualistic insults have existed since the earliest English, but have undergone change in both form and function, with ritualistic insults coming to serve an exclusively ludic function, and with personal insults of a sexual or scatological nature appearing only from Middle English on. It is likely that non-ludic insulting such as we see in cases of flyting is possible only in contexts of discernment politeness, as in Old English, where social relationships are based on one's position in society.

5.6   Thanks and Responses to Thanks

Thanks: Thanking is an expression of appreciation or gratitude. A hearer is thanked for an action that has benefited the speaker. In the speech act of thanking, the sincerity and the essential conditions overlap. Whether or not the speaker feels grateful, the speaker wants the expression to count as an expression of gratitude (Searle 1969: 67). In the Brown and Levinson framework (1987[1978]: 101ff.), thanking is a form of positive politeness; by claiming indebtedness to the hearer, the speaker addresses the positive face and raises the esteem of the hearer. But it may also be a FTA against the speaker's positive face, since the speaker is humbled by being placed in the hearer's debt. For Leech (2014: 196–200), thanking expresses the Maxim of Obligation (of speaker to hearer). Thanking a person involves expressing one's obligation to them, assigning a positive value to them, and thus enhancing their face. It is therefore an example of pos-politeness in his framework as well. Thanks can be intensified (e.g., *thank you very much*). There are a number of thanking strategies:
- Thanking explicitly (e.g., *thanks*)
- Expressing or stressing one's gratitude (e.g., *I am grateful, I must thank you*)
- Expressing appreciation to the addressee (e.g., *that's kind of you*)
- Expressing appreciation for an act (e.g., *that's lovely*)
- Acknowledging a debt (e.g., *I owe you a debt of gratitude*)
- Expressing emotion (e.g., *oh (thank you)*)
- Suppressing one's own importance (e.g., *I am an ingrate*) (Aijmer 1996: 37).
While thanking is intrinsically polite, it may also function ironically, of course:

(7)   Politico, for instance, was slammed on social media for declaring that Trump's claim that "one in three women is sexually assaulted on the long journey north" to America was only partly true – because it's actually 31 percent. . . . "Well **thank you** politico for pointing out to us that he rounded up 2% in his quote," another user responded. (2019 Fox News; COCA)

In Present-day English, thanking may serve a number of discourse functions, such as in proposal–acceptance sequences (i.e., closing a conversation) or in adjacency pairs (e.g., compliment–thank you), where the expression of thanking may be secondary to the discourse function (see Aijmer 1996: Ch. 2). In fact, Aijmer finds that the most common function of thanks in Present-day English is that of bringing a conversation to an end (1996: 68).

The verb *þancian* originates in Old English, and functions as a performative verb beginning in Middle English:

(8) For ye so kyndely this oother day/ Lente me gold; and as I kan and may,/ **I thanke yow**, by God and by Seint Jame! (1387 Chaucer, *Canterbury Tales* B. Sh 353–5)

'For you so kindly the other day lent me gold, as I know how and may I thank you, by God and Saint James'

Historical studies of thanking are infrequent: see Jacobsson (2002) and Taavitsainen and Jucker (2020) on thanking in Early Modern English (in the *Corpus of English Dialogues*), Taavitsainen and Jucker (2010a; also Jucker 2020: 127–134) on thanking in the eighteenth century, and El-Mahallawi (2018) on thanking expressions in three plays in each of the EModE, LModE, and PDE periods.

In Early Modern English, *thank you* and *thanks* (as a noun) are the most common forms, and *I thank you*, *I give you thanks* are preferred over the shortened forms we use today: *thanks* is rare in this period (OED, s.v. *thank*, n., P1) and *thank you* arises even later (Jacobsson 2002: 67; El-Mahallawi 2018: 906–907). Infrequent variants are *obliged to*, *beholden*, *bound*, and *owe*. The change from *I thank you* to *thank you/thanks* is seen as a change from an explicit performative to an implicit one, and may be a case of what Jucker (2019) calls speech act attenuation (see Chapter 9, §9.2). Intensifiers accompanying expressions of thanks in Early Modern English are frequently deferential (*thank you kindly/ forsooth/hartily/humbly/very moch*, *a thousand/great/most hartye thanks*), as are accompanying vocatives (*your ladyship*, *your grace*). Compound thanking (e.g., *thank you, that's very nice of you*) is rare. The expression of thanks as a means to close discourse segments, while possible, is not yet frequent. Some ironic uses of thanking, which are actually cases of impoliteness, can be found, especially in comedic dramas. Jacobsson tentatively suggests that at the beginning of the EModE period, the low occurrence of thanks with intensifiers and the rare use of responders (see below) are a sign of positive politeness, or intimacy between interlocutors. At the end of the period, the more frequent use of intensifiers and the occurrence of deferential responders are a sign of negative politeness, or increased distance between interlocutors.

Thanking in the eighteenth century is characterized by ornate and elaborate ways of expressing thanks, with thanks embedded in longer turns (Taavitsainen and Jucker 2010a; see also Jucker 2020: 127–134). Expressions of gratitude overlap with feelings of obligation. Thus, thanking often involves the acknowledgment of favors or debts, and *(much) obliged* is a common idiom. Thanking is also intertwined with compliments, boosted with acts of deference. The "address of thanks" is "a formalized part of a ceremonial compliment" (Jucker 2020: 131). Instructional manuals of letter writing in the eighteenth century provide models for "letters of thanks" suitable for almost any occasion. What is rare in Early Modern and still inchoate in the eighteenth century is the use of *thank you* in the most common use today, as a means of responding to a proposal and thus closing the discourse, as shown in (9):

(9)   And then, "I'd like to do it outside, if we can." # "I'll see what I can manage." # **"Thank you."** # This settled, she turned away . . . (2019 *Michigan Quarterly Review*; COCA)

Responses to thanks: The polite correlative to thanking is the response to thanks. When A thanks B, A is in B's debt, and this is a FTA against A's own positive face (because it is humbling). When B accepts the thanks, B minimizes that debt and thus seeks to restore equilibrium. Responses to thanks provide "reduction of the thanker's indebtedness and thus the reduction of the imbalance between the thanker and the thankee" (Bieswanger 2015: 528). For Leech, responses to thanks are oriented toward the thanker (the speaker giving the thanks) and involve the Maxim of Obligation, where the responder (the hearer of the thanks) rates the hearer's obligation (indebtedness) to him- or herself as low; they are thus an example of neg-politeness (2014: 200–201).

A number of different strategies may be used in responses to thanks, all of which serve to minimize debt (see Table 5.3). For example, expressing pleasure or appreciation mitigates the need for gratitude, returning thanks balances the debt, and acknowledging thanks denotes that the expression of thanks was

Table 5.3 *Typology of responses to thanks (adapted from Brinton 2021)*

Category	Possible formal realizations
Express appreciation	*you're welcome, absolutely, anytime, anything for you, you bet, you got it, sure*
Express pleasure	*(it was) my pleasure, the pleasure is/was mine, absolutely, any time, anything for you*
Minimize the favor	*don't mention it, think nothing of it, it was nothing, no problem/worries/ bother, not at all, that's alright, that's okay, (it is/was) no trouble, {no need to, don't} thank me, that's alright*
Return thanks	*thanks*
Verbally acknowledge	*yeah, mh-hm, right, okay, alright, of course*
Non-verbally acknowledge	<head nod>

sufficient recompense. Reponses to thanks are actually fairly uncommon, possibly because they occur only when there is significant distance between the interlocutors, the debt incurred is quite significant, or the thanks have been effusively expressed (Leech 2014: 200).

The history of responses to thanks has received brief mention by Jacobsson (2002: 69–70, 75–76), Jucker (2020: 128, 130), and Taavitsainen and Jucker (2020: 117, 118) and more complete treatment in Brinton (2021). Thanking responders are less common in Early Modern than they are in Present-day English, perhaps because thanks are embedded in longer discourses. The responders found in the *Corpus of English Dialogues* can be classified as expressions of deference (*I am your most humble Servant*), expressions of appreciation (*You are heartily welcome, sir*), minimizers (*It is not worth thankes*), or returns of thanks, sometimes in combination. The deference usage is a category not recognized in contemporary English. In eighteenth-century letter-writing manuals, explicit examples of answers to letters of thanks are rare, though letters that "return thanks" for advice rendered or offers made can be found.

Many of the forms used for responses to thanks in Present-day English are of quite recent origin. While *you're welcome/welcome* has served as a greeting of pleasure at the sight or arrival of a person since Old English (see Chapter 6 §6.7) and is found as a responder to thanks in Early Modern English, it is not frequent in the latter function until the twentieth century (OED, s.v. *welcome*, n.1, adj., and int., def. B3d). COHA provides only three nineteenth-century examples:

(10)   a. No, I mean I thank you very much. [Davy] **You're welcome**, miss (1862 Murdoch, *Davy Crockett*; COHA)
       b. "Thank you," he said to the teamster. "**You're welcome**," returned that gentleman, (1882 Harte, *Found at Blazing Star*; COHA)
       c. for which complimentary expression of opinion he gravely thanked her. "**You are very welcome**, sir," she said, (1891 Finley, *Elsie's Vacation and After Events*; COHA)

Very few examples of *The pleasure is/was mine, It is/was my pleasure, My pleasure* are found in COHA before the 1960s:

(11)   a. BILLY HOLLIDAY Thank you very much. MRS. TEMPLE **The pleasure is mine**, I assure you. (1915 *Hit-the-Trail-Holiday*; COHA)
       b. Thank you for dropping me off, Colonel Darly. **It was my pleasure**, Miss Smith. (1944 *Meet Me in St. Louis*; COHA)
       c. There you are, Johnny. Thank you, Ricky. **My pleasure**, Johnny (1957 *I Love Lucy*; COHA)

A contemporary minimizing response to thanks, *no problem, not a problem* (also *no prob, no problemo*) (OED, s.v. *problem*, n., Phrases) is a twentieth-century addition.

(12)   a. Thanks, Ernie. – **No problem**. (1974 *The Swinging Cheerleaders*; COHA)
        b. Hi. Thanks for coming. **No prob**, heh (1986 *Witchboard*; *The Movies Corpus* [Movies])
        c. Thanks for coming, lieutenant. **Not a problem**. (2003 *Requiem for Mutants: The Score of 'X2'*; Movies)

A number of sociolinguistic studies (see, e.g., Schneider 2005; Mulo Farenkia 2012; Bieswanger 2015; Dinkin 2018) have shown that *no problem* is a common response to thanks in British, Irish, and Canadian English. In Canadian English, for example, its use ranges from 11.4 percent or 25 percent of the responses (in covertly elicited data; Bieswanger 2015; Dinkin 2018) to 48 percent of the responses (in written questionnaires; Mulo Farenkia 2012). Dinkin finds that younger speakers use *no problem* as the preferred form whether in response to informal *thanks* or the more formal *thank you, thank you very much*; older speakers use it only in the informal case and thus view it as a less polite response. While this might suggest that young speakers simply do not recognize different levels of politeness among the thanking formulas, Dinkin finds that they do indeed make formality distinctions, using *you're welcome* in response to the formal *thank you (very much)* and *no worries* more often with the more informal *thanks*. These results point to a change in progress toward *no problem* as the preferred response to thanks. This usage has attracted the attention of prescriptivists and language commentators, who see it as a rude form associated with younger speakers and recommend its elimination, especially in service contexts. For example, Noë (2015) argues that *no problem* negates the gratitude by transforming it into a debt, suggesting that the courtesy or assistance was not given freely but was a problem foisted upon the giver. He sees this usage as "a fairly recent change" and "accelerating." Interestingly, in the case of *you bet*, where the response to thanks function is the most common one in the spoken section of COCA (see Hirota and Brinton 2023), this usage has escaped prescriptive attention, perhaps because it is somewhat older (13) or has a lower frequency than *no problem*:

(13)   Thanks. Thank you, sir. **You bet**. (1947 *Welcome Stranger*; Movies)

5.7   Non-imposition Politeness: Indirect Directives

Non-imposition politeness is one aspect of negative politeness. It encompasses attempts by the speaker not to impose on the wants or needs of the hearer, typically by giving the hearer as many choices as possible. Non-imposition politeness is seen most clearly in the case of directives. Directives (commands) express the speaker's desires and are an attempt to get the hearer to perform an action, thus, in Brown and Levinson's framework, a FTA against the hearer's negative face. Negative politeness dictates that we avoid such attacks by using indirect forms. Indirect forms of directives are based on the Tact Maxim, that of giving low value to the speaker's wants (Leech 2014). The need for indirect forms is relative: the greater the power of the speaker over the hearer (the vertical distance), the more socially distant the speaker and hearer (horizontal distance), and the greater the debt incurred in the command, the more indirect the forms used should be. But it turns out that less indirectness is needed at both ends of the scales (greater distance and lesser distance) than in the middle (Leech 2014:139). That is, we can be less polite both with those we have most power over and those with whom we are closest. Indirect strategies for the performance of directives, arising in the modern period, are "emblematic of non-imposition negative politeness" (Culpeper and Demmen 2011: 75). As Leech (2014: 295) observes, contemporary English "seems to be strongly if not exceptionally associated with indirect requests ... [and] the Tact Maxim appears to have taken over a key position in the politeness of present-day English."

Most typical of indirect directives in Present-day English are forms with *can you, could you, would you, will you, won't you*, which Wierzbicka (2006) calls "whimperatives." Aijmer (1996: 157) finds questions about the hearer's ability to do something expressed by *could/can/would/will* to be the most common indirect forms in her corpus. But there is a wide variety of similarly indirect constructions (e.g., *you might like to, you might consider, I would suggest, perhaps you could, if you would like to, I wonder if would/could, can I ask you*, and so on, see Table 6.2 in Chapter 6).

Wierzbicka (2006) argues that this type of non-imposition politeness is not a universal of language but is part of what she calls "Anglo culture," where individuals are seen as autonomous, and putting pressure on them is considered unfair, unreasonable, and rude. Three principles are at work: (1) one can't tell other people what to do; (2) it is bad to impose one's will on other people, and (3) it is good to avoid telling people that we want them to do something (49). The use of whimperatives and related indirect request expressions is a way of "acknowledg[ing] the addressee's autonomy while at the same time making clear what the speaker wants" (49). Wierzbicka suggests four stages of historical development for requests (without giving diachronic evidence) (53–54):

Stage I: free use of imperatives and performative verbs of requesting: *I pray thee, do it*

Stage II: decline in the use of imperatives and performatives, rise of whimperatives: *Could you/would you do it?*

Stage III: rise of "suggestions" of various kinds: *I would suggest ... /Perhaps you could ... /You might like to ...*

Stage IV: From suggestion to thought: *I was wondering if you could/if you'd like to ...*

Let us consider what we know about directives in the history of English. In Old English, as we will see in Chapter 6 §6.5, the use of explicit performative verbs, especially of what Kohnen called the 'ask' and 'order' class, second-person imperatives, and other constructions giving direct expression to directives was the norm; indirect directives, including verbs of the 'suggest/advise' class, did not occur. Even in Early Modern English, directives were still almost exclusively expressed directly (with performatives, imperatives, and statements of hearer obligation or speaker wants) and the use of indirect forms was uncommon, typically focused on the hearer's volition (e.g., *if you please to*) rather than the hearer's ability or willingness (Culpeper and Archer 2008). As Wierzbicka notes (2006, 2012), the most common verbs were *beseech, exhort, command, entreat, beg, plead, implore,* and *pray/prithee,* all of which put pressure on the speaker to fulfill the request. There are no examples of directives with *(if you) please* in Shakespeare or other forms that ask about the hearer's willingness to perform an action; rather, directives use *(I) pray (you), prithee,* which focus on the speaker's sincere wishes for the hearer to perform the action (Busse 2002).

Culpeper and Demmen (2011) find no evidence for indirect directives of the *could you/can you* type in the eighteenth century. Even in the nineteenth century, evidence is scanty; a small number of examples, occurring mainly in trial proceedings, which are unambiguously requests, is suggestive but not conclusive.

(14)   a.   The Judge [...] **can you** tell me the last occasion when you saw him? — It would be in December 1888 when I saw him professionally (1899 The Maybrick Case; Culpeper and Demmen 2011: 73)
        b.   Then, too, **could you** lend me your small geological map? i.e., if you don't want it at all (1862 Letter from J.R. Green to W. Boyd Dawkins; Culpeper and Demmen 2011: 71)

Culpeper and Demmen date the rise of these indirect directives to after 1900, when the use of *can* and *could* is known to increase. They argue that a rising importance of the individual – an "ethos of the self" – resulted from sociocultural change in the nineteenth century (e.g., secularization, Protestantism, social and geographical mobility); this combined with the Victorian value of work resulting from the Industrial Revolution led to the emergence of indirect directives of the *could you/can you* type which focused on the abilities of individuals yet strove not to impose.

Jucker (2020: 170–183) provides a study of non-imposition politeness in American English using COHA and COCA (i.e., from the nineteenth century on). First, he finds that *please* increases over time, leveling off in the second half of the twentieth century. *Please* is assumed to be derived from *if you please, please you* (OED, s.v. *please,* adv. and int.), a form which makes the fulfilling of a request contingent on the hearer's will or pleasure. Second, a study of *would/can/could you* used as indirect requests shows an overall increase over time, with a decline in the last three decades of COHA (1980–2000) paralleled by a decrease from 1990 to 2017 in COCA brought about mainly by a decrease in the use of *would you*. The collocation of these three indirect forms with *please*, which marks them unambiguously as requests (cf. *Can you answer the door?* vs. *Can you answer the door, please?*), is very rare in the nineteenth century but rises dramatically from the mid-twentieth century. Again, a decline in both the most recent periods is brought about by a decline in *would you*.

Jucker dates the rise of *could/can/would you (please)* to the mid-twentieth century in American English, while Culpeper and Demmen suggest a rise in British English somewhat earlier (after 1900), but their corpus data do not extend beyond the nineteenth century and thus their proposed date must be seen as speculative.

The falling off of usage of the indirect *can/could/would* forms in the most recent periods could be a case of what Kohnen called "hidden manifestations" (see Chapter 6, §6.3), where other – perhaps not yet identified – forms are taking their place. Jucker also suggests that there may be a movement toward further indirectness, where requests are merely hinted at. This might suggest arrival at Wierzbicka's Stage III ('suggest' verbs, as also noted by Kohnen, see Chapter 6, §6.5) and Stage IV (*I wonder if* constructions). Leech sees the *wonder if* constructions as "toward the most indirect and most polite end of the pragmalinguistic politeness scale" (2014: 162) because the speaker does not directly question the hearer but merely expresses uncertainty about the hearer's state of mind. What Leech calls "deliberative and appreciative openings" are, in fact, quite recent in the history of English, arising only in the later part of the nineteenth–early twentieth century (15–18):

(15) a. "Now, Rollo," said Mr. George, "I have got a great deal to do to-day, and there are our passports to be stamped. **I wonder if** you could not attend to that." "Yes," said Rollo, "if you will only tell me what is to be done." (1854 Abbott, *Rollo in Switzerland*; COHA)

      b. "**I wonder if** you could tell me what it is? I wonder if it is really there at all?" said Giovanni. (1887 Crawford, *Saracinesa*; CEN)

(16) a. "Yes, yes, I dare say. **Do you think** you could make it convenient to keep the cat for the present, if I paid you for its food?" (1884 Gissing, *The Unclassed*; CEN)

      b. "and then tomorrow I shall write a letter to her and beg her to forgive me. If I do so, **do you think** you could stay?" (1887 Gissing, *Thyrza*; CEN)

(17) a. "**We would greatly appreciate it if** you would be with us and say a few words." (1922 Morley, *Where the Blue Begins*; COHA)

      b. **I shall appreciate it if** you together with the chief librarian, Prof. M. Anasaki, and Dr. Takuma Dan will act as a committee of three (1925 *Time Magazine*; COHA)

(18)   a. "**I should be grateful** if you would at once release me from our engagement and permit me to leave your employment," said Ishmael, (1876 Southworth, *Ishmael in the Depths*; COHA)
       b. "But **it would be kind of you – I should be grateful if** you would tell me – has any woman ever loved you dearly?" (1891 Crawford, *Don Orsino*; CEN)

5.8   Camaraderie Politeness

Present-day English has seen the rise of "camaraderie politeness" (a term coined by Lakoff 1973). This does not displace non-imposition politeness but coexists with it as well as with other forms of trivalent (interactional) politeness, such as inviting, thanking, and apologizing and so on. Camaraderie politeness refers to strategies to enhance rapport, increase solidarity, and eliminate distance between individuals. It is thus an aspect of positive politeness and can be used to mitigate FTAs in Brown and Levinson's terms. Evidence of this type of politeness includes:

• the declining use of respectful titles (*sir, madam, Mr., Mrs.*), of politeness markers such as *please*, and of introductory salutations and more familiar closings in written communications (*Dear X > Hi X, Sincerely yours > Best wishes*), along with
• the increasing use of first names, nicknames, and pet names, of familiarizing vocatives (*guys, folks, man, dude, mate, bro*), of endearments (*honey, dear, love*), of familiar greetings and closings (*Hi, Hey, Cheers, See ya*), of interjections to open conversations (*Hey*), of pragmatic markers (*y'know, I mean*), and of direct terms rather than euphemisms or technical terms for intimate aspects of life (e.g., sex, money, disease) (see Chapter 7, §7.6).

Lakoff notes that these forms look like "spontaneous expression of true feelings replacing stuffy old meaningless formalities," but they are actually highly conventionalized and may represent only a superficial show of friendship (2005: 34). When the speaker and hearer are equally ranked or the speaker is more highly ranked than the hearer, camaraderie politeness produces a sense of equality, but when the speaker is more lowly ranked than the hearer, the speaker may be seen as "taking liberties." Leech argues that the increasing use of familiar language is a continuation of the trend toward reduction of vertical and horizontal distances between individuals. It contrasts with bivalent politeness, which is based on unequal relationships, and its rise is hence a sign of the loss of bivalent politeness: here, "everyone is equal and can claim instant solidarity with other individuals" (2014: 298).

   Leech attributes these changes to three factors:
• individualism and democratization, eliminating overt signs of power asymmetries and emphasizing the right of individuals to make their own choices;

- informalization, leading to the shortening of the distance between speaker and hearer, banning displays of superiority, and contributing to a more engaging and less impersonal style; and
- colloquialization, moving written language toward spoken norms and incorporating oral features (see Mair 2006: 183–193; Leech et al. 2009: 239–249; this topic is discussed in more detail in Chapter 8).

Lakoff (2005) also suggests that the increasing diversity and multiculturalism of today's society is breaking down the symbolic differences that in the past led to the use of distancing and deferential forms.

5.9   Chapter Summary

This chapter covered the following topics:

- different pragmatic approaches to politeness, that is, politeness as the avoidance of face-threatening acts and politeness as the maintenance of communicative concord;
- pragmatic approaches to impoliteness;
- pragmatic approaches to changing politeness in the history of English, with the rise, for example, of discernment politeness, the politeness of humility and gentleness, deference politeness, and solidarity politeness;
- four case studies showing changing norms of politeness in English:
  - compliments, showing change from ritual to personal compliments and the predominance of highly formalized compliments in the eighteenth century;
  - insults, showing change from ritual to personal insults and from non-ludic to ludic (ritual) insults;
  - thanking, showing the rise of elliptical forms (*thanks*, *thank you*), conventionalization in the eighteenth century, and the development of a function in closing discourse;
  - responses to thanks, showing increasing frequency after Early Modern English and the development of different types and forms in the modern period;
- non-imposition politeness, focused on indirect directives of the *can*/*could*/*will*/*would you* type in the twentieth century; and
- camaraderie politeness, involving the declining use of honorifics and increasing use of first names in the twentieth century.

5.10   Further Reading

The literature on (im)politeness is extensive; for a discussion of the study of politeness, see Jucker (2020: Ch. 1) and for impoliteness, see Culpeper (2011b: Ch. 1). On politeness in the history of English, see Jucker (2020) and the many references therein, as well as Nevala (2010) and Leech (2014: Ch. 11). Culpeper, Haugh, and Kádár (2017) is a comprehensive collection of articles on all aspects of (im)politeness. Jucker and Kopaczyk (2017) provides a useful summary of scholarship and a general overview of historical (im)politeness. On democratization, colloquialization, informalization, see Farrelly and Seoane (2012). Jucker (2009b) discusses challenges for the study of compliments. The Unferð episode in *Beowulf* has been thoroughly discussed in both the literary and linguistic literature; for a new interpretation, see Williams (2017). On thanks and responses to thanks in Present-day English, see Aijmer (1996: Ch. 2) and Leech (2014: §7.3). A classic study of politeness in Shakespeare's plays is Brown and Gilman (1989); see also Magnusson (1999).

5.11   Exercises

1. (a) Use COCA to see if you can locate the first use of *no worries* as a response to thanks. Note that *no worries* is most often used in the sense of 'You have nothing to worry about,' not as a response to thanks. It can also be used as a response to apologies. It will help to narrow your results by searching for "no worries" in collocation with "thanks" or "thank you."
   (b) Use COHA to locate the earliest examples of indirect requests of the form:
      (i) *do you happen to . . . /you don't happen to . . .*
      (ii) *you might like to . . .*
      (iii) *will/would you be so good/kind as . . .*
      (iv) *can/may I ask you to . . .*
   Also see whether these expressions are found in the OED. Based on these two sources of data, when would you date the rise of these constructions?

2. In the following Shakespearian examples, describe what the speaker is trying to do or achieve. Describe whether this is a case of positive or negative politeness (according to Brown and Levinson) and identify Leech's Maxim of Politeness (if possible – given the partial list you have been given above) at work. (Examples are taken from Kopytko 1995 and Brown and Gilman 1989, quoted from *Open Source Shakespeare*)
   (a) HAMLET: I am sorry they offend you, heartily;/ Yes, faith, heartily. (1599–1601 *Hamlet* I.v)
   [Hamlet is speaking to his good friend Horatio.]
   (b) DUKE OF ALBANY: Methought thy very gait did prophesy/ A royal nobleness. I must embrace thee./ Let sorrow split my heart if ever I/ Did hate thee (1605–6 *King Lear* V.iii)

[The Duke of Albany (Lear's daughter Goneril's husband) is speaking to Edgar, the Earl of Gloucester's son.]

(c) OTHELLO: Most potent, grave, and reverend signiors,/ My very noble and approved good masters,/ That I have ta'en away this old man's daughter,/ It is most true; (1603–4 *Othello* I.iii)

[Othello is speaking about the fact that he has married Desdemona. He is addressing the Duke of Venice and the Venetian Senators (one of whom is Brabantio, Desdemona's father).]

(d) DUKE OF VENICE: There is no composition ['consistency'] in these news/ That gives them credit.

FIRST SENATOR: Indeed, they are disproportioned./ My letters say a hundred and seven galleys. (1603–4 *Othello* I.iii)

[The Duke of Venice has received contradictory reports about the size of the Turkish fleet approaching the Venetian possession, Cyprus. His advisor responds.]

(e) MENENIUS AGRIPPA: Hear me one word;/ Beseech you, tribunes, hear me but a word. (1608 *Coriolanus* III.i)

[Menenius Agrippa, a Senator of Rome, wishes to give advice to the assembled tribunes of Rome; he asks to give "one word."]

(f) CASSIO: Yet, I beseech you,/ If you think fit, or that it may be done,/ Give me advantage of some brief discourse/ With Desdemona alone. (1603–4 *Othello* III.i)

[Cassio, Othello's captain, asks Emilia, Desdemona's maidservant, to speak to Desdemona alone.]

(g) OTHELLO: All's well now, sweeting; come away to bed (1603–4 *Othello* II.iii)

[Othello is trying to placate his wife, Desdemona, and requesting that she retire to their bedroom.]

3. Discuss strategies of impoliteness in this selection from Jane Austen's *Pride and Prejudice* (1813). The haughty and arrogant Lady Catherine de Bourgh demands that Elizabeth tell her whether she is engaged to marry her nephew, Mr. Darcy, who, she claims, has been promised to her daughter. Elizabeth refuses to say whether she is engaged or not:

"Obstinate, headstrong girl! I am ashamed of you! Is this your gratitude for my attentions to you last spring? Is nothing due to me on that score? Let us sit down. You are to understand, Miss Bennet, that I came here with the determined resolution of carrying my purpose; nor will I be dissuaded from it. I have not been used to submit to any person's whims. I have not been in the habit of brooking disappointment."

"*That* will make your ladyship's situation at present more pitiable; but it will have no effect on *me*."

"I will not be interrupted. Hear me in silence. My daughter and my nephew are formed for each other. They are descended, on the maternal side, from the same noble line; and, on the father's, from respectable, honourable, and ancient—though untitled—families. Their fortune on both sides is splendid. They are destined for each other by the voice of every member of their respective houses; and what is to divide them? The upstart pretensions of a young woman without family, connections, or fortune. Is this to be endured! But it must not, shall not be. If you were sensible of your own good, you would not wish to quit the sphere in which you have been brought up."

"In marrying your nephew, I should not consider myself as quitting that sphere. He is a gentleman; I am a gentleman's daughter; so far we are equal."

"True. You *are* a gentleman's daughter. But who was your mother? Who are your uncles and aunts? Do not imagine me ignorant of their condition."

"Whatever my connections may be," said Elizabeth, "if your nephew does not object to them, they can be nothing to *you*."

"Tell me once for all, are you engaged to him?"

Though Elizabeth would not, for the mere purpose of obliging Lady Catherine, have answered this question, she could not but say, after a moment's deliberation:

"I am not."

Lady Catherine seemed pleased.

"And will you promise me, never to enter into such an engagement?"

"I will make no promise of the kind."

"Miss Bennet I am shocked and astonished. I expected to find a more reasonable young woman. But do not deceive yourself into a belief that I will ever recede. I shall not go away till you have given me the assurance I require." (www.gutenberg.org /files/1342/1342-h/1342-h.htm)

6   Speech Acts

6.1   Introduction

The concept of a speech act is based on the view that all of our utterances are performing social actions, whether they are serving as promises, commands, apologies, threats, congratulations, or even representations of the world. The idea of a speech act originated in the work of the British philosopher J. L. Austin (1962) and the American philosopher John Searle (1969) and has generated a rich area of pragmatic research, both synchronic and diachronic.

In this chapter you will be introduced to the structure of speech acts and a typology of speech acts. The study of speech acts poses difficulties for the form-to-function approach and for corpus pragmatic study, as the most explicit form for expressing speech acts, performative verbs such as *I command [you to leave]*, are infrequently used and may change over time. Speech acts thus call out for a function-to-form approach, but such is fraught with difficulties. We will consider a number of "work-arounds" that scholars have proposed. After briefly looking at performative verbs, the remainder of the chapter exemplifies in detail changes in a selection of speech acts in the history of English, including directives (commands), commissives (promises), and a variety of expressives (apologies, curses, greetings, leave-takings).

6.2   Speech Acts and a Typology of Speech Acts

A speech act consists of a "locutionary act" (a concrete utterance) with a certain "propositional content" (or primary meaning). In addition, the "illocutionary force" of this sentence is the communicative purpose, or intention of the speaker, in making the utterance. For example, the propositional content [it rains] can be used for different illocutionary forces to perform various speech acts:

> To ask a question: "Is it raining?";
> To state a belief about the world: "It is raining"; or
> To express a wish: "If only it would rain." "I wish it would rain."

The most explicit way in which a speaker can perform a speech act is by using a performative verb, a first-person singular, simple present-tense verb, such as in these examples:

(1)   a. I **promise** you to keep it faithfully between ourselves. (1835 Kennedy, *Horse Shoe Robinson*; COHA)
       b. I **congratulate** you upon the success of your labors, (1866 Optic, *Outward Bound*; COHA)
       c. I **command** you to leave this place, and go with me. (1851 *Harpers*; COHA)
       d. I **pronounce** you a good, well-made, and worthy Mason. (1835 Thompson, *The Adventures of Timothy Peacock, Esquire*; COHA)

Simply by uttering these sentences, the speaker performs the action named. Speech acts can also be performed in a variety of ways without performative verbs. For example, in place of *I promise* in (1a), you could say "I will keep it faithfully between ourselves," "I won't tell anyone. That's a promise." "Let me assure you that I'll keep it faithfully between ourselves," "Don't worry; I will keep it to myself," or countless other ways. As we will see later in the chapter, speech acts are in fact more commonly performed in these varied ways rather than with performative verbs.

Speech acts may also have both expected and unexpected "perlocutionary effects"; these denote the consequences that speech acts have on the beliefs or behavior of the hearer, such as annoyance, alarm, persuasion, and so on. A simple speech act such as "It is raining," for example, might depress the mood of the hearer or persuade them to take an umbrella.

Speech act scholars have come up with a variety of typologies of speech acts. The most prototypical class of speech acts is what Searle calls "declaratives." In a declarative, a speaker performs an action simply by uttering a statement, such as "I declare you man and wife," "I resign," "I find you guilty as charged." These utterances bring about the actions referred to: the couple is married, the person has resigned, the criminal is found guilty. In most cases, the speaker has to have a position in an extralinguistic institution in order to perform the declarative successfully; a random person on the street cannot find you guilty of a crime; rather, they must be a judge or magistrate speaking in the context of a courtroom. This is true of the directive in (1d), where the person pronouncing this must be a high-ranking Mason.

In classifying speech acts, Searle argues that three factors are most important: illocutionary force, direction of fit, and sincerity condition (1976: 5). Direction of fit refers to how the verbal utterance relates to the external world. In a statement of fact (e.g., *It is raining*), the speaker believes that the words match the world ("word-to-world"). In an order (e.g., *Open the window*), the speaker wants the world to come to resemble the words ("world-to-word").

The sincerity condition is the speaker's psychological state in uttering a speech act, such as belief, intention, desire/want, pleasure, and so on (Searle 1976: 4)

In this chapter, we will look in detail at three types of speech acts: directives, commissives, and expressives:

- A **directive** is a command, order, request, invitation, question, and so on (see 1c). It constitutes an attempt by the speaker to get the addressee to do something, such as carry out an action or provide an answer (its illocutionary force). The direction of fit is world-to-word. For a command to "work," however, a number of conditions must be met. The sincerity condition is that the speaker must want the action to be performed. And the addressee must be able to perform the action. It makes no sense, for example, to say "Please bring me a glass of water" when you do not want water, or to command someone to "Grow taller" since it is humanly impossible for a person to will this to happen. The person issuing a command often stands in a position of power (or perceives themselves to stand in a position of power) over the recipient, sometimes in an extralinguistic institution. For example, (1c) may require that the speaker and addressee hold positions in the military chain of command, or minimally that the speaker be in a position of power over the addressee. The utterance counts as a command by virtue of the speaker's authority over the addressee.
- A **commissive** is a promise, vow, pledge, guarantee, and so on (see 1a). The direction of fit is also world-to-word. Here the sincerity condition is that speakers commit themselves to carrying out an action. "I promise to visit you tomorrow, but I do not intend to" is nonsensical. Also, the action promised must be within the human control of the promiser; I cannot successfully promise to make it stop raining at noon. Finally, the promiser must believe that the addressee wants the action performed.
- An **expressive** is the speaker's articulation of a feeling or attitude about a situation in the world, typically one that bears some relation to the addressee (see 1b). Expressives encompass of range of speech acts, including congratulating, expressing regret/sorrow/happiness, consoling, insulting, complimenting, welcoming, greeting, thanking, and so on. An expressive has no direction of fit because the situation in the world is presupposed. If I thank a friend for a gift, I assume the friend is the one who has given me the gift. If the friend has not done so, then the thanking does not "work." The issue of the speaker's sincerity is also not really at issue. You can congratulate a colleague on a promotion even when you think it is unwarranted or you envy the colleague. What is important is that you are seen to be expressing congratulations (what Searle calls the "essential condition").

In addition to the sincerity condition and the essential condition, a number of other conditions may need to hold in order for a speech act to be successful (so-called "felicity conditions"). For example, for a commissive or a directive to work, it must not be obvious that the speaker or hearer is already going to undertake (or undertaking) the action promised or requested (the "non-obvious condition"); I would not order you to open the window as you are in the process of doing so. Congratulating depends on the speaker believing that the event the hearer is being congratulated on is in the hearer's interest (the "preparatory condition"); I would not normally congratulate you on your firing. Apologizing depends on the speaker believing that their action has offended the hearer. The relation of the speaker and the hearer must be understood by the interlocutors as appropriate; for example, commanding, pleading, and urging depend on different relations between the interlocutors. The strength of the speaker's commitment must also be appropriate to the propositional content; for example, one would suggest going to a movie, but not normally insist upon doing so. All speech acts have a unique set of felicity conditions.

6.3   The Study of Speech Acts

How can we go about studying speech acts in the discourse of the past? One way would be to take a form-to-function approach (see Chapter 2, §2.3) and tabulate the range and frequency of performative verbs used to carry out the speech act in question over time. But there are several problems with this approach.

- First, the performative verbs used at earlier stages of the language undoubtedly differ from those used today, and we must correctly identify the performative verbs used in each period and carefully track the changes over time.
- Second, the same performative verb can be used to carry out several different speech acts, and for this reason, simple tabulations of performative verbs can be misleading. For example, *I insist* can be a directive, as in *I insist that you leave now*, but it can also be used as one of the strongest expressions of belief, as in *I insist this is the right place*. In the second sentence, *I insist* functions as a performative verb in what Searle calls a "representative." Here, a speaker represents a state of affairs and is committed to the truth of the representation, but the speaker's degree of commitment can range from weak (as with *think* or *predict*) to strong (as with *insist* or *promise*).
- Finally, and more importantly, it turns out that explicit performative verbs are a rather infrequent means used by speakers to carry out speech acts, except in the case of the most formulaic types of acts, such as greeting, thanking, or apologizing. Thus, the form-to-function approach exemplified by the study of performative verbs is, on the whole, not very fruitful.

What interests us in speech act research is the relationship between illocutionary forces and the wide variety of forms that speakers use to express such forces. This necessitates a function-to-form approach (see Chapter 2, §2.3). If we decide we are studying a particular illocutionary force and we are working with a text or a corpus, then we need to identify all of the possible realizations of that particular illocutionary force. For formal work with a corpus, we need a precise set of search terms. However, compiling a complete inventory of forms can be very difficult since a speech act is typically expressed in a wide variety of expected – and unexpected – ways, both directly and indirectly.

When studying speech acts in historical texts, the problems of the function-to-form approach are multiplied. As speakers of Present-day English, we may not necessarily have intuitive access to the means used to express speech acts in earlier periods, or even to the speech acts used in those periods. Thus, compiling a complete inventory of forms which signal a particular speech act may be quite difficult: the manifestations of speech acts can be "unpredictable" (Kohnen 2015b). According to Kohnen (2004, 2015b), this difficulty leads to either an "illustrative eclecticism," where scholars collect illustrative examples of speech acts which they consider typical in a text or corpus, or to "structural eclecticism," where scholars begin with a set of formal manifestations of a speech acts (e.g., performative verbs) and systematically search for them in a text or corpus. Kohnen (2007b) also refers to the problem of "hidden manifestations," the fact that some ways of expressing speech acts will invariably go unnoticed. You might find, for example, a decrease of a particular way of expressing a speech act over time, but you cannot be certain whether this represents a change in the frequency of the speech act or whether other means used to express the speech act (of which you are unaware) have come in to fill the void. Finally, functions (i.e., illocutionary forces) are not necessarily stable and may change over time. For example, if we are studying compliments, we must recognize that what actually counts as a compliment may change depending on societal and cultural norms (as we saw in Chapter 5).

Given these difficulties, the diachronic study of speech acts may seem to pose insurmountable obstacles. However, a number of successful approaches have been undertaken. Kohnen (2008c) suggests an essentially traditional, philological, and bottom-up approach, involving the micro-analysis (close reading) of a single genre – Old English sermons – in order to identify all of the ways in which directives are expressed. Once the forms of directives are identified in this single genre, these can be searched for in other genres or in multi-genre corpora. This approach is obviously labor-intensive and time-consuming, though it ensures accuracy and completeness. We will examine Kohnen's finding below in the section on directives (§6.5).

A different approach is to annotate a corpus for each instance of a speech act, as was done by Archer (2005) and Culpeper and Archer (2008) for the trial and drama sections of the *Corpus of English Dialogues*. The annotation was done not on the basis of form, but on the basis of the effect of the speech act. For example, only those directives which were either received by the recipient as a request or carried out were annotated as such. This technique, like traditional approaches, is very time-consuming and labor-intensive, and as we discussed in Chapter 2, has met with limited success.

Jucker (2013: 7–13, also Taavitsainen and Jucker 2007; Jucker and Taavitsainen 2014a) sets out three ways to study speech acts in historical texts:

(a) The first method involves focusing on "illocutionary-force-indicating devices" (IFIDs), or formal devices that are conventionally used to signal a specific speech act. These include performative verbs but also words such as *sorry, excuse (me), (I beg your) pardon, afraid, excuse* for apologies, or *please* for requests, as in the example below:

(2)   "Can I ride up with you, **please**? I am so tired." (1875 *Galaxy*; COHA)

Such searches will miss instances of the speech acts without these IFIDs and will retrieve irrelevant examples (e.g., the use of *please* as a verb), but if the search can be refined to include syntactic information, this approach can be quite effective. Note that this is essentially an expanded form-to-function approach.

(b) The second method involves searching for syntactic patterns typical of a speech act. It has been shown (Manes and Wolfson 1981) that compliments in Present-day English are quite formulaic, many fitting into one of three syntactic patterns: Noun Phrase {*is, looks*} (*really*) Adjective, *I* (*really*) {*love, like*} Noun Phrase, or Pronoun *is* (*really*) (*a*) Adjective Noun Phrase, as in *The dinner is really good, That suit looks good on you, I love your idea*, or *This is an attractive prospect*. While these constructions seem too restrictive for compliments in older texts, it might be possible to search for positive-evaluative adjectives such as *good, fine*, or *pretty* (see Chapter 5, §5.5, for more on compliments). Similarly, thanks may involve *I am grateful, much appreciated*, and directives might include patterns such as *I'd like it if you, Would you be willing to, Would you kindly*, as in the following (as was discussed in Chapter 5, §5.7):

(3)   "She, and I, **would like it if** you do the reading to-night. Will you?" (1876 Warner, *Wych Hazel*; COHA)

But determining all of the relevant patterns would be challenging, and this approach risks resulting in what Kohnen calls "structural eclecticism," as noted above. It is likely that some, or even many, of the patterns used in older texts could be overlooked.

(c) The third method is to focus on the speech act labels, or metacommunicative expressions, used to talk about speech acts, such as *insult, greet*, or *compliment*. In example (4) we see *order* used as a speech act label. In (4a), *ordered* occurs in a speech reporting clause, with the actual speech act expressed in the preceding clause, whereas in (4b), the narrator describes the character's speech as an order, or as interpreted as an order by the butler. As we saw in Chapter 4, however, the occurrence of a full range of reporting verbs is not common before the LModE period, and thus the use of speech act labels in reporting clauses cannot always be used as a useful heuristic in earlier periods.

(4) a. "Sit there and write what I tell you," **ordered** Thorny, with all the severity of a strict schoolmaster. (1870 Alcott, *Under the Lilacs*; COHA)
     b. "Here, Francis, fill a bumper and drink to the new baronet." The gray-headed butler did as **ordered** with a very good grace, (1835 Cooper, *The Monikins*; COHA)

While the use of speech act labels is an indirect means of identifying speech acts, it shows us how a speech act is evaluated by the interlocutors or intended by the writer. We can identify who uses a speech act, to whom, and on what occasion. And often we can also determine how the speech act is received by the recipient, that is, what its perlocutionary effect is.

6.4 Performative Verbs

Speech act verbs such as *promise*, *command*, or *declare* can be used either performatively or descriptively (Taavitsainen and Jucker 2007: 112–114). The performative use, as shown in example (1), is the first-person singular present-tense use of the verb. It represents the actual performance of the speech act. Here is an example of the performative verb *congratulate* from Early Modern English:

(5) i much reioyce to see you here in england; and **i congratulate** your coming to this our vniuersity of oxford. (1630 Clare, *The Conuerted Iew*; EEBO)

In (5), *congratulate* is used in a sense that is now obsolete (OED, s.v. *congratu-late*, v., def. 2a), namely 'to express joy of the occasion of' something (cf. the modern use of *congratulate* in (1b)). The descriptive use, which is more common, represents the characterization of a speech act that has occurred before, performed either by the speaker or another. The descriptive use is what was termed above as "metacommunicative." The actual wording of the speech act may be reported, as in (6a), or the content of the speech act may be briefly characterized or summarized, as in (6b), along with other speech acts ("complained," "pray'd")

(6) a. we sent backe our Boates for those low Countrie Captaines afterward; who vpon their arriuall **congratulated** our good successe, in taking so strong a peece of ground, fortified, and guarded with so many men: (1625 Purchas, *Purchas his Pilgrimes*; EEBO)
     b. she **congratulated** his recovery, she civilly complained of his incivility, and pray'd him not onely to see her, but also to write vnto her: (1638 d'Audiguier, *Love and Valour*; EEBO)

Though indirect, the descriptive use can be an effective means of capturing the way in which speakers and addressees conceptualize speech acts. The range of verbs and expressions used to describe a speech act is broader than the performative verb itself. Thus, instead of *congratulate* one can *praise (good work)*, *give/express congratulations, applaud, commend, salute, laud*, et cetera.

Diachronic studies of these verbs (both in their performative and descriptive uses) have shown how performative verbs develop over time. Traugott and Dasher (2002: 204–214, also Traugott 1997) identify pragmatic changes in the verb *promise*. The verb is derived from the noun *promise*, a French and Latin borrowing in Middle English (OED, s.v.v. *promise*, v., and *promise*, n.). Like the development of performative verbs in general, it is first used in a descriptive (non-performative) sense in the middle of the fifteenth century. The performative use arises by the end of the fifteenth century, as in (7).

(7)   **I promise** you that I shall help you to my power for to make your apoyntmente wyth the kyng (1489 Caxton (trans.), *The Right Plesaunt and Goodly Historie of the Foure Sonnes of Aymon*; CMEPV)

According to Traugott and Dasher, the change from non-performative to performative use is a pragmatic change from the domain of content semantics to the domain of pragmatic function. A parenthetical use, *I promise you*, develops at about the same time from the performative use:

(8)   He shall not spede, **I yow promysse**. (a1500(a1450) Gener.(2) (Trin-C O.5.2; MED)

       'He shall not succeed, I promise you'

Here *I yow promysse* functions as a comment clause, as was discussed in Chapter 5, and would appear to arise out of the main clause, thus conforming to the matrix clause hypothesis. The comment clause use is interpersonal: it denotes the speaker's degree of certainty concerning the attached sentence while at the same time recognizing that there might be some doubt in the hearer's mind.

Valkonen (2008) searches for the most common performative verbs of promising (*promise, pledge, vow, swear, vouch for, guarantee*) in the *Eighteenth-Century Fiction* collection in four patterns: *I* Verb, *I* Modal Verb, *I* Adverb Verb, and *I* Modal Adverb Verb. He finds that *promise*, *swear*, and *vow* constitute 97.6 percent of the verbs used, with *pledge* and *vouch* rare, though he also finds idiosyncratic differences among authors. The two most common patterns are *I* Verb and *I* Modal Verb. While recognizing that performative verbs represent only a restricted set of ways in which speech acts are realized, Valkonen feels that automatic searches show promise for the historical study of speech acts.

Finally, pointing out that no studies have attempted to study different types of speech acts in relation to one another, Kohnen (2015b) studies performative verbs expressing commissives, directives, representatives, declaratives, expressives, and "rogatives" (questions) in three corpora over time (fifteenth to nineteenth centuries). Consistent with other studies, he finds that performatives are rare and

Table 6.1 *Performative verbs expressing directives over time (based on Kohnen 2015b: 81)*

15th century:	advise, ask, beseech, bidde, command, charge/give in charge, counsel, crave, forbid, pray, recommend, redde, require, warn
Late 17th century:	adjure, advise, ask, beg, beg leave, beg pardon, beseech, call, charge, command, commend, crave, defy, intreat, pray, propose
Late 19th century:	appeal, ask, beg, beg pardon, command, forbid, give admonition, implore, insist, pray, propose

that they decrease over time, from 10.19/million to 4.7/million. But the different types of speech acts show different patterns. Commissives, which may be expressed by a wide variety of verbs in the fifteenth century, drop dramatically. Directives show the most extreme decline, with neutral 'asking' verbs (rather than 'ordering' or 'suggesting' verbs), which are absent in Old English (see below), being most common through time (see Table 6.1). Expressives, which encompass a wide range of different speech acts, are relatively stable. Thanking and complaining are basic types in all periods, whereas repenting and cursing are more common in Middle English; congratulating is quite recent. Declaratives and rogatives are marginal types. Representatives are perhaps most interesting, beginning low in the fifteenth century, with verbs expressing strong commitment (*ensure*, *affirme*) being predominant, rising to a high in the late seventeenth century, with a wider spread of verbs, and falling somewhat in the late nineteenth century, with verbs of admitting and (dis)agreeing being most common. Kohnen postulates that the rise of representatives in Early Modern English may be due to genre considerations, the fact that treatises and handbooks, which are a rich source of representatives, predominate in this period.

We turn now to detailed studies that have examined directives, commissives, and expressives from a diachronic perspective.

6.5 Directives

Directives (orders, commands, requests) are perhaps the most easily recognizable type of speech act, given the existence of the imperative sentence type (e.g., *Close the door*), which goes back to Old English, as well as performative verbs (e.g., *I command/order/request you to close the door*). The issuing of directives places an imposition on the addressee and is often considered impolite. Thus, we make use of a number of indirect and face-saving strategies to perform directive speech acts. These are what are called "indirect speech acts" (Searle 1975). In an indirect speech act, two speech acts are performed simultaneously, an explicit locutionary act, which is secondary, and an implicit illocutionary act, which is primary. For example, in asking your neighbors to turn down their music, you might say (9a) when you actually intend (9b). Your neighbors will understand the intended (implicit) speech act because typically the explicit speech act articulates one of the conditions on the implicit speech act (in this case, the fact that there is a reason for turning down the music). Of course, the neighbors might be uncooperative interlocutors and respond to the explicit speech act (e.g., "I don't think it's too loud").

(9)   a.   explicit speech act (a statement of belief, i.e., a representative): *Your music is too loud.*
       b.   implicit speech act (a request, i.e., a directive): *Please turn your music down.*

Directives are especially susceptible to indirect expression, as the direct form may be considered impolite. Table 6.2 presents a range of ways in which we can perform directives indirectly. In Chapter 5, §5.7, we looked at examples belonging to the volitional and ability/possibility categories. You will notice in the table that statements generally focus on the speaker's wants or needs (*I want you to*) or the hearer's obligations (*you must/should/need to*), while questions focus on the hearer's ability or willingness (*will/would you?*).

Leech also notes that there are a wide variety of "pragmatic modifiers" which contribute to indirectness, including the politeness marker *please*, hedged performatives (e.g., *May I ask you to*), downtoners (e.g., *Can I just have a brief word with you?*), deliberative openings (e.g., *I wonder if (you'd mind), Do you think*

Table 6.2 *Strategies for performing directives indirectly (based on Leech 2014: 147–159)*

Statements	
Prediction	e.g., *You will be responsible for the shipping costs.*
Strong obligation	*You must/have got to/had better do* X
Weaker obligation	*You should/need to do* X, *I need you to do* X
Volitional	*I want you to/would like you to do* X
Ability/possibility	*You can/may/might want to do* X
Questions	
Volitional	*Will/would you do* X?
Ability/possibility	*Can/could you do* X?
Non-sentential strategies	
	Idioms: *How about? What about?*
	e.g., *Another cup of coffee. A one-way ticket to Chicago.*
Hints	
Statements	e.g., *The neighbors can hear you.*
Questions	e.g., *Do you have any ripe bananas?*

(you could)), appreciative openings (e.g., *I'd appreciate it if/be very grateful if, Would you be so good as*), happenstance indicators (e.g., *You don't happen to*), temporal availability queries (e.g., *Do you have the time to*), past tense, progressive aspect, and tag questions (2014: 159–171).

As we discussed briefly in Chapter 5, directives in Old English display a number of differences from those in Present-day English. The most frequent Old English directive performative verbs are *biddan* 'ask, request', *(be)beodan* 'command', *halsian* 'beseech, entreat', and *læran* 'instruct'. Contemporary directive performative verbs, *order*, *command*, and *request*, are all French borrowings appearing in the Middle English period (OED, s.v.v. *order*, v., *command*, v., *request*, v.). In two studies (2000, 2008a), Kohnen finds that the use of explicit performative verbs (as in 10) is uncommon, as is also the case today. Over the history of English, the use of performative verbs for directives never rises above 5 percent (Kohnen 2007b: 154). Nonetheless, the use of performatives is seven times more frequent in Old English than in Present-day English:

(10)   **ic bidde** þinre dohtor me to gemæccan. (ApT 4.8; DOEC; Kohnen 2000: 304)

      'I ask for your daughter as my wife'

The performative verbs of Old English fall into two classes, what Kohnen calls the 'ask' class (e.g., *biddan*) and the 'order' class (e.g., *beodan*), both encapsulating an unequal relationship between speaker and addressee. In the former, the speaker is subordinate or equal to the hearer, while in the latter, the speaker is superordinate to the hearer. What is distinctive about Old English is the lack of performatives belonging to what Kohnen calls the 'suggest' class, which point to an equal relationship between the interlocutors. As he points out, "Anglo-Saxon speakers quite often used directive performatives which today would appear mostly inappropriate, whereas 'face-saving' performatives seem to have been uncommon" (Kohnen 2008a: 32–33). He attributes this to the strictly hierarchical society of the times. In a later study, Kohnen (2011) does find some directives with *ic wolde* 'I wished, wanted' and *ic wille* 'I wish, want', which sound more like the polite and indirect directives of Present-day English. Note that the anomalous verb *willan* in Old English has a meaning of 'volition' and does not have the modalized meaning we find in Present-day English. Moreover, *wolde* forms are restricted to translations of Latin texts and reflect Latin conventions, and *wille* forms, which occur mainly in laws and charters, reflect the speaker's sovereign authority; thus, they can "hardly be called polite" (236) in present-day terms.

Other means for expressing directives in Old English include the following:

• *þu scealt, ge sculan* – a second-person modal form meaning 'you [singular/ plural] shall', as in *you should empty the garbage*;

• *uton* + infinitive – a first-person plural imperative meaning 'let's' (Bosworth-Toller, s.v. *witon*), as in *Let's see a movie tonight*; and

- *(neod)þearf* + first- or second-person pronoun + *þæt* clause – an impersonal form meaning 'there is need for me/us/you that ...' (Bosworth-Toller, s.v. *þearf*), as in *It's necessary for you to check the oil in your car regularly.*

The modal form is used in secular texts, invariably by a superior speaker to a subordinate, thus again showing no need for any face-saving. The other two forms are restricted to religious texts and reflect Christian ideals rather than a movement toward increased politeness. Kohnen concludes that indirectness was not typical of Old English communication and that negative politeness (see Chapter 5) played a small role.

In two articles examining directives in sermons in the history of English (2007b, 2008c), Kohnen shows that over time, directives have decreased. But the story is more complex. In Old English, the most common forms are first- and third-person modals, which express common ground or impersonality and are hence quite face-saving, as in *we should follow that path* or *he must leave now*. First-person plural imperatives (with *uton* 'let's'), standard second-person imperatives, and third-person imperatives (e.g., *Let him wash the dishes*) also occur. A decline in the various types is seen in Middle English, with the exception of second-person imperatives, which signal the superior position of the speaker vis-à-vis the addressee. These imperative forms increase substantially in Early Modern English, with a slight decline in twentieth-century English. Thus, the overall decrease in frequency of directives is not necessarily accompanied by an increase in politeness. More polite and face-saving forms begin to appear in the modern period. The *let's* form appears in the sixteenth century. Indirect forms of directives (such as questions of the hearer's abilities or willingness or statements of the hearer's obligations) appear in the same century but are rare until quite recently (Kohnen 2015b). Present-day English continues the trend toward indirectness, with the increase of the *let's* construction and indirect forms, as well as performative verbs using 'suggest/advise' verbs. Direct imperatives do not disappear, but tend to focus on mental rather than physical action and hence be less face-threatening.

In the corpus annotation study mentioned above, Culpeper and Archer (2008) look at directives in Early Modern English trials (1640–1760) and find them "dramatically different" from those in Present-day English. In their data, 73 percent of directives belong to what they call the "direct impositive" category (imperatives, (hedged) performatives, statements of hearer obligations and speaker wants; see example (11)), whereas only 10 percent belong to this category in modern English. Of the impositive type, three-quarters are direct imperatives. The use of "conventionally indirect forms," or suggestions, such as *let me, will you V, if you will, please to, you may,* does not rise above 17 percent, whereas they are the majority form today.

(11)   Mrs. DOTTEREL. Lookee, Mr. Daffodil, **you must** curb your Passions, and keep your Distance – Fire is catching, and one does not know the Consequences when once it begins to spread. (1757 Garrick, *The Male-Coquette*; Culpeper and Archer 2008: 49)

Surprisingly, the indirect forms are typically used by speakers of high social status. Nearly one-half of the directives in Early Modern English have no modification to soften the blow. Vocatives and forms of *pray* (*prithee*) may occur, but "grounders" (which give the reason for the request) – the most common present-day way to mitigate the directness of an order – are not common. But Culpeper and Archer (2008) argue that one should not infer that Early Modern English is "less polite." In the hierarchical society of the time, one could simply assume the right to make a request, with no sense of infringing upon the rights of others. Indirect forms were typically used by speakers of higher social status in order to appeal to the addressee's desire to be liked (appealing to people's willingness to act or granting permission to act).

In sum, these studies of directives in the history of English, while not entirely comparable, have shown movement away from the direct directives to indirect directives. (See Chapter 5, §5.7, for changes in directives in the modern period.)

6.6   Commissives

Studies of promises in the history of English have shown changes in form and pragmatic function. In Old English, promises could be expressed in a simple sentence with 'shall' or 'will' (Arnovick 1999), as in Beowulf's boast:

(12)   ond nu wið Grendel **sceal**, wið þam aglæcan ana **gehegan** ðing wið þyrse (Beo 424b–26a; DOEC)

     'And now against Grendel, I shall alone achieve the deed, against the monster, against the demon'

Performative uses of 'promise' verbs (*behatan* 'promise, vow', *gehatan* 'promise, vow', *(ge)beotian* 'promise (in a boastful manner)', *swerian* 'swear (an oath)', *beweddian* 'ensure by pledge') also occurred (see Traugott and Dasher 2002: 211–214).

(13)   **Ic** hit þe **gehate,** no he on helm losaþ, ne on foldan fæþm, ne on fyrgenholt, ne on gyfenes grund, ga þær he wille. (Beo 1392–5; DOEC)

     'I promise you this: he will not escape under cover, nor into the bosom of the earth, nor into the mountain-woods, nor to the sea bottom, go where we will'

Arnovick (1999) argues that the grammaticalization of *will* and *shall* as markers of epistemic modality (and the future) led to the need for more "expanded" forms for promising. In Middle English, a variety of 'promise' verbs were used (*bihoten, plighten* 'promise, pledge', *sweren, wedden*), including performatively (14a); expressions with the nouns *biheste* 'promise' and *treuth* 'truth', such as 'have truth' in (14b) were also common (see Pakkala-Weckström 2008):

(14)   a.   And heere **I swere** that nevere willyngly,/ In werk ne thoght, I nyl yow
             disobeye, (1387 Chaucer, *Canterbury Tales* E.Cl 362–3; Pakkala-
             Weckström 2008: 149)

             'And I hereby swear that never willingly in deed or thought I not-will you
             disobey'

        b.   Sire, I wol be youre humble trewe wyf;/ **Have heer my trouthe**, til that
             myn herte breste (1387 Chaucer, *Canterbury Tales*, F.Fkl 758–9; Pakkala-
             Weckström 2008: 142)

             'Sir, I will be your humble true wife – have hereby my promise – until my
             heart breaks'

As discussed above, the verb *promise* (a French borrowing) was not used performatively until the end of the fifteenth century. By the eighteenth century it was the most common performative verb used in commissives, along with *swear* and *vow* (Valkonen 2008).

The pragmatics of promises involve a sincerity condition (that the speaker intends to perform the action) and an essential condition (that the speaker intends for the utterance to place them under an obligation to perform the action) (Searle 1969: 60). It has been argued that ME promises did not conform to these conditions. In a study of promises in the *Canterbury Tales*, Pakkala-Weckström (2008) finds that there are formulaic ways in which promises are made. In the chivalric and courtly society depicted in the tales, honor dictates that promises must be fulfilled, whether or not the promiser was sincere in making the promise, whether it was made in desperation, or whether it was made out of stupidity and greed. The uttering of the words alone constitutes a "binding promise." For Pakkala-Weckström, this means that the essential condition is overruled in these cases and the sincerity condition is void. The promise made by the character Dorigen in "The Franklin's Tale" is an example. In order to rid herself of an unwanted suiter, Aurelius, Dorigen promises to love him if he removes all the rocks from the coastline of Brittany (in order to ensure the safe return of her husband). It is clear that Dorigen does not see the essential condition as being met because she notes that her promise is made *in pley* 'in jest' and with the belief that what she asks *shal never bityde* 'shall never happen'. That is, she has no intention of carrying out her promise. However, when Aurelius, with the help of a magician, seems to have removed the rocks, she feels compelled to honor her promise, and even her husband agrees. She has pledged her *trouthe*, her faith or loyalty (OED, s. v. *troth*, n. and adv. (and int.), def. 3), and this overrides her lack of intent (Pakkala-Weckström 2005). Thus, "the defective speech act is highly successful."

Arnovick (2006) takes a somewhat different view. She argues that Dorigen's utterance, though in the conventional form of a promise, does not in fact constitute a promise, as the context makes clear. Not only is the essential condition invalid, but, more importantly, the utterance fails the sincerity condition on promising. Arnovick provides evidence that in the legal framework holding at the time, Dorigen's "promise" is invalid, as it promises that she will commit a sin (adultery), she could not envisage the magical removal of the rocks, and it was rashly made. Rather, Dorigen's utterance functions as a rejection of her admirer, an assertion of her intention not to love him: it is an "insincere promise embedded within a larger rejection" (170). Arnovick sees this promise as a kind of indirect speech act (see above): the explicit speech act is Dorigen's promise, but the implicit speech act is her rejection, a kind of expressive. Arnovick argues that by taking her promise literally, Aurelius is flouting the inferential principles that hold in conversations, because it is clear from his original response (*Is ther noon oother grace in you?* 'Is there no other mercy in you?') that he recognizes it as an insincere promise.

6.7 Expressives

Expressives cover a wide range of speech acts. In this section, we will look at some historical studies of apologies, curses, and greetings/farewells.

Apologies: An apology is a "speech act performed by an apologizer, who has done something annoying or damaging or violated social norms, to restore equilibrium and social harmony" (Su 2020: 117). In a prototypical apology, there is some offense, someone who has caused the offense or takes responsibility for it, someone who has been offended, and some remedy (such as a sign of regret or other reparation), but all four features may not be present, and there is a range of related speech acts, such as excuses or general expressions of sorrow. In Present-day English, we have a set of formulaic devices for expressing apologies (*(I'm) sorry, I'm afraid, excuse me, pardon me*, etc.), but care must be taken because these same expressions may be used in many instances that are not true apologies, such as *I'm sorry it's raining* (an expression of regret), *Excuse me for interrupting* (an attention-getter), *Excuse me, can you speak up* (introduction to a directive), or *I'm sorry, I just don't understand the purpose of that* (a preface to a disagreement) (Leech 2014: Chs. 5 and 6).

Kohnen (2017a, 2017b; see also Williams 2018: Ch. 4) finds that apologies do not occur in Early Medieval England: "none of the patterns of apologizing typical of present-day English ... are found in Old English" (2017b: 315). While there are words expressing 'sorrow' and 'regret' in the first person and 'excuse', and 'forgive' in the imperative, they are not used in apologies. 'Sorrow' expressions are used to convey general repentance (for sins committed), 'regret' expressions are used in penitence when addressing God, 'excuse' expressions are used when seeking to be excused from a duty or obligation, and 'forgive' expressions are addressed to God to request forgiveness for sins. All of these are restricted to Christian texts (religious instruction and prayers). The concept of apologizing seems to have been incompatible with the Germanic secular warrior society in which transgressions were met with retribution or were appeased through payment. Kohnen believes that acts of penitence, which he calls "pre-apologies," later developed into apologies when the entity transgressed against was not God but a fellow Christian, but these were rare in Old English.

Williams (2018) finds that secular apologies – what he calls "affective apologies" – do not occur until the late fourteenth century. While most early apologies in the medieval period relate to cardinal sins and major transgressions, apologies for minor acts also begin to appear. These serve the purpose of maintaining good social relations. Here is an early occurrence of *I am sorry* in such an apology from *The Book of the Duchess*, where the Dreamer apologizes to the Knight for interrupting his thoughts:

(15)   "A!, goode sir, nor fors," quod y,/ **"I am ryght sory** yif I have ought/ Destroubled yow out of your thought./ Foryive me, yif I have mystake." (1369–70 Chaucer, *Book of the Duchess* 522–5; Williams 2018: 143)

"'A, good sir, no matter," said I, "I am right sorry if I have disturbed you at all out of your thought. Forgive me if I did wrong'"

By Early Modern English, apologies are much more common, but they differ in both form and function from modern apologies. Jucker and Taavitsainen (2008a) study apologies in Renaissance fiction and drama by searching their corpus using a set of IFIDs (*sorry, excuse me, I apologize for, forgive me, pardon me for, I regret that, I'm afraid*). What they find is that while present-day apologies are often one or two words in length ("Sorry," "Excuse me"), Renaissance ones are embedded in more complex structures, as in example (16), with the apology preceded by an interpersonal plea ("I beg your") and followed by an explanation ("for th'vnciuill speech"):

(16)   IAGO: Th'exceeding happinesse to see you well, / Is more then ioy can vtter: On my knees/ I beg your pardon for th'vnciuill speech/ My ignorant tongue committed. (1620 Swetnam, *The Woman-Hater, Arraigned by Women* I.iii; ED)

Moreover, while modern speakers most often apologize for not hearing/not understanding or interrupting/failing to pay attention, a common cause for apologies in the Renaissance drama is for "lack of decorum in speech," such as speaking too long, with too much emotion, in an apparently rude or outspoken manner, and above one's rank, as we see in the case of the "uncivil speech" in (16). The question of whether Renaissance drama is characteristic of the everyday usage of the time must, of course, be kept in mind.

Jucker and Taavitsainen (2008a) see two types of apologies:

- addressee-oriented ones, which ask for the addressee's forgiveness (*pardon me / excuse me*) and
- speaker-oriented ones, which express the speaker's regret (*I am sorry/ I regret*).

Addressee-oriented apologies are more common in the Renaissance, while speaker-oriented ones prevail in the present day. An expression such as "pardon me" is more of an imposition than one such as "I'm sorry" since the former is asking the addressee to show generosity and forgive an offense, while the latter is simply expressing the speaker's remorse and does not call for any change in the addressee.

A study of apologies in the fiction subcorpus of COHA (Jucker 2018) confirms that speaker-oriented apologies (*I'm sorry, I regret*) have clearly come to predominate at the expense of addressee-oriented apologies (*pardon me, forgive me*); see Figure 6.1. *Apologize*, a Renaissance borrowing from Greek via Latin, appears only at the beginning of the seventeenth century and is rare; it is a frequent metaexpression describing apologies (17a), but less often serves as a performative verb (17b).

(17) a. "Not that I think old maids can not be very acceptable women," he **apologized** (1894 Page, *The Burial of the Guns*; COHA)
      b. **I apologize** to you and the owner for my rudeness, (1888 Optic, *Taken by the Enemy*; COHA)

Su (2020), using all subcorpora of COHA, likewise finds that *sorry* and *excuse* have increased and *regret*, *forgive*, and *apologize* have decreased. Identifying an exhaustive set of patterns, he sees increasing frequency of *sorry* forms: three patterns (*Sorry*; *I'm sorry*; *I'm sorry,* [vocative]) show a large increase and three (*Sorry about* X; *Sorry,* [vocative]; [vocative], *I'm sorry*) a lesser increase. Stand-alone *Sorry* is identified only in the 1900s. Three patterns with *sorry* decline, but all include intensifiers (*Really sorry*; *I'm truly sorry*; *I'm sincerely sorry for that*); Su attributes their loss to the reduction of social distance among individuals (2020: 130). The other decreasing pattern is the direct imperative *Forgive me,* [vocative], and its decrease could be expected given the more general decline of second-person imperatives, as discussed above. However, in contrast to Jucker and Taavitsainen's findings, Su finds that several addressee-oriented patterns with direct imperatives (including *Forgive me, Forgive my* X, *God forgive me*) fluctuate but do not decrease.

Looking at metaexpressions of apologies, Jucker (2018) finds an overall increase in apologies over time, consistent with what is shown in Figure 6.1. In this context, apologies with explicit IFIDs increase (especially the simple form *sorry*), as apologies that take responsibility (as in 18a) or offer an explanation

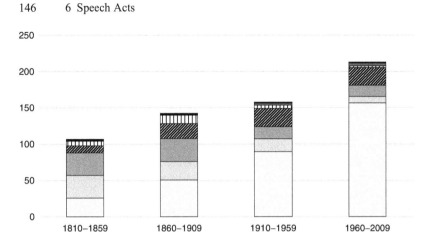

Figure 6.1 Performative apology expressions in the fiction section of COHA (frequency per million words) (from Jucker 2018: 388)

(Andreas H. Jucker. 2018. Apologies in the history of English: Evidence from the *Corpus of Historical American English*. *Corpus Pragmatics* 2(4). 388. Reprinted under the Creative Commons Attribution 4.0 International license.)

(as in 18b) decrease; also, apologies are more often performed non-verbally over time:

(18)   a. "I was woolgathering," he said by way of **apology**. (1971 Epstein, *Dream Museum*; COHA; Jucker 2018: 393)
        b. "It's awful hard to find anybody in a crowd like this," he **apologized**. (1930 Dobie, *The False Talisman*; COHA; Jucker 2018: 393)

As apologies have become more and more frequent, they have become increasingly routinized, conventionalized, and empty of content, correlated with reduction in form: "[w]hat used to be a heart-felt expression of regret for having committed an offence has in many cases turned to a conventionalized phrase with little meaning" (Jucker 2019: 396). Or as Williams (2018: 30) notes, "when we say *sorry* today it is often more of a matter of sociability rather than an actual expression of feeling bad about something." Furthermore "Present-day English-speaking culture is extensively apologetic, and we use apologies for the most minor everyday social infractions ... as well as for more serious wrongs committed against those closest to us" (Williams 2018: 121–122).

Jucker (2019) depicts changes in the illocutionary force of apologies in Figure 6.2. Apologies originate in acts of penitence in Old English, then develop into "pre-apologies" to fellow Christians at the end of the period.

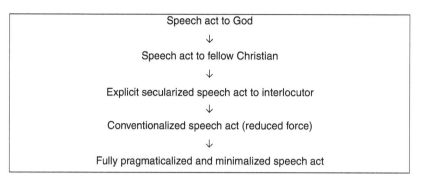

Figure 6.2 The diachrony of apologies (adapted from Jucker 2019: 7)

(Andreas H. Jucker. 2019. Speech act attenuation in the history of English: The case of apologies. *Glossa: A Journal of General Linguistics* 4(1). 45. 7. Reprinted under Creative Commons Attribution 4.0 license.)

Explicit secular apologies arise later in the Middle English period, followed in the Early Modern English period by conventional expressions of regret whose force tends to weaken over time. Finally, fully pragmaticalized, empty tokens (e.g., *oops*, *my bad*) evolve in the modern period; their main purpose is perlocutionary, that is, serving to maintain social cohesion.

Curses: In one conception, a curse is an expressive; it consists of a wish that something bad will happen to the target, but it does not imply any necessary effect of this wish (OED, s.v. *curse*, n., def. 2). We see this in example (19a) where *curse* means 'wish ill'. Archer (2010) calls this an "exclamatory" curse. But curses can also be interpreted as declaratives (see above), that is, as expressions which – by their mere uttering – bring some evil upon the target (OED, s.v. *curse*, n., def. 1), as in (19b). Archer (2010) calls this an "execra-tory" curse. For an execratory curse to "work" the speaker has to be in a pact with the devil (or be supernatural). Execratory curses are found in Old and Middle English, in both Christian and pagan traditions; Arnovick (1999: Ch. 5) dates the rise of the exclamatory curse to Middle English.

(19) a. i have served him fourescore and six yeares, and he never hurt me in any thing: how shall i **curse** him who hath saved mee? (1639 Gouge, *A Recovery from Apostacy*; EEBO)
      b. She confessed to him y^t ['that'] she had **cursed** 2 childeren of Parkers and that they languished immediately (1645 Suffolk Witches, p. 293; Culpeper and Semino 2000: 102)

In a study of witchcraft narratives in Early Modern English, Culpeper and Semino (2000) show that people accused as witches are typically poor and marginalized members of society, often women. When these people utter a curse or simply express anger at a neighbor, their speech acts may be interpreted as a declarative, as a speech act that inevitably results in misfortune falling upon the target. In the witchcraft context of the seventeenth century, witches are thus people who, because of their dealings with the devil, have the power to perform declaratives.

Greetings: A greeting has no sincerity condition, and only the essential condition is important: it counts as a courteous recognition of the hearer by the speaker (Searle 1969: 67). Leech (2014) sees greetings (and leave-takings) as manifestations of the Sympathy Maxim, in which the speaker gives value to the hearer's opinion. Both the beginning and end of a conversation are potentially face-threatening; for this reason, greetings are often accompanied by inquiries about the hearer's health or well-being. Although many such expressions are highly stereotyped and devoid of feeling, their presence is necessary for polite discourse. Moreover, greetings may be accompanied by elements that serve to establish and strengthen social relationships or to structure discourse.

Grzega (2008) provides an extensive inventory of the changing form of greetings in the history of English. In Old English, the forms of greetings were quite restricted, mainly concerned with wishes for well-being: *beo gesund* 'be in good health', *wes þu hal* 'be you hale'. (The paucity of Old English texts with represented speech limits our data.) In Middle English, *heil (þu)* continues this tradition. Forms expressing wishes for the time of day (*Good morn(ing)*, *Good morrow, Good even(ing)*) and inquiries about well-being (*How fare you?*, *What chere?* 'What mood') begin to appear, as do borrowed forms such as *Ave* (< Latin), *Bienvenu* (< French), *Hail* (< Old Norse), and *Benedicite* (< Latin). Other greetings express happiness about seeing one another (OE *wilcomen* 'welcome') and wishes for God's protection (ME *God bless you* and *God save you*, EModE *God speed* and *God bless you*). In a detailed study of greetings in Chaucer's *Canterbury Tales*, Jucker (2011a) identifies these same categories as well as interjections (*now, o, what (ho)*); he points out that ME greetings very often occur with nominal terms of identification and are less routinized than modern ones. Crystal and Crystal (2002: 206) and Salmon (1967: 43–44, 54) provide an inventory of the varied types of greetings found in Shakespeare. In addition to the categories already identified, they record special greetings for monarchs (e.g., *Hail to your Grace*). Salmon notes that blessings are reserved for more formal greetings, whereas wishes for the time of day and inquiries about well-being are used among friends.

The earliest recorded instances of the common contemporary greetings – *Hello, Hi, How are you (doing)? How do you do?* – are from the nineteenth century. *Hello* and *hi* as well as the more recent *hey* are all attention-getters. In a study of greetings in COHA, Jucker (2017), finds that *hello* takes over from

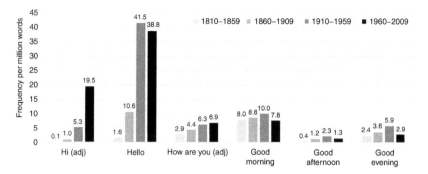

Figure 6.3 Greetings in COHA (frequency per million words) (adapted from Jucker 2017: 47)

(Andreas H. Jucker. Speech acts and speech act sequences: Greetings and farewells in the history of American English. *Studia Neophilologica* 89(s1). 47. Copyright © 2017, reprinted by permission of Taylor & Francis Ltd. www.tandfonline.com. Redrawn with data supplied by author.)

good morning in the mid-nineteenth century and *hi* shows a large rise in the twentieth century. See Figure 6.3 (values for *hi* and *how are you* are adjusted here to exclude false hits).

In the early period, *How are you?* and *How do you do?* can be real questions and elicit responses concerning the recipient's well-being. But over time they become more and more conventionalized and devoid of their original meaning. Both increase over time in COHA, except for a decrease in *How do you do* in the mid-twentieth century. Jucker attributes this decline to its almost completely formulaic nature – the typical response being the reciprocal *How do you do?* – and its use between strangers in formal contexts. The original meaning may persist to some degree with *How are you?* Similar to the stylistic change of *How do you do?* Grzega notes that a marked form may become neutral, as in the case of *Hi* and *Hello*, now used as general salutations but originally used to greet a person from a distance (i.e., with an attention-getting function), as in the following example:

(20)   "**Hallo**! who comes there? shouted the sentinel. (1823 McHenry, *The Wilderness*; COHA)

Leave-takings: A leave-taking is the reverse of a greeting. Like greetings, leave-takings can be seen as having no propositional content but serve only as an expression of good wishes at parting. But they are potentially face-threatening since the speaker is implying that they no longer wish to share the hearer's company. For this reason, they often involve good wishes (*Have a nice day, take care, good to talk to you, glad to see you*) (Leech 2014: 213–214).

Grzega (2005) finds only one possible expression of leave-taking in Old English, the wish for health *wes þu hal*, also used as a greeting. In Middle English, new leave-taking forms appear, including further wishes for health (*farewell/fare thee well, well be you*), wishes for a good time of day (*good night, have you good day*), wishes for God's blessing (*God thee speed, God save you, peace be with you, to God/Christ I commend you*), and borrowed expressions (*adieu* < French). As with greetings, Jucker (2011a) finds that it is common for the leave-taking expression in Chaucer to be accompanied by a personal name. Shakespeare was quite inventive in the formulation of leave-taking expressions, including farewells with kind regards (e.g., *I do commend me to you*), farewells with concerns for well-being (e.g., *Rest you merry*), and simple dismissals (e.g., *Go thy ways, There lies your way, Be gone, Hence and avaunt*) (Crystal and Crystal 2002: 170; Salmon 1967: 44, 54). *Farewell* and *adieu* are neutral, blessing and wishes for a good time of day are deferential, and dismissals are typically used by a master to a servant (Salmon 1967: 54). *Farewell* was the most common expression in the LModE period. Distance alternatives are *adieu*, which falls almost out of use in the modern period, and *good night*, which remains steady. *Goodbye* overtakes *farewell* in the 1950s in COHA (Jucker 2017, see Figure 6.4).

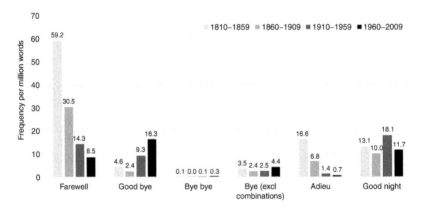

Figure 6.4 Leave-taking expressions in COHA (frequency per million words) (adapted from Jucker 2017: 49)

Some categories of leave-takings are of quite recent vintage, such as expressive elements (*ta-ta*, *cheerio*), directives to take care (*take care*), and predictions for seeing one another again (*see you*). Leech notes that *see you*, which he sees as modeled on German *Auf Wiedersehen* and French *Au revoir*, softens the discourtesy of leave-taking by suggesting that the parting is only temporary (2014: 213).

Two common leave-taking expressions in Present-day English have disputed etymologies. *So long* – first appearing in the mid-nineteenth century – may be a reduced form of *(it will seem) so long until we meet again*, or disputedly a calque on German *so lange*, or a corruption of Arabic *salaam* or Hebrew *shalom* 'peace', or a clipping and calque from Norwegian *så lenge* (Grzega 2005: 60–61). *Goodbye* is standardly seen as a reduction of the blessing *God be with you*, attested since at least the fifteenth century, with *good* substituted for *god* in the late seventeenth century perhaps by analogy with *good night, good day* (OED, s.v. *goodbye*, n., int., and adj.). But an origin in *God buy you* 'God redeem you' has also been suggested, and the derivation of *bye* from *buy you* is phonologically more plausible than from *be with you* (see Grzega 2005: 61–62). Arnovick (1999: 112–113) attributes the loss of the religious element in this leave-taking formula to cultural change, namely secularization in the seventeenth and eighteenth centuries (but see Grzega 2005: 62).

Leave-taking may be effected by using direct imperatives (e.g., *Farewell, Have a good day*) which on first glance appear rude (attacks on negative face, see Chapter 5), but as Brown and Levinson (1987[1978]: 99) point out, leave-taking is a situation where the speaker anticipates the hearer's reluctance to leave (and its possible affront to the speaker) by issuing a particularly firm command.

6.8 Chapter Summary

This chapter covered the following topics:
- the nature of speech acts and their categorization;
- methods devised for the study of speech acts, given the challenges posed by the function-to-form approach, including close readings of texts/corpora, speech-act annotations of corpora, or focus on performative verbs, illocutionary-force-indicating devices, and/or metacommunicative labels;
- the evolution of performative verbs from descriptive to performative to comment clause uses;
- directives in the history of English, with a focus on the overt nature of directives in earlier English and on the rise of indirect directives in the modern period (see also Chapter 5, §5.7);
- commissives in the history of English, with discussion of a differing conceptualization of promises in ME society;

- a selection of expressives in the history of English:
  - apologies, where we see the rise of secular apologies in the ME period, the predominance of speaker-oriented apologies in the LModE and PDE periods, and the weakening of the force of apologies in contemporary society;
  - curses, which evolve from execratory (declarative) to exclamatory (expressive) in nature;
  - greetings, where we see a proliferation of forms over time, the predominance of *hello/hi* in the nineteenth and twentieth centuries, and the conventionalization of greetings such as *how do you do?* and *how are you?*;
  - leave-takings, which show a similar proliferation of forms and replacement of *adieu* and *farewell* with *goodbye/bye* in the twentieth century.

6.9   Further Reading

For good overviews, begin with Archer (2010), Kohnen (2015b), and Jucker (2019). On speech acts in Early Modern English, see Archer (2012). Jucker and Taavitsainen (eds.) (2008b) is an older, but still good collection of articles on diachronic speech acts.

Studies of directives, commissives, and expressives (of various types) in the history of English are common, but the study of representatives and declaratives has been neglected (except Kohnen 2015b on representatives). In addition to the sources discussed in the chapter, Rudanko (1993: Chs. II and V) is an early study of speech acts in *Othello* and *Coriolanus*, U. Busse (2008) looks at directives in Shakespeare, and Moessner (2010) is a cross-genre comparison of directives in legal, religious, and scientific discourse in Early Modern English and Present-day English. Rudanko (2004) is a study of threats (a special kind of commissive) in Chaucer's wooing scenes. A variety of expressives have been studied, see Arnovick (1999: Ch. 5) on cursing, (1999: Ch. 6) on *good-bye*, (1999: Ch. 7) on *bless you*, and (2006: Ch. 8) on book curses.

For good treatments of apologies and requests in contemporary English, see Aijmer (1996: Chs. 3 and 4) and Leech (2014: Chs. 5 and 6).

6.10   Exercises

1. Identify the speech acts in the following passage from Jane Austen's *Pride and Prejudice* (1813). Elizabeth Bennet has just received a proposal of marriage from the pompous Mr. Collins, which she has refused. Her mother, Mrs. Bennet, wants her to accept the proposal and is urging her husband to make Elizabeth accept the offer. Focus on directives and commissives (threats) in the following passage. Some are "infelicitous" for a variety of reasons.

"Oh! Mr. Bennet, you are wanted immediately; we are all in an uproar. You must come and make Lizzy marry Mr. Collins, for she vows she will not have him, and if you do not make haste he will change his mind and not have *her*."

Mr. Bennet raised his eyes from his book as she entered, and fixed them on her face with a calm unconcern which was not in the least altered by her communication.

"I have not the pleasure of understanding you," said he, when she had finished her speech. "Of what are you talking?"

"Of Mr. Collins and Lizzy. Lizzy declares she will not have Mr. Collins, and Mr. Collins begins to say that he will not have Lizzy."

"And what am I to do on the occasion? It seems an hopeless business."

"Speak to Lizzy about it yourself. Tell her that you insist upon her marrying him."

"Let her be called down. She shall hear my opinion."

Mrs. Bennet rang the bell, and Miss Elizabeth was summoned to the library.

"Come here, child," cried her father as she appeared. "I have sent for you on an affair of importance. I understand that Mr. Collins has made you an offer of marriage. Is it true?" Elizabeth replied that it was. "Very well—and this offer of marriage you have refused?"

"I have, sir."

"Very well. We now come to the point. Your mother insists upon your accepting it. Is it not so, Mrs. Bennet?"

"Yes, or I will never see her again."

"An unhappy alternative is before you, Elizabeth. From this day you must be a stranger to one of your parents. Your mother will never see you again if you do *not* marry Mr. Collins, and I will never see you again if you *do*." (from www .gutenberg.org/files/1342/1342-h/1342-h.htm)

2. Identify the forms used to express a direct or indirect directive speech act in each of the following Old English examples (taken from Kohnen 2007b, 2008a, 2011):

(a) Uton we þonne þæs geþencean (HomU 20 (BlHom 10) 148; DOEC)
    'Let us then be mindful of this'

(b) Ic bidde eow þæt ge gymon eowra sylfra (ÆLet 1 (Wulfsige X a) 117; DOEC)
    'I ask you to take care of yourselves'

(c) Þa men þu scealt smerwan mid þy ele (LchII (2); DOEC)
    'those men thou shall smear with the oil'

(d) Ac us is mycel neodþearf, þæt we geþencan (HomS 6 (Ass 14) 7; DOEC)
    'But we have great need to consider . . .'

(e) Ne beo nænig man her . . . on his geþohte to modig (HomU 20 (BlHom 10) 48; DOEC)
    'Let no man here be . . . in his thoughts too proud'

(f) & scyldað eow wið galscypas (WHom 8c 163; DOEC)
    'And protect yourselves against luxury'

(g) Nu mote we habban maran rihtwisnysse (ÆHom 16 120; DOEC)
    'Now we must have more righteousness'

(h) Wolde ic þæt ðu funde þa (El 1079; DOEC)
'I would like you to find them'

3. Imperatives in Shakespeare could take a number of different forms. Identify
   the form used in each example (examples taken from U. Busse 2008: 87)
   and say how they compare with imperatives in Present-day English:
   (a) Go, and be rul'd; ... (1608 *Coriolanus* III.ii.90)
   (b) come you to me at night (1596–7 *Merchant of Venice* II.ii.256–7)
   (c) Toads stoole, lerne me the Proclamation (1600–2 *Troilus and Cressida* II.
       ii.21–2)
   (d) We pray you throw to earth/This vnpreuayling woe, (1599–1601 *Hamlet* I.
       ii.106–7)
   (e) Doe thou amend thy Face (1596–97 *Henry IV, Part I* III.iii.23)
   (f) Giue me your answer, yfaith doe (1599 *Henry V* V.ii.129–30
   (g) haue done your foolishness, (1594 *The Comedy of Errors* I.ii.72)
   (h) Vp sword, (1599–1601 *Hamlet* III.iii.88)
   (i) Then go we neare her (1598–9 *Much Ado About Nothing* III.ii.32)
   (j) And pawse vs, till these Rebels, now a-foot,/ Come vnderneath the yoake of
       Gouernment (1597–8 *Henry IV, Part II* IV.iii.9–10)
   (k) let vs take our leaue (1589–91 *Two Gentlemen of Verona* I.i.56)
   (l) let vs hence (1598–9 *Much Ado About Nothing* V.iii.30)

4. Like greetings, expressions of leave-taking can be quite varied in form and
   can be based on different principles. Explain the elements that constitute the
   following farewells from Chaucer's *Canterbury Tales* (examples taken from
   Jucker 2011a):
   (a) "farewel, have good day!" (B.Sh 320)
   (b) "And, goode lemman ['sweetheart'], God thee save and kepe!" (A.Rv 4247)
   (c) "And God be with yow, where ye ['you'] go or ryde!" (C.Pard 748)
   (d) "Now, goode sire, go forth thy wey and hy ['make haste'] the" (G.CY 1295)
   (e) "Allas! go forth thy wey anon,/ Help us to scape ['escape'], or we been dede
       ['dead'] echon ['everyone']!" (A.Mil 3607–8)
   (f) "Go now thy wey, and speed thee heer-aboute" (A.Mil 3562)
   (g) "Fare weel, Malyne, sweete wight ['creature']!/ The day is come, I may no
       lenger byde ['remain'];/ But everemo, wher so I go or ryde,/ I is thyn awen
       ['own'] clerk, swa have I seel ['happiness']!" (A.Rv 4236–9)
   (h) "God save yow, that boghte agayn mankynde" (C.Pard 766)

5. Research the development of *my bad* as an apology in contemporary
   English.
   (a) Check out the OED. Is there an entry for "my bad"? If so, what
       definition and usage label are given? What is the earliest citation
       given? What do the citations tell you about its origin?

(b) Go to Google NGrams (https://books.google.com/ngrams) and search for "My bad" (be sure to use a capital "M"). You will see that there is a sudden increase in about 2000. Look at some of the examples. How accurate is search for finding examples of the apology?

(c) Search for "my bad PUNC" in COCA. Discuss your results. How accurate is this search; that is, does it return exclusively (or mostly) examples of the apology form? What is the earliest example of *my bad* as an apology? How is the form developing over time? In which genre(s) is this apology form most common? Why might it be found in some genres but not in others?

7   Address Terms

7.1   Introduction

Address terms are forms used by the speaker to denote the intended hearer of an utterance. They include nominal terms of address (vocatives) and second-person pronouns. Over time we can see the obsolescence and rise of terms of address, semantic changes in the terms of address, and, more importantly, changes in the social distinctions that they make.

In the history of English, there has been a fundamental change in the second-person pronoun system. The pronouns of Old English, *þū* 'thou' and *ȝē* 'you', which distinguished singular and plural addressees, changed in Middle English, most probably under French and Latin influence, to forms that expressed intimacy/closeness or deference/distance, respectively. How this system worked in the ME and EModE periods is a matter of great scholarly debate. The intimate form *thou* became increasingly infrequent in the seventeenth century, and by about 1700, it had been replaced by *you* for most users; *you* no longer carried social meaning but came to be used indistinguishably for singular and plural addressees in all social contexts. *Thou* was then restricted to use in specialized domains (e.g., certain religious groups, archaizing poetry, biblical discourse [see Chapter 8, §8.5]) and in regional dialects.

Nominal terms of address have not undergone such systematic change, but the individual lexical and semantic changes have been extensive. This chapter begins by illustrating nominal change with the term *lady*. We then turn to the pronominal system. The use of *thou* and *you* can be approached in a number of different ways. We look at the pronominal system in Middle English, when the honorific system of use is arising, and in Early Modern English, when it falls out of use. EModE evidence from trial records and depositions, from personal letters, and from literary records, especially Shakespeare, presents a complex and often contradictory picture that often proves difficult to interpret. We then turn to the nominal system, beginning with an overview of this system in Present-day English. OE and ME studies of vocatives, where they exist, are summarized. In Early Modern English, we look at the relevant data from Shakespeare – where an interesting study looks at the cooccurrence of *thou/*

you forms with different nominal terms of address – from salutations and subscriptions in personal letters, and from vocatives in trial transcripts.

7.2 Case Study: *Lady*

As an illustration of change in terms of address, let's consider the address term *lady* (OED, s.v. *lady*, n.). This term was used in medieval and early modern times as the female equivalent of *lord*. It functioned as an honorific form of address for a woman of distinction (the female head of a household; a female ruler, a queen; a member of the nobility, the wife or daughter of a duke, baron, earl, viscount, etc.); in courtly love, the name was conferred upon the object of the nobleman's affection. It was typically used deferentially, often with a positive adjective such as *gentle* or *noble*, see (1a) where the Host is addressing the Prioress (in the *Canterbury Tales*) or (1b) where Gratiano is addressing Portia (in *The Merchant of Venice*). However, it could also be used with negative adjectives to express anger, when the Earl of Gloucester is addressing Regan (in *King Lear*) (1c) or in an ironic way when Prince Henry addresses Mistress Quickly, the innkeeper (in *Henry IV, Part 1*) (1d). In Present-day English, *lady* may still be used to denote a woman of rank (1e) or distinction, as in the "First Lady" of the United States. (Though the origin of her name is disputed, Stefani Germanotta, aka Lady Gaga, claims to have chosen "Lady" because "Lady has such connotations."[1])

(1)   a. "My **lady** Prioresse, by youre leve,/ So that I wiste I sholde yow nat greve,/ I wold demen that ye tellen sholde/ A tale next, if so were that ye wolde. (1387 Chaucer, *Canterbury Tales* B.Sh 447–50)

            'My lady Prioress, by your leave, if I knew I should not grieve you, I would judge that you should tell a tale next, if it were so that you would'

        b. GRATIANO: My lord Bassanio and **my gentle lady**,/ I wish you all the joy that you can wish; (1596–97 *Merchant of Venice* III.ii; OSS)

        c. EARL OF GLOUCESTER: **Naughty lady**,/ These hairs which thou dost ravish from my chin/ Will quicken, and accuse thee. (1605–6 *King Lear* III. vii; OSS)

        d. HOSTESS QUICKLY: O Jesu, my lord the prince!
            HENRY V: How now, **my lady** the hostess! what sayest thou to me? (1596–7 *Henry IV, Part I* II.iv; OSS; quoted from U. Busse 2003: 198–199)

        e. 7TH CALLER: Evansville, Indiana I was wondering, **Lady Thatcher**, do you have a hobby? (1995 CNN_King; COCA)

Lady is now more often used in polite contexts without any reference to rank (as in 2a). In such cases, there may be an implication that the lady possesses genteel qualities, as shown in the quotation in (2b).

---

[1] See www.thelist.com/281348/the-bizarre-story-of-how-lady-gaga-got-her-name.

(2)   a. MARTIN: … Thank you, **ladies**, so much for joining us. Ms-WATERS: Thank you for having me. Ms-SWANK: Thank you so much. (2010 *Tell Me More*; COCA)

b. "Doctor, don't you offer chairs to **ladies**?" "Certainly. If they are **ladies**." (1970 Hazzard, *Bay of Noon*; COHA)

Ladies and gentlemen is a vocative used in formal contexts (3a), and the expression may also be used entirely formulaically, especially in welcoming addresses, with bleaching of the honorific aspect. Nonetheless, the sense of *ladies* (and *gentlemen)* as referring to people of distinction or refinement is not entirely lost (see 3b).

(3)   a. Your Excellency, Mr. Mayor, Governor Pataki, Senators Schumer and Clinton, distinguished guests on the dais, **ladies and gentlemen**, I am honored to join you this evening. (2001 Fox_HC; COCA)

b. Well, our patrons are **ladies and gentlemen**, and they'll ignore any protesters that may be there. (2002 Associated Press: An Interview with Augusta's Hootie Johnson; COCA)

Lady has undergone pejoration as a term of address, when it is used in bare form with "overtones of brusqueness or hostility" (OED, s.v. *lady*, n., def. 4), as in "Hey, lady" or "Look, lady." This usage appears in the first quarter of the twentieth century (4a). Polite uses of bare *lady* can occur but seem dialectal (4b).

(4)   a. Hey, **lady**, you better answer to what I ask him. (1932 *Number 17*; Movies)

b. Gee, please, **lady**, can I have a dance?' (1992 NPR_ATC; COCA)

Young lady and *little lady* are often impolite terms of address, used in cases of anger or impatience (5a) or in a patronizing manner (5b); *young lady* is rarely used in a neutral sense (5c) except when plural (*several young ladies were present*).

(5)   a. Go to your room, **young lady**, you're grounded." (2007 CBS SatEarly; COCA)

b. You'll recognize it, **little lady**, when you see it. There is nothing in the world looks like it except more gold (1998 ABC_GMA; COCA)

c. Good for you, **young lady**. I am glad. (2002 *Literary Review*; COCA)

Finally, since the rise of feminism in the 1960s there has been a reaction against the use of *lady* as a synonym for *woman* since the genteel qualities it seems to imply (of a demure, modest, or subservient creature) are seen as demeaning and patronizing.[2] There is also a sense that it objectifies women as sexual objects. This backlash can be seen in (6a), where the older Terry Gross is questioning the younger Lena Dunham about the name of her television series, *Girls*. The

---

[2] See https://helloclue.com/articles/culture/lets-talk-about-word-lady

use of *ladies* in service contexts (where "polite" forms are used between both server and customer and customer and server; see Leech 1999: 112–113) points to the difficulty it can cause for nonbinary and trans people (6b).

(6)   a.   When I was in my late teens and 20s, my friends and I insisted on calling each other and having other people call us women. It was the era of the women's movement, and we weren't girls, we were women, and we certainly weren't dames, we were women, and we weren't, like, **ladies**, we were women. (2013 Fresh Air; COCA)

         b.   For example, like, once I start to see myself as nonbinary, if a host at a restaurant says, right this way, **ladies**, I just, like – I start to get really angry 'cause I'm like, I'm dressed like a man. (2017 Fresh Air; COCA)

7.3   Pronominal Terms of Address – Approaches

In a landmark article, Brown and Gilman (1960) discuss the origin of the politeness uses of the second-person pronouns, which they describe as T and V (using the Latin pronouns, singular *tu* and plural *vos*). The plural form was used to address the Latin emperor in the fourth century. In the medieval vernacular languages, this usage spread to other figures of power, including within the family, though Brown and Gilman admit that "[t]here was much inexplicable fluctuation between T and V" (255). The usage in medieval Europe was based on an asymmetric "power semantic": the superior says T and receives V. Also, among equals, V was used in the upper classes and T in the lower classes. While this system holds in a relatively static and hierarchical society, Brown and Gilman see it gradually being replaced by a symmetrical "solidarity semantic" as social mobility and equalitarianism grow. Here, among equals, differences (which are not based on power) lead to the use of V and similarities lead to the use of T. But the spread of this system to unequals puts the two systems in conflict in two cases: when an inferior addresses a superior with whom they are in solidarity (is the V of the power system or the T of the solidarity system appropriate?) and when a superior addresses an inferior with whom they are not in solidarity (is the T of the power system or the V of the solidarity system appropriate?). These are resolved in favor of solidarity, so, for example, a child uses T to a parent and an employer uses V to an employee, respectively. The triumph of the solidarity principle gives rise to the informal/formal T/V distinction we see at work in modern European languages such as French, German, and Italian. But Brown and Gilman recognize that English followed a rather different path in which the two-tier system was lost. They also recognize that violations of the norms of usage can have expressive effects, such as the use of T (in place of V) to express contempt and anger, or the use of V (in place of T) to express admiration or respect.

The apparent lack of systematicity in the use of second-person pronouns in Middle and Early Modern English calls into question the validity of the Brown and Gilman model. As Lass notes, English never developed a rigid hierarchical opposition, but rather functioned with a "loose, unstable and pragmatically more subtle" system (1999: 149). Especially problematic are the frequent and apparently arbitrary fluctuations between the pronouns that we see in English. This is what Brown and Gilman (1989: 178) call "retractability," the possibility for speakers to switch back and forth between *you* and *thou*, even within the same turn. Retractability distinguishes the English system from the systems found in modern European languages, where once the shift from formal to familiar occurs, there can be no change back. Wales (1983) argues that Brown and Gilman's system cannot explain the fluctuations in English, nor can it explain the emotive functions of *thou*. For Brown and Gilman, the emotive use arises out of the "solidarity semantic" which comes to replace the "power semantic," but in English we see the two types of uses coexisting in the medieval period. Wales argues, rather, that the use of *thou* "for the expression of deep emotions and intimacy of feeling is the natural outcome of its common occurrence in informal, especially private speech" (115). While *you* would be associated with "polite" usage, *thou* would be "non-polite" (either familiar or non-polite).

An alternative approach to understanding the use of the second-person pronouns is in terms of markedness. This concept was first introduced by Quirk (1971). He argues that *you* is unmarked, "not so much 'polite' as 'not impolite' ... [and] not so much 'formal' and 'not informal'." This means that *thou* is the marked or "conspicuous" form that serves a number of special functions: to mark solemnity and formality in religious discourse, and to express contempt, anger, intimacy, (filial) affection, and so on. The concept of markedness here has been criticized, perhaps unfairly. It is said that this theory reduces *thou* to expressive uses and that it fails to recognize that *you* may be marked in certain contexts. But Quirk recognizes that the use of *thou* and *you* is a matter of "active contrast": both the use of *thou* where *you* is expected and the use of *you* where *thou* is expected can carry special meaning. It is also argued that the norm/deviant model suggested by the concept of markedness cannot explain the frequent examples of switching found in literary texts. While this is perhaps true – because as we will see below, interpreting such switches in Shakespeare in particular depends on complex literary interpretations of character and plot – the concept of markedness provides a useful benchmark for measuring the use of *you* and *thou*.

7.4   The *Thou/You* Distinction in Middle English

There is no evidence in Old English for a distinction between *þū* and *ȝē* other than for one of number. But sporadic uses of singular *ye* begin to appear in early

Middle English, and by the fourteenth century, it is common, especially among the upper ranks: by one scholar's count there are 1,426 instances of singular *ye/ you/your* and 1,734 instances of singular *thou/thee/thy* in Chaucer's work (Mazzon 2000: 136). The medieval system is succinctly expressed by Walter Skeat in his edition of Chaucer's works:

Thou is the language of the lord to a servant, of an equal to an equal, and expresses also companionship, love, permission, defiance, scorn, threatening; whilst *ye* is the language of a servant to a lord, and of compliment, and further expresses honour, submission, or entreaty (1894: V, 175).

By the fifteenth century, we find instances of the verbs *thouen* 'to address (a person) with the pronoun *thou*, esp. as a sign of familiarity or contempt' (MED, s.v. *thouen*; OED, s.v. *thou*, v.) and *yēen* 'to address (a person) by the pronoun *you*, esp. as a mark or respect, deference, or formality' (MED, s.v. *yēen*; OED, s.v. *you*, v.).

What has puzzled scholars about Middle English is the flexibility of second-person pronominal usage and its apparent randomness, especially the "retract-ability" of the system, involving switches back and forth between *you* and *thou* among the same interlocutors, even in the same turn. Burnley (1983, 2003) establishes a flowchart to explain the usage of *thou* and *ye* in Chaucer (see Figure 7.1). The criteria determining usage include power, familiarity, intimacy, age, and status as well as genre. He makes a distinction between non-courtly genres (learned, religious, and "unsophisticated" discourse among the peasant class), where *thou* is the norm, and courtly genres, where an unfamiliar addressee is always addressed as *ye* and a familiar addressee receives *thou* or *ye* depending on intimacy, age, and social status. The diagonal line path represents the choice made when any one or more of these criteria are not salient; that is, *ye* is the norm. This use of *ye* is a reflection of negative politeness (see Chapter 5), or "part of the value system which medieval people called *curtesie*," the code of deference and respect (2003: 35). Importantly, Burnley also recognizes that speakers may choose pronominal forms that do not follow the flowchart but are "contextually deter-mined"; that is, there are no "unbreakable rules" in Middle English. He divides these non-conforming choices into "affective," "rhetorical," and "genre" switches. The affective switch from *thou* to *ye* may indicate detachment, distancing, formal-ity, objectivity, rejection, or repudiation. The switch from *ye* to *thou* may be used to intimidate or insult, to address children, or in a joking or patronizing way. It may also express solidarity or intimacy. Rhetorical switches refer to role-playing, or changes in modes of address, as in an adult being addressed in the mode appropri-ate for a child, or an equal addressed in the mode appropriate for an inferior. Finally, the genre criterion refers to different pronominal uses promoted by different genres, such as the fabliaux, heroic tales, courtly romances, saints' lives, sermons, and so on. The many factors involved in the use of *thou* and *ye*

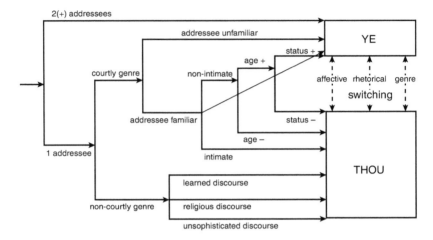

Figure 7.1 Flowchart for the use of *thou* and *ye* in Middle English (from Burnley 2003: 29)

(David Burnley. 2003. The *T/V* pronouns in Middle English literature. In Irma Taavitsainen and Andreas H. Jucker (eds.), *Diachronic perspectives on address term systems*. Amsterdam: John Benjamins, 29. https://benjamins.com/catalog/pbns .107.03bur. Reprinted with permission.)

and the changes the system undergoes during the ME period leave Burnley skeptical about the possibility of explaining all instances of pronominal usage.

In a series of articles, Jucker (2000b, 2006b, 2020) argues that pronoun usage in Middle English is "more principled than previously assumed" (2020: 54). He sees three factors determining pronoun usage:

• social status;
• the relation between interactants; and
• situational status.

The first two are both relatively stable and fixed, though Jucker differs from Burnley in seeing the latter as scalar, not binary. He agrees that familiarity, social status, and age are basic criteria, but for him, interactional status – which incorporates both the affective and rhetorical criteria identified by Burnley – is the most important dimension and may override the others. Interactional status is temporary and unstable, with interactants having to make "on-the-spot" choices between pronoun forms, depending on how the interaction is developing. Thus, he brings Burnley's affective and rhetorical factors to the fore, giving them precedence over the relatively stable norms set out in Figure 7.1. But knowledge of these stable norms must, I would argue, underlie any on-the-spot decision to either conform with or flout expected usage. Jucker (2006b, 2020) analyzes episodes from several tales in the *Canterbury Tales* (see also Mazzon 2000). Unlike Burnley and other scholars who consider pronoun choice to be a matter of default choices with deviations, Jucker believes that the analysis of individual dialogues is necessary on the micro-level. For example, in "The Wife of Bath's Tale," when the Knight meets the old woman who will ultimately help him answer the question he has been posed ("What do women most desire?"), they initially address each other deferentially with *ye*. As the old woman realizes her power over the Knight, she begins to address him with *thou* (7a). In addressing the queen, the Knight, of course, uses the deferential *ye* (7b). Later the old woman reminds the Knight that he must fulfill his promise to marry her, and she again uses *thou* (7c), though in combination with the deferential *sir knyght*. Once married, however, the old woman treats the Knight with the deference due husbands by addressing him as *ye* (7d). The Knight is unhappy in this marriage because of his wife's age and ugliness: *So wo was hym, his wyf looked so foule.* 'So woeful was he, his wife looked so ugly'. In this context, he addresses her as *thou* (7e). After being chastised by the old woman and lectured on the nature of nobility, the Knight realizes the need to cede power to her; this again leads to the use of deferential *ye* along with highly deferential nominal terms of address (7f).

(7)   a. "Plight me **thy** trouthe heere in myn hand," quod she, (l. 1009)

        "'Pledge your word to me here in my hand" she said,'

    b. "Dooth as **yow** list; I am heer at **youre** wille." (l. 1042)

        "'Do as you please; I am here subject to your will.'"

    c. "Bifore the court thanne preye I **thee**, sir knyght,"/ Quod she, "that **thou** me take unto **thy** wyf; (ll. 1054–5)

        "'Before the court then I pray you, sir knight,"/ Said she, "that thou take me as thy wife,'

    d. And seyde, "O deere housbonde, *benedicitee*!/ Fareth every knyght thus with his wyf as **ye**?" (ll. 1087–8)

        'And said, "O dear husband, bless me! Does every knight behave in this way with his wife as you do?"'

    e. "**Thou** art so loothly, and so oold also,/ . . . That litel wonder is thogh I walwe and wynde." (ll. 1100–2)

        "'You art so loathsome, and so old also, ... That there is little wonder is though I toss and twist about.'"

    f. "My lady and my love, and wyf so deere,/ I put me in **youre** wise governance;" (ll. 1230–1)

        "'My lady and my love, and wife so dear, I put myself in your wise governance;'"

Jucker's claim is that *ye* is a marker of deference (of politeness and respect), often associated with the speaker's inferiority, but it is not a marker of distance. *Thou* is used when no deference is needed, and in situations of the speaker's superiority. Jucker does not see affection and intimacy, which have been suggested as underlying the use of *thou* in non-canonical contexts, as explanatory principles; he points out, for example, that husbands and wives typically use *ye* to each other out of respect, but this does not indicate a lack of affection.

7.5   The *Thou/You* Distinction in Early Modern English

The use of *you* and *thou* in Early Modern English has been the subject of exhaustive scholarly study and debate, in main focused on usage in Shakespeare, where switches between the pronouns among interlocutors are frequent, and affective uses are complex and subject to varying interpretations. As Roger Lass observes, "The history of this system is intricate and not well understood (alternatively, not entirely coherent)" (1999: 148). What all scholars seem to agree on is that the change to singular *you* was well under way in the sixteenth century, with *you* the choice for the middle and upper ranks of society and increasingly also for the lower classes. *You* outnumbered *thou*. *Thou*, though it could denote asymmetries in rank, was very frequently used to express heightened emotion. During the seventeenth century *thou* retreated to specialized (religious and literary) contexts and dialectal use. Thus, Shakespeare wrote during a crucial time in the development of the second-person pronominal system. However, we cannot be confident that Shakespeare's literary usage actually represents contemporary norms; it has been suggested that it might be old-fashioned, overusing *thou* forms, which are recessive by his time. It has even been claimed that it "is unlikely to mirror actual usage in the Early Modern period" (Hope 2003: 77). The partial and perhaps biased nature of literary evidence (such as Shakespearian usage) is thus evidence of the "bad data" problem that historical pragmaticists must contend with (see Chapter 2, §2.5). For this reason, we try to garner as much and as varied evidence as possible and, more importantly, look at what we know about the use of *thou* and *you* in records of actual speech of the period, that is, in trials, depositions (written transcripts of oral statements made by witnesses, plaintiffs, and defendants), and personal letters. Although we cannot know what changes have been introduced by transcribers and scribes in these records (further aspects of the bad data problem), we can be fairly confident that we are close to the authentic speech of the period.

Trial records and depositions: Using the trial and deposition records contained in the *Corpus of English Dialogues* (1560–1760), Walker (2007) finds that *thou* decreases in frequency but does not disappear. In trials, *thou* is rare – only 8 percent of the total – becoming extremely uncommon in the seventeenth and obsolete by the eighteenth century. Walker attributes the rarity of *thou* to the formal setting and social distance of the courtroom. Apart from its use in formulaic phrases (e.g., *art thou guilty or not guilty?*), *thou* may be used by the higher-ranked participants (judges and lawyers), sometimes to express impatience/anger or to bully/cajole witnesses but also sometimes to express fatherly concern/condescension. The case of depositions is more complex, although there is a general decline in the use of *thou* during the period, from a high of 62 percent to a low of 21 percent at the end of the period. The more informal nature of depositions, often concerning emotional or intimate affairs, is obviously more conducive to the use of *thou* for expressing both negative and positive affect. Rank is an important determinant in the use of the pronouns here. The upper classes use *you* almost exclusively among themselves, even in emotional contexts. The upper commoners (well-to-do farmers, retailers, urban craftsmen) increasingly prefer *you*, with the use of *thou* for strong emotion dropping off. Evidence for lower commoners (poorer farmers, rural craftsmen, servants, apprentices) is rather scanty, and most in this rank are women, but it appears that *thou* is the pronoun of choice. Servants give *you* to masters and receive *you* or *thou* (in emotional contexts). An intermediate, and perhaps somewhat socially insecure rank, is professionals (frequently clergymen), who give *you* to commoners but receive *thou*, and rarely use *thou* for emotional purposes. Apart from this, the usage is as one would expect by rules of deference (e.g., the higher ranks give *thou* and receive *you*, parents give *thou* to their children and receive *you*). Interestingly, Walker does not find that husbands address their wives with *thou* or are addressed by their wives with *you*, a commonly held belief.

An earlier study of depositions by Hope (1993) (using depositions held at Durham University) is not entirely consistent with Walker's study since he argues that *you* is the majority form as early as the 1560s and hence the "default, or neutral" pronoun, while *thou* is the marked form. The use of *thou* is motivated by positive (affectionate) or negative (angry, insulting) emotion, but there are many cases where *you* is used where *thou* would be expected, such as in exchanges among the lower classes. Like Walker, he does not find that spouses use asymmetric *thou/you* pronouns of address, nor is *thou* used among siblings. A more complete study of depositions from throughout England for the period 1560–1760 by Walker and Kytö (2011) shows that region is an important factor and confirms some initial findings by Walker. While *thou* declines over time after a peak in the period 1600–1649, there is a significant difference between the East and London, where *thou* is all but obsolescent by the early seventeenth century, and the North, where there is no real pattern of decline and *thou* represents 30 percent of second-person pronoun usage. The North is precisely the area where *thou* continues to have a dialectal presence. A similarly high frequency of *thou* usage is also found in Scottish depositions (Leitner 2013), where *thou* is also used dialectally. Unsurprisingly, Walker and Kytö find that the gentry do not use *thou*; merchants, professionals, and well-to-do commoners disfavor *thou*, but lesser farmers, craftsmen, servants, and laborers continue to use *thou* more than *you*. The evidence of lower-class usage is rather scanty and difficult to interpret, with *thou* falling out of use gradually in different periods at different times. It may be that the context –*you* in business contexts and *thou* for emotional contexts – is more important than rank or region.

Personal letters: Lass (1999) presents a brief study of pronoun usage in the fifteenth-century Paston and Cely family letters as well as in later personal correspondence. Early letters tend to be formal and focused on business matters and fairly consistently use *you*. By the sixteenth century, the topics of letters become more intimate, addressing personal concerns, gossip, and matters of the heart, and a distinction arises: *you* is "distal," used in business contexts, to one's superiors, and in unreal conditions; *thou* is used within the family unit and focuses on the factual and present events. Lass (1999: 151) provides an example from Katherine Paston's letter to her son William, dated 1664:

(8)   My good child the Lord bless **the** euer more in they goings ovtt and thy Cominges in. I was very glad to here by **your** first letter that **you** wer so saffly arriued at **your** wished portt. but more glad to read **thy** louing promises ... which I hope ... shall always redound to **thy** chiefest good ... I could wish that **you** would settle **your self** to certin howers tasks euery day **you** rise ...

Katherine begins with intimate *thou*, but then shifts to *you* when discussing more general aspects of the journey; she returns to *thou* when reflecting on her son's inner state, and again reverts to the less personal *you* when issuing a maternal command. Lass's findings thus give support to the claim that *thou* retreated to the private sphere in Early Modern English (Nevalainen 2006a).

   Nevala's (2002) study of the pronoun forms in letters among family and friends in the *Corpus of Early English Correspondence* shows that *you* is the preferred form throughout the period. *Thou* use increases in the seventeenth century, with more users of *thou* and more frequent use of *thou*, with a regional spread of use from London to the outlying areas, and a social spread in users from the gentry to other classes and in the recipients of *thou* from children and siblings to a greater range of relations (spouses, cousins, nieces, nephews). But there is an "abrupt decline" in the eighteenth century. Age, power, and social role (but not rank) may influence the use of *thou*, as may intimacy and affection, but some uses of *thou* are "obscure." For example, Nevala finds it difficult to explain the pronoun switches by Katherine Paston – a prolific user of *thou* – in an earlier letter to her (young) son (dated 1625):

(9)   and seinge I goe not to London this summer **thow** mayst wear **thy** damaske sute for I wold not haue it growe to littell for **the**:/ but wear it fayerly: I send **you** now **your** Crimson sattin sute: to wear in whot wether. (quoted in Nevala 2002: 135)

Literary texts: U. Busse (2002) finds that in the corpus of Shakespeare's plays, *you* predominates, by a ratio of 1 to 0.7, and that *thou* regresses over time. In the early plays, including the history plays and early tragedies (1598 and earlier), *thou* is more common, while in the later plays (>1600), *you* is more common. In the comedies, which date from the span of Shakespeare's career, *thou* has the lowest frequency, contrary to expectation. The higher use of *thou* in the tragedies and histories is due to its use for emotional effect, while the higher use of *you* in comedies is evidence, for U. Busse, that "*you* was the 'normal' pronoun of rapport between middle and also lower-class characters from 1600 onwards" (2003: 284). In a sampling of comedies from the *Corpus of English Dialogues*, Walker (2007) also finds a decline in the use of *thou* from 24 percent to 5 percent; while *thou* can be used for expressing positive and negative emotion, *you* is "the pronoun used, especially in less emotional contexts, by characters of all ranks" (234).

Shakespeare's usage of *thou* and *you* has been the subject of extensive study by both literary and linguistic scholars. His plays exhibit a sophisticated and subtle use of the pronoun forms, where many instances follow the expected power dynamic, but pronoun usage can also serve purposes of characterization and plot development, and switches back and forth between the pronouns within dialogues can capture transient changes in status or emotion between characters. The switches often require subtle and nuanced interpretation and many "remain unexplained" (Mazzon 2010: 262). However, as Stein points out, "There could be no meaningful variation if there was not constancy enough to establish what is normal, socially determined use" (2003: 252). Stein finds that *you* is the unmarked form in most cases. The mutual use of *thou* is infrequent; it is the unmarked form when addressing servants or attendants, among (common as opposed to court) servants, among members of the lower classes, and for addresses to oneself or to gods/goddesses; among fools, jesters, and the insane *thou* is frequent, though there is considerable fluctuation. Hope (2003) adds that *thou* is "almost mandatory" in asides or apostrophes, when addressing an absent person, a ghost or spirit, or an animal, and in certain religious, legal, or chivalric contexts, which are formal and archaic. But Stein finds that approximately 30 percent of the pronominal forms represent marked uses, where *thou* and less frequently *you* is used for its expressive potential, both positive and negative: *thou* can express intimacy, affection, or respect on the one hand or scorn, disapproval, anger, or insult on the other, while *you* can express distance or disapproval on the one hand or elevation, respect, or formality on the other. Marked uses do not occur in the very highest and lowest ends of the social scale, but primarily among the middle and higher classes.

The details of Shakespeare's pronominal usage can only be touched on here (see, e.g., Mazzon 2003). Social inferiors frequently receive *thou* and return *you*, as in this conversation between Portia and her maid-in-waiting Nerissa (10), but servants can also be addressed with *you*:

(10)   NERISSA: But what warmth is there in **your** affection towards any of these princely suitors that are already come?
        PORTIA: I pray **thee**, over-name them; and as **thou** namest them, I will describe them; (1596–7 *Merchant of Venice* I.ii; OSS)

Among male characters, the pronominal term is determined by rank and intimacy, and may mark in- and out-group membership. Othello addresses the high-born Cassio with *you* (11a) and the lower-ranked Iago with *thou* (11b):

(11)   a.   CASSIO: The duke does greet **you**, general, . . .
             OTHELLO: What is the matter, think **you**? (1603–4 *Othello* II.i; OSS)
        b.   IAGO: Ha! I like not that.
             OTHELLO: What doest **thou** say?
             IAGO: Nothing, my lord: or if – I know not what. (1603–4 *Othello* III. iii; OSS)

Since *you* is the usual form of address among men of high status, the use of *thou* can be insulting. In a famous passage in *Twelfth Night*, Sir Toby Belch advises Sir Andrew Aguecheek to use *thou* in his challenge to his rival "Cesario" (Viola in disguise). At the same time, Sir Toby is condescending (and perhaps insulting) in addressing Sir Andrew with *thou*:

(12)   TOBY BELCH: Go, write it in a martial hand; . . . taunt him with the licence of ink: if **thou thou**'st him some thrice, it shall not be amiss; (1602 *Twelfth Night* III.ii; OSS)

Spouses use *you* to one another but may switch to *thou* to express strong emotion. In (13) Desdemona addresses her husband with *you*; Othello initially addresses her with the endearment *chuck* but switches to *thou* as he becomes suspicious of her:

(13)   DESDEMONA: . . . Come now, **your** promise.
        OTHELLO: What promise, chuck?
        DESDEMONA: I have sent to bid Cassio come speak with **you**.
        OTHELLO: I have a salt and sorry rheum offends me;/ Lend me **thy** handkerchief. (1603–4 *Othello* III.iv; OSS)

Lovers also use *you*, as in example (14), where *you* accompanies the intimate terms of address "my most fair Bianca" and "sweet love"; but lovers may also switch to *thou* in moments of intimacy:

(14)   BIANCA: Save **you**, friend Cassio!
        CASSIO: What make **you** from home?/ How is it with **you**, my most fair Bianca?/ I' faith, sweet love, I was coming to **your** house. (1603–4 *Othello* III.iv; OSS)

While parents and (adult) children generally exchange *you*, a parent may use *thou* to express tenderness or parental concern. For example, Gertrude often uses *thou* in addressing her son Hamlet, but he invariably returns *you*. In (15) Gertrude begins with intimate *thou*. Hamlet's *you*, though seemingly respectful, is cold and distancing, and she rebukes him for his reply using *you*:

(15)   HAMLET: Now, mother, what's the matter?
        GERTRUDE: Hamlet, **thou** has thy father much offended.
        HAMLET: Mother, **you** have my father much offended.
        GERTRUDE: Come, come, **you** answer with an idle tongue. (1599–1601 *Hamlet* III.iv; OSS)

Finally, the use of *thou* among the lower classes is somewhat less clear. As we saw above, in authentic texts, the lower classes (in southern England) use *you*. For Shakespeare, the unmarked form among servants is *thou*, as in (16a); his usage may thus be seen as somewhat old-fashioned. In (16b), Rosalind, the daughter of a Duke but disguised here as the forester "Ganymede," begins by addressing the shepherd Corin with *you*; while he continues to use *you*, she slips into using *thou*. Finally, in (17) we see the use of *you/ye* between the professional characters, Holofernes, a schoolmaster, and Nathaniel, a curate.

(16)   a. SERVANT 2: Let's follow the old Earl, and get the bedlam/ To lead him where he would . . .
            SERVANT 3: Go **thou**. I'll fetch some flax and whites of eggs/ To apply to his bleeding face. (1605–6 *King Lear* III.vii; OSS)
        b. ROSALIND: Peace, I say. Good even to **you**, friend.
            CORIN: And to you, gentle sir, and to **you** all.
            . . .
            CORIN: The young swain that **you** saw here but erewhile,/ That little cares for buying any thing.
            ROSALIND: I pray **thee**, if it stand with honesty,/ Buy **thou** the cottage, pasture, and the flock,/ And **thou** shalt have to pay for it of us. (1599–1600 *As You Like It* II.iv; OSS)

(17)   HOLOFERNES: The deer was, as **you** know, sanguis, in blood . . .
        NATHANIEL: Truly, Maser Holofernes, the epithets are sweetly varied, . . . But, sir, I assure **ye**, it was a buck of the first head. (1594–5 *Love's Labours Lost* IV. ii; OSS)

Jucker (2020) concludes that while Chaucer's use of the second-person pronouns is related to politeness (see Chapter 5), in Shakespeare, the concept of affect is much more important. He surmises that the loss of *thou* may relate to its increased emotionality, which dictated against its use in neutral contexts. Mazzon (2010) mentions that *thou* may have been lost because it became "offensive." Wales (1983) suggests a number of sociolinguistic factors accounting for the loss of *thou*:

- standardization, which favored the *you* form;
- "change from above," with *you* forms spreading down the social scale in either conscious or unconscious imitation of the habits of the upper classes;
- urbanization and the breakdown of the medieval social stratification and a subsequent blurring of social ranks (leading to the use of polite *you* to avoid offense) and the rise of a nouveau-riche middle class of merchants and tradesmen, who followed upper-class usage;
- the (negative) association of *thou* with dissenting and radical religious groups such as the Quakers and the Levellers, who had adopted *thou* as their standard pronoun; and
- the association of *thou* with biblical and archaic language, such as the King James Bible and the Book of Common Prayer.

The result is that *thou* becomes a special form, removed from normal, everyday usage, and *you* the all-purpose second-person form. Of course, this leaves English without a singular/plural distinction in the second person.

7.6   Nominal Terms of Address in Present-day English

A vocative can be defined as follows: "an optional element, usually a noun phrase, denoting the one or more persons to whom the sentence is addressed. It is either a CALL, drawing the attention of the person or persons addressed, singling them out from others in hearing ... or an ADDRESS, expressing the speaker's relationship or attitude to the person or persons addressed" (Quirk et al. 1985: 773). Among the three functions – getting someone's attention, identifying someone as the addressee, and establishing or reinforcing social relationships – it is the last which often determines which vocative term is used: "vocative terms generally convey a considerable amount about the speaker's social relations or emotive attitude toward the address, and their primary or sole purpose is often to give expression to this kind of meaning" (Huddleston and Pullum 2002: 523).

Most vocatives can be used in two ways, as vocatives proper (18a) and as referring terms (18b); however, some are more often vocative than referring (e.g., *Mommy*) and others are more often referring than vocative (e.g., *niece*).

(18)   a. You forget, **cousin**, how very little any man might have to gain by compromising me." (2012 Archer, *Demon's Bride*; COCA)
         b. My **cousin** Anatoly said I could trust him. (2019 *The Magazine of Fantasy and Science Fiction*; COCA)

Vocatives fall into a number of different categories, as shown in Table 7.1. Most vocatives can be expanded by (a range of) modifiers: *good Margaret, you smart young fellow, my dear old friend, you filthy liar, my sweet love.*

Table 7.1 *Range of vocative forms (based on Quirk et al. 1985: 773–775; Biber et al. 1999: 1108–1109; Leech 1999; Huddleston and Pullum 2002: 522–523)*

Category	Examples
Personal names	
Given or first name	*Barbara, Jing, Abdul, Mai*
Surname or last name	*Jones, Singh, Wu, Nguyen*
Familiarized form of first name (shortened or pet names)	*Babs, Patsy, Ron, Kim*
Kinship terms (formal and familiar)	
Family	*brother, sister, father, papa, mother, mummy*
Extended family	*aunt, auntie, grandmother, granny, cousin, nephew*
"Familiarizers" or general terms	*guys, man, dude, mate, buddy, folks, bro, ladies and gentlemen, son, old chap, young man, young lady*
Titles	
Honorific titles (of respect or status)	*sir, lady, lord, ma'am, madam, your Majesty, your Excellency, your Honour, Mr./Mrs.* + surname, *Miss, Ms., father* (priest), *sister* (nun), *admiral*
Professions or occupational titles (may be combined with surname)	*doctor, nurse, officer, professor, (Mr./ Madam) president, prime minister, bishop, cabbie, conductor, Vicar*
Endearments	*honey, baby, babe, sweetheart, love, dear/darling, sweetie(pie)*
Epithets (expressing an evaluation)	
Favorable	*my love, my darling, my beauty*
Unfavorable	*(you) bastard, idiot, liar, slowpoke, swine*
Second-person pronouns	*you there, you with the glasses, you guys*
Indefinites	*somebody, anybody, someone, anyone, whoever you are, whoever said that, What's your name*

The use of first names is becoming increasingly common in Present-day English and has become almost the norm (see Chapter 5, §5.8, on "Camaraderie Politeness"). In Leech's study (1999), first names (full and shortened) represent 60 percent of the vocatives used, while title + surname combinations are less than 5 percent and honorifics less than 1 percent. The use of the last name alone is receding, but may still be found in male (or female)-bonding in contexts such as boarding schools, sports teams, or the military. Use of the full name is restricted to certain contexts. Some kinship terms, such as *Mother* or *Daddy*, have become proper nouns (19a), but other kinship names seldom function this way (e.g., *daughter*). In contemporary discourse, familiarizers are also becoming increasingly common, especially in American English. In Leech's corpus study, familiarizers constitute 22 percent of all vocatives; they express camaraderie rather than intimacy and may be somewhat disrespectful (19b). *Guys* is often thought to be gender-neutral (19c) (though a recent informal poll of my Canadian undergraduate students suggests this is not the case). Note that familiarizers (like honorifics, endearments, epithets, especially unfavorable ones, and second-person pronouns) do not require that the speaker know the addressee, while others (personal names and kinship terms) do require the speaker and addressee to be acquainted (or introduced).

(19)   a. And he said to her, You know, **Mother**, I am not a comedian. (2003 NPR_TalkNation; COCA)
       b. "No offense, **guys**, but we need some new blood." (2019 Campbell, *Quarterway House*; COCA)
       c. Jenna-Bush-Hager: Welcome back this Tuesday. Meredith is in for Hoda. Earlier, **guys**, I spit out my gum in a little piece of paper (2019 NBC_Today; COCA)

With the increase of familiarizers and first names, honorific titles have declined and become more marked. Thus, we find a "progressive familiarization of addressing and naming habits" (Leech 1999: 114), with familiarizers, endearments, and kinship terms twice as common as honorifics and title + surname combinations. Honorific titles and occupational titles, which frequently overlap, may be used either alone or in conjunction with names (20a–b). Some titles (*professor*, *doctor*, *vicar*) are applied at all times, while others only when the person is acting in that capacity (*cabbie*, *waiter*, *conductor*).

(20)   a. Martin: So given all that, **Professor**, what is your take on the students' decision to paint over the poem with one of their choosing? (2018 NPR_ATCW; COCA)
       b. Mr-Mac-Neil: What do you see, **Father Greeley**, as the Pope's role in the political debate in America right now on welfare programs? (1995 PBS_Newshour; COCA)

Endearments and positive epithets also overlap. Endearments signal affection and intimacy, though many are used as conventionalized terms of address (such as *love* in British English or *dear* in American English) (compare 21a and 21b).

(21)   a. Every time Isabelle said, "Kelle, I need this or I want that," he'd be like, "Okay, here, **dear**, here's the credit card." (2009 ABC_20/20; COCA)
       b. Out to the lines. Christine in Louisiana. Hi, Christine. Hi, **dear**, whats [sic] your question? (2011 CNN_Grace; COCA)

An epithet expresses "some quality or attribute which the speaker or writer regards as characteristic of the person or thing described" (OED, s.v. *epithet*, n., def. 1a). Note that favorable epithets often occur with *my*, unfavorable with *you* (22a–b). The use of the second-person pronouns as vocatives is "markedly impolite," according to Quirk et al. (1985), as are indefinites (22c):

(22)   a. "Let me tell your fortune, **my beauty**," she said. # I waved my hand at her. (2003 *Success d'Estime*; COCA)

    b. Sledge hung from the door of the car and shouted. "Hey, **you, jackass**! You up there in the cab. Both your pals are dead." (2001 Jakes, *On Secret Service*; COCA)

    c. "So tell me, **whoever you are**," she went on, "what are you doing here in the middle of the night?" (2004 Wolitzer, *The Wife: A Novel*; COCA)

Terms of address exist on a scale from closest/most familiar and intimate to most remote/least friendly/most respectful. Leech (1999) suggests the following ordering:

> endearments > family terms (e.g., *mommy*, *grandma*, *dad*) > familiarizers > familiarized first names (i.e., shortened and pet names) > full first names > titles + surname > honorifics

It is possible to equate this to a scale ranging from positive politeness (expressing camaraderie or solidarity) to negative politeness (expressing deference and respect), as was discussed in Chapter 5. In her study of Early Modern English, Raumolin-Brunberg (1996: 171) suggests a scale, encompassing both adjectival modifiers and nominal terms of address. Most positively polite are terms of endearment and nicknames collated with positive adjectives such as *kind* and *loving*. Somewhat less positive are family terms. Moving toward the negative end of the scale, we find titles (e.g., *captain*), and at the far end of the negative scale are honorific titles (*lord*) and respect adjectives (e.g., *worshipful*, *honored*). Below we look in more detail at how this can be applied to historical stages of English.

7.7 Nominal Terms of Address in Old and Middle English

Historically, the study of nominal address terms has focused on two areas: represented speech (in narrative and drama) and personal letters. One rewarding area of study has examined the interaction of nominal terms with the pronominal forms, *you* and *thou*.

Only one study has researched the use of nominal terms of address in Old English. Kohnen (2008b) focuses on three positive address terms, all of which occur primarily in religious texts: *leof* 'dear one', *broþor* 'brother', and *hlaford* 'lord'. *Leof* may be used by superiors to subordinates and vice versa; it may thus combine with intimate or family terms (*bearn* 'child', *cild* 'child', *dohter* 'daughter'), neutral terms (*men*), and authoritative terms (*cyning* 'king', *hlaford*). *Broþor* may indicate a blood brother, a fellow Christian, or a member of a religious order. Both *broþor* and *leof* express friendliness and affection. *Hlaford* is used to address God, Jesus, and saints, and in its rare uses as a term of address outside religious texts it indicates a fixed rank in a hierarchical society. Kohnen concludes that whereas the use of *broþor* and *leof* may represent positive politeness, it is more correct to see all three terms as a case of "discernment politeness" (see Chapter 5, §5.4), in which the speaker recognizes the principles of mutual obligation and kin loyalty which guide life in the hierarchical society of Early Medieval England (see Chapter 6, §6.5, on directives).

In Middle English we find a much expanded set of nominal terms of address, ranging from deference to endearment, which point to a system of positive/ negative politeness at work. However, scholarly work in this area remains scant, with a focus on individual fictional texts. Making generalizations can be difficult since the address terms used are often negotiated in context or may be used ironically or parodically. As Mazzon observes, "the pragmatic element of the situation seems as important as the social status of the addressee" (2000: 149). Nonetheless, considering the cooccurrence of address terms with *you* and *thou* in the *Canterbury Tales*, Mazzon is able to identify a number of terms as deferential (mostly occurring with *you*), including *sire*, *lord*, *lady*, *dame*, *madame*, and *maister*, and a number of non-deferential and intimate terms, including *freend*, *brother*, *cook*, *squyer* 'squire', *somnour* 'summoner', *messager* 'messenger', *juge* 'judge', *prest* 'priest', as well as terms of abuse and endearment. First names are used among intimates, generally in the lower classes. Already in Middle English, *sire* is being extended to men of all ranks as a polite term of address, as we see in this address of the Host to the socially lowly ranked shipman. Note the cooccurrence of polite *maister* and familiar *thou*:

(23)   "Wel seyd, by *corpus dominus*," quod oure Hoost,/ "Now longe moote thou saille by the cost/ **Sire** gentil maister, gentil maryneer!" (1387 Chaucer, *Canterbury Tales* B.Sh 435–7)

        "'Well said, by the body of our Lord," said our Host, "Now long may you sail by the coast, Sir gentle master, gentle mariner!'"

Given the complexity of *thou/you* use in Middle English, however (see above), we can find subtly nuanced interactions between nominal and pronominal address terms. For example, Palamon addressing his cousin Arcite (both knights) in "The Knight's Tale" uses *thou* in combination with *my leeve brother* to express solidarity (24a) but *thou* in combination with *false Arcite* to express contempt (24b) (Honegger 2003).

(24)   a. Neither of us in love to hyndre oother,/ Ne in noon oother cas, **my leeve brother**;/ But that **thou** sholdest trewely forthren me (1387 Chaucer, *Canterbury Tales* A.Kn 1135–1137)

           'Neither of us in love should hinder the other, nor in any other case, my dear brother, But rather you should truly help me'

        b. Nay, certes, **false Arcite, thow** shalt nat so. (1387 Chaucer, *Canterbury Tales* A.Kn 1145)

           'Nay, certainly, false Arcite, thou shalt not (do) so.'

While god(s) and goddesses are generally addressed with *thou*, Honegger (2003) finds interesting shifts between nominal and pronominal terms in Chaucer's "The Knight's Tale." Addressing the goddess Diana, Emelye begins with the expected combination of *goddess* and *thou*, but shifts to *lady* and deferential *you* as the goddess is humanized. Honegger also discusses the shifting terms of address among lovers. In the initial stage of wooing, where lovers are negotiating their relationships, they focus on the social hierarchy and are concerned with saving negative face, using deferential terms such as *dame/ madam/lady* with modifiers such as *swete* 'sweet', *dere* 'dear', and *my* and *sir/ lord* with similarly positive adjectives. Once the relationship has been success-fully established, the lovers switch to more familiar and intimate terms of address focused on positive face. These include designations of belovedness (*lemman*), sweetness (*sweting*), preciousness (*dere*), importance (*herte*), joy (*joye*), respect (*sire*), and so on.

7.8 Nominal Terms of Address in Early Modern English

Shakespeare: One branch of scholarship on vocatives in Early Modern English has focused on the extremely rich inventory of naming forms in Shakespeare. B. Busse (2006) finds 3,111 different types of vocatives in seventeen plays by Shakespeare, averaging about 500 tokens per play. For Replogle (1973), vocatives in Shakespeare "minutely trace all the vagaries of the political and social hier-archy" (172). Elizabethans were punctilious in their use of titles; usage was highly codified, taught in etiquette handbooks, and learned from childhood. Superiors were addressed with the honorific form corresponding to their highest honor, equals with more abbreviated forms, and inferiors with regular forms or no forms at all. Change in status, whether involving gain or loss, was properly denoted. Deviations from proper usage "made natural vehicles for dramatic emphasis which Shakespeare assumed his audience understood and which he fully exploited" (181). For example, inappropriate use of titles, such as the use of overly familiar forms, could constitute an insult. Omission of forms of address indicated extreme distress and lack of self-possession. Or the use of forms could indicate character, such as Mistress Quickly's overuse of vocatives as an indica-tion of her status as a social climber (in *Henry IV, Part 2*). Salmon (1967) provides an inventory of vocatives in Shakespeare; she includes personal names, relation-ship terms, generic terms of address (e.g., *man, woman, gentleman/woman, gentles, boy, lad, maid, wench*), terms indicating occupations, titles of courtesy (e.g., *lord, lady, sir, madam, mistress, sirrah, goodman/wife, dame*), and terms of endearment (e.g., *sweet, wag, bully, chuck, my joy, my heart*) and of abuse (e.g., *knave, rascal, rogue, slave, varlet, villain*) (see also Mazzon 2003; U. Busse 2003: 196). Brown and Gilman (1989) attempt to assign titles in Shakespeare absolute values based on power and distance: an adorned title (e.g., *gentle lady*) is +2, an unadorned title (e.g., *madam*), an honorific adjective and name (e.g., *good Hamlet*), and a name alone when used as an in-group marker are +1 or otherwise a neutral 0, while *sirrah* is −1. However, such a rigid scale is obviously unworkable. In a monograph-length study of vocatives in Shakespeare, B. Busse (2006) presents a detailed picture of vocatives as experiential, interpersonal, and textual markers that are highly multifunctional:

[Vocatives] are crucial to how interactants accumulate symbolic capital, construe their emotions, their relationships, their attitudes, their character, and their habitus … Vocatives construe the interplay between macro-contextual factors (institutions, power, social order) and micro-contextual aspects of the immediate situation (see Busse and Busse 2010: 258–259).

As in Present-day English, the value of address terms was not fixed. They could express a range of meanings in use; for example, *sirrah* could be used authoritatively, contemptuously, familiarly, or in a playful manner. Crystal and Crystal (2002: 8) conclude that for Shakespeare "[t]he naming practice performs a variety of expressive functions, shading from courtesy through endearment into sarcasm and insult."

U. Busse (2002: Ch. 6, 2003) is a systematic study of the relation of nominal terms of address (omitting personal names) and *thou/you* pronouns in Shakespeare. He finds that there is no absolute correlation between categories of vocatives and the two pronouns, but all vocatives exist on a scale of "*thou*fulness" or "*you*fulness." As would be expected, titles of courtesy, names of occupations, and terms denoting family relationships are strongly *you*ful, while generic terms, terms of abuse, and terms of endearment are strongly *thou*ful. But within each category, there is a range from *thou* to *you* cooccurrence, which demonstrates the nuanced differences between vocatives. For example, although *you* is the normal pronoun used with *lady*, there are several occasions where *thou* is used by a male speaker to a lady of rank, such as to a lover, from a husband to a wife, or from a royal father to a daughter. This makes it less *you*ful than *mistress*. Terms of family relationships range on the *you*ful scale from the highest (*sister*, *brother*) to the lowest (*husband*, *wife*). *Husband* and *wife* are almost equally balanced between the two pronouns, with frequent pronoun switches; this variability leads U. Busse to think that relationship was highly "negotiable." But there is not entire consistency here between the findings in the plays and findings in correspondence (see below). In between these two sets are *cousin* and *coz*. In earlier English, *cousin/coz* had much wider use than in Present-day English, applied to a range of relatives and in-laws as well as to non-relatives of the same rank (see Häcker 2019). Perhaps most surprising are U. Busse's findings concerning generic terms and terms of abuse, which both present a very mixed bag. For the latter, see Figure 7.2 (here

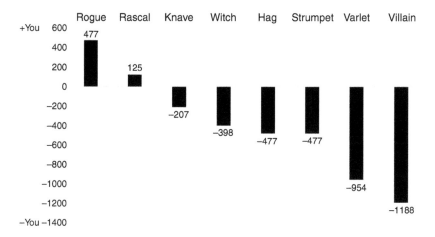

Figure 7.2 Terms of abuse on the scale from *you* to *thou* cooccurrence in Shakespeare (adapted from U. Busse 2003: 213)

a logarithmic scale is used; i.e., +1000 means that *you* is 10 times more frequent than *thou*, and −1000 means that *thou* is 10 times more frequent than *you* for the particular term). *Rogue, rascal,* and to a lesser extent *knave* could be used less abusively. *Rogue* can cooccur with both negative (*damnable, bastardly*) and positive (*sweet little, poor*) adjectives. While it may be used in cases of serious abuse (in conjunction with *thou*), *rogue* as well as *rascal* may also be used in a playful, even endearing manner to denote a mischievous person. Both *rogue* and *knave* can be used to chide a servant, in which case they occur with *you*.

What has been the fate of the multitude of address terms found in Shakespeare? We find a number of changes affecting terms of address (see Salmon 1967: 49–54, 56–59; Crystal and Crystal 2002: 8–9):

- loss or obsolescence: *ancient* (=ensign), *biddy* 'chicken', *bully* 'sweetheart, fine fellow', *coz* (now used colloquially for *cousin*), *gallant* 'fine gentleman', *gentles* 'people of good birth', *goodman* 'male head of household', *goodwife* 'female head of household', *gossip* 'friend, neighbor', *masters* (plural of *master*), *sirrah*, and endearments such as *bawcock* 'fine fellow' (from French *beau coq* 'fine hen'), *chuck* (from *chick*), *sweeting, wag* 'fellow';
- extension in meaning, from men and women of high rank to men and women more generally (no longer dependent on land ownership), as a polite term of

address: *dame, lady, master, mistress, sir*; or other kinds of extension: *captain* 'senior person, no particular rank';

- pejoration of meaning: *dame* 'old hag', *goodman* (a term for one below the rank of gentleman), *lording* (a lord > a term of contempt for a minor or inferior lord), *sirrah* (a term for boys > a term of contempt for men).

Personal letters: As an example of authentic language use, letters provide another view into address terms in the Early Modern period and beyond. Both salutations (forms used at the beginning of letters) and subscriptions (forms used to close the letter) can be elaborate and varied, including kinship terms, endearments, first and last names, and titles as well as possessive pronouns, modifiers (e.g., *good, reverent, honorable, loving, kind*), and intensifiers (e.g., *right, most, well, beloved, very*). The inventory of forms does not change very much over time, but the constructions used and their application to different addressees do. Nevala (2003) provides a detailed scale ranging from positive politeness (intimate, affectionate, and familiar) to negative politeness (deferential and distanced) among the various combinatory possibilities of address terms (see Table 7.2) (see also Chapter 5).

While usage is quite complex, and there is not complete agreement among the different studies, a number of overarching trends seem to be evident in address terms in letters over the period (see Nevalainen and Raumolin-Brunberg 1995; Raumolin-Brunberg 1996; Nevala 2003, 2004):

- simplification in the structure of salutations: for example, from *right trusty sir and brother* to *good brother* to *John*;
- movement to more positively polite forms, especially within the family and among equals: for example, from *mine own good sister and lady* to *my dear Lucille*; those of equal rank may use negative or positive forms depending on distance;
- continuing importance of power among those of unequal rank, with status and power overriding distance: social superiors use positive politeness to inferiors; inferiors use negative politeness to superiors; and
- increasing routinization of simple forms such as *sir* and *madam*.

Nevala (2003, 2004, 2010) sees the change to positive politeness beginning with spouses. Inequality in status impedes the movement to positive politeness forms. Also, among the royalty, the change to positive politeness lags by a century; deferential terms remain the norm until the eighteenth century. Rather than casting the decline in honorific forms and rise of friendly terms as a change from negative to positive politeness, Leech (2014) sees a change in vertical distance, from a more socially stratified society to a more egalitarian one. Leech also notes that it has always been the custom (since Old English) to address inferiors in a complimentary (and positively polite) way. Thus, "in Shakespeare's day, as in earlier times, politeness was not just a unidirectional

Table 7.2 *Address terms in Early Modern English letters, aligned from most positive to most negative (adapted from Nevala 2003: 154)*

Positive	Neutral	Negative
Endearment (*dearest*)	Intensifier + positive modifier + kinship (*right beloved son*)	Status (+ last name) (*good Madam, Mr. Thynne*)
First name (*John*)	Kinship + first/last name (*brother Edmund*)	Intensifier + modifier + honorific (*right worshipful sir*)
Modifier + first name (*my dear John*)	Possessive pronoun + kinship (*my father*)	
Positive modifier + kinship term (*my dearest brother*)	*Right* + deferential modifier + positive modifier + kinship (*right reverend and kind mother*)	
	Right + deferential modifier + kinship (*right worshipful husband*)	
	Positive modifier + status + kinship (*mine own good lady and sister*)	

tribute paid by the lowly to the rich and powerful but also had a reciprocal element" (2014: 291).

Trials: Another authentic example of terms of address comes from trials (see Nevalainen 2006a). During the trial of Alice Lisle in 1685, she is addressed by the Clerk of Arraignments as "Alice Lisle" (in combination with *thou*) in a formulaic expression, by the Lord Chief Justice alternatively as "Mrs. Lisle" or "Lady Lisle" (in combination with *you*); both titles are appropriate because her husband was born in the gentry (hence "Mrs.") but also a member of Cromwell's House of Lords (hence "Lady"). Many of the witnesses are of the non-gentry class (including a baker and a farmhand) and use the deferential "Lady Lisle."

7.9   Chapter Summary

This chapter covered the following topics:
- ways to understand the second-person (*thou/you*, T/V) distinction in respect to power/solidarity, and markedness;
- *thou/you* in Middle English, where power, intimacy, age, rank, and interactional status all contribute to the choice of pronoun, with "retractability" (switches in pronoun use) often motivated by affect, rhetorical function, or genre;
- *thou/you* in Early Modern English, where a change in progress (loss of *thou*), the partial nature of available data, and genre differences together present a complex picture:
  - the loss of *thou* being more rapid in trial records than in depositions, with regional differences;
  - *you* being the preferred form in letters throughout the period, with *thou* continuing to be used;
  - *you* being the majority form in Shakespeare, with genre differences (e.g., comedy vs. history) and frequent switches (retractability) serving subtle purposes of plot and characterization;
- the rich vocative system of Present-day English, ranging from endearments to honorifics;
- the expanding set of vocative terms from Old English to Middle English;
- the rich inventory of vocatives in Early Modern English, with great attention to different genres:
  - the elaborate set of vocatives used in letters showing a change over the period to more positively polite (familial, affectionate), syntactically simpler, and more routinized naming forms;
  - in Shakespeare, a relative but not absolute relation between *thou/you* forms and different vocatives;

• change toward the use of personal names (especially first names), kinship terms, "familiarizers" (e.g., *guys*, *dude*), and endearments and decline in the use of titles and honorifics in Present-day English, both characteristic of "camaraderie politeness" (see Chapter 5, §5.8).

7.10   Further Reading

For a general introduction to the historical study of address terms, see Mazzon (2010). Pakkala-Weckström (2010) and Jucker (2006b, 2020) provide useful overviews of research on *thou* and *ye* in Middle English, while Walker (2007: Ch. 4) is a good summary of research on *thou* and *you* in Early Modern English and different theoretical approaches to address pronouns. U. Busse (2002: Ch. 2) focuses on research on Shakespeare's use of the second-person pronouns; see also Stein (2003). A clear introduction to Shakespeare's usage with examples is provided by Hope (2003). For a brief overview of nominal terms of address in the history of English, see Taavitsainen and Jucker (2016). B. Busse (2006) is a comprehensive account of vocatives in Shakespeare. Jucker (2020: Ch. 6) is an analysis of nominal and pronominal terms of address in Shakespeare's *Romeo and Juliet*. Arguments against the application of Brown and Gilman's model to English are provided by Wales (1983).

7.11   Exercises

1. Chaucer's "The Nun's Priest's Tale" is a beast epic presenting the vain and prideful cock Chauntecleer and his hen Pertelote as courtly characters. Chauntecleer has a dream which bodes ill, but he recklessly ignores it. One day he is approached by a fox, fooled by the fox's flattery into closing his eyes and singing, and captured by him. Chauntecleer ultimately devises a way to trick the fox into releasing him by getting him to open his mouth.

    See if you can explain the usage of *thou* and *ye* as well as nominal terms of address in these extracts:

    (a) Pertelote addressing Chauntecleer:

    > She was agast and seyde, "Herte deere,/ What eyleth **yow**, to grone in this manere?" (2889–80)
    > 'She was aghast and said, "Dear heart, what ails you, to groan in this manner?"'

    (b) Chauntecleer addressing Pertelote:

    > And he answerde, and seyde thus: "Madame,/ I pray **yow** that ye take it nat agrief." (2892–3)
    > 'And he answered, and said thus: "Madame, I pray you that you take it not amiss."'

(c) Narrator addressing Chauntecleer when he recklessly leaves his perch:

O Chauntecleer, acursed be that morwe/ That **thou** into that yerd flaugh fro the bemes! (3230–1)

'O Chauntecleer, cursed be that morning that thou flew from the beams into that yard!'

(d) The Fox addressing Chauntecleer upon first encountering him:

the fox anon/ Seyde, "Gentil sire, allas! wher wol **ye** gon?/ Be **ye** affrayed of me that am **youre** freend?" (3283–5)

'the fox straightway Said, "Gentle sir, alas, where will you go? Are you afraid of me who is your friend?"'

(e) The Fox asking Chauntecleer to sing:

"Now syngeth, sire, for seinte charitee;/ Lat se, konne **ye** youre fader countrefete?" (3320–1)

"'Now sing, sir, for Saint Charity; Let's see; can you imitate your father?"'

(f) The Narrator praying to Venus:

O Venus, that art goddesse of plesaunce,/ Syn that **thy** servant was this Chauntecleer,/ ... Why woldes**tow** suffre hym on **thy** day to dye? (3342–6)

'O Venus, who art goddess of pleasure, since this Chauntecleer was thy servant, ... Why wouldest thou allow him to die on thy day?'

(g) The Narrator complaining to the writer Geoffrey of Monmouth:

Why ne hadde I now **thy** sentence and **thy** loore, (3350)

'Why had I not now thy wisdom and thy learning'

(h) Chauntecleer (caught by the Fox) is being chased by all of the denizens of the barnyard:

And seyde, "Sire, if that I were as **ye**,/ Yet sholde I seyn, as wys God helpe me,/ 'Turneth agayn, **ye** proude cherles alle! A verray pestilence upon **yow** falle!'" (3407–10)

'And said, "Sir, if I were you, yet should I say, as God may help me, 'Turn again, all you proud churls! May a true pestilence fall upon you'"'

(i) The Fox trying to coax Chauntecleer down (after Chauntecleer has tricked him into opening his mouth and has escaped):

"Allas!" quod he, "O Chauntecleer, allas!/ I have to **yow**," quod he, "ydoon trespas" (3419–3420)

"'Alas!" said he, "O Chauntecleer, alas! I have to you," said he, "done offense"'

(j) Chauntecleer responding to the Fox:

"Nay thanne," quod he, "I shrewe us bothe two./ And first I shrewe myself, bothe blood and bones,/ If **thou** bigyle me ofter than ones." (3426–28)

"'Nay then," said he, "I curse both of us two. And first I curse myself, both blood and bones if thou trick me more often than once."'

2. Are the following uses of *thou* and *you* in Shakespeare motivated by socially
   determined rules or are they "affective" uses? Explain the switches in
   pronouns (if they are present). Note any nominal terms of address (examples
   taken from Crystal and Crystal 2002: 450–451):

   (a) Romeo and Juliet – lovers belonging to the aristocracy:

      JULIET: … Therefore stay yet; **thou** need'st not to be gone.

      ROMEO: Let me be ta'en, let me be put to death;/ I am content, so **thou** wilt have
      it so. (1595 *Romeo and Juliet* III.v; OSS)

   (b) Hamlet and the ghost of his father:

      HAMLET: Whither wilt **thou** lead me? Speak! I'll go no further …

      HAMLET: Alas, poor ghost!

      FATHER'S GHOST: Pity me not, but lend **thy** serious hearing/ To what I shall
      unfold. (1599–1601 *Hamlet* I.v; OSS)

   (c) Orlando (nobleman) and the servant Adam:

      ADAM: Yonder comes my master, **your** brother.

      ORLANDO: Go apart, Adam, and **thou** shalt hear how he will shake me. (1599–
      1600 *As You Like It* I.i; OSS)

   (d) Snug and Quince – a joiner and a carpenter (friends and neighbors)

      SNUG: Have **you** the lion's part written? pray **you**, if it be, give it me, for I am
      slow of study.

      QUINCE: **You** may do it extempore, for it is nothing but roaring. (1595
      A Midsummer Night's Dream I.ii; OSS)

   (e) Hamlet and Ophelia – lovers belonging to the aristocracy

      OPHELIA: Good my lord,/ How does **your** honour for this many a day?

      HAMLET: I humbly thank **you**; well, well, well. …

      HAMLET: Get **thee** to a nunnery! Why wouldst **thou** be a breeder of sinners? …
      Go **thy** ways to a nunnery. Where's **your** father?

      OPHELIA: At home, my lord. (1599–1601 *Hamlet* III.i; OSS)

   (f) Polonius (Lord Chamberlain) to his son Laertes:

      POLONIUS: Yet here, Laertes? Aboard, aboard, for shame!/ The wind sits in the
      shoulder of **your** sail,/ And **you** are stay'd for. There – my blessing with
      thee! … My blessing season this in **thee**!

      LAERTES: Most humbly do I take my leave, my lord.

      POLONIUS: The time invites **you**. Go, **your** servants tend. (1599–1601 *Hamlet*
      I.iii; OSS)

   (g) Hamlet (son of the former king) and Rosencrantz (courtier):

      HAMLET: Denmark's a prison …

      ROSENCRANTZ: We think not so, my lord.

      HAMLET: Why, then 'tis not to **you**; for there is nothing either good or bad but
      thinking makes it so. To me it is a prison.

      ROSENCRANTZ: Why, then **your** ambition makes it one. 'Tis too narrow for **your**
      mind. (1599–1601 *Hamlet* II.ii; OSS)

(h) Hamlet and his friend Horatio:

HORATIO: Here, sweet lord, at **your** service.

HAMLET: Horatio, **thou** art e'en as just a man/ As e'er my conversation cop'd withal.

HORATIO: O, my dear lord!

HAMLET: Nay, do not think I flatter;/ For what advancement may I hope from **thee**,/ That no revenue hast but thy good spirits/ To feed and clothe **thee**? (1599–1601 *Hamlet* III.ii; OSS)

3. As discussed at the beginning of the chapter, the term *lady/ladies* has undergone pragmatic change over time. Where initially it was a form devoting an elevated social rank, it may now be used formulaically with little appeal to rank (*ladies and gentlemen*), as a pejorative term (*hey lady, lady of the night* 'prostitute'), and a term denoting 'female' (*lady doctor*), as a term denoting women possessing certain refined qualities (*lady with impeccable manners*) and so on. Use the OED and COCA to see what changes the partner term *gentleman* has undergone. For example, can the singular, *gentleman*, be used as a vocative in Present-day English? If not, can you suggest why it differs from *lady* in this respect? What pejorative qualities or extended meanings, if any, has *gentleman* acquired. Have these arisen in certain contexts? Are there purely formulaic uses of *gentleman*?

8   Discourse: Register, Genre, and Style

8.1   Introduction

In this last chapter we turn to the level above that of the sentence, that is, to the level of discourse. Following an introduction to terminology, the chapter presents an overview of the scope of discourse studies, using developments in news discourse as an example. The stylistic change from oral to literate in the history of English, using a multidimensional model of variation, is the next topic of discussion. We then examine in detail changes in the history of English of one register (the religious register) and one genre (recipes).

8.2   Terminology

As was discussed briefly in Chapter 2, terminology in this area is rather confusing, but in this chapter "discourse" includes both spoken and written "texts." Beyond that there are differing uses of the terms "register" or "domain," "genre," "text type," and "style" in the literature. As Claridge notes, a "complicating factor . . . is the variable usage of the basic terminology – what is one researcher's style may be another's register" (2012: 249).

I will adopt the following (somewhat simplified) definitions. Register refers to the "situational, social, and professional contexts and the field or domain of discourse" (Claridge 2012: 238). Texts belonging to the same register share a communicative situation and a set of contextual features, such as subject matter and the nature and role of the participants. Thus, register refers broadly to the discourse of law, science, medicine, religion, sports, news, fiction, and so on. Within any register, there are a variety of genres. A genre is a socially determined form, shaped primarily by its communicative function, but to a lesser extent by its conventional structure and a set of stylistic features: genres are "texts which share a specific communicative purpose and a conventional text structure" (Claridge 2017a: 186). Genres are shaped by the expectations of readers/hearers and their understanding of the prototypical functions and features of a text. Examples of genres include fairy tales, prayers, eulogies, weather forecasts, obituaries, sonnets, haikus, recipes, sermons, book reviews, crossword puzzles, commercials, emails, marriage vows, footnotes, editorials, IOUs, shopping lists, and hundreds more. In fact, Görlach (2001) compiles a list of 2,100 terms from the OED which reference a genre in some way (2001: 64–81). Jucker and Taavitsainen (2013: 147–148) point out that genres are not always clearly delineated but may overlap and blend into one another. They suggest that a prototype or family resemblance approach to genre is thus warranted.

Another way to view genre is as "social action." That is, genre encompasses "the whole of the rhetorical situation, including not only audience but also purpose, writer, setting, medium, and other cultural and contextual constraints" (Devitt 2020: 61). "Genre exists not as a set of linguistic features tied to sociocultural variables but as performances enacting these features in socially recognized ways" (Devitt 2020: 49). If you think, for example, of the genre of "eulogy," you will recognize that this is not simply a discourse with certain structural or stylistic features serving a particular function (i.e., to praise a deceased person), but it must be delivered in a particular social setting (a funeral or memorial service) by a designated speaker (typically a friend or relative of the deceased) to a specific audience (those attending the funeral), even in a particular solemn tone of voice. We cannot deliver a eulogy at a cocktail party, though we might say that a speech for a retiring person at a company party is a eulogy "of sorts" (hence the blurry boundaries between genres). In the view of genre as social action, it is important that genres are constructed, defined, and named by a community of users. Thus, for example, what constitutes a eulogy may differ significantly from one culture to another. Genres must be recurrent and stable enough to be identified as such by their users, but they are always changing as the community of users changes and new contexts of use arise (as we will see below in our discussion of the recipe genre). At the same time, the concept of a named and recognized entity, a genre, has a normalizing and ideological force which inhibits change. One can imagine a speech at a funeral which hearers would not accept as a eulogy, if it criticizes rather than exalts the person spoken about, for instance, or if it is delivered by a complete stranger. Finally, genres do not exist in isolation but always in relation to surrounding genres.

A text type is defined by internal linguistic features. These may be determined by multidimensional analysis (as described below). Often reference is made here to five broad categories: narration, description, exposition, argumentation, and instruction. These cut across genres and may be found in combination within a single genre. Defining features are action-recording verbs in the past tense in narration, existential statements in description, phenomenon-identifying statements in exposition, quality-attributing statements in argumentation, and action-demanding imperatives in instruction (Jucker and Taavitsainen 2013: 155). In the broadest sense, style is choice. It denotes "a conglomeration of textual features which are not inherently necessary for the register or genre but due to certain choices, for example aesthetic ones, by the language user" (Claridge 2017a: 199). Often, style is seen as idiosyncratic and individual, referring to a writer's (speaker's) choice of linguistic forms. But style can be a matter of genre, register, or period. We will examine in detail later in the chapter the wide-ranging shift from "oral" to "literate" style which occurs in the history of English, which is differently realized in the various genres and registers. Individual writers in any one period may participate more or less in this stylistic shift.

8.3   Scope of Discourse Studies

The registers that have attracted the most scholarly attention are scientific and medical discourse, news discourse, legal or courtroom discourse, religious discourse, and fictional discourse. Each of these warrants a monograph by itself in order to trace the changes in generic forms within each register.

Take, for example, the case of news discourse. Here we see significant changes in the formats in which news is conveyed and in the publication types used, that is, the medium, physical appearance and layout, and periodicity of news texts (Claridge 2010: 595). There is also a proliferation of different genres within the news register. The earliest news publication type was the "pamphlet," beginning in the early sixteenth century with the advent of printing, which permitted large print runs and attracted wider audiences (Jucker and Taavitsainen 2013: 184–185, 187). Pamphlets were non-periodical (one-time) publications addressing topical, often controversial, political or social issues. They ranged from one to a hundred pages and could include a range of genres, such as speeches, petitions, letters, sermons, and dialogues. Precursors of the newspaper appeared in the seventeenth century. These included biannual news collections, "corantos" (periodical news publications covering foreign news presented in narrative form), and newsbooks (quarto-size periodical publications); all of these resembled pamphlets in having full title pages, but their periodic nature represented a "revolutionary change" (Jucker and Taavitsainen 2013: 187). Newspapers as we understand them – with no separate title page, headlines, printed in columns – appeared first on the Continent. The earliest English newspapers were the twice-a-week *Oxford* (later *London*) *Gazette* in 1665 and *The Daily Courant* in 1703 (Fries 2012: 1065). Early newspapers focused on simple news reports presented as a series of (largely unordered) dispatches, or letters, from foreign correspondents. "[T]ypical newspaper features only evolved gradually, over a period of around 150 years" (Claridge 2010: 599).

During the eighteenth century, a number of features of newspapers developed, including national as well as international news, editorials, and a range of non-political or "soft news"; among the latter, the *Zurich English Newspaper Corpus* of seventeenth- and eighteenth-century newspapers recognizes shipping news, crimes, accidents, birth, wedding, and death notices, advertisements, lost and found, proclamations, announcements, letters, essays, and reviews (Claridge 2010: 605). Many of these, such as editorials and obituaries, represent distinct genres (e.g., see Fries [2009] on crime reports in early newspapers). Headlines are an interactive feature of newspapers, used to attract readers. Over time they have changed from expressing the place of origin and date of a news report (e.g., *Berlin, May 7*) to expressing concrete topics, they have grown in length and complexity, and they have changed from more nominal to more verbal (e.g., *The Russian Epidemic* vs. *German Cabinet Resigns*).

Speech presentation (see Chapter 4) has always been important in news discourse as it attests to the credibility of the news and provides newsworthy statements. In a study of *The Times*, Jucker and Berger (2014) found an increasing use of direct and free direct speech rather than indirect speech in newspapers, especially in the more popular press. Perhaps the most important structural change has been the development of a "top-down" or "inverted pyramid" organization, starting with a "lead" paragraph which summarizes the who/what/where/when/why/how of the event, followed by descriptive background. This emerged about 1900 (Claridge 2010: 606). This approach allows readers to get a full account of the events without reading to the end and also gives editors the option of cutting the end of reports, if necessary (Jucker and Taavitsainen 2013: 193).

The internet has "drastically changed the dissemination of news" (Jucker and Taavitsainen 2013: 195–197). While news was formerly broadcast by newspapers and, in the twentieth century, by radio and television, typically under the control of professional journalists or news organizations, the internet allows news to be disseminated by individuals through a variety of channels, including tweets, Instagram, Facebook, TikTok, blogs, and rapidly changing instruments. News producers in these contexts may be addressing more specialized audiences (e.g., Twitter followers, members of Facebook groups) than are assumed for other, more traditional news outlets, which generally assume a large and anonymous audience. Features such as comment sections and discussion forums allow news to become more interactive than letters to the editor, with the distinction between producers and consumers of news discourse breaking down. Finally, news on the internet is highly fluid and can be almost continuously updated. Thus, since its inception in the sixteenth century, we have seen several "revolutionary" changes in the domain of new discourse.

Like other aspects of historical pragmatics, there are three ways to approach the study of genre (see Chapter 2, §2.2). In historical pragmatics (proper), the structural and linguistic characteristics of a genre at a particular time are examined; for example, one might trace the generic conventions of chronicles in the Early Medieval period. In diachronic pragmatics, changes in genres over time are studied. Such changes may be brought about by external factors such as the printing press, which led to the rise of genres such as the pamphlet and the newspaper. Or they may be the result of text-internal factors, such as the increasingly "reader-friendly" layout, eye-catching headlines, "human interest" content, and informal language we find in contemporary tabloid newspapers (Claridge 2017a: 192–193). Finally, in pragmahistorical linguistics, the focus is on the role of genre in linguistic change, for instance on how changes may occur earlier or more frequently or not at all in certain genres rather than others.

Because the scope of this chapter does not allow a discussion of all (or even many) of the discourse registers nor of the genres within these registers, we will present a case study of one register (religious discourse) and one genre (recipes). But first we consider the question of style change over time.

8.4 "Drift" from Literate to Oral Style

One overwhelming change observed in the history of English genres has been the "drift" across genres from features characteristic of written/literate style to those characteristics of oral style. Ground-breaking work in this area was undertaken by Biber and Finegan (1989, 1992) using a multidimensional model of variation. Examining a set of historical text extracts from the seventeenth to the twentieth century, falling into a number of conventionally recognized genres (letters, essays, fiction narrative, dialogue in drama, dialogue in fiction), they automatically identified syntactic and lexical features of the texts using a computer program. The 1989 study includes three written genres; the 1992 study adds two oral genres. They found that the features they isolated cooccurred along a set of dimensions, which they interpreted as functional (see Table 8.1):
• more information-rich to more interpersonal (Dimension A);
• from more elaborate to more situation-dependent (Dimension B); and
• from more abstract to more concrete (Dimension C).
They interpreted these changes as a "drift" from a more "literate" to a more "oral" style. By "literate" they mean "language produced in situations that are typical for writing" and "oral" is "language produced in situations typical of speaking" (1989: 493). But this does not necessarily correspond to the mode of production, as letters are typically written but highly "oral." This drift is similar to what has been called "colloquialization" (Leech et al. 2009: 239–249).

Dimension A ranges from "informational" to "involved." The informational style is characterized by the heavy use of nouns, adjectives, and prepositions,

Table 8.1 *Three dimensions of style (adapted from Biber and Finegan 1992: 690)*

Dimension A	Dimension B	Dimension C
Information vs. Involved Style	Elaborated vs. Situation-Dependent Style	Abstract Style
Positive Features	Positive Features	[Positive Features]
nouns	pied-piping	conjuncts
word length	*wh*-relatives – on subject	agentless passives
prepositions	*wh*-relatives – on object	*by*-passives
attributive adjectives	phrasal coordination	past participial adverb clauses
high type-token ratio	nominalizations	past participial WHIZ deletion
		other adverbial subordinators
Negative Features	Negative Features	
private verbs	time adverbials	
that-deletion	place adverbials	
contractions	other adverbs	
1st/2nd-person pronouns		
present-tense verbs		
DO as pro-verb		
analytic negation		
demonstrative pronouns		
emphatics		
IT pronoun		
BE as main verb		
causative subordination		
discourse markers		
indefinite pronouns		
hedges and amplifiers		
sentence relatives		
wh-questions/clauses		
possibility modals		
non-phrasal coordination		
sentence-final prepositions		

long words, and a high type-to-token ratio; it represents discourse where information is carefully integrated, lexical choice is precise, and careful editing may occur. The involved style is characterized by:

- *that*-deletions (e.g., *I said ~~that~~ it was hot*);
- stranded prepositions (e.g., *Who did you speak to?*);
- contractions;
- first- and second-person pronouns;
- private verbs (e.g., *think, feel, believe*); and
- pragmatic markers (see Chapter 3).

When present, these features are said to be "positive" in Table 8.1. Such discourse is more interactional and affective, and is often expressed using reduced forms. Dimension B ranges from "elaborated" (referents are explicitly identified in the text) to "situation-dependent" (reference is to places, times, and things outside the text); the former is characterized by nominalizations (e.g., *involvement, conclusion, representation* cf. *involve, conclude, represent*), *wh*-relative clauses (e.g., *The paper which I wrote was published*), and pied-piping constructions (e.g., *To whom did you speak?*), the latter by time, place, and other adverbs. Finally, Dimension C ranges from "abstract" to "non-abstract." The abstract style deemphasizes the agent, is frequently passive, refers to inanimate entities, and is technical in content. It is identified by:

- conjuncts (e.g., *moreover, however, meanwhile*);
- agentless passives (e.g., *The dog was fed*);
- past participial adverbial clauses (e.g., *toppled by the wind*);
- adverbial clauses and other adverbial subordinators;
- *by*-passives (e.g., *The dog was walked by the dogwalker*); and
- past participial WHIZ deletions (e.g., *the textbook ~~which was~~ used in that class*).

Tracing changes from the seventeenth to the twentieth centuries, Biber and Finegan do not find, however, that the changes follow a direct path: "17th-century texts are relatively oral; 18th-century texts become more literate in style; and later texts then gradually shift to more oral styles. By the modern period, the three genres are usually considerably more oral than their 17th-century counterparts" (1989: 498–499). This can be clearly seen in the development of fiction essays, and letters along the elaborated/situation-dependent dimension (Dimension B; see Figure 8.2), where we see, for example, that eighteenth-century fiction is most elaborated and twentieth-century fiction is most situation-dependent, while seventeenth- and nineteenth-century fiction fall in between.

Eighteenth-century fiction also ranks highly on the informational scale (Dimension A). In (1) is a passage from eighteenth-century fiction (Horace Walpole, *The Castle of Otranto*, 1764) which shows many of the positive features of the informational dimension, including a predominance of nouns, prepositions, and attributive adjectives (*afflicted parent, equal duty, same time, warmest sympathy, little felicity, destined bridegroom, severe temper, causeless rigour, amiable princesses* [adjectives are underlined in (1)]), a high type-token ratio, and long words. Moreover, it rates highly on the elaborate dimension, with relative clauses (*who doted, who had been, who returned, which she saw, which had promised, who had imprinted*), pied-piping (*for whom*), phrasal coordination (*assisting and comforting, endeavouring to partake*), and (verb > noun) nominalizations (*amazement, assisting, comforting, affection, endeavouring, weight, situation, commiseration, marriage, indulgence* [nominalizations are double-underlined in (1)]); it also exhibits features of the abstract dimension, including a *by*-passive (*had been treated by Hippolita*), an agentless passive (*to be delivered*), and adverbial subordinators (*at the same time, though*).

(1)   Matilda, who doted on her mother, smothered her own grief and amazement, and thought of nothing but assisting and comforting her afflicted parent. Isabella, who had been treated by Hippolita like a daughter, and who returned that tenderness with equal duty and affection, was scarce less assiduous about the Princess; at the same time endeavouring to partake and lessen the weight of sorrow which she saw Matilda strove to suppress, for whom she had conceived the warmest sympathy of friendship. Yet her own situation could not help finding its place in her thoughts. She felt no concern for the death of young Conrad, except commiseration; and she was not sorry to be delivered from a marriage which had promised her little felicity, either from her destined bridegroom, or from the severe temper of Manfred, who, though he had distinguished her by great indulgence, had imprinted her mind with terror, from his causeless rigour to such amiable princesses as Hippolita and Matilda.
(www.gutenberg.org/files/696/696-h/696-h.htm)

The general patterns of change hold despite the different intrinsic nature of the genres: essays are primarily literate and information-rich, letters are primarily interpersonal and oral, and fiction is a mixed form, literate but not for informational purposes. Dialogue in fiction and drama, though most consistently oral in nature, likewise moves more toward the oral end, at least in respect to concreteness and situation-dependency. Literary dialogue is considerably more informational and literate than actual dialogue, leading Biber and Finegan to conclude that "authors have probably not accurately represented ... conversation in earlier periods," perhaps due to the need for dialogue to carry or advance the story line (1992: 701–702).

Biber and Finegan see the eighteenth century as a period of flux in genre norms, with experimentation producing a range of oral and literate styles. They explain this apparent reversal of the literate to oral trend in terms of conflicting views about readership and aesthetic style during this period; on the one hand, expansion of the general reading public promoted a more colloquial and structurally simple style, while, on the other hand, many of the writers of the period still saw themselves as addressing an elite audience using a more elaborated, abstract style. But in the nineteenth-century, Romantic ideals of "natural" language and colloquial style came to prevail and have continued into the modern period.

Note that Biber and Finegan include only a limited number of genres in their study. A similar study of legal, scientific, and medical discourse would likely not confirm this oral drift, as here there has been a consistent trend toward the more literate norms of academic prose, including more information, less narrative, more explicit reference, dense modification patterns, and less overt expression of persuasion (e.g., Atkinson 1999).

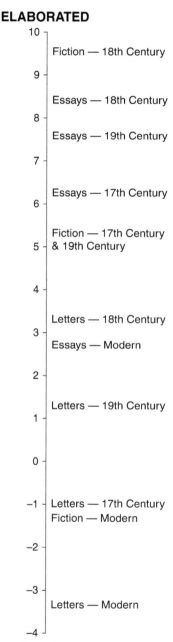

ELABORATED

10 ⌐
    Fiction — 18th Century

9 ⊣
    Essays — 18th Century

8 ⊣
    Essays — 19th Century

7 ⊣
    Essays — 17th Century

6 ⊣
    Fiction — 17th Century
5 ⊣ & 19th Century

4 ⊣

    Letters — 18th Century
3 ⊣
    Essays — Modern

2 ⊣

    Letters — 19th Century
1 ⊣

0 ⊣

−1 ⊣ Letters — 17th Century
    Fiction — Modern

−2 ⊣

−3 ⊣
    Letters — Modern
−4 ⌐

SITUATION-DEPENDENT

Figure 8.1 Drift from elaborated to situation-dependent in essays, fiction, and letters, seventeenth-century to modern period (from Biber and Finegan 1989: 502)

(Douglas Biber and Edward Finegan. Drift and the evolution of English style: A history of three genres. *Language* 65(3). 502. © 1989 Reprinted with permission.)

8.5   Religious Register

The religious register is good place to begin our pragmatic study of discourse because it encompasses a rich inventory of genres that have been relatively stable over time. Moreover, because of the social import-ance of religious texts and their prestige, many have been preserved and come down to us today. However, despite their prominence and impact, they have been relatively neglected by historical pragmaticists and are underrepresented in standard historical corpora. This relative neglect may be due to the waning importance of religious writing in contemporary Western Christian society.

Kohnen (2010, 2015a) provides a comprehensive introduction to religious discourse and its place in the history of English. As a way to systematically classify the wide range of genres within the religious domain, Kohnen suggests considering who is addressing whom and how they interact. Using these criteria, he identifies three major categories, as shown in Figure 8.2. First, God addresses the entire Christian community through the Bible. As the "word of God," the Bible enjoys a privileged status and prestige, though it contains a range of genres (prayers, laws, poems, chronicles, and so on) and represents a rather heterogeneous collection of texts. Second, the Christian community,

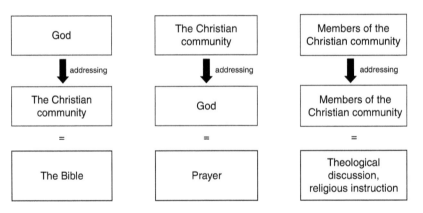

Figure 8.2 The religious register, classified by addresser/addressee (adapted from Kohnen 2015a: 179)

either individually (private prayer) or communally in an institutionalized context (liturgical prayer), may pray to God or some other transcendent being (the Virgin Mary, a saint). Third, some members of the Christian community may address other members of the Christian community; this might involve clergy or scholars addressing one another (theological discussion) or clergy addressing laypeople (religious instruction).

In the *Corpus of English Religious Prose* (COERP) that Kohnen and his team are compiling they have identified three classes of genre:

- The core class is fundamentally religious, including sermons, treatises, catechisms, prayers, religious biographies, and hymns.
- The minor class is also fundamentally religious, but is restricted in regard to the producers or users of the texts, including monastic rules, penitentials, and exegetical commentaries.
- The associated class exists outside the religious domain, but becomes linked to it through its content, including pamphlets, prefaces, religious letters, and religious articles in newspapers (see Kohnen 2010: 534–535, 2015a: 181).

In part because of the longevity of religious genres and their apparent stability, but also in part because of the archaic nature of the language of the 1611 King James Bible (Kohnen 2012a), it is often assumed that the language of the religious register is conservative. Kohnen et al. (2011), using prayers, catechisms, sermons, and religious biographies dated 1500–1699 from COERP and comparing their results to contemporary letters from the *Corpus of Early English Correspondence*, challenge this assumption. They compare a number of linguistic features typically thought to be conservative. The first feature is the retention of *thou*, replaced by *you* during this period (see Chapter 7). Only prayers are "typically religious" in consistently using *thou/thee*. All of the other genres follow the general trend of replacing *thou* with singular *you*. This trend is especially marked when one considers that many of the resistant *thou*s in these genres are "secondary" or indefinite *thou* (*Thou shalt not beare false witness*) or contained within Bible passages. The second feature is retention of the third-person singular verbal ending *-th*. Here, only Bible passages retain *-th* exclusively, and prayers are rather reluctant to use *-s*. In the other religious genres, the shift to *-s* occurs, but later and more slowly than in letters. The third feature, Northern *are* replacing *be*, actually seems to occur earlier in the religious texts than in the secular letters, and the fourth feature, use of *which* rather than *the which*, occurs at a high frequency already at the beginning of the period in all genres. Thus, it is only the prayer genre but not other religious genres generally that clearly exhibits conservative features, and here only in the use of *thou* rather than *you* and of *-th* rather than *-s*. Another common assumption for which there seems to be little evidence is that the King James Bible has had a profound effect on the development of the English language; there appears to be little evidence for such influence apart from some minor effects in the area of lexis and idiom (Kohnen 2012a: 1047–1048).

Religious writing was the predominant register in Early Medieval England, with most genres represented. Even secular (oral Germanic) texts such as *Beowulf* were or became imbued with religious content. The users and producers of texts during this period were primarily members of the clergy. While a complete vernacular Bible in Old English did not exist, there were partial translations, as well as free paraphrases and interlinear glosses (Kohnen 2012a). Early ME literature is almost exclusively religious, with the vast majority of the secular texts not appearing until the late fourteenth and fifteenth centuries. A complete Bible translation attributed to John Wycliffe (d. 1384), existing in two versions, was extremely popular and widely circulated (Kohnen 2012a).

Religious instruction formed a significant part of ME religious writing. Early Modern English might be seen as the height of religious writing in English. William Tyndale's (d. 1536) translation of the New Testament (1534) and parts of the Old Testament proved immensely popular. It served as the basis of a number of complete Bible translations in the mid-sixteenth century, such as the Puritan Geneva Bible (1560) and the Anglican Bishop's Bible (1568). The Bible and Book of Common Prayer (1549) were most popular, but other genres of religious writing were equally important, and new genres such as catechisms arose. Religion and politics were intrinsically linked during this period. The King James Bible (1611) was an attempt to reconcile the two major divisions (Anglicanism/Calvinism); it achieved a "sacred" status, and as a consequence no new translation of the Bible appeared until the late nineteenth century (Kohnen 2012a). After the EModE period, religious writing waned in popularity, but many genres continued to be well represented.

In a number of studies, Kohnen (2008c, 2010, 2012b) has examined the generic features of prayers. Prayers are a "conservative genre which does not seem to have changed a lot during the centuries" (2012b: 177). Prayers in English were rare before Early Modern English, when they came to be collected in "primers"; these were initially used by the middle ranks and later by those lower on the social scale, but the contents remained unchanged. Primers were central in daily life and perhaps the most important product of print culture of the time: "Thus one can say that in terms of reception, popularity and circulation prayers were among the most important genres in Late Medieval and Early Modern England" (Kohnen 2012b: 167). The communicative situation of prayers has remained unchanged over time, consisting of the supplicant addressing their God; it is hence unidirectional. The speaker may also talk about God (*God be to the father*), invite others to praise God (*Prayse ye the lorde*), and ask others to join in prayer (*Let us pray*) Kohnen argues that prayers are interactive and performative. Evidence of interactivity is the high proportion of personal pronouns – *I/we* (supplicant(s)) and *thee* (God) – both in EModE and modern prayers. The percentage of such pronouns found in EModE prayers is comparable to that found in EModE letters, trials, and drama, which are all recognized as speech-related genres. This points to the oral and speech-like nature of prayers. Nominal terms of address, most frequently *Lord*, are also common, with even higher frequency in modern prayers than in EModE prayers. The nominal term is often accompanied by an appositive and relative clause which may be used to emphasize essential qualities of religious faith (as in (2)):

(2)   O My souerayne **lorde Ihesu the veray sone of almyghty god and of the moost clene & glorious vyrgyn Mary/ that suffred the bytter deth for my sake and all mankynde vpon good fryday & rose agayne the thyrde daye.** I beseche the lorde haue mercy vpon me that am a wreched synner but yet thy creature. **And for thy precyous passion saue me** & kepe me from all perylles bothe bodyly & goostly/ (Prymer of Salysbury Vse, 1527, ccviir; Kohnen 2010: 538)

A number of speech acts (see Chapter 6) are typical of prayers, including directives to God, thanking God, confessing/professing one's sins, and praising/ worshipping God. These are often performed with explicit performative verbs: *pray, beseech, entreat, ask*; *thank*; *worship, praise*; *confess*. Directives are the most common, as "petitions form the most significant and prevailing element of the genre" (Kohnen 2008c: 302). In fact, the percentage of directives in prayers surpasses that in letters and sermons and is higher than in almost any other genre, except OE laws. Kohnen hypothesizes that in both laws and prayers the use of explicit performatives is a means by which the speaker "ensures the proper performance and validity of the speech act" (2012b: 174). The most common manifestation of directives is second-person imperatives (e.g., *saue me & kepe me from all perylles*), with some performative verbs (e.g., *I beseche the lorde*). In this respect, prayers are somewhat like letters, but with higher rates of directives; also, explicit performatives are not found in modern letters.

Like prayers, "[s]ermons seem to be among the more stable genres in the history of English" (Kohnen 2007a: 290). In late Middle English/Early Modern English, cycles of liturgical sermons, serving as templates for sermons to be delivered on Sundays throughout the year and on saints' feast days, were widely circulated. One of the best known is John Mirk's *Festial* cycle, dating from the late fourteenth century, parts of which were published by William Caxton in 1483, with eighteen subsequent print editions. Sermons were an early and popular type of print publication. Rütten (2012) argues that sermons thus constitute the first form of "mass communication," as they served the purpose of disseminating identical messages (i.e., theological doctrine) to a large and heterogeneous social group (i.e., largely illiterate Christians). According to

Rütten (2012), sermons follow a similar structure, with clearly identifiable functional parts. Most important are the exhortation (addresses to the audience urging certain beliefs or actions), the exegesis (Biblical interpretation), and the narration. The section breaks are identified with headings ("Narracio" 'narration' in example (3)), pragmatic markers, markers of topic change, tense changes, and prefabricated formulas. Typical topics include sins, repentance, and forgiveness. Rütten (2012) sees sermons, like prayers, as interactive and performative. They often contain conversational markers between the preacher (*I*) and the congregation (*ye*), though designation of the congregation necessarily remains abstract or indefinite (*gode men, somme, he wyl faste, ye that faste, He that fasteth* in example (3)). Directives expressed by performatives (*I warne you*) and less directly (*ye shal have ye common to chyrch . . . and heren a masse*) are a common feature of sermons, as are pleas to God. Kohnen (2008c) finds that sermons used a mixed set of directive forms, mostly modal constructions, but also first- and second-person imperatives; performatives are rare. From the tenth to the seventeenth century the number of directives decreases in sermons, with a slight increase in the late twentieth century. While this might represent an increase in politeness followed by a decrease, Kohnen (2010: 539–540) argues that this is not the case. Modern sermons tend to include the preacher in the directive and use indirect means.

(3)   Gode men, **suche a day** ye schal have the fest of Seynt Margrete. And thagh it be a lyght halyday, save theras the schyrch is edyfyed in hur name, yitte **I warne yow**, for as **I suppose ther ben somme that** have suche love to hure, **that he wyl fasten** hur evon. Bot than **ye that faste** hur evyn, ye quyte yow not to hyr os ye schulde bot if ye common to chyrch on morrowun and heren a masse of hure; . . . **He that fasteth** the evyn, he helpyth hymselfe, and no forthur. Than to styrron youre devocion the more to this holy maydon, I wil schewen in party of hyr lyfe, and whate scheo suffred for Goddys love. **Narracio** I rede in hir lyf that scheo hadde a grete man to hir fadurh . . . (John Mirk, *Sermon on the life of St. Margaret*, a1400; Rütten 2012: 299–300).

'Good men, on this day shall you celebrate the Feast of St Margaret. And even though it is only a minor holiday, except where the church is dedicated to her, yet I warn you, because I suppose there are some that adore her so much that they wish to fast the evening before her feast day. But then you that fast on the evening, you do not behave to her as you should, unless you [also] come to church the [next] morning and hear a mass in her honour . . . He that fasts on the evening [only] helps himself and no one else. But to stir your devotion more towards this holy maid, I will tell a little of her life story and what she suffered for God's love. Narration. I read in the story of her life that she had a great man as her father . . .'

Kohnen (2007a) is a study of coordinating and subordinating conjunctions in sermons over time. Late ME sermons have a high number of coordinators (especially *and*), formulaic use of subordinators, and a high frequency of

subordinate noun clauses (*show that, see how, tell us that*), while EModE
sermons have fewer coordinators and subordinate noun clauses, but a large
number of subordinators of condition and concession. This confirms the
impression that ME sermons are more "oral" in nature and EModE ones
more "literate." Late twentieth-century sermons are more like ME sermons,
with more *ands* and subordinate noun clauses and fewer conditional and
concessive subordinators. Kohnen concludes that "connective profiles" of
this type "may be reliable indicators of the respective distance of texts and
text types from spoken and written language" (2007a: 304). Kohnen thus finds
a drift to orality similar to that found by Biber and Finegan (see above, §8.4).

8.6   Recipe Genre

The goal of genre study is to identify the possible genres and their characteristic
features in a historical period and then to trace changes in these genres over
time by comparing the synchronic descriptions.

   Genres can be fairly stable over time, as we saw in the last section in the case
of prayers and sermons. But they may also fall out of use, such as saints' lives
(a genre popular in the Early Medieval period), or beast fabliaux (a genre
popular in Middle English) or telegrams (a genre important from the mid-
nineteenth to the mid-twentieth century but now rarely used). Of course, genres
may also arise, such as the pamphlet in the sixteenth century or the email or text
message in the latter part of the twentieth century. New genres may come into
being because of the appearance of new technology, such as printing or the
internet. Some genres develop within certain registers, media, or publication
types, such as editorials, obituaries, and weather forecasts in the news domain
(Claridge 2012: 246). And genres may change and develop over time, as in the
development of the "top-down" approach in news reports; sometimes such
changes may result from borrowing from other genres, as in the case of
newspapers borrowing from the letter genre (Claridge 2017a: 191).

   In this section, we will look at the genre of recipes. Recipes would seem to be
rather stable historically as they appear early and their function remains
virtually unchanged, namely to offer instructions on how to prepare something:
"the basic function and generic features have remained constant throughout the
long history of the genre" (Pahta and Taavitsainen 2012: 569). Because of the
functional stability of the genre, we might expect a high degree of standardization with little change over time. Nonetheless, we do observe variation in form
and significant changes in the structural and linguistic features of recipes. In
part, these changes are due to the range of topics that recipes have been
concerned with. For medieval recipes, we generally focus on two types,
medical and culinary recipes, but many medieval recipes remain unedited
and unstudied. Alchemical recipes, that is, recipes giving instruction for

turning base metals into silver or gold, are also found (see Grund 2003), as are recipes for the preparation a wide variety of other substances apart from medicants and food items, including dyes, laces, gunpowder, soap, artificial jewels, glue, gunpowder, wax, wine, and so on.

The term *recipe* was not initially used to name this genre. According to the OED, *recipe* (derived from the Latin imperative *recipe* 'take') was first used to denote medical recipes in 1533 and culinary recipes in 1631 (s.v. *recipe*, n.), though both existed well before these dates. As a verb (s.v. *recipe*, v.), the term was used for medical recipes and culinary recipes in 1300 and 1500, respectively. The MED records *receit(e* (n.) in reference to recipes (mostly alchemical and medical recipes); the term *recipe* (in its Latin sense 'take') is found frequently in the quotation database but is not given as a headword. The term *receipt* (OED, s.v. *receipt*, n., defs. IV 12 and 14) is also used for medicinal (1398), alchemical (1405), and cookery (1595) recipes. *Recipe book* is first cited in 1803, with *cookbook* noted as an Americanism the same year.

The earliest recipes in English are medicinal recipes in Old English dating from the late ninth/early tenth century, some translated from Latin, but others with no known Latin sources. Here are two examples that involve the preparation of a medicant for sore eyes and a treatment for baldness, both from *Bald's Leechbook*, a well-known ninth-century collection of recipes:

(4)   a.   Wið eagena sar genim þære ylcan wyrte wyrttruman, seoð on wætere to þriddan dæle; & of þam wætere beþa þa <eagan> (Lch I (Herb); DOEC; quoted in Carroll 2004: 175).

             'For sore eyes, take the same plant root. Boil it in water reducing it to a third, and with the water bath the [eyes]'

        b.   gif man calu sie, plinius se micla læce segþ þisne læcedom, genim deade beon, gebærne to ahsan & linsæd eac, do ele to on þæt, seoþe swiþe lange ofer gledum, aseoh þonne & awringe & nime welies leaf, gecnuwige, geote on þone ele, wylle eft hwile on gledum, aseoh, þonne smire mid æfter baþe. (Lch II (1); DOEC; quoted in Görlach 2008: 126)

             'if a man is bald, Plinius the great doctor gives this recipe, take dead bees, burn to ashes and linseed also, put oil on that, boil a long time over live coals, then strain and wring and take a willow leaf, pound, and put oil on, boil again a while over live coals, strain, then smear with after bathing'

The earliest medicinal recipes in the ME period are in Anglo-Norman, translated into English in the early fourteenth century. Original English recipes are recorded in the later fourteenth century. Medical recipes in this period are found in two different types of sources, in so-called "remedybooks" and in scholarly treatises. While these two types of recipes share many characteristics, they are addressed to distinct audiences and serve rather different functions, and thus exhibit some different linguistic features. Remedybooks are collections of recipes directed primarily at the layperson. These recipes are practical cures of a folkloristic nature. They often occur in manuscripts with other types of practical advice interspersed, such as charms, dietary advice, herbals, prognostications regarding diseases, astrological rules, and so on (Taavitsainen 2001: 91–93). Remedybooks are assumed to have been widely consulted and used as handbooks for quick reference. For this reason, the layout and form of the recipes serve to make them easily accessible. Headings generally state the purpose of the recipe (the ailment it cures) rather than naming the medicant, which might not have been known to the lay reader. They assume a familiar and intimate relationship with the reader, and if authority is invoked, it is either to vague "good leeches" or "wise men" or to God.

The organization of recipes within remedybooks, while it is sometimes *de capite ad pedem* ('from head to foot') is usually not entirely coherent. Recipes in scholarly or surgical treatises are embedded at points within the text either to exemplify a practical cure or illustrate a theoretical point. The audience of such texts is assumed to be professionals, with the author "communicating advancement and experience to colleagues working in the same field" (Taavitsainen 2001: 107). These recipes are less standardized and more varied in form than those in remedybooks. They may not be clearly set off from the rest of the text. A heading for the recipe, if it occurs at all, may be given in Latin. Classical authorities, such as Greek physicians or Arabic scientists, may be invoked. The style may include more adjectives to give weight and a "professional style" (Sylwanowicz 2016), and use of the first person lends the recipe an authoritative voice. In fact, scholarly recipes may include a first-person narration of the physician's treatment of his patient, which sounds almost like a case report (Taavitsainen 2001: 104–106).

Below is an example of a fifteenth-century medicinal recipe:

(5)   Pro male videntibus uel oculos rubeos habentibus. [t]ake white gyngire, and robbe hit on a whestoon in a fayre bacin of metal, and take as mykel salt, as þow hast pouder, and grynd hem wel to gedur in þe bacin, and temper hem wyþ white wyn, and let hit stond a day and a nyȝt, & þenne take þe þynne, þat stondes aboue, & do hit in to a viol of glas, and when þe seke goos to bedde, take a feþer, and wete þer ynne, & anoynt wel þe sore eyen, þer wyþ, & he shal be hool. (c. 1450 https://archive.org/details/einmittelenglisc00heinuoft [p. 68]; cited in Carroll 2004: 177–178)

> 'For sick eyes and having red eyes. Take white ginger and rub it on a whetstone in a good basin of metal, and take as much salt as you have powder, and grind them well together in the basin, and temper them with white wine, and let it stand a day and a night, and then take the runny fluid that stands above and put it into a glass vial and when the sick person goes to bed, take a feather and wet therein, and anoint well the sore eyes therewith, and he shall be well.'

No culinary recipes are extant from Old English. The earliest cooking recipes found in England are written in Anglo-Norman and date from the thirteenth century. These were translated into English. A well-known compilation of medieval culinary recipes (existing in a number of different manuscripts dating from the late fourteenth century) is the *Form of Curye* 'Manner of Cooking.' Below is a typical recipe from this collection:

> (6)   Rysshews of fruyt. Take fyges and raisouns; pyke hem and waisshe hem in wyne. Grynde hem wiþ apples and peeres ypared and ypiked clene. Do þerto gode powdours and hole spices; make balles þerof, frye in oile, and serue hem forth. (a.1425(a1399) Form Cury (Add 1506); MED; www.godecookery.com /mtrans/mtrans13.htm)
>
> 'Rissole of fruit. Take figs and raisins, pick them and wash them in wine. Grind them with apples and pears, pared and picked clean. Add to them good powders and whole spices; make balls out of this, fry in oil and serve them forth.'

Cooking recipes were often collected together in manuscripts with other types of practical instruction, such as advice on food, hygiene, table manners, and types of foods to be served at a feast et cetera. The recipes themselves did not necessarily appear in a logical order. Culinary and medicinal recipes could be intermixed, or the same recipe might serve either purpose. As Carroll notes, "users of Middle English did not have a strong distinction between culinary and medicinal recipes, but ... both were considered to be tokens of the same text" (1999: 38).

A number of aspects of medieval culinary recipes make it highly unlikely that they were written as instructions for the amateur cook or peasant housewife. As can be seen in (6), medieval recipes did not give exact measurements and provided only very general explanations of the cooking procedures involved. Knowledge about ingredients, tools, and cooking techniques were all assumed. Moreover, the recipes often called for a wide range of ingredients, many of which, such as pepper, saffron, or cinnamon, would have been very expensive in medieval times: "one can only wonder who would have been able to afford such exquisite culinary pleasures" (Arendholz et al. 2013: 131). These facts have led scholars to assume that the audience consisted of experienced cooks or professional chefs, likely in noble, aristocratic, or clerical households. Moreover, the recipes were perhaps not intended so much as instruction as a memory aid to be consulted when the need arose. As Bator points out, the extant manuscripts containing recipes are "clean" and do not show any evidence of having actually been used in the kitchen: "All in all, it seems that despite the recipe being an instruction on how to prepare a certain dish, the medieval recipes were not so much supposed to instruct; and even though hardly any indication of the reader can be found, food historians ... restrict the audience to professional cooks, clergy or nobility" (2016: 12). Pursuing the question of readership further, Arendholz et al. (2013: 132–133) point out that the fine foodstuffs found in many of the medieval recipes seem "unseemly" in a clerical context, and that the cooks in noble and aristocratic kitchens were likely to have been illiterate, unless the recipes were read out to them by the noblewoman of the house.

Recipes in Middle English are typically quite short (40–120 words) (Carroll 2004: 182). Medicinal and culinary recipes share a common function, a number of clearly recognizable structural elements and linguistic characteristics.

Function: Both medicinal and culinary recipes belong to a utilitarian genre whose purpose is to instruct the reader on how to PREPARE things, medications or culinary dishes. Carroll (2004: 188) argues that both types of recipes also instruct the reader on how to DO things; for instance, she cites recipes which show how to salvage meat which has gone bad or how to fasten together two pieces of flesh.

Structural elements: According to Taavitsainen, "The most pervasive feature of recipe composition is the overall structure, which shows a very clear communicative principle or text strategy" (2001: 98). Scholars characterize and name the sections of recipes somewhat differently. I will follow Bator and Sylwanowicz (2017: 13) in identifying three parts:

• Heading (or title). This is present in culinary recipes and in medical recipes appearing in remedybooks. In medical recipes, the heading typically expresses the purpose of the recipe and is denoted by a prepositional phrase (*For nose-bledingge*) or infinitive (*To make poplyan* 'to make poplar ointment'). When multiple recipes for the same ailment are provided, an anaphoric reference occurs (*Another*). In culinary recipes, it is more common to name the dish with a noun phrase (*Leche Lumbard* 'a jellylike dessert cut in strips after the Lombard fashion') or, especially in Anglo-Norman recipes, to denote the purpose of the recipe in an infinitive (*For to make Grene Sawce*). In (5–6), we see a heading in Latin in the medicinal recipe (*Pro male videntibus uel oculos rubeos habentibus*) and in English in the culinary recipe (*Rysshews of fruyt*).

• Procedure (including ingredients and preparation). This is the only (nearly) obligatory section of the recipe, occurring 90 percent of the time or more. What characterizes medieval recipes is a unified discussion of ingredients and preparation. No separate list of ingredients is supplied. Temporal sequence is followed in the instructions. What is also characteristic of these recipes is almost no specification of quantities, or at best very vague expressions (*a quantyte, nowt to moche, a lytil of, a handful, a sawcerful, a good porcion of*). Neither of the recipes in (5–6) provides any specification of quantity. Time allotted to the steps is also typically not indicated, though it may be indirectly referenced (*Te space of iii pater-nosteres and iii aves* 'the time of three Our Fathers and three Hail Marys'). As Arendholz et al.

observe, "our Middle English recipe tells us about How, but nothing about the How Much and How Long" (2013: 130).

- Application. Medicinal recipes usually explain how the medicant should be used or dosed (*anoynt wel þe sore eyen, and ley on his heued*). In culinary recipes, "application" refers to how the dish should be served (*And ete hem with clere hony*).
- Additional comments. These are not typical of culinary recipes, but a common element of the medicinal recipe is the "efficacy statement"; "the function of efficacy statements is to insist on the value of a given remedy in the form of prognostication" (Alonso-Almeida and Cabrera-Abreu 2002: 145).

Linguistic features:
- Medieval recipes consist of short, paratactic sentences, in parallel structure, with few complex sentences. Sentence linkage is effected by the use of connective *and (then)*.
- Imperative verbs, "one of the defining syntax features" of recipes throughout the ages (Diemer 2013: 140), are the predominant verbal form.
- Imperative "*Take …* " is conventional, though other 'take' verbs (*accipe, nim, recipe*) and more specific cooking terms (*roast, scald, pare*) may be substituted. *Take and* [verb] "seems to internally structure the text by sectioning the sequential steps of description" (Arendholz et al. 2013: 131).
- An ending formula of the type & *serue it forth* is typical of culinary recipes. Medicinal recipes end with a range of formulaic efficacy statements: the Latin phrase *probatum est* or English expressions such as *for þis is prouen/ for þis is medicine wel proved* attest to the success of the remedy, while expressions such as & *þou shalt be hool, it sall do hym gude, thou schalt ben hole by goddis grace* would appear to function as promises for the patient's recovery. However, Alonso-Almeida and Cabrera-Abreu (2002) argue that the illocutionary force of the promise is often undercut by conditional phrases such as *by goddis grace* and *til the seke be hool þourgh þe grace of God*.
- A "reader-oriented" attitude may be produced by the use of second-person possessive pronouns (as in "take thy hare" or "take your hare"). In the medieval alchemical recipes he examined, Grund (2003) found that the possessive pronouns often occurred with direct addresses with *ye* or *thou*. He concludes that this represents "reader-friendliness or writer-reader involvement" (470), with *the/your* being more formal and *thy* more informal (cf. Görlach 2008: 129; see Chapter 7 on *thou/you*).
- The lexis of recipes encompasses culinary terms, plant and meat names, minerals, organic substances, body parts, and diseases. A small set of verbs occurs in recipes, especially *take, do,* and *put*. Verbs specific to cooking (*fry, seethe, strain, boil*) occur in culinary recipes, but verbs of combining

(*meddle, mix, temper*) and general active verbs (*beat, burn, cut, turn, put, stamp, gather, draw, drink, bruise*) are common to all recipes (Taavitsainen 2001: 99–100). The verbs are almost exclusively Germanic in origin. In contrast, nouns in recipes are predominantly of French origin, whether referring to herbs, plants, and organic substances used in medicants or to spices and other foodstuffs used in cooking dishes.

Three linguistic features that arise later in the history of the genre are more or less absent from medieval recipes: telegraphese, article elision, and zero or null objects (e.g., *Fry onions. Add ∅ to meat mixture*). Sentences in medieval recipes are generally complete. Article omission does not occur. The omission of pronoun objects is very uncommon – Culy (1996) finds that it happens in less than 5 percent of the cases in medieval recipes – though it can occur. For example, we see it in the OE recipe given in (4b), *nime welies leaf, gecnuwige* 'take a willow leaf, pound (it)'. Arendholz et al. (2013: 122) find several examples of object deletion in a fifteenth-century recipe: *Take fayre beef of þe rybbys of þe fore quarterys, an smyte* 'take fair beef off the ribs and the forequarters, and smite (it)' or *an let boyle onys* 'let (it) boil once'.

The EModE period saw a large increase in the number of cookbooks (see Görlach 2008: 131). But Alonso-Almeida (2013: 85) finds no substantial changes in the structure and form of recipes in the period 1600–1800. Most of the following discussion concerns culinary recipes, but medical and culinary recipes continue to be aligned until the eighteenth century (Görlach 2008: 131).

Below is an example of an EModE culinary recipe:

(7)   To boyle a Rabbet with Hearbes on the French fashion
        Fit your Rabbet for the boyling, and seeth it with a little Mutton broth, white Wine, and a peece of whole Mace: then take Lettuce, Spynage, Parsley, winter Sauory, sweet Marioram: all these being pickt, and washy cleane, bruise them with the backe of a Ladle (for the bruising of the Hearbes wil make the broth looke very pleasantly greene.) Thicken it with a crust of Manchet [good quality wheat bread], being steeped in some of the broth, and a little sweet Butter therein. Season it with Uergis [verjuice?], and Pepper, and serue it to the Table vpon Sippits [toasted bread used as spoons]. Garnish your Dish with Barberyes [barberries]. (1615 Murrell, *The New Book of Cookery*; cited in Bator 2016: 11)

While it is still uncommon to provide exact quantities, you will notice that this recipe gives more elaborate instructions (with more specific verbs such as *bruise, thicken, season, steep, fit*) and a more fulsome specification of ingredients (*Mace, Lettuce, Spynage, Parsley, winter Sauory, sweet Marioram*), and is generally more exhaustive and systematic. The majority of names of ingredients are still of French origin (e.g., *rabbit* rather than *hare*), and ingredients are not listed separately. An important change is that EModE recipes are no longer anonymous (as we see here). Also, the readership is assumed to be fundamentally different from that of medieval recipes. With printing and increasing literacy, culinary recipes acquired a larger readership and became more popular. It is assumed that EModE recipes were now addressed to the lay (not professional) chef and primarily to women (housewives) (Diemer 2013: 144).

While LModE recipes follow the trends of the previous period, they have not yet acquired all the features we expect to find in modern recipes:

(8)   To make hasty fritters:
       TAKE a stew-pan, put in some butter, and let it be hot: in the mean time take half a pint of all-ale not bitter, and stir in some flour by degrees in a little of the ale; put in a few currants, or chopped apples, beat them up quick, and drop a large spoonful at a time all over the pan. Take care they don't flirt together, turn them with an egg-flice, and when they are fine brown, lay them in a dish, and throw some sugar over them. Garnish with orange cut into quarters (1774 Glasse, *The Art of Cookery*; quoted in Diemer 2013: 146)

As in Early Modern English, culinary recipes are addressed to the amateur cook and the audience is exclusively female (Görlach 2008:132, Diemer 2013: 146). In the eighteenth century, social distinctions may be apparent, between those recipes that are expressed in "genteel diction" and those that eschew professional terminology and are written in a plain style. Diemer (2013: 147) notes the appearance of what he calls "supporter" and "controller" statements. Supporters accompany steps that might be problematic (*Take care they don't flirt together*) and controllers provide information on the completion of steps (*when they are fine brown*). By the middle of the nineteenth century, many of the features of modern recipes have begun to appear (see the example given in exercise 3).

The following contemporary recipe can be found online:

(9)   **Fresh Fruit Fritters**

> Preparation: 15 mins
> Cooking time: 10 mins
> Total time: 25 mins
> Servings: 24 servings
> Yield: 24 fritters

These easy fruit fritters are made with chunks of fresh fruit or berries dipped in a simple fritter batter. Use slices of banana, peaches, apples, or fresh berries.

Ingredients

1 C sifted flour	1 tbsp. sugar
1 tsp. baking powder	½ tsp. salt
2 eggs, separated	½ C milk
4 C banana, chunks; or peach slices, apple chunks, or fresh berries of your choice	
1 C cinnamon sugar	

Steps
Sift together flour, baking powder, sugar, and salt.
In a bowl, combine egg yolks, milk, and 1 tbsp. vegetable oil; blend well for a smooth batter.
In a metal or glass bowl, beat the egg whites to stiff peaks with an electric mixer.
Gently fold the beaten egg whites into the batter.
Pour oil into a deep fryer or heavy deep pan and heat to 370° F.
Put some of the banana or fruit chunks in the batter; gently stir to coat.
With tongs, fork, or spoon, lower the battered fruit pieces into hot deep oil and fry for 3 to 4 minutes. Work in small batches.
Drain on paper towels.
Sprinkle hot fritters with powdered sugar or roll in cinnamon sugar mixture.
(adapted from www.thespruceeats.com/fresh-fruit-fritters-3056337)

As can be seen in (9), modern English recipes have a bipartite structure with distinct sections for ingredients and procedural steps, often set off visually from one another. The procedure is described in a chronological, step-wise fashion, with the steps numbered or bulleted. Exact measurements are given, and steps are exhaustively explained, with controlling and supporting statements. Headings typically express the name of the dish with a noun phrase, but may also summarize ingredients, explain how the dish is cooked, denote the ease or short duration of preparation ("easy," "quick"), name the author of the recipe, or specify a suitable occasion for the dish (Bator 2016: 11). An introductory statement may describe the recipe or summarize the preparation time and servings, both of which we see in (9). Final statements may provide additional information, such as calories, nutritional facts, price, and so on. Photographs of the dishes are often included, and online recipes may even have videos demonstrating the preparation of the recipe. A "comment" section makes online recipes interactive. Clearly, modern recipes are addressed to any conceivable audience and are gender-neutral (Diemer 2013: 149).

The tradition of using imperatives and simple syntax, with paratactic connectives, and addresses to the reader in the second person (either explicit or implicit) remains constant, though the language of contemporary recipes is not as formulaic as it was in earlier periods. We see the appearance of new linguistic features, including the use of telegraphic style, with the omission of articles (*sift together [the] flour, pour [some/the] oil, sprinkle [the] hot fritters*) and frequent object omission (*blend [them] well, work [them] in small batches, drain [them] on paper towels*). As noted above, zero objects are found only occasionally in earlier periods, but are now considered "the hallmark of the recipe" (Görlach 2008: 140). Culy (1996: 98) finds a significant increase in elliptical objects in recipes in the last quarter of the nineteenth century. He argues that this feature cannot be explained syntactically or morphologically (since it differs from normal object deletion) but must be pragmatically motivated; he is unclear about how this change proceeds historically and why the change occurs, though he postulates it might be due to increases in literacy in the nineteenth century and a widening market for cookbooks (Culy 1996: 102).

In conclusion, we see a number of changes over time in culinary recipes, many of which can be attributed to their focus on a wider and less professional audience: the development of a clearly delineated internal structure, a more elaborately articulated set of procedural steps, the precise specification of measurements (ingredients, cooking times, and temperatures), a decrease in lexis requiring a high degree of specialized knowledge, the addition of extraneous information, and a more personalized tone and even interactive features (cf. Diemer 2013: 139, 151).

8.7   Chapter Summary

This chapter covered the following topics:

- change in a discourse domain, using the development of modern newspapers from EModE pamphlets as an example, where we see extensive changes in the publication type (medium, physical appearance and layout, periodicity) and structure (the "top-down" approach);
- "drift" in style from written/literate to oral in the history of English, along three dimensions (informational > involved, elaborated > situation-dependent, abstract > non-abstract) but not on an entirely straightforward path;
- the religious register, which exhibits longevity and stability, with a range of genres:
  - prayers, a "conservative," speech-like, and historically important genre which is both performative (directive) and interactive;
  - sermons, perhaps the first form of mass communication, showing a fixed structure (exhortation – exegesis – narrative), interactive and performative features, and a drift from literate to oral;
- the recipe genre, which shows functional stability but significant changes in form:
  - medieval culinary and medical recipes being relatively brief, featuring short, paratactic sentences and imperatives, being inexact in respect to amounts, times, and procedures; culinary recipes appearing to be addressed to the professional cook and medical recipes to either the lay healer (in remedybooks) or to the professional (in scholarly treatises);
  - culinary recipes over time developing a bipartite structure (ingredients, procedural steps), giving more elaborate instructions and exact measurements, adding various types of extraneous information, and coming to address the

amateur cook; stylistically, continuing the use of imperatives but acquiring a "telegraphic" style (omission of articles and objects).

8.8   Further Reading

For an overview of registers, see the chapters in Jucker and Taavitsainen (eds.) (2010): Claridge (2010) on news discourse, Doty (2010) on courtroom discourse, Kohnen (2010) on religious discourse, Fitzmaurice (2010) on literary discourse, Pahta and Taavitsainen (2010) on scientific discourse, and Palander-Collin (2010) on letters. Historical pragmatic treatments of fiction overlap with literary stylistic, corpus stylistic, and narratological approaches, such as Leech and Short (2007[1981]), Semino and Short (2004), or Fludernik (1993).

The history of the newspaper in England has been well studied. Collections of articles which focus on the language of newspapers include Brownlees (2006) and Jucker (2009b). Facchinetti et al. (2012) gives a chronological account of the development of the register, as does Fries (2012). Conboy (2010) is a sociohistorical approach to the language of newspapers.

A collection of articles on genres in the history of English is Diller and Görlach (2001). Two volumes of articles on recipes are DiMeo and Pennell (eds.) (2013) (covering different types of recipes) and Gerhardt et al. (eds.) (2013) (focusing on culinary recipes). The ME recipe has received considerable attention: see Carroll (1999, 2004), Taavitsainen (2001), Alonso-Almeida and Cabrera-Abreu (2002), Alonso-Almeida (2008), Quintana-Toledo (2009), and Sylwanowicz (2016). Overviews of the history of culinary recipes are provided by Görlach (2008), Diemer (2013), and Bator (2016). Taavitsainen (2001) is concerned with the difference between scholarly and remedybook recipes, Alonso-Almeida (2013) examines recipes from 1600 to 1800, Bator and Sylwanowicz (2017) provide a quantitative comparison of the features of some 2,800 medieval medical and culinary recipes. On readership of medieval and modern recipes, see Sylwanowicz (2017) and Arendholz et al. (2013). For a study of the alchemical recipe, which bears close similarity to medicinal and culinary recipes, both in structure and linguistic features, see Grund (2003).

Archives of many historical newspapers are available in ProQuest Historical Newspapers™. For example, included are *The Washington Post* (1877–2005), *The New York Times* (1851–2018), *The Guardian* (1821–2003), and *The Observer* (1791–2003), as well as papers from India, China, Canada, Israel, Australia, Ireland, France, and Scotland.[1] These are available through subscription and can be accessed through university libraries. As mentioned in Chapter 2, two newspaper corpora exist: *Zurich English Newspaper Corpus* (ZEN) covering 1661–1791 and *Newsbooks at Lancaster* covering 1653–1654.

---

[1] See https://about.proquest.com/en/products-services/pq-hist-news/.

(On newspaper sources, see also Fries 2012: 1064.) EModE pamphlets can be found in *The Lampeter Corpus of Early Modern Tracts* and in EEBO.

Several corpora contain texts from the religious register and the recipe genre. Not all of these are publicly available. The *Corpus of English Religious Prose* (COERP) includes a variety of religious genres dating from 1150 to 1800. *The Lampeter Corpus* also includes religious tracts dating from 1640 to 1740. The *Corpus of Early English Medical Writing* contains both remedybook and scholarly recipes; the corpus is published in three periods, Middle English (c.1375–1500, c. 0.5 million words), Early Modern English (1500–1700, c. 2 million words), and Late Modern English (1700–1800, more than 2 million words). Under construction is the *Corpus of Early English Recipes* (CoER); it will cover the period 1375–1850/1900, comprise 3 million words, and include all possible types of recipes.

8.9   Exercises

1. In the following sermon, discuss the structural and linguistic elements of the sermon genre that are present. The sermon is taken from *Mirk's Festial: A collection of homilies by Johannes Mirkus (John Mirk)*, Vol. 1, ed. by Theodor Erbe. EETS, 96. London: Kegan Paul, Trench, Trübner & Co., 1905 (https://archive.org/details/mirksfestialcoll01mirkuoft/page/n1/mode/2up).

    Good men and woymen, þat ben ytaght by Goddys lawes forto come þys day to holy chyrch, forto worschip God and þys holy martyr Seynt Thomas þat was slayn for þe lawes of holy chyrch and for þe right of þe rem. This holy Seynt Thomas was born yn þe cyte of London, and had a fadyr was callet Gylbert, þat was scheryue of London.
    Þen felle hit, as þys Gylbert went to þe holy lond, he was taken and put yn dysstres. Þen come þer a worschypfull woman of þe contrey to hym and sayde, yf he wold plight hys troth to wed hur, scho wold helpe hym out of his doses. And soo scho dyd. (De Festo Sancti Thome, Martiris et Eius Solempnitate – p. 38)

    'Good men and women, who have been taught by God's laws to come this day to the holy church for the purpose of worshipping God and his holy martyr Saint Thomas that was slain for the right of the realm. This holy Saint Thomas was born in the city of London, and had a father called Gilbert, who was sheriff of London.
    'Then it happened that, as this Gilbert went to the holy land, he was taken and put into prison. Then came there a virtuous woman of the country to him and said, if he would give his word to wed her, she would help him out of his distress. And so she did.'

2. Identify the features of ME recipes in the fourteenth-century culinary and medicinal recipes given below:
    a. Benes yfryed. Take benes and seeþ hem almost til þey bersten. Take and wryng out þe water clene. Do þerto oynouns ysode and ymynced, and garlec þerwith;

frye hem in oile oþer in grece, & do þereto powdour douce, & serue it forth. (a1399 Form Cury (Add 5016); www.godecookery.com/mtrans/mtrans12 .htm)

'Fried beans. Take beans [fava beans?] and boil them almost until they burst. Take and wring out the water completely. Add to this boiled and minced onions and garlic; fry them in oil or in grease and add sweet powder and serve forthwith.'

b. Pro vermibus in ventre. Take nepte, & stampe it, & temper hit wyþ hote wyn, & drinke hit, when þou felyst þe wormes gruen þe, þou shalt be hool. (quoted in Taavitsainen 2001: 99)

'For worms in the stomach. Take catmint and crush it, and mix it with hot wine, and drink it, when you feel the worms grieving you, you shall be healed.'

c. For ache in þe joynte. Take mogworte and stamp it and do þerto eysyll and fresche grece of a swyne and bete yt to-gedry and make a playster þer-of and ley it on þe sore. (https://archive.org/stream/beitrgezurmittel00schf/beitrgezurmit tel00schf_djvu.txt [p. 233])

'For ache in the joint. Take mugworte and pound it and add vinegar to it and fresh grease of a swyne and beat it together and make a plaster thereof and lay it on the sore.'

3. How does this Late Modern English (mid-nineteenth-century) culinary recipe foreshadow the form of modern recipes? This recipe occurs in one of the most popular cookbooks of the time, Mrs. Beeton's *The Book of Household Management* (1861) (https://onlinebooks.library.upenn.edu/web bin/gutbook/lookup?num=10136):

TOAD-IN-THE-HOLE (a Homely but Savoury Dish).

INGREDIENTS. – 1-1/2 lb. of rump-steak, 1 sheep's kidney, pepper and salt to taste. For the batter, 3 eggs, 1 pint of milk, 4 tablespoonfuls of flour, 1/2 saltspoonful of salt.

Mode. – Cut up the steak and kidney into convenient-sized pieces, and put them into a pie-dish, with a good seasoning of salt and pepper; mix the flour with a small quantity of milk at first, to prevent its being lumpy; add the remainder, and the 3 eggs, which should be well beaten; put in the salt, stir the batter for about 5 minutes, and pour it over the steak. Place it in a tolerably brisk oven immediately, and bake for 1-1/2 hour.

Time. – 1-1/2 hour. *Average cost*, 1s. 9d. *Sufficient* for 4 or 5 persons. *Seasonable* at any time.

Note. – The remains of cold beef, rather underdone, may be substituted for the steak, and, when liked, the smallest possible quantity of minced onion or shalot may be added. (https://onlinebooks.library.upenn.edu/webbin/gut book/lookup?num=1013)

4. The letter genre can be traced back to the earliest English. Although there are many different types of letters, ranging from the personal to the professional, and although the conventions of letter writing have changed over time, all letters ave certain characteristics. They are written in order to share information or to conduct some business. Structurally, they have a salutation and a closing formula and use address terms. They typically have a known addressee and addresser, who share some sort of relationship with one another. They tend to be original and spontaneous productions which undergo little editing (although the epistolary novel exploits this genre for literary purposes and letters therein are crafted and edited productions). They are closer to the "oral" (informal, colloquial) rather than literate end of the spectrum. Finally, they may be written by anyone, by men and women, and by people of all social ranks and levels of education.

   Look at the letters below, which range in time from Middle English to the twentieth century. All are private letters (written from one brother to another, between friends and confidantes, and from a man to his cousin). Private letters show interactive features and a dialogic structure. They foreground the relationship between the correspondents and may be based on shared knowledge.

   What common generic features (both structural and linguistic) are present in all of the letters below? What features are different? To what extent are Biber and Finegan's (1992) features of "involved" style present in these letters? Is there a "drift" toward more oral style evident in the letters?

Middle English letter

The Cely family were wealthy wool merchants living in London but traveling frequently to Calais and Flanders. Their surviving letters date from 1475 to 1488. In this letter Richard Cely writes from London to his brother George in Calais:

Anno Jhesu M^{1}iiij^{c}iiij^{xx}j [1481]
   Riught whellbelouid brother I recomend me wnto yow wyth aull myne hart, informeyng yow at the makyng of thys howr fathe[r] and mother wher whell comforttyd and sendys yow ther blessyngys. Hyt whos so that be the menys of Brandon howr father and I wher indytted for scleyng ['slaying'] of an hartte ['hart, deer'] that whos dreuyn into Kent, the qwheche whe newyr se ['saw'] ner knew of, and thys day I haue ben wyth mastyr Mwngewmbre [Sir Thomas Montgomery, member of the Privy Council to Edward VI and Steward of the King's Forest of Essex], and geuyn hym the whalew ['value'] of a pype whyn ['cask holding 126 gallons of wine'] to haue ws ['us'] howt of the boke heuir ['whenever'] hyt be schewyd the Kyng, and so he has promysyd me, and to be good master to howr father and ws in the matter betwhene Brarddon and hus. John Froste, foster [forester], brohut me to hys mastyrschyp and aqwaynttyd me wyth a genttyllmane of hys hos

name ys Ramston, that ys a ny mane ['a close associate'] to master Mongewmbre, and so I mwste informe hym my matters at aull tymys and he whyll sche[w] them to hys master, etc. ... And I wndyrstonde that ʒe haue sowlde yowr grehyt gray hors, and I am ryught glade therof, for ij ys as good as xx. I wndyrstonde that ʒe haue a fayre hauke. I am ryught glade of hyr, for I trwste to God sche schall make yow and me ryught grehyt sporte. ʒefe ['if'] I whor sewyr ['sure'] at what passayge ['passage across the channel'] ʒe whollde send her I whowlde fett ['fetch'] hyr at Dowyr [Dover] and kepe hyr tyll ʒe cwm. A grehyt inforttewin ys fawlyn on yowr beche ['bitch'], for sche had xiiij fayr whelpys, and aftyr that sche hade whelpyd sche wholde newyr hett ['eat'] mette, and so sche ys deyd and aull her whelpys ... No mor to yow at thys tym. Jhesu kepe you. Whritte at London the v day of Nowembyr.

per yowr brother,
Richard Cely.
Source: Hanham (1975: 119–120)

Early Modern English letter

Lady Anne Conway (1631–1671), a seventeenth-century philosopher, corresponded regularly with the Cambridge Platonist, Henry More (1614–1687), about matters both philosophical and personal. In this letter, Henry More writes to Anne Conway:

"To the honourable the Lady Conway at Kensington these. Leave these at Dr Gells house in Bow-lane."

Madame

I am heartily sorry to hear that your head-ache increases so much upon you, and that your Physick has had no better success ... I do not at all mislike your resolution in giving over Physick if there be no better effect of it. Ease of minde, fresh ayr and diet, may leasurely do that, which Physick could not effect so suddenly. And you must absteine not onely from reading but from thinking too intensely. This Interpretation of mine you desire too see I have not yett completed, but I shall doe what I can to make an end of it this week, because I am to goe into Lincolnshire with these 10 dayes. When I come back, God willing, I shall transcribe it by parts and send it you ... Thus with my hearty prayers to God that he would bestow that upon you that Physicions can not procure you, in hast I take leave and rest,

Your Ladiships very affectionate friend and servant,
Hen. More.

Aprill 18 [1653]

Source: Nicolson (1992: 80–81)

Late Modern English letter

In the following letter, Charles Darwin writes to his second cousin, William Darwin Fox, in July 1835 from Lima, Peru, during the voyage of the HMS *Beagle* (1831–1836):

My dear Fox,

I have lately received two of your letters, one dated June and the other November, 1834 (they reached me, however, in an inverted order). I was very glad to receive a history of this most important year in your life. Previously I had only heard the plain fact that you were married. You are a true Christian and return good for evil, to send two such letters to so bad a correspondent as I have been. God bless you for writing so kindly and affectionately; if it is a pleasure to have friends in England, it is doubly so to think and know that one is not forgotten because absent. This voyage is terribly long. I do so earnestly desire to return, yet I dare hardly look forward to the future, for I do not know what will become of me . . ..

From this most wretched 'City of the Kings' we sail in a fortnight, from thence to Guayaquil, Galapagos, Marquesas, Society Islands, etc., etc. I look forward to the Galapagos with more interest than any other part of the voyage. They abound with active volcanoes, and, I should hope, contain Tertiary strata . . .

I shall indeed be glad once again to see you and tell you how grateful I feel for your steady friendship. God bless you, my very dear Fox.

Believe me, Yours affectionately, CHAS. DARWIN.

Source: Darwin (1887)

Present-day English letter

In this letter, the American poet Robert Lowell (who signs himself "Cal") writes to the British poet Ezra Pound:

November 8, 1957

Dear Ezra:

We expect to be in Washington the week-end of December 6, and I look forward to seeing you. Here are some poems, I've been writing like a house a-fire for the last three months. I hope you'll like some of them. I've been bolder about meter, and taken no count of the scansion in many of the new ones. I like regular meter too though, and don't feel I have to choose. Still after twenty years of writing in harness, it's not suicidal to cut loose a bit. My stuff is small and self-centered compared with yours and perhaps needs a certain tightness to come off.

We've enjoyed seeing Omar, and will have an evening with him again before I see you. He is tireless about his teaching and has little time to loaf. I guess next year will be a lot lighter for him. Hope you are booming and flourishing as you were last year.

My love to Dorothy,

Cal

Source: Hamilton (2005: 303–304)

9   Concluding Remarks

This chapter provides a summary of the book, which has attempted to describe the scope and nature of historical pragmatics in the first quarter of the twenty-first century and bring together a wide range of studies in the field. The chapter then reflects on issues arising from such studies and on gaps or limitations of existing work. Finally, it looks ahead to future research possibilities in the field of historical pragmatics.

9.1   Summary

This book begins with two chapters delimiting the field of historical pragmatics. These set the groundwork for six focused, topical chapters exemplifying the range and scope of historical pragmatic study.

Historical pragmatics has been defined as "a field of enquiry that investigates patterns of language use in earlier periods, the diachronic development of such usage patterns, and pragmatic explanations for language change in general" (Jucker 2012b: 510). It represents a convergence of historical linguistics (the study of language variation and change) and pragmatics (the study of language in use). The rise of historical pragmatics in the mid-1990s was the result of changes in both linguistics and pragmatics. The field of linguistics in the post-generative era underwent a number of paradigmatic shifts: a reawakened interest in historical study in the latter part of the twentieth century, combined with an emphasis on language as performance, not competence, on the everyday and sometimes ephemeral aspects of language, on meanings as negotiated in use rather than inherently stable, with the importance of social and cultural factors in shaping language use, and the increased importance of the collection and analysis of empirical data, made easier by the development of computer corpora. Changes in the field of pragmatics also enabled the development of historical pragmatics. Early work in pragmatics focused exclusively on oral conversational data as the source of pragmatic meaning. However, it came to be acknowledged that all discourse, whether spoken or written, consisted of communicative acts produced in a social and cultural context and is thus a valid subject of pragmatic study. We see the scope of historical pragmatics spanning the two branches of pragmatics, the Anglo-American or "micro-pragmatic" branch and the European Continental or "macro-pragmatic" branch, with two aligned fields – historical sociolinguistics and historical sociopragmatics – having affinity with the latter.

The field of historical pragmatics encompasses "historical pragmatics (proper)," with a synchronic focus on pragmatic forms and functions in an earlier stage of the language, and "diachronic pragmatics," with a dynamic focus on changes in pragmatic forms and functions over time. Within each subfield, it is also possible to study different linguistic levels, from either a synchronic or a diachronic perspective (either in or over time). On the level of expressions – words, phrases, and clauses – the approach taken is typically form-to-function, moving from a concrete linguistic form to its discourse-pragmatic functions. On the level of utterance – for example, speech acts or strategies of politeness – the approach taken is typically function-to-form, moving from a speech act function or politeness phenomenon to its formal exponents. And on the level of discourse, including register and genre, the approach may move from the formal conventions of a genre to their pragmatic functions or from the pragmatic dimensions of a genre to their formal expression. The lack of naturally occurring oral conversation and oral narrative from the past, where pragmatic meaning, especially relating to speaker attitude and speaker–hearer interaction, would be most obviously manifest, has been termed the "bad data" problem and seen as a challenge for historical pragmatic study. Nonetheless, the recognition that there is not an absolute dichotomy between speech and writing goes some way in addressing this concern. Medieval prose and verse growing out of the ancient oral tradition is known to retain many oral features. Moreover, from early periods, we have records which, while they come down to us in written form, represent authentic ("speech-based") dialogue (court transcripts, depositions, parliamentary proceedings), constructed or "speech-purposed" dialogue (dramatic and fictional dialogue), or material intended for oral delivery (sermons, prayers), and "speech-like" texts that are more or less colloquial in nature (personal letters, diaries). It is the "digital turn" in linguistics that has made many of these documents accessible for study in multi-genre and more specialized single-genre electronic corpora. The pragmatic annotation of these corpora, however, remains in its infancy.

A central area of study within historical pragmatics concerns the rise and function of pragmatic markers – or discourse markers – in the history of English. Here, the focus may be either on the function of pragmatic markers during a particular period or on their development over time. An underlying assumption of diachronic study is that pragmatic markers develop from content words, phrases, or clauses that acquire a distinctive syntactic form and discourse-pragmatic functions over time. In their development pragmatic markers follow various pathways, from adverb > conjunction > pragmatic marker, from sentence-internal adverb > sentential adverb > pragmatic marker, from main clause > ambiguous clause > parenthetical, from adverbial or imperative clause > pragmatic marker. Detailed studies of pragmatic markers in the history of English have shown that the historical data may be inconclusive about the pathway followed and require nuanced interpretation. The "matrix clause hypothesis" – the hypothesis that clausal pragmatic markers begin as main clauses and develop through an indeterminate stage following *that*-deletion into moveable parentheticals – does not always find confirmation in the historical data. The process of language change that best accounts for the development of pragmatic markers, including lexicalization, pragmaticalization, grammaticalization, and cooptation, is still a matter of scholarly debate, though the majority view is that if "grammar" is broadly understood, pragmatic markers are best seen as undergoing grammaticalization (including decategorialization and desemanticization).

The choices one makes for how the speech and thought of others is incorporated onto one's discourse are pragmatically motivated by, for example, how one evaluates this speech and thought or how one wishes to organize the discourse by foregrounding or backgrounding the quoted material. The categories of speech and thought representation have undergone change over time, as have the norms of speech and thought representation in different genres. Tracing the norms of speech and thought representation and the distribution of the different categories over time poses difficulties because different categories predominate in different genres, and existing historical studies do not give a comprehensive account of all genres in different periods. Overall, we can say with confidence that in all periods, speech presentation is more common than thought presentation and there is a general trend from more indirect (narrator-controlled, summarizing) forms of representation, such as indirect speech and narrative representation of thought, to more direct (autonomous or non-narrator-controlled, verbatim) forms, such as direct thought. (Free) direct speech is almost universally the norm for speech representation. In Old and Middle English we find mixed forms involving "slippage" between direct and indirect speech, but the conventionalization of quotation marks in Early Modern English led to the clearer marking of direct speech. For the representation of thought, internal narration takes over in the modern period from narrative representation of thought and indirect thought. Free indirect discourse did not exist in earlier English, arising perhaps in proto-form in the seventeenth century, but conventionalized fully only in the course of the nineteenth century. It is now used more often for the representation of thought than of speech. The inventory of reporting verbs has also changed over time. The most common verb of Old English, *cweþan*, developed into an invariable quotative marker, *quoth*, which then became obsolete. It was replaced in Middle English by *seien* 'say', which has remained the most common, neutral reporting verb. Present-day English is characterized by the rise of new reporting verbs, especially *go* and *be like*.

Politeness is at its core a pragmatic phenomenon, and we see changes in both the types of politeness and the forms of politeness used over time. Politeness has been conceptualized as the avoidance of face-threatening acts or as the enhancement of communicative concord. The Old English period was an era of "discernment" politeness, stemming from the fixed social hierarchy of the time; Christianity introduced politeness of humility. The Middle English period saw the rise of "deference" politeness following the French fashion (i.e., the honorific system of second-person pronouns). A face-based system began in Early Modern English, but studies are not consistent in finding this to be a positive or negative politeness system. Changing social structures led to the loss of the deference politeness system. The eighteenth century extolled polite manners and behavior and the use of highly formalized compliments, thus earning the designation "compliment culture." The modern period is characterized by "non-imposition" politeness, most obvious in the development of indirect directives (negative politeness) of the *can/could/will/would you* type in the twentieth century. At the same time, a system of "camaraderie" politeness, which increases solidarity and eliminates distance between individuals, coexists (positive politeness). Four case studies of politeness exemplify changing politeness forms in the history of English: (i) compliments, showing a change from ritual to personal compliments; (ii) insults, likewise changing from ritual to personal insults, with ludic ritual insults continuing in certain cultural contexts; (iii) thanking, showing the rise of elliptical expressions (*thanks, thank you*), highly codified forms in the eighteenth century, and the development of a discourse (closing) function for thanks in the modern period; and (iv) responses to thanks, showing increasing frequency after Early Modern English and the development of different types and forms in the modern period (*no problem, no worries*).

The study of speech acts presents a number of challenges for historical pragmatics. Given the relatively rare use of performative verbs, the form-to-function approach offers limited possibilities, though it has been shown that speech-act uses of verbs develop from non-performative origins. Identifying speech-act functions in historical texts/periods and their formal manifestations (i.e., the function-to-form approach) is fraught with difficulties. Methods that have been devised for the study of speech acts that address these difficulties include close readings of texts/corpora and speech-act annotations of corpora, or focus on performative verbs, illocutionary-force-indicating devices, and/or metacommunicative labels. Historical studies of a range of speech acts, including directives, commissives, and expressives, have exposed changes not only in the formal manifestations of speech acts over time but also in the nature of the speech acts themselves. Directives in earlier English would seem to be more direct than we find today, but this can be attributed to the more fixed social structure, not to less politeness. In Middle English society, commissives were "binding," regardless of the conditions under which they were uttered, whereas now they rest fundamentally upon the sincerity condition of the speaker. Apologies, curses, greetings, and leave-takings represent expressives that have undergone change in the history of English, both in respect to their formal expression and their functional profile. Secular apologies begin to appear in Middle English, with speaker-oriented (*I'm sorry*) coming to replace addressee-oriented (*excuse me*) apologies and a weakening of the force of apologies in general in contemporary society. Curses evolved from execratory (declarative) to exclamatory (expressive) in nature. Forms of greeting and leave-taking proliferated over time and often weakened in meaning, such as *how do you do* no longer serving as an inquiry about one's well-being or *goodbye* (< *God be with you*) no longer serving as a blessing.

Address terms, both second-person pronouns and nominal terms of address (used vocatively), serve essential pragmatic functions in negotiating interpersonal relations, for example in expressing closeness, affection, distance, respect, and so on, and are fundamentally related to matters of politeness. Both systems have changed in the history of English in the direction of less honorific-based, more camaraderie-based systems. While data in Old English are scanty, in Middle English we begin to have texts in which address terms are common, including constructed dialogue (in drama and fiction) and authentic dialogue (in personal letters, court proceedings, and witness depositions). Second-person pronouns, originally distinguishing singular and plural in Old English, began in Middle English to distinguish differences between interlocutors, with the singular *thou* denoting lesser rank/status/age/power or increased solidarity, intimacy, or informality and the plural *you* denoting higher rank/status/age/power or greater social/emotional distance or formality. The use of these pronouns for a range of affective purposes became prominent in Early Modern English, especially in literary texts, where sometimes bewildering shifts between the pronouns (what has been called "retractability") were used for literary purposes. Nonetheless, loss of *thou* for a variety of sociolinguistic reasons was complete by 1700 or even earlier in the "standard" dialect of London and the East, leaving English without an honorific form or a number distinction in the second person. The nominal system of address underwent less systematic change, but moved in the same general direction. The elaborate vocative system we see in Early Modern English, which carefully delineated a person's rank and status, was replaced by a more diffuse collection of vocative terms, with preference increasingly given to personal names (especially first names), familiar family names, "familiarizers," and endearments, all of which serve to increase rapport between individuals and create a sense of equality. They are part of the phenomenon of camaraderie politeness, which is dominant in Present-day English.

Finally, pragmatic factors operate on the discourse level, including register, genre, and style. Applying a multidimensional analysis to style, Biber and Finegan (1989, 1992) reveal a gradual drift from "literate" to "oral" style over the history of English, but not by an entirely direct path and not in all genres universally. Registers, or discourse domains, are shaped by pragmatic factors over time. For example, the news register has undergone substantial change with the rise of the newspaper in the seventeenth century leading to the introduction of numerous new types of publications, such as television, radio, and internet news, and new genres, such as editorials, obituaries, or weather forecasts. In contrast, the religious register has a history going back to Old English and has shown remarkable stability. Two genres within the religious register, prayers and sermons, have undergone little change in respect to function, structure, and linguistic characteristics. The recipe genre, in contrast, exhibits a substantial set of changes. While the function of recipes remained constant (i.e., instructions on how to prepare or do something), thus accounting for the imperative as the defining linguistic form, we find differences in the content of recipes (medicinal vs. culinary, with the gradual demise of medicinal recipes over time), in the audience of recipes (e.g., the professional vs. the amateur cook, or the professional doctor vs. the lay healer), in the structural elements found in recipes (e.g., separation of the ingredients and the procedural steps), and in characteristic linguistic features (such as the introduction of null objects and telegraphic style).

9.2   Future Directions

This book has focused on historical pragmatic study exclusively in English. While early work in the field was primarily (though not exclusively) focused on English, the expansion of the field has led to historical pragmatic studies in a large variety of languages, including ancient (e.g., Greek, Latin, Egyptian), medieval (e.g., Old Occitan, Old Italian, Old High German), and contemporary (e.g., Italian, French, German), as well as non-Indo-European languages (e.g., Japanese, Korean, Chinese), as is obvious by a glance through the table of contents of the *Journal of Historical Pragmatics*. We can expect that an ever increasing variety of languages will come under the scrutiny of historical pragmatists.

As we have seen throughout this book, electronic corpora have played a central role in (almost) all historical pragmatic study and have become the methodological norm today. We can expect to see the increasing development of genre-specific ("second generation") corpora which are more and more sophisticated (with access to source manuscripts, variant editions, original and standardized spelling and so on, and with part-of-speech and syntactic tagging). Indeed, a number of genre-specific corpora are currently under construction, partially completed, or recently released; others are available, but not in the public domain. A few of these include the following:[1]

- *A Corpus of Irish English Correspondence* (CORIECOR) – Some but not all of this corpus (letters dated from 1731 to 1940) is available (*CORIECOR visualized. Irish English in writing across time [a longitudinal historical perspective]*).[2]
- *Corpus of Early English Recipes* (CoER) – See Alonso-Almeida et al. (2012).
- *Coruña Corpus of English Scientific Writing* – This corpus includes subcorpora on chemistry, life sciences, history, and astronomy[3] – See also Moskowich et al. (2021).
- *The Málaga Corpus of Early English Scientific Prose* – The Late Middle English (1350–1500)[4] and Early Modern English (1500–1700)[5] subcorpora are available; these include unedited material dealing with medicine. A Late Modern English subcorpus (1700–1900) of printed texts is being prepared. See Miranda García and Calle-Martín (2012).

We also look forward to more of *The Old Bailey Proceedings Online* being coded as part of the *Old Bailey Corpus* (a 3rd edition is to be released), as well as further updates and expansions of the ARCHER corpus.[6] We would also hope to see advances in the automatic pragmatic annotation of (historical) corpora, which a decade ago, Jucker (2013: 4) was pessimistic about ("Pragmatic information still seems to defy automatic processing").

A number of the distinctions set out in the first two chapters of this book may need to be re-evaluated. First, as many of the studies summarized here have made obvious, the distinction between form-to-function and function-to-form is often difficult to maintain, as form and function are intrinsically interconnected. Nor is it necessarily a useful distinction or one that can always easily be made. Second, also difficult to maintain is the division between the subfields of historical pragmatics (proper) and diachronic pragmatics. The function of pragmatic forms, like all linguistic forms, is in constant flux, responding to the needs of interlocutors and the effects of contextual interactions. When viewing large periods of time, such as Middle English or Early Modern English, we should have no expectation that pragmatic forms and functions would remain unchanged. The extent to which the separation between historical pragmatics (proper) and diachronic pragmatics can be maintained, however, rests on the focus in the latter on the syntactic origins of and processes of semantico-syntactic change affecting pragmatic forms; this emphasis is especially the case in regard to pragmatic markers, which are assumed to originate

---

[1] See https://varieng.helsinki.fi/CoRD/corpora/corpusfinder/index.html for more complete and updated information.
[2] https://corviz.h.uib.no   [3] https://ruc.udc.es/dspace/handle/2183/21846
[4] https://hunter.uma.es   [5] https://modernmss.uma.es/Corpus
[6] Version 3.3; see www.projects.alc.manchester.ac.uk/archer/archer-versions/

in fully referential forms and undergo semantic and syntactic change on their path to pragmatic markers (whether they are understood to undergo grammaticalization, pragmaticalization, or cooptation). Third, the division between historical pragmatics and what has been termed "historical sociopragmatics" is often blurred. The two approaches in fact work in tandem: historical sociopragmatics seeks to understand how the sociohistorical conditions of language use provide motivations for pragmatic forms and processes over time, while historical pragmatics examines the ways in which pragmatic forms and processes of pragmatic change give us insight into the sociohistorical context. As Archer notes, it might be better to speak of "historical (socio)pragmatic linguistics," since pragmatic is by definition social: "[m]any studies with historical pragmatics combine the sociopragmatic and the pragmalinguistic perspective ... or the component and perspective views" (2017: 332).

In coming years, register and genre offer many new possibilities for pragmatic study. Chapter 8 was able only to scratch the surface by looking at the register of religion (the genres of prayer and sermons) and the genre of recipes, with briefer attention to the news register and the genre of the personal letter. Within the field at large, the focus of such studies to date has been the registers of science and medicine, religion, law (and the courtroom), news, and correspondence and their associated genres. But there are a myriad of other registers and genres awaiting pragmatic study. One area that is receiving increased attention is the "pragmatics of fiction" (see, for example, Locher and Jucker 2017). But in many ways, this is not new. The field of "literary pragmatics" can be traced back to the early 1990s (e.g., Sell 1991). Linking pragmatic theory with literary analysis, it "uses ideas from pragmatics to the benefit of literary analysis" and is "inevitably interpretive" (Pilkington 2010: 251). Pragmatic concepts such as deixis, presupposition, implicature, relevance, the cooperative principle, speech acts, (im)politeness, and turn-taking are analyzed in literary texts (plays, novels, poems) in order to enhance or justify particular literary interpretations of those texts. In contrast, the focus of the "pragmatics of fiction" is essentially not interpretive. Jucker (2015: 67) argues "that a pragmatic analysis might possibly provide some additional layers of literary interpretation but also – and perhaps more importantly – that fictional language provides a fertile data source for pragmaticists if it is not seen as a deviation from more basic forms of language but as a specific form of communication with its own characteristic features that warrant an analysis in and of itself." Jucker (2015: 63) first emphasizes that fictive language may in many ways "seem an unlikely candidate for pragmatic analyses" because it is far removed from spontaneous oral conversation (the usual data for pragmatic analysis); fiction is typically written (though drama is intended for oral delivery), carefully planned and edited, and often subject to artificial conventions such as meter and rhyme. But Jucker argues that if fiction is accepted for what it is and not apologized for as an imperfect representation of "actual speech," then pragmatic analysis is possible. More importantly, the pragmatics of fiction has as its focus the identification of the pragmatic features of a genre, that is, the pragmatic forms which characterize fictive texts in general. Areas of interest include the pragmatic resources used for characterization, voice, stance, emotion, (im)politeness, speech representation, et cetera. The pragmatics of fiction has not to date had a strong historical focus (see the handbook by Locher and Jucker [2015], which has only one chapter on language change, but see Fitzmaurice [2010]). However, as we have seen throughout this book, historical pragmaticists have relied heavily on literary texts for their data sources, because until recently, non-literary texts were not always easily available and conversational data was nonexistent. For example, historical pragmatic studies for Middle English have relied heavily on Chaucer and for Early Middle English on Shakespeare. While it is not necessary to throw out such studies, it is perhaps necessary to moderate the pragmatic conclusions arrived at in these earlier studies in light of what is emerging within the growing field of the pragmatics of fiction. That is, it cannot be assumed that the use of *thou* and *you* in Shakespeare, for instance, is consonant with the everyday language of the time, but it must be recognized that it is shaped by the demands of the dramatic genre. We have actually seen quite a few examples in the course of the preceding chapters where genre plays a highly significant role, whether in the use of *thou* and *you* in witness depositions as opposed to trial proceedings and in contrast to Shakespeare or in the representation of speech in witness depositions in contrast to that in novels or newspapers.

Despite thirty years of concentrated work, there remains much to be done in the study of pragmatics in the history of English. While there are always more and newly emerging pragmatic markers to be studied (see, e.g., McColm and Trousdale 2019 on *whatever*) and more debate about the process(es) responsible for the development of pragmatic markers (see, e.g., Heine et al. 2021), a fruitful approach taken in recent work by Traugott (2020, 2022) is a historical constructionalist perspective. Examining an interrelated set of discourse structuring markers, including elaborative markers (*also, further(more), moreover*), contrastive markers (*but, all the same, instead*), digressive markers (*by the way, by the by, incidentally, parenthetically*), and 'return to topic' markers (*to return to X point, back to X point/topic*), Traugott argues that these constitute a constructional schema generalizing over individual micro-constructions which develop from different sources, generally circumstance adverbials, occurring in recurrent discourse contexts, following similar paths, and progressing either to the stage of "minimally pragmatic," monofunctional discourse structuring markers or conjuncts (e.g., *in addition, instead*) or to the stage of fully pragmatic, multifunctional Discourse markers (e.g., *after all, by the way*) by processes of "constructionalization" and "post-constructionalization." No matter what theoretical perspective one adopts, Traugott's work shows clearly the importance of seeing pragmatic markers not as individual and autonomous forms but rather as parts of larger (and overlapping) networks of similarly behaving (and similarly developing) constructions. We might, for example, wish to examine the rise of epistemic parentheticals in a similar framework, where we see some as more fully pragmaticalized, such as *I reckon, I gather, I find*, and others as more contentful, such as *I think, I believe, I guess*. Do these arise in similar discourse contexts and follow similar paths of development?

In the chapter on speech and thought representation, we saw that it was difficult to compare studies because they were disparate not only in period covered but also in genre or register examined. Register/genre seems to be a strong factor in respect to the types and norms of speech and thought representation used. There is considerable room, therefore, for historical studies (similar to that of Semino and Short [2004] for Present-day English) that take a cross-genre approach. In addition, although we have studies of Middle English and Early Modern English speech and thought representation, with the exception of B. Busse's study of the nineteenth-century novel and research on free indirect discourse (e.g., Fludernik 1993; Vandelanotte 2009) mainly focused on contemporary English, the Late Modern English period has been relatively neglected.

While we have a recent monograph on politeness in the history of English (Jucker 2020), there remain unanswered questions. As we saw, for example, scholars are divided as to whether Early Modern English can be characterized as a period of positive or negative politeness and what changes, if any, occurred over the course the period. Jucker's (2020: 187–188) description of the period as one of both "deference" and "solidarity" politeness is not entirely successful in avoiding the contradiction between "negative" and "positive" politeness. Likewise, Present-day English has been characterized as a period of both negative (non-imposition) politeness and positive (camaraderie) politeness. Leech (2014) ends his discussion of politeness by questioning whether politeness is declining in English. He cites Lakoff's (2005) examples of instances where politeness has come under pressure, in large part from electronic media, where interactions are frequent, multiple, and often anonymous, where speaker and hearer are unlikely ever to enter into a social relationship, where informalization is predominant, and where an adversarial system (adopted from politics and law) is institutionalized. Lakoff lists nine cases of "impoliteness," such as cursing and non-politically correct language, sexual coarseness in public, violence in the media, "agonism" (unwillingness to acknowledge middle ground), negative political advertising, displays of hostility (e.g., road/air rage), "flaming" on the internet and/or loss of polite conventions (e.g., *thank you, please*). Nonetheless, Leech believes that impoliteness is a "minority phenomenon," and that while bivalent politeness has declined, trivalent politeness remains strong. This is certainly a question that requires further investigation.

Speech acts are a functional category, depending on the illocutionary force of an utterance, or the communicative intention of the speaker. The study of speech acts thus requires a function-to-form approach, which would seem to necessitate a close reading of a text or corpus extract. In order to study speech acts (semi-)automatically in a corpus – which requires a search string – a number of work-arounds have been developed, namely, searches for performative verbs, for illocutionary-force-indicating devices (IFIDs), for syntactic patterns typical of particular speech acts, and for metacommunicative speech-act labels. These are all essentially form-to-function approaches and are thus fundamentally problematic: they require pre-existing knowledge of the relevant speech-act forms in earlier stages of the language. We can hope that with improved pragmatic annotation of corpora (see above), we will have more trustworthy means of studying speech acts in earlier English corpora. Not only do the forms used for expressing the speech acts change in significant ways over time, but also the very nature of the speech act, its illocutionary force, or what Jucker (2018) calls its "functional profile," may change over time. And this can pose a problem since we usually take the illocutionary force of a speech act as the starting point of diachronic studies. What counts as a particular speech act in earlier English and in Present-day English may be very different. For example, we have seen that curses, which originally served as declaratives that (were believed to) bring the wrath of God upon their recipients, have become expressives, merely giving voice to the ill will of the speaker against the hearer. Promises, which in the "binding promises" of medieval times did not depend upon the sincerity condition of the speaker, now rest fundamentally upon this condition. The religious invocation expressed by the leave-taking expression *God be with you/God by you* has now become a neutral form of leave-taking, *Goodbye*. Greetings such as *How are you?* and especially *How do you do?*, originally serving as requests concerning the well-being of the recipient, are now conventionalized and propositionally empty greetings. In the case of thanking, fully performative forms (*I give you thanks/I thank you*) have given way to shortened forms (*thank you/thanks*), which Aijmer (1996: 72, 76–77) says do not express "real gratitude" but are used more in response to polite greetings or in response for minor services or trivial acts of kindness. Moreover, thanking is frequently used as a means to close a discourse segment, where it serves as a "discourse marker" and has "very little meaning" (Aijmer 1996: 52–66). *Thank you/thanks* can also be used ironically (e.g., *thank you for nothing*). Similarly, responses to thanks that express pleasure or appreciation (e.g., *my pleasure, you're welcome*) or those that minimize the favor (e.g., *don't mention it, it was no trouble*) are being replaced by simple acknowledgments (e.g., *okay, all right*). Responses to thanks also come to reinforce the discourse function of thanking, and an ironic use of *you're welcome* is also possible (see Brinton 2021).

Jucker (2019) sees these changes in speech acts as a unidirectional process of weakening or "attenuation." He notes that apologies have become more common, often uttered for minor infractions, which the apologizer playfully calls attention to with new expressions such as *oops, whoops, my bad*. Thus, the "illocutionary potential [of apologies] has been maximally weakened, i.e. attenuated, and they are fully pragmaticalized, i.e. the semantic transparency has largely been lost and their interpretation increasingly relies on the specific context in which they occur" (16). Jucker suggests that other speech acts such as promises (which have become insincere and devoid of commitment) may undergo similar attenuation. Leech (2014) sees the bleaching of meaning in these cases as what he calls "pragmaticalization," in which forms become devoid of meaning and develop into pragmatic markers (e.g., in the case of *pardon*). This is a topic which requires further study. We know that in language change processes of weakening are typically balanced by processes of strengthening. We also know that new IFIDs for the expression of speech acts are always entering the language (e.g., *apologize* for apologies) or IFIDs are coopted for new purposes (e.g., *promise* or *insist* as strong representatives). Thus, a unidirectional and irreversible process of speech-act weakening would deplete the language of true speech acts and reduce language to a series of minimal speech acts with reduced or empty force.

While the use of *thou* and *you* and the eventual replacement of the former by the latter in English would seem to have been exhaustively studied, we saw that scholarly attention has been strongly focused on the use of these pronouns in Shakespeare. In these dramatic texts, intricate switches between *thou* and *you* – or what has been termed "retractability" – make it clear that the pronouns' use is in large part motivated by literary demands (of characterization, plot development, and so on). Thus, the use of the second-person pronouns in Shakespeare perhaps tells us more about the dramatic genre in Elizabethan times than it does about contemporary (non-literary) usage. As U. Busse notes at the conclusion of his study of the use of *thou* and *you* in Shakespeare, "Although we should not believe that Shakespeare had any reason to present inauthentic language, it must be emphasised that some of the pronoun choices may have been made for the sake of rhyme and metre, the requirements of genre, plot or a particular scene, to achieve a certain dramatic effect, etc. ... we should not conclude that the language of drama with its carefully constructed speeches bore any close resemblance to real people talking ..." (2003: 216). As more studies appear on the use of *thou* and *you* in non-literary genres, such as witness depositions, trial proceedings, and personal letters, we may begin to acquire a somewhat clearer understanding of pronoun usage in Elizabethan England and the extent to which sociolinguistic factors, including socioeconomic class, gender, age, and regional variety, influenced usage – and ultimately led to the loss of *thou*.

Another aspect of pronoun usage which bears closer study is the way in which speakers have restored the singular–plural distinction in the second person by innovating new plural forms. A wide variety of these new pronouns are found in regional American English dialects (as well as other dialects), including *yous* (variously *youse, yez, yiz, yooz, youze,* etc.), *you-all, y'all, youse-all, you-uns, you-uns all, you guys,* and *youse guys.* There is some evidence that *y'all,* characteristic of the Midland and Southern US, is now spreading throughout American English (see Black 2019). The *Dictionary of American English* (DARE) cites all of these forms from the early to mid-nineteenth century; similar datings are given for most of these recorded in the OED. The editors of DARE admit, however, that for *you-all* "its early history is poorly documented." Examples of *y'all* appear in EModE verse, for example, where the contractions would seem to be required by the demands of the verse:

(1) a. The captiue men of strength I gaue to you,
         The weaker sold; and this **y'all** know is true,
         The free-borne women ransom'd, or set free
         For pittie sake, the seruile sort had yee: (1631 Lisle, *The Faire Æthiopian*;
         cited in Black 2019; https://quod.lib.umich.edu/e/eebo/A02903.0001.001?
         view=toc)
     b. Ta. A race of Criples, are **y'all**
         Issue of Snayles, he could not else have scap't us.
         Now, what newes bring you? (1646 Suckling, *The Goblins*; ED)

Fuller historical study is obviously called for. Interestingly, both *you-all/y'all* (DARE, s.v. *you-all,* pron, def. A2) and *youse* (DARE, s.v. *youse,* pron, def. 2) can be used for singular reference as well. According to DARE, *you guys* (DARE, s.v. *you guys,* pron), though originally referring to males, is "now generally used as a genderless pron[oun]." This statement may need to be re-evaluated, however, given contemporary views of gender and pronoun usage. Black (2019) speculates that *y'all* may be developing as the gender-neutral form of *you guys.* In general, of course, gendered/non-gendered pronoun usage has become a pragmatically fraught area deserving of more careful study.

With obsolescence of the honorific system of second-person pronouns in English, the pragmatic importance of vocatives has grown. Yet apart from B. Busse's monumental study of vocatives in Shakespeare (2006) and some attention to vocatives in letters of the time (e.g., Nevala 2003, 2004, 2010), historical study of vocatives has been limited. Changing patterns of vocative use over time call for more careful and detailed study (see, for example, the sample study of *lady* which begins Chapter 7).

In conclusion, while we have witnessed the expansion and growing maturity of the field of historical pragmatics since its inception in the 1990s, it remains in some respects an emerging field which presents a rich potential for future research.

References

Adamson, Sylvia. 1994. From empathetic deixis to empathetic narrative: Stylisation and (de-)subjectivisation as processes of language change. *Transactions of the Philological Society* 92(1). 55–88. https://doi.org/10.1111/j.1467-968X.1994.tb00428.x

Adamson, Sylvia. 2001. The rise and fall of empathetic narrative: A historical perspective on perspective. In Willie van Peer and Seymour Chatman (eds.), *New perspectives on narrative perspective*, 83–99. Albany, NY: State University of New York Press.

Aijmer, Karin. 1996. *Conversational routines in English: Convention and creativity.* New York: Longman. https://doi.org/10.4324/9781315845128

Aijmer, Karin. 2015. Quotative markers in *A Corpus of English Dialogues 1560–1760.* In Arendholz et al. (eds.), 231–254. https://doi.org/10.1515/9783110427561-011

Aijmer, Karin and Christoph Rühlemann (eds.). 2015. *Corpus pragmatics: A handbook.* Cambridge: Cambridge University Press. https://doi.org/10.1017/CBO9781139057493

Alonso-Almeida, Francisco. 2008. The pragmatics of *and*-conjunctives in Middle English medical recipes: A Relevance Theory description. *Journal of Historical Pragmatics* 9(2). 171–199. https://doi.org/10.1075/jhp.9.1.02alo

Alonso-Almeida, Francisco. 2013. Genre conventions in English recipes (1600–1800). In DiMeo and Pennell (eds.), 68–92.

Alonso-Almeida, Francisco and Mercedes Cabrera-Abreu. 2002. The formulation of promise in medieval English medical recipes: A Relevance-Theoretic approach. *Neophilologus* 86. 137–154. https://doi.org/10.1023/A: 1012940619214

Alonso-Almeida, Francisco, Ivalla Ortega-Barrera, and Elena Quintana-Toledo. 2012. Corpus of Early English recipes: Design and implementation. In Vázquez (ed.), 37–50.

Ameka, Felix. 1992. Interjections: The universal yet neglected part of speech. *Journal of Pragmatics* 18. 101–118. https://doi.org/10.1016/0378-2166(92)90048-G

Archer, Dawn. 2005. *Questions and answers in the English courtroom (1640–1760): A sociopragmatic analysis.* Amsterdam: John Benjamins. https://doi.org/10.1075/pbns.135

Archer, Dawn. 2010. Speech acts. In Jucker and Taavitsainen (eds.), 397–417. https://doi.org/10.1515/9783110214284.6.379

Archer, Dawn. 2012. Early Modern English: Pragmatics and discourse. In Bergs and Brinton (eds.), vol. 1, 652–667. https://doi.org/10.1515/9783110251593.652

Archer, Dawn. 2014. Exploring verbal aggression in English historical texts using USAS: The possibilities, the problems and potential solutions. In Taavitsainen, Jucker, and Tuominen (eds.), 277–301. https://doi.org/10.1075/pbns.243.17arc

Archer, Dawn. 2017. Context and historical (socio)pragmatics twenty years on. *Journal of Historical Pragmatics* 18(2). 315–336. https://doi.org/10.1075/jhp.00008.arc

Archer, Dawn and Jonathan Culpeper. 2003. Sociopragmatic annotation: New directions and possibilities in historical corpus linguistics. In Andrew Wilson, Paul Rayson, and Tony McEnery (eds.), *Corpus linguistics by the Lune: A Festschrift for Geoffrey Leech*, 37–58. Frankfurt: Peter Lang.

Archer, Dawn and Jonathan Culpeper. 2009. Identifying *key* sociophilological usage in plays and trial proceedings (1640–1760): An empirical approach via corpus annotation. *Journal of Historical Pragmatics* 10(2). 286–309. https://doi.org/10.1075/jhp.10.2.07arc

Archer, Dawn, Jonathan Culpeper, and Matthew Davies. 2008. Pragmatic annotation. In Anke Lüdeling and Merja Kytö (eds.), *Corpus linguistics: An international handbook*, vol. 1, 613–642. Berlin: De Gruyter Mouton.

Arendholz, Jenny, Wolfram Bublitz, Monika Kirner, and Iris Zimmermann. 2013. Food for thought – or, what's (in) a recipe: A diachronic analysis of cooking instructions. In Gerhardt et al. (eds.), 119–137. https://doi.org/10.1075/clu.10.05are

Arendholz, Jenny, Wolfram Bublitz, and Monika Kirner-Ludwig (eds.). 2015. *The pragmatics of quoting now and then*. Berlin: De Gruyter Mouton. https://doi.org/10.1515/9783110427561

Arnovick, Leslie K. 1999. *Diachronic pragmatics: Seven case studies in English illocuttionary development*. Amsterdam: John Benjamins. https://doi.org/10.1075/pbns.68

Arnovick, Leslie K. 2006. *Written reliquaries: The resonance of orality in medieval English texts*. Amsterdam: John Benjamins. https://doi.org/10.1075/pbns.153

Atkinson, Dwight. 1999. *Scientific discourse in sociohistorical context: The Philosophical Transactions of the Royal Society of London, 1675–1975*. Mahwah, NJ: Lawrence Erlbaum Associates. https://doi.org/10.4324/9781410601704

Austin, John L. 1962. *How to do things with words*. Cambridge, MA: Harvard University Press.

Banfield, Ann. 1982. *Unspeakable sentences: Narration and representation in the language of fiction*. London: Routledge. https://doi.org/10.4324/9781315746609

Bator, Magdalena. 2016. On the development of the English culinary recipe. *Academic Journal of Modern Philology* 5. 7–15.

Bator, Magdalena and Marta Sylwanowicz. 2017. The typology of medieval recipes – culinary vs. medical. In Jacek Fisiak, Magdalena Bator, and Marta Sylwanowicz (eds.), *Essays and studies in Middle English. 9th International Conference on Middle English, Philological School of Higher Education in Wrocław, 2015*, 11–33. Frankfurt: Peter Lang.

Beeching, Kate. 2016. *Pragmatic markers in British English: Meaning in social interaction*. Cambridge: Cambridge University Press. https://doi.org/10.1017/CBO9781139507110

Bergs, Alexander and Laurel J. Brinton (eds.). 2012a. *English historical linguistics: An international handbook*, 2 vols. Berlin: De Gruyter Mouton.

Bergs, Alexander and Laurel J. Brinton. 2012b. History of English historical linguistics: Overview. In Bergs and Brinton (eds.), vol. 2, 1289–1295. https://doi.org/10.1515/9783110251609.1289

Biber, Douglas. 2004. Historical patterns for the grammatical marking of stance. *Journal of Historical Pragmatics* 5(1). 107–136. https://doi.org/10.1075/jhp.5.1.06bib

Biber, Douglas and Edward Finegan. 1989. Drift and the evolution of English style: A history of three genres. *Language* 65(3). 487–517. https://doi.org/10.2307/415220

Biber, Douglas and Edward Finegan. 1992. The linguistic evolution of five written and speech-based English genres from the 17th to the 20th centuries. In Matti Rissanen, Ossi Ihalainen, Terttu Nevalainen, and Irma Taavitsainen (eds.), *History of Englishes: New methods and interpretations in historical linguistics*, 688–704. Berlin: Mouton de Gruyter. https://doi.org/10.1515/9783110877007.688

Biber, Douglas, Stig Johansson, Geoffrey Leech, Susan Conrad, and Edward Finegan. 1999. *Longman grammar of spoken and written English*. Harlow, Essex: Longman.

Bieswanger, Markus. 2015. Variational pragmatics and *responding to thanks* – revisited. *Multilingua* 34(3). 527–546. https://doi.org/10.1515/multi-2014-0106

Black, Bill. 2019. Why is everyone suddenly saying "y'all"? *Mel Magazine*. https://melmagazine.com/en-us/story/why-is-everyone-suddenly-saying-yall (accessed October 20, 2022)

Boye, Kasper and Peter Harder. 2007. Complement-taking predicates: Usage and linguistic structure. *Studies in Language* 31(3). 569–606. https://doi.org/10.1075/sl.31.3.03boy

Brinton, Laurel J. 1980. "Represented perception": A study of narrative style. *Poetics* 9. 363–381. https://doi.org/10.1016/0304-422X(80)90028-5

Brinton, Laurel J. 1996. *Pragmatic markers in English: Grammaticalization and discourse functions*. Berlin: Mouton de Gruyter. https://doi.org/10.1515/9783110907582

Brinton, Laurel J. 2008. *The comment clause in English: Syntactic origins and pragmatic development*. Cambridge: Cambridge University Press. https://doi.org/10.1017/CBO9780511551789

Brinton, Laurel J. 2010. Discourse markers. In Jucker and Taavitsainen (eds.), 285–314. https://doi.org/10.1515/9783110214284.5.285

Brinton, Laurel J. 2014. The extremes of insubordination: Exclamatory *as if! Journal of English Linguistics* 42(2). 93–112. https://doi.org/10.1177/0075424214521425

Brinton, Laurel J. 2015. Historical discourse analysis. In Deborah Tannen, Heidi E. Hamilton, and Deborah Schiffrin (eds.), *The handbook of discourse analysis*, 2nd ed., 222–243. Chichester: Wiley-Blackwell. https://doi.org/10.1002/9781118584194.ch10

Brinton, Laurel J. (ed.). 2017a. *English historical linguistics*. Cambridge: Cambridge University Press. https://doi.org/10.1017/9781316286562

Brinton, Laurel J. 2017b. *The evolution of pragmatic markers in English: Pathways of change*. Cambridge: Cambridge University Press. https://doi.org/10.1017/9781316416013

Brinton, Laurel J. 2017c. Historical pragmatic approaches. In Brinton (ed.), 245–275. https://doi.org/10.1017/9781316286562.010

Brinton, Laurel J. 2021. Responding to thanks: From *you're welcome* to *you bet. Journal of Historical Pragmatics* 22(2). 180–201. https://doi.org/10.1075/jhp.00052.bri

Brinton, Laurel J. and Elizabeth Closs Traugott. 2005. *Lexicalization and language change*. Cambridge: Cambridge University Press. https://doi.org/10.1017/CBO9780511615962

Brown, Keith (ed.). 2006. *Encyclopedia of language and linguistics*, 2nd ed. Amsterdam: Elsevier.

Brown, Penelope and Stephen C. Levinson. 1987[1978]. *Politeness: Some universals in language use*. Cambridge: Cambridge University Press. https://doi.org/10.1017/CBO9780511813085

Brown, Roger and Albert Gilman. 1960. The pronouns of power and solidarity. In Thomas A. Sebeok (ed.), *Style in language*, 256–276. Cambridge, MA: MIT Press.

Brown, Roger and Albert Gilman. 1989. Politeness theory and Shakespeare's four major tragedies. *Language in Society* 18(2). 159–212. https://doi.org/10.1017/S0047404500013464

Brownlees, Nicholas (ed.). 2006. *News discourse in Early Modern Britain. Selected Papers of CHINED 2004*. Bern: Peter Lang.

Bublitz, Wolfram and Monika Bednarek. 2006. Reported speech: Pragmatic aspects. In Brown (ed.), 540–553. https://doi.org/10.1016/B0-08-044854-2/00369-2

Buchstaller, Isabelle. 2014. *Quotatives: New trends and sociolinguistic implications*. Malden, MA: Wiley-Blackwell. https://doi.org/10.1002/9781118584415

Burnley, David. 1983. *A guide to Chaucer's language*. London: Macmillan. https://doi.org/10.1007/978-1-349-86048-7

Burnley, David. 2003. The T/V pronouns in Middle English literature. In Taavitsainen and Jucker (eds.), 27–45. https://doi.org/10.1075/pbns.107.03bur

Busse, Beatrix. 2006. *Vocative constructions in the language of Shakespeare*. Amsterdam: John Benjamins. https://doi.org/10.1075/pbns.150

Busse, Beatrix. 2020. *Speech, writing and thought presentation in 19th-century narrative fiction: A corpus-assisted approach*. Oxford: Oxford University Press. https://doi.org/10.1093/oso/9780190212360.001.0001

Busse, Ulrich. 2002. *Linguistic variation in the Shakespeare corpus: Morpho-syntactic variability of second person pronouns*. Amsterdam: John Benjamins. https://doi.org/10.1075/pbns.106

Busse, Ulrich. 2003. The co-occurrence of nominal and pronominal address forms in the Shakespeare corpus: Who says *thou* or *you* to whom? In Taavitsainen and Jucker (eds.), 193–221. https://doi.org/10.1075/pbns.107.10bus

Busse, Ulrich. 2008. An inventory of directives in Shakespeare's King Lear. In Jucker and Taavitsainen (eds.), 85–114. https://doi.org/10.1075/pbns.176.06bus

Busse, Ulrich and Beatrix Busse. 2010. Shakespeare. In Jucker and Taavitsainen (eds.), 247–281. https://doi.org/10.1515/9783110214284.4.247

Butters, Ronald R. 1980. Narrative *go* "say." *American Speech* 55(4). 304–307. https://doi.org/10.2307/454573

Campbell, Lyle. 2021. *Historical linguistics: An introduction*, 4th ed. Cambridge, MA: MIT Press.

Carroll, Ruth. 1999. The Middle English recipe as text-type. *Neuphilologische Mitteilungen* 100(1). 27–42. www.jstor.org/stable/43315278

Carroll, Ruth. 2004. Middle English recipes: Vernacularisation of a text-type. In Irma Taavitsainen and Päivi Pahta (eds.), *Medical and scientific writing in late Medieval English*, 174–196. Cambridge: Cambridge University Press.

Chapman, Don. 2008. "You belly-guilty bag": Insulting epithets in Old English. *Journal of Historical Pragmatics* 9(1). 1–19. https://doi.org/10.1075/jhp.9.1.02cha

Cichosz, Anna. 2018. Parenthetical reporting clauses in the history of English: The development of quotative inversion. *English Language and Linguistics* 23(1). 183–214. https://doi.org/10.1017/S1360674317000594

Claridge, Claudia. 2010. News discourse. In Jucker and Taavitsainen (eds.), 587–620. https://doi.org/10.1515/9783110214284.7.587

Claridge, Claudia. 2012. Styles, registers, genres, text types. In Bergs and Brinton (eds.), vol. 1, 237–253. https://doi.org/10.1515/9783110251593.237

Claridge, Claudia. 2013. The evolution of three pragmatic markers: *As it were, so to speak/say* and *if you like. Journal of Historical Pragmatics* 14(2). 162–184. https://doi.org/10.1075/jhp.14.2.01cla

Claridge, Claudia. 2017a. Discourse-based approaches. In Brinton (ed.), 185–217. https://doi.org/10.1017/9781316286562.008

Claridge, Claudia. 2017b. Voices in medieval history writing. *Nordic Journal of English Studies* 17(1). 7–40. https://doi.org/10.35360/njes.393

Claridge, Claudia. 2021. Discourse representation in Early Modern English historiography. In Grund and Walker (eds.) 212–237. https://doi.org/10.1093/oso/978019091 8064.003.0009

Claridge, Claudia and Leslie Arnovick. 2010. Pragmaticalisation and discursisation. In Jucker and Taavitsainen (eds.), 165–192. https://doi.org/10.1515/9783110214284 .3.165

Claridge, Claudia and Merja Kytö (eds.). 2020. *Punctuation in context: Past and present perspectives*. Bern: Peter Lang. https://doi.org/10.3726/b16021

Cohn, Dorrit. 1978. *Transparent minds: Narrative modes for presenting consciousness in fiction*. Princeton, NJ: Princeton University Press. https://doi.org/10.1515/ 9780691213125

Collins, Daniel E. 2001. *Reanimated voices: Speech reporting in a historical-pragmatic perspective*. Amsterdam: John Benjamins. https://doi.org/10.1075/pbns.85

Conboy, Martin. 2010. *The language of newspapers: Sociohistorical perspectives*. London: Continuum.

Crystal, David. 2015. *Making a point: The persnickety story of English punctuation*. London: Profile Books.

Crystal, David and Ben Crystal. 2002. *Shakespeare's words: A glossary and language companion*. London: Penguin Books.

Culpeper, Jonathan. 1996. Towards an anatomy of impoliteness. *Journal of Pragmatics* 25. 349–367. https://doi.org/10.1016/0378-2166(95)00014-3

Culpeper, Jonathan. 2009. Historical sociopragmatics: An introduction. *Journal of Historical Pragmatics* 10(2). 179–186. (Reprinted in Culpeper [ed.] 2011a.) https:// doi.org/10.1075/jhp.10.2.02cul

Culpeper, Jonathan. 2010. Historical pragmatics. In Cummings (ed.), 188–192.

Culpeper, Jonathan (ed.). 2011a. *Historical sociopragmatics*. Amsterdam: John Benjamins (Originally published as *Journal of Historical Pragmatics* 10(2) 2009.) https://doi.org/10.1075/bct.31

Culpeper, Jonathan. 2011b. *Impoliteness: Using language to cause offence*. Cambridge: Cambridge University Press. https://doi.org/10.1017/CBO9780511975752

Culpeper, Jonathan and Dawn Archer. 2008. Requests and directives in Early Modern English trial proceedings and play texts, 1640–1760. In Jucker and Taavitsainen (eds.), 45–84. https://doi.org/10.1075/pbns.176.05cul

Culpeper, Jonathan and Jane Demmen. 2011. Nineteenth-century English politeness: Negative politeness, conventional indirect requests and the rise of the individual self. *Journal of Historical Pragmatics* (Special issue on "Understanding historical (im)politeness" ed. by Marcel Bax and Dániel Z. Kádár) 12(1–2). 49–81. https://doi .org/10.1075/jhp.12.1-2.03cul

Culpeper, Jonathan and Merja Kytö. 2000. Data in historical pragmatics: Spoken interaction (re)cast as writing. *Journal of Historical Pragmatics* 1(2). 175–199. https://doi.org/10.1075/jhp.1.2.03cul

Culpeper, Jonathan and Merja Kytö. 2010. *Early Modern English dialogues: Spoken interaction as writing*. Cambridge: Cambridge University Press.

Culpeper, Jonathan and Elena Semino. 2000. Constructing witches and spells: Speech acts and activity types in Early Modern England. *Journal of Historical Pragmatics* 1 (1). 97–116. https://doi.org/10.1075/jhp.1.1.08cul

Culpeper, Jonathan, Michael Haugh, and Dániel Z. Kádár (eds.). 2017. *The Palgrave handbook of linguistic (im)politeness*. London: Palgrave Macmillan. https://doi.org/ 10.1057/978-1-137-37508-7

Culy, Christopher. 1996. Null objects in English recipes. *Language Variation and Change* 8. 91–124. https://doi.org/10.1017/S0954394500001083

Cummings, Louise (ed.). 2010. *The pragmatics encyclopedia*. New York: Routledge. https://doi.org/10.4324/9780203873069

Cummins, Chris. 2019. *Pragmatics*. Edinburgh: Edinburgh University Press. https://doi .org/10.1515/9781474440042

D'Arcy, Alexandra. 2017. *Discourse-pragmatic variation in context: Eight hundred years of LIKE*. Amsterdam: John Benjamins. https://doi.org/10.1075/slcs.187

D'Arcy, Alexandra. 2021. Reconfiguring quotation over time and the system-internal rise of BE *like*. In Grund and Walker (eds.), 73–101. https://doi.org/10.1093/oso/978 0190918064.003.0004

Davidse, Kristen, Simon De Wolf, and An Van Linden. 2015. The development of modal and discourse marker uses of *(there/it is/I have) no doubt. Journal of Historical Pragmatics* 16(1). 25–58. https://doi.org/10.1075/jhp.16.1.02dav

Devitt, Amy J. 2020. The blurring boundaries of genres-in-use: Principles and implications for rhetorical genre studies for English historical linguistics. In Peter Grund and Megan Harman (eds.), *Studies in the history of the English language VIII: Boundaries and boundary-crossings in the history of English*, 45–72. Berlin: De Gruyter Mouton. https://doi.org/10.1515/9783110643282-003

Diemer, Stefan. 2013. Recipes and food discourse in English – a historical menu. In Gerhardt et al. (eds.), 139–155. https://doi.org/10.1075/clu.10.06die

Diewald, Gabriele. 2011. Pragmaticalization (defined) as grammaticalization of discourse functions. *Linguistics* 49(2). 365–390. https://doi.org/10.1515/ling.2011.011

Diller, Hans-Jürgen and Manfred Görlach (eds.). 2001. *Towards the history of English as a history of genres*. Heidelberg: Universitätsverlag C. Winter.

DiMeo, Michelle and Sara Pennell (eds.). 2013. *Reading and writing recipe books 1500–1800*, 68–92. Manchester: Manchester University Press.

Dinkin, Aaron J. 2018. It's no problem to be polite: Apparent-time change in responses to thanks. *Journal of Sociolinguistics* 22(2). 190–215. https://doi.org/10.1111/josl .12278

Doty, Kathleen. 2010. Courtroom discourse. In Jucker and Taavitsainen (eds.), 621–650. https://doi.org/10.1515/9783110214284.7.621

El-Mahallawi, Basma Mahmoud Mohamed. 2018. The use of thanking expressions and their intensifiers from Early Modern to Present Day English. *FJHJ* (Journal of

Arts and Humanities, Minia University) 86(4). 903–920. https://journals
.ekb.eg/article_174628.html (accessed August 24, 2021).

Enkvist, Nils Erik. 1986. More about the textual functions of the Old English adverbial *þa*. In Dieter Kastovsky and Aleksander Szwedek (eds.), *Linguistics across historical and geographical boundaries: In honour of Jacek Fisiak on the occasion of his fiftieth birthday*, vol. 1, 301–309. Berlin: Mouton de Gruyter. https://doi.org/10.1515/9783 110856132.301

Enkvist, Nils Erik and Brita Wårvik. 1987. Old English *þa*, temporal chains, and narrative structure. In Anna Giacalone Ramat, Onofrio Carruba, and Giuliano Bernini (eds.), *Papers from the 7th International Conference on Historical Linguistics*, 221–237. Amsterdam: John Benjamins. https://doi.org/10.1075/cilt.48.17enk

Erman, Britt and Ulla-Britt Kotsinas. 1993. Pragmaticalization: The case of *ba'* and *you know*. *Studier i modern språkvetenskap* (Acta Universitatis Stockholmiensis, Stockholm Studies in Modern Philology, New Series 10), 76–93 Stockholm: Almqvist & Wiksell.

Evans, Mel. 2021. "Saying the woordes or the lyke": Speech representation in sixteenth-century correspondence. In Grund and Walker (eds.), 183–211. https://doi.org/10 .1093/oso/9780190918064.003.0008

Evans, Nicholas. 2007. Insubordination and its uses. In Irina Nikolaeva (ed.), *Finiteness: Theoretical and empirical foundations*, 366–431. Oxford: Oxford University Press.

Facchinetti, Roberta, Nicholas Brownlees, Birte Bös, and Udo Fries. 2012. *News as changing texts: Corpora, methodologies and analysis*. Newcastle upon Tyne: Cambridge Scholars Publishing. https://doi.org/10.1515/east-2012-0006

Farrelly, Michael and Elena Seoane. 2012. Democratization. In Nevalainen and Traugott (eds.), 392–401. https://doi.org/10.1093/oxfordhb/9780199922765.013.0033

Fischer, Kerstin (ed.). 2006. *Approaches to discourse particles*. Amsterdam: Elsevier. https://doi.org/10.1163/9780080461588

Fischer, Olga. 2007. *Morphosyntactic change: Formal and functional perspectives*. Oxford: Oxford University Press.

Fischer, Olga, Anette Rosenbach, and Dieter Stein (eds.). 2000. *Pathways of change: Grammaticalization in English*. Amsterdam: John Benjamins. https://doi.org/10 .1075/slcs.53

Fitzmaurice, Susan M. 2004. Subjectivity, intersubjectivity and the historical construction of interlocutor stance: From stance markers to discourse markers. *Discourse Studies* 6. 427–448. https://doi.org/10.1177/1461445604046585

Fitzmaurice, Susan M. 2010. Literary discourse. In Jucker and Taavitsainen (eds.), 679–704. https://doi.org/10.1515/9783110214284.7.679

Fitzmaurice, Susan M. and Irma Taavitsainen (eds.). 2007. *Methods in historical pragmatics*. Berlin: Mouton de Gruyter. https://doi.org/10.1515/9783110197822

Fleischman, Suzanne. 1990. Philology, linguistics, and the discourse of the medieval text. *Speculum* 65. 19–37. https://doi.org/10.2307/2864470

Fludernik, Monika. 1993. *The fictions of language and languages of fiction: The linguistic representation of speech and consciousness*. New York: Routledge.

Fraser, Bruce. 1988. Types of English discourse markers. *Acta Linguistica Hungarica* 38. 19–33.

Fries, Udo. 1983. Diachronic textlinguistics. In Shiro Hattori and Kazuko Inoue (eds.), *Proceedings of the XIIIth International Congress of Linguists, August 29–September 4, 1982*, 1013–1015. Tokyo: Tokyo Press.

Fries, Udo. 2009. Crime and punishment. In Jucker (ed.), 13–30. https://doi.org/10
    .1075/pbns.187.04fri

Fries, Udo. 2012. Newspapers. In Bergs and Brinton (eds.), vol. 1, 1063–1075. https://
    doi.org/10.1515/9783110251593.1063

Gehweiler, Elke. 2008. From proper name to primary interjection: The case of *gee!*
    Journal of Historical Pragmatics 9(1). 71–93. https://doi.org/10.1075/jhp.9.1.05geh

Gerhardt, Cornelia, Maximiliane Forbenius, and Susanne Ley (eds.). 2013. *Culinary
    linguistics: The chef's special.* Amsterdam: John Benjamins. https://doi.org/10.1075/
    clu.10

Görlach, Manfred. 2001. A history of text types: A componential analysis. In Diller and
    Görlach (eds.), 47–88.

Görlach, Manfred. 2008. Text types and language history: The cooking recipe. In *Text
    types and the history of English*, 121–140. Berlin: Mouton de Gruyter. https://doi.org/
    10.1515/9783110197167.121

Grund, Peter. 2003. The golden formula: Genre conventions of alchemical recipes in the
    Middle English period. *Neuphilologische Mitteilungen* 104(4). 455–475. www
    .jstor.org/stable/43343990

Grund, Peter. 2007. From tongue to text: The transmission of the Salem witchcraft
    examination records. *American Speech* 82(2). 119–150. https://doi.org/10.1215/000
    31283-2007-005

Grund, Peter. 2017a. Description, evaluation and stance: Exploring the forms and
    functions of speech descriptors in Early Modern English. *Nordic Journal of English
    Studies* 16(1). 41–73. https://doi.org/10.35360/njes.394

Grund, Peter. 2017b. Sociohistorical approaches. In Brinton (ed.), 218–244. https://doi
    .org/10.1017/9781316286562.009

Grund, Peter. 2018. Beyond speech representation: Describing and evaluating speech in
    Early Modern English prose fiction. *Journal of Historical Pragmatics* 19(2).
    265–285. https://doi.org/10.1075/jhp.00022.gru

Grund, Peter. 2020. What it means to describe speech: Pragmatic variation and change
    in speech descriptors in Late Modern English. In Merja Kytö and Erik Smitterberg
    (eds.), *Late Modern English: Novel encounters*, 295–314. Amsterdam: John
    Benjamins. https://doi.org/10.1075/slcs.214.13gru

Grund, Peter. 2021a. The metalinguistic description of speech and fictional language:
    Exploring speech reporting verbs and speech descriptors in Late Modern English. In
    Grund and Walker (eds.), 102–130. https://doi.org/10.1093/oso/9780190918064.003.0005

Grund, Peter. 2021b. *The sociopragmatics of stance: Community, language, and the
    witness depositions from the Salem witch trials.* Amsterdam: John Benjamins. https://
    doi.org/10.1163/9789004390652_009

Grund, Peter J. and Terry Walker. 2021a. Speech representation in the history of
    English: Introduction. In Grund and Walker (eds.), 1–28. https://doi.org/10.1093/oso/
    9780190918064.003.0001

Grund, Peter J. and Terry Walker (eds.). 2021b. *Speech representation in the history of
    English: Topics and approaches.* Oxford: Oxford University Press. https://doi.org/10
    .1093/oso/9780190918064.003.0001

Grzega, Joachim. 2005. *Adieu, bye-bye, cheerio*: The ABC of leave-taking in English
    language history. *Onomasiology Online* 6. 56–64. www1.ku.de/SLF/EngluVglSW/
    grzega1051.pdf (accessed August 24, 2021)

Grzega, Joachim. 2008. *Hāl, Hail, Hello, Hi*: Greetings in English language history. In Jucker and Taavitsainen (eds.), 165–193. https://doi.org/10.1075/pbns.176.10grz

Güldemann, Tom, Manfred von Roncador, and Wim van der Wurff. 2002. A comprehensive bibliography of reported discourse. In Tom Güldemann and Manfred von Roncador (eds.), *Reported discourse: A meeting ground for different linguistic domains*, 363–415. Amsterdam: John Benjamins. https://doi.org/10.1075/tsl.52.23gul

Häcker, Martina. 2019. Kinship or friendship? The word *cousin* as a term of address for non-relatives in Middle English. *Journal of Historical Pragmatics* 20(1). 96–131. https://doi.org/10.1075/jhp.17005.hac

Haselow, Alexander. 2012. Discourse organization and the rise of final *then* in the history of English. In Irén Hegedüs and Alexandra Fodor (eds.), *English historical linguistics 2010*, 153–175. Amsterdam: John Benjamins. https://doi.org/10.1075/cilt.325.07has

Heine, Bernd, Gunther Kaltenböck, Tania Kuteva, and Haiping Long. 2021. *The rise of discourse marke*rs. Cambridge: Cambridge University Press. https://doi.org/10.1017/9781108982856

Herlyn, Anne. 1999. So he says to her, he says, "Well," he says . . . Multiple dialogue introducers from a historical perspective. In Andreas H. Jucker, Gerd Fritz, and Franz Lebsanft (eds.), *Historical discourse analysis*, 313–330. Amsterdam: John Benjamins. https://doi.org/10.1075/pbns.66.13her

Hernández-Campoy, Juan Manuel, and Juan Camilo Conde-Silvestre. 2012. *The handbook of historical sociolinguistics*. Chichester, West Sussex: Wiley-Blackwell. https://doi.org/10.1002/9781118257227

Hirota, Tomoharu and Laurel J. Brinton. 2023. "You betcha I'm a Merican": The rise of YOU BET as a pragmatic marker. *International Journal of Corpus Linguistics* Published online February 23, 2023. https://doi.org/10.1075/ijc121060.hir

Höglund, Mikko and Kaj Syrjänen. 2016. Corpus of Early American Literature. *ICAME Journal* 40(1). 17–38. https://doi.org/10.1515/icame-2016-0003

Holmes, Janet. 1988. Paying compliments: A sex preferential politeness strategy. *Journal of Pragmatics* 12(4). 445–465. https://doi.org/10.1016/0378-2166(88)90005-7

Honegger, Thomas. 2003. "And if ye wol nat so, my lady sweete, thane preye I thee, [. . .].": Forms of address in Chaucer's Knight's Tale. In Taavitsainen and Jucker (eds.), 61–84. https://doi.org/10.1075/pbns.107.05hon

Hope, Jonathan. 1993. Second person singular pronouns in records of Early Modern "spoken" English. *Neuphilologische Mitteilungen* 94(1). 83–100. www.jstor.org/stable/43345931

Hope, Jonathan. 2003. *Shakespeare's grammar*. London: The Arden Shakespeare.

Hopper, Paul J. 1991. On some principles of grammaticization. In Traugott and Heine (eds.), vol. 1, 17–35. https://doi.org/10.1075/tsl.19.1.04hop

Hopper, Paul J. and Elizabeth Closs Traugott. 2003. *Grammaticalization*, 2nd ed. Cambridge: Cambridge University Press. https://doi.org/10.1017/CBO9781139165525

Huang, Yan. 2010. Anglo-American and European continental traditions. In Cummings (ed.), 13–15.

Huang, Yan. 2017a. Introduction: What is pragmatics. In Huang (ed.), 1–18.

Huang, Yan (ed.). 2017b. *The Oxford handbook of pragmatics*. Oxford: Oxford University Press. https://doi.org/10.1093/oxfordhb/9780199697960.001.0001

Huddleston, Rodney and Geoffrey K. Pullum et al. 2002. *The Cambridge grammar of the English language*. Cambridge: Cambridge University Press. https://doi.org/10.1017/9781316423530

Hundt, Marianne and Anne-Christine Gardner. 2017. Corpus-based approaches: Watching English change. In Brinton (ed.), 96–130. https://doi.org/10.1017/9781316286562.005

Jacobs, Andreas and Andreas H. Jucker. 1995. The historical perspective in pragmatics. In Jucker (ed.), 3–33. https://doi.org/10.1075/pbns.35.04jac

Jacobsson, Mattias. 2002. *Thank you* and *thanks* in Early Modern English. *ICAME Journal* 26. 63–80.

Jucker, Andreas H. (ed.). 1995. *Historical pragmatics: Pragmatic developments in the history of English*. Amsterdam: John Benjamins. https://doi.org/10.1075/pbns.35

Jucker, Andreas H. 1997. The discourse marker *well* in the history of English. *English Language and Linguistics* 1(1). 91–110. https://doi.org/10.1017/S136067430000037X

Jucker, Andreas H. 1998. Historical pragmatics: An interdisciplinary approach. In Raimund Borgmeier, Herbert Grabes, and Andreas H. Jucker (eds.), *Anglistentag 1997 Giessen proceedings*, 3–7. Trier: Wissentschaftlicher Verlag Trier.

Jucker, Andreas H. 2000a. Slanders, slurs and insults on the road to Canterbury: Forms of verbal aggression in Chaucer's *Canterbury Tales*. In Irma Taavitsainen, Terttu Nevalainen, Päivi Pahta, and Matti Rissanen (eds.), *Placing Middle English in context*, 369–390. Berlin: Mouton de Gruyter. https://doi.org/10.1515/9783110869514.369

Jucker, Andreas H. 2000b. *Thou* in the history of English: A case for historical semantics or pragmatics? In Christiane Dalton-Puffer and Nikolaus Ritt (eds.), *Words: Structure, meaning, function: A Festschrift for Dieter Kastovsky*, 153–163. Berlin: Mouton de Gruyter. https://doi.org/10.1515/9783110809169.153

Jucker, Andreas H. 2002. Discourse markers in Early Modern English. In Richard Watts and Peter Trudgill (eds.), *Alternative histories of English*, 210–230. London: Routledge.

Jucker, Andreas H. 2006a. Historical pragmatics. In Brown (ed.), 329–331. https://doi.org/10.1016/B0-08-044854-2/00340-0

Jucker, Andreas H. 2006b. "Thou art so loothly and so oold also": The use of *ye* and *thou* in Chaucer's *Canterbury Tales*. *Anglistik* 17(2). 57–72.

Jucker, Andreas H. 2008. Historical pragmatics. *Language and Linguistics Compass* 2 (5). 894–906. https://doi.org/10.1111/j.1749-818X.2008.00087.x

Jucker, Andreas H. (ed.) 2009a. *Early Modern English news discourse: Newspapers, pamphlets and scientific news discourse*. Amsterdam: John Benjamins. https://doi.org/10.1075/pbns.187

Jucker, Andreas H. 2009b. Speech act research between armchair, field and laboratory: The case of compliments. *Journal of Pragmatics* 41(8). 1611–1635. https://doi.org/10.1016/j.pragma.2009.02.004

Jucker, Andreas H. 2011a. Greetings and farewells in Chaucer's *Canterbury Tales*. In Päivi Pahta and Andreas H. Jucker (eds.), *Communicating early English manuscripts*, 229–240. Cambridge: Cambridge University Press.

Jucker, Andreas H. 2011b. Positive and negative face as descriptive categories in the history of English. *Journal of Historical Pragmatics* (Special issue on "Understanding historical (im)politeness" ed. by Marcel Bax and Dániel Z. Kádár) 12(1–2). 178–197. https://doi.org/10.1075/jhp.12.1-2.08juc

Jucker, Andreas H. 2012a. Changes in politeness cultures. In Nevalainen and Traugott (eds.), 422–433. https://doi.org/10.1093/oxfordhb/9780199922765.013.0036

Jucker, Andreas H. 2012b. Pragmatics in the history of linguistic thought. In Keith Allan and Kasia M. Jaszczolt (eds.), *The Cambridge handbook of pragmatics*, 495–512. Cambridge: Cambridge University Press. https://doi.org/10.1017/CBO9781139022453.027

Jucker, Andreas H. 2013. Corpus pragmatics. In Jan-Ola Östmann and Jef Verschueren (eds.), *Handbook of Pragmatics (2013)*, 1–17. Amsterdam: John Benjamins. https://doi.org/10.1075/hop.17.cor3

Jucker, Andreas H. 2015. Pragmatics of fiction: Literary uses of *uh* and *um*. *Journal of Pragmatics* 86. 63–67. https://doi.org/10.1016/pragma.2015.05.012

Jucker, Andreas H. 2017. Speech acts and speech act sequences: Greetings and farewells in the history of American English. *Studia Neophilologica* 89(s1). 39–58. https://doi.org/10.1080/00393274.2017.1358662

Jucker, Andreas H. 2018. Apologies in the history of English: Evidence from the *Corpus of Historical American English*. *Corpus Pragmatics* 2(4). 375–398. https://doi.org/10.1007/s41701-018-0038-y

Jucker, Andreas H. 2019. Speech act attenuation in the history of English: The case of apologies. *Glossa: A Journal of General Linguistics* 4(1). 1–25. https://doi.org/10.5334/gjgl.878

Jucker, Andreas H. 2020. *Politeness in the history of English: From the Middle Ages to the present day*. Cambridge: Cambridge University Press. https://doi.org/10.1017/9781108589147

Jucker, Andreas H. and Manuel Berger. 2014. The development of discourse presentation in *The Times* 1833–1988. *Media History* 20(1). 67–87. https://doi.org/10.1080/13688804.2013.879793

Jucker, Andreas H. and Joanna Kopaczyk. 2017. Historical (im)politeness. In Culpeper et al. (eds.), 433–459. https://doi.org/10.1057/978-1-137-37508-7_17

Jucker, Andreas H. and Irma Taavitsainen. 2000. Diachronic speech act analysis: Insults from flyting to flaming. *Journal of Historical Pragmatics* 1(1). 67–95. https://doi.org/10.1075/jhp.1.1.07juc

Jucker, Andreas H. and Irma Taavitsainen. 2008a. Apologies in the history of English: Routinized and lexicalized expressions of responsibility and regret. In Jucker and Taavitsainen (eds.), 229–244. https://doi.org/10.1075/pbns.176.12juc

Jucker, Andreas H. and Irma Taavitsainen (eds.). 2008b. *Speech acts in the history of English*. Amsterdam: John Benjamins. https://doi.org/10.1075/pbns.176

Jucker, Andreas H. and Irma Taavitsainen (eds.). 2010. *Historical pragmatics*. (Handbooks of Pragmatics, vol. 8.) Berlin: De Gruyter Mouton. https://doi.org/10.1515/9783110214284

Jucker, Andreas H. and Irma Taavitsainen. 2013. *English historical pragmatics*. Edinburgh: Edinburgh University Press. https://doi.org/10.1515/9780748644704

Jucker, Andreas H. and Irma Taavitsainen. 2014a. Complimenting in the history of American English: A metacommunicative expression analysis. In Taavitsainen et al. (eds.), 257–276. https://doi.org/10.1075/pbns.243.16juc

Jucker, Andreas H. and Irma Taavitsainen. 2014b. Diachronic corpus pragmatics: Intersections and interactions. In Taavitsainen et al. (eds.), 3–26. https://doi.org/10.1075/pbns.243.03juc

Jucker, Andreas H., Irma Taavitsainen, and Gerold Schneider. 2012. Semantic corpus trawling: Expressions of "courtesy" and "politeness" in the Helsinki Corpus. In Carla

Suhr and Irma Taavitsainen (eds.), *Developing corpus methodology for historical pragmatics* (Studies in Variation, Contacts and Change in English, vol. 11) https://varieng .helsinki.fi/series/volumes/11/jucker_taavitsainen_schneider/ (accessed June 7, 2022)

Kohnen, Thomas. 2000. Explicit performatives in Old English: A corpus-based study of directives. *Journal of Historical Pragmatics* 1(2). 301–321. https://doi.org/10.1075/ jhp.1.2.07koh

Kohnen, Thomas. 2004. Methodological problems in corpus-based historical pragmatics. The case of English directives. In Karin Aijmer and Bengt Altenberg (eds.), *Advances in corpus linguistics. Papers from the 23rd International Conference on English Language Research on Computerized Corpora (ICAME 23) Göteborg 22– 26 May 2002*, 237–247. Amsterdam: Rodopi.

Kohnen, Thomas. 2007a. "Connective profiles" in the history of English texts: Aspects of orality and literacy. In Ursula Lenker and Anneli Meurman-Solin (eds.), *Connectives in the history of English*, 289–308. https://doi.org/10.1075/cilt.283.14koh

Kohnen, Thomas. 2007b. Text types and the methodology of diachronic speech act analysis. In Fitzmaurice and Taavitsainen (eds.), 139–166. https://doi.org/10.1515/9 783110197822.139

Kohnen, Thomas. 2008a. Directives in Old English. Beyond politeness? In Jucker and Taavitsainen (eds.), 27–44. https://doi.org/10.1075/pbns.176.04koh

Kohnen, Thomas. 2008b. Linguistic politeness in Anglo-Saxon England? A study of Old English address terms. *Journal of Historical Pragmatics* 9(1). 140–158. https:// doi.org/10.1075/jhp.9.1.11koh

Kohnen, Thomas. 2008c. Tracing directives through text and time. Towards a methodology of a corpus-based diachronic speech act analysis. In Jucker and Taavitsainen (eds.), 295–310. https://doi.org/10.1075/pbns.176.16koh

Kohnen, Thomas. 2010. Religious discourse. In Jucker and Taavitsainen (eds.), 523–547. https://doi.org/10.1515/9783110214284.7.523

Kohnen, Thomas. 2011. Understanding Anglo-Saxon "politeness": Directive constructions with *ic wille / ic wolde. Journal of Historical Pragmatics* (Special issue on "Understanding historical (im)politeness" ed. by Marcel Bax and Dániel Z. Kádár) 12 (1–2). 230–254. https://doi.org/10.1075/jhp.12.1-2.10koh

Kohnen, Thomas. 2012a. Bible translations. In Bergs and Brinton (eds.), vol. 1, 1039–1050. https://doi.org/10.1515/9783110251593.1039

Kohnen, Thomas. 2012b. Prayers in the history of English: A corpus-based study. In Merja Kytö (ed.), *English corpus linguistics: Crossing paths*, 165–180. Amsterdam: Rodopi. https://doi.org/10.1163/9789401207935_009

Kohnen, Thomas. 2015a. Religious discourse and the history of English. In Irma Taavitsainen, Merja Kytö, Claudia Claridge, and Jeremy Smith (eds.), *Developments in English: Expanding electronic evidence*, 178–194. Cambridge: Cambridge University Press.

Kohnen, Thomas. 2015b. Speech acts: A diachronic perspective. In Aijmer and Rühlemann (eds.), 52–83. https://doi.org/10.1017/CBO9781139057493.004

Kohnen, Thomas. 2017a. Anglo-Saxon expressives: Automatic historical speech-act analysis and philological intervention. *Anglistik* 28(1). 43–56.

Kohnen, Thomas. 2017b. Non-canonical speech acts in the history of English. *Zeitschrift für Anglistik und Amerikanistik* 65(3). 303–318. https://doi.org/10.1515/zaa-2017-0030

Kohnen, Thomas, Tanja Rütten, and Ingvilt Marcoe. 2011. Early Modern English religious prose: A conservative genre? In Paul Rayson, Sebastian Hoffmann, and

Geoffrey Leech (eds.), *Methodological and historical dimensions of corpus linguistics* (Varieng: Studies in Variation, Contacts and Change, vol. 6). https://varieng.helsinki.fi/series/volumes/06/kohnen_et_al/

Kopytko, Roman. 1995. Linguistic politeness strategies in Shakespeare's plays. In Jucker (ed.), 515–540. https://doi.org/10.1075/pbns.35.27kop

Krug, Manfred. 1998. British English is developing a new discourse marker, *innit*? A study in lexicalisation based on social, regional and stylistic variation. *Arbeiten aus Anglistik und Amerikanistik* 23. 145–197.

Kryk-Kastovsky, Barbara. 2006. Impoliteness in Early Modern English courtroom discourse. *Journal of Historical Pragmatics* 7(2). 213–243. https://doi.org/10.1075/jhp.7.2.04kry

Kytö, Merja. 2010. Data in historical pragmatics. In Jucker and Taavitsainen (eds.), 33–67. https://doi.org/10.1515/9783110214284.2.33

Kytö, Merja and Terry Walker. 2003. The linguistic study of Early Modern English speech-related texts: How "bad" can "bad" be? *Journal of English Linguistics* 31(3). 221–248. https://doi.org/10.1177/0075424203257260

Kytö, Merja, Peter J. Grund, and Terry Walker. 2011. *Testifying to language and life in Early Modern England*. Amsterdam: John Benjamins. CD-ROM, https://doi.org/10.1075/z.162

Labov, William. 1972. Some principles of linguistic methodology. *Language in Society* 1(1). 97–120. https://doi.org/10.1017/S0047404500006576

Labov, William. 1994. *Principles of linguistic change*. Vol. 1: *Internal factors*. Cambridge, MA: Blackwell.

Lakoff, Robin Tolmach. 1973. The logic of politeness; or, minding your p's and q's. In Claudia Corum and T. Cedric Smith-Stark (eds.), *Papers from the Ninth Regional Meeting of the Chicago Linguistic Society*, 292–305. Chicago, IL: Chicago Linguistic Society.

Lakoff, Robin Tolmach. 2005. Civility and its discontents: Or, getting in your face. In Robin T. Lakoff and Ide Sachiko, *Broadening the horizon of linguistic politeness*, 23–43. Amsterdam: John Benjamins. https://doi.org/10.1075/pbns.139.05lak

Landert, Daniela. 2019. Function-to-form mapping in corpora: Historical corpus pragmatics and the study of stance expressions. In Carla Suhr, Terttu Nevalainen, and Irma Taavitsainen (eds.), *From data to evidence in English language research*, 169–190. Leiden: Brill. https://doi.org/10.1163/9789004390652_009

Lass, Roger. 1999. Phonology and morphology. In Roger Lass (ed.), *The Cambridge history of the English language*. Vol. III, *1476–1776*, 56–186. Cambridge: Cambridge University Press. https://doi.org/10.1017/CHOL9780521264761.004

Leech, Geoffrey. 1983. *Principles of pragmatics*. New York: Routledge. https://doi.org/10.4324/9781315835976

Leech, Geoffrey. 1999. The distribution and function of vocatives in American and British English conversation. In Hilde Hasselgård and Signe Oksefjell (eds.), *Out of corpora: Studies in honour of Stig Johansson*, 117–118. Amsterdam: Rodopi.

Leech, Geoffrey. 2014. *The pragmatics of politeness*. Oxford: Oxford University Press. https://doi.org/10.1093/acprof:oso/9780195341386.001.0001

Leech, Geoffrey and Mick Short. 2007[1981]. *Style in fiction: A linguistic introduction to English fictional prose*, 2nd ed. Harlow: Pearson Education.

Leech, Geoffrey and Martin Weisser. 2003. Generic speech act annotation for task-oriented dialogues. In Dawn Archer, Paul Rayson, Andrew Wilson, and Tony McEnery (eds.), *Proceedings of the Corpus Linguistics 2003 Conference*, 441–446. Lancaster: Centre for Computer Corpus Research on Language Technical Papers, Lancaster University. https://citeseerx.ist.psu.edu/viewdoc/download?do i=10.1.1.371.4462&rep=rep1&type=pdf (accessed October 19, 2021)

Leech, Geoffrey, Marianna Hundt, Christian Mair, and Nicholas Smith. 2009. *Change in contemporary English: A grammatical study*. Cambridge: Cambridge University Press. https://doi.org/10.1017/CBO9780511642210

Lehmann, Christian 2015[1995]. *Thoughts on grammaticalization*, 3rd ed. Language Science Press. https://langsci-press.org/catalog/book/88 (accessed June 7, 2022)

Leitner, Magdalena. 2013. *Thou* and *you* in Late Middle Scottish and Early Modern Northern English witness depositions. *Journal of Historical Pragmatics* 23(1). 100–129. https://doi.org/10.1075/jhp.14.1.04lei

Lenker, Ursula 2000. *Soþlice* and *witodlice*: Discourse markers in Old English. In Fischer et al. (eds.), 224–249. https://doi.org/10.1075/slcs.53.12len

Lenker, Ursula. 2010. *Argument and rhetoric: Adverbial connectives in the history of English*. Berlin: De Gruyter Mouton. https://doi.org/10.1515/9783110216066

Lewis, Diane M. 2012. Late Modern English: Pragmatics and discourse. In Bergs and Brinton (eds.), vol. 1, 901–915. https://doi.org/10.1515/9783110251593.901

Locher, Miriam A. and Andreas H. Jucker (eds.). 2017. *Pragmatics of fiction*. Berlin: De Gruyter Mouton. https://doi.org/10.1515/9783110431094

Longacre, Robert E. 1976. Mystery particles and affixes. In Salikoko S. Mufwene, Carol A. Walker, and Sanford B. Steever (eds.), *Papers from the twelfth regional meeting of the Chicago Linguistic Society*, 468–475. Chicago, IL: Chicago Linguistic Society.

López-Couso, María José and Belén Méndez-Naya. 2014. On the origin of parenthetical constructions: Epistemic/evidential parentheticals with *seem* and impersonal *think*. In Taavitsainen et al. (eds.), 189–212. https://doi.org/10.1075/pbns.243.12lop

Los, Bettelou and Ans van Kemenade. 2012. Information structure and syntax in the history of English. In Bergs and Brinton (eds.), vol. 2, 1475–1490. https://doi.org/10 .1515/9783110251609.1475

Louviot, Elise. 2016. *Direct speech in* Beowulf *and other Old English narrative poems*. Cambridge: D. S. Brewer. www.jstor.org/stable/10.7722/j.ctt19x3hzx

Lutzky, Ursula 2012a. *Discourse markers in Early Modern English*. Amsterdam: John Benjamins. https://doi.org/10.1075/pbns.227

Lutzky, Ursula. 2012b. *Why* and *what* in Early Modern English drama. In Manfred Markus, Yoko Iyeiri, and Reinhard Heuberger (eds.), *Middle and Modern English corpus linguistics: A multi-dimensional approach*, 177–189. Amsterdam: John Benjamins. https://doi.org/10.1075/scl.50.16lut

Lutzky, Ursula. 2015. Quotations in Early Modern English witness depositions. In Arendholz et al. (eds.), 343–367. https://doi.org/10.1515/9783110427561-016

Lutzky, Ursula. 2021. Initiating direct speech in Early Modern prose fiction and witness depositions. In Grund and Walker (eds.), 51–72. https://doi.org/10.1093/oso/97801 90918064.003.0003

Magnusson, Lynne. 1999. *Shakespeare and social dialogue: Dramatic language and Elizabethan letters*. Cambridge: Cambridge University Press. https://doi.org/10 .1017/CBO9780511483745

Mair, Christian. 2006. *Twentieth-century English: History, variation and standardization.* Cambridge: Cambridge University Press. https://doi.org/10.1017/CBO9780511486951

Manes, Joan and Nessa Wolfson. 1981. The compliment formula. In Florian Coulmas (ed.), *Conversational routine: Explorations in standardized communication situations and prepatterned speech*, 115–132. The Hague: Mouton. https://doi.org/10.1515/9783110809145.115

Mazzon, Gabriella. 2000. Social relations and forms of address in the *Canterbury Tales*. In Dieter Kastovsky and Arthur Mettinger (eds.), *The history of English in a social context: A contribution to historical sociolinguistics*, 135–168. Berlin: Mouton de Gruyter. https://doi.org/10.1515/9783110810301.135

Mazzon, Gabriella. 2003. Pronouns and nominal address in Shakespearean English: A socio-affective marking system in transition. In Taavitsainen and Jucker (eds.), 223–249. https://doi.org/10.1075/pbns.107.11maz

Mazzon, Gabriella. 2010. Address terms. In Jucker and Taavitsainen (eds.), 351–376. https://doi.org/10.1515/9783110214284.5.351

McColm, Daniel and Graeme Trousdale. 2019. Whatever happened to *whatever*? In Nuria Yáñez-Bouza, Emma Moore, Linda van Bergen, and Willem Hollman (eds.), *Categories, constructions and change in English syntax*, 81–104. Cambridge: Cambridge University Press.

McHale, Brian. 1978. Free indirect discourse: A survey of recent accounts. *PTL: A Journal for Descriptive Poetics and Theory of Literature* 3. 249–287.

McIntyre, Dan and Brian Walker. 2011. Discourse presentation in Early Modern English writing: A preliminary corpus-based investigation. *International Journal of Corpus Linguistics* 6(1). 101–130. https://doi.org/10.1075/ijcl.16.1.05mci

Meehan, Teresa. 1991. It's like, "What's happening in the evolution of like?" A theory of grammaticalization. *Kansas Working Papers in Linguistics* (ed. by Kumiko Ichihasi and Mary Sarah Lim) 16. 37–52. https://doi.org/10.17161/KWPL.1808.423

Mey, Jacob L. 2001. *Pragmatics: An introduction*, 2nd ed. Oxford: Blackwell.

Miranda García, Antonio and Javier Calle-Martín. 2012. Compiling the Málaga Corpus of Late Middle English Scientific Prose. In Vázquez (ed.), 51–65.

Moessner, Lilo. 2010. Directive speech acts: A cross-generic diachronic study. *Journal of Historical Pragmatics* 11(2). 219–249. https://doi.org/10.1075/jhp.11.2.03moe

Moore, Colette. 2002. Reporting direct speech in Early Modern slander depositions. In Donka Minkova and Robert Stockwell (eds.), *Studies in the history of the English language: A millennial perspective*, 399–416. Berlin: Mouton de Gruyter. https://doi.org/10.1515/9783110197143.3.399

Moore, Colette. 2006. The use of *videlicet* in Early Modern slander depositions: A case of genre-specific grammaticalization. *Journal of Historical Pragmatics* 7(2). 245–263. https://doi.org/10.1075/jhp.7.2.05moo

Moore, Colette. 2011. *Quoting speech in early English*. Cambridge: Cambridge University Press.

Moore, Colette. 2015. Histories of talking about talk: *Quethen, quoth, quote*. In Arendholz et al. (eds.), 254–270. https://doi.org/10.1515/9783110427561-012

Moore, Colette. 2016. Visual pragmatics: Speech presentation and Middle English manuscripts. In Merja Kytö and Päivi Pahta (eds.), *The Cambridge handbook of English historical linguistics*, 481–496. Cambridge: Cambridge University Press. https://doi.org/10.1017/CBO9781139600231.029

Moore, Colette. 2020. The path not taken: Parentheses and written direct speech in Early Modern printed books. In Claridge and Kytö (eds.), 85–101.

Moore, Colette. 2021. Before quotation marks: Quotative parentheses in early printed works. In Grund and Walker (eds.), 29–50. https://doi.org/10.1093/oso/9780190918064 .003.0002

Moskowich, Isabel, Luis Puente-Castelo, Begoña Crespo-García, and Gonzalo Camiña-Rioboó. 2021. *The Coruña Corpus of English Scientific Writing: Challenges and reward.* www.researchgate.net/publication/348338219_The_Coruna_Corpus_of_ English_Scientific_Writing_Challenge_and_Reward

Mulo Farenkia, Bernard. 2012. Face-saving strategies in responding to gratitude expressions: Evidence from Canadian English. *International Journal of English Linguistics* 2(4): 1–11.

Narrog, Heiko and Bernd Heine. 2021. *Grammaticalization.* Oxford: Oxford University Press.

Nevala, Minna. 2002. *Youre moder send a letter to the*: Pronouns of address in private correspondence from Late Middle to Late Modern English. In Helena Raumolin-Brunberg, Minna Nevala, Arja Nurmi, and Matti Rissanen (eds.), *Variation past and present: VARIENG studies on English for Terttu Nevalainen*, 135–159. Helsinki: Société Néophilologique.

Nevala, Minna. 2003. Family first: Address and subscription formulae in English family correspondence from the fifteenth to the seventeenth century. In Taavitsainen and Jucker (eds.), 147–176. https://doi.org/10.1075/pbns.107.08nev

Nevala, Minna. 2004. Inside and out: Address forms in 17th- and 18th-century letters. *Journal of Historical Pragmatics* 5(2). 273–298. https://doi.org/10.1075/jhp .5.2.07nev

Nevala, Minna. 2010. Politeness. In Jucker and Taavitsainen (eds.), 419–450. https://doi .org/10.1515/9783110214284.6.419

Nevalainen, Terttu. 2006a. *An introduction to Early Modern English.* Edinburgh: Edinburgh University Press. https://doi.org/10.1515/9780748626366

Nevalainen, Terttu. 2006b. Synchronic and diachronic variation. In Brown (ed.), 356–363. https://doi.org/10.1016/B0-08-044854-2/01521-2

Nevalainen, Terttu and Helena Raumolin-Brunberg. 1995. Constraints on politeness. The pragmatics of address formulae in early English. In Jucker (ed.), 541–601. https://doi .org/10.1075/pbns.35.28nev

Nevalainen, Terttu and Helena Raumolin-Brunberg. 2003. *Historical sociolinguistics: Language change in Tudor and Stuart England.* London: Longman.

Nevalainen, Terttu and Elizabeth Closs Traugott (eds.). 2012. *The Oxford handbook of the history of English.* Oxford: Oxford University Press. https://doi.org/10.1093/ oxfordhb/9780199922765.001.0001

Noë, Alva. 2015. A case against the phrase "no problem." *NPR: Cosmos & Culture, Commentary on Science and Society* 13(7). February 11. www.npr.org/sections/13.7/ 2015/02/01/383060338/a-case-against-the-phrase-no-problem (accessed August 24, 2021).

Overstreet, Maryann and George Yule. 2021. *General extenders: The forms and functions of a new linguistic category.* Cambridge: Cambridge University Press. https:// doi.org/10.1017/9781108938655

Pahta, Päivi and Irma Taavitsainen. 2010. Scientific discourse. In Jucker and Taavitsainen (eds.), 549–586. https://doi.org/10.1515/9783110214284.7.549

Pakis, Valentine. A. 2011. Insults, violence, and the meaning of *lytegian* in the Old English *Battle of Maldon*. *Journal of Historical Pragmatics* 12(1). 198–229. https://doi.org/10.1075/jhp.12.1-2.09pak

Pakkala-Weckström, Mari. 2005. *The dialogue of love, marriage and* maistrie *in Chaucer's* Canterbury Tales. (Mémoires de la Société Néophilologique de Helsinki, LXVII.) Helsinki: Société Néophilologique.

Pakkala-Weckström, Mari. 2008. "No botmeles bihestes." Various ways of making promises in Middle English. In Jucker and Taavitsainen (eds.), 133–162. https://doi.org/10.1075/pbns.176.08pak

Pakkala-Weckström, Mari. 2010. Chaucer. In Jucker and Taavitsainen (eds.), 219–245. https://doi.org/10.1515/9783110214284.4.219

Palander-Collin, Minna. 1997. A medieval case of grammaticalization, *me thinks*. In Matti Rissanen, Merja Kytö, and Kirsi Heikkonen (eds.), *Grammaticalization at work: Studies of long-term developments in English*, 371–403. Berlin: Mouton de Gruyter. https://doi.org/10.1515/9783110810745.371

Palander-Collin, Minna. 2010. Correspondence. In Jucker and Taavitsainen (eds.), 651–677. https://doi.org/10.1515/9783110214284.7.651

Parkes, M. B. 1992. *Pause and effect: An introduction to the history of punctuation in the West*. Abingdon: Routledge.

Pilkington, Adrian. 2010. Literary pragmatics. In Cummings (ed.), 251–253.

Pons-Sanz, Sara M. 2019. Speech representation as a narrative technique in *Sir Gawain and the Green Knight. The Review of English Studies* 70(294). 209–230. https://doi.org/10.1093/res/hgy094

Quintana-Toledo, Elena. 2009. Middle English medical recipes. *Studia Anglica Posnaniensia* 45(2). 21–38. https://doi.org/10.2478/v10121-009-0014-5

Quirk, Randolph. 1971. Shakespeare and the English language. In Kenneth Muir and S. Schoenbaum (eds.), *A new companion to Shakespeare studies*, 67–82. Cambridge: Cambridge University Press. (Reprinted in Salmon and Burgess (eds.) 1987, 3–21.)

Quirk, Randolph, Sidney Greenbaum, Geoffrey Leech, and Jan Svartvik. 1985. *A comprehensive grammar of the English language*. London: Longman.

Raumolin-Brunberg, Helena. 1996. Forms of address in early English correspondence. In Terttu Nevalainen and Helena Raumolin-Brunberg (eds.), *Sociolinguistics and language history: Studies based on the Corpus of Early English Correspondence*, 167–181. Amsterdam: Rodopi.

Replogle, Carol. 1973. Shakespeare's salutations: A study in stylistic etiquette. *Studies in Philology* 70(2). 172–186. (Reprinted in Salmon and Burgess (eds.), 101–116.)

Richman, Gerald. 1986. Artful slipping in Old English. *Neophilologus* 70(2). 279–291. https://doi.org/10.1007/BF00553322

Romaine, Suzanne and Deborah Lange. 1991. The use of *like* as a marker of reported speech and thought: A case of grammaticalization in progress. *American Speech* 66 (30). 227–279. https://doi.org/10.2307/455799

Rudanko, Juhani. 1993. *Pragmatic approaches to Shakespeare: Essays on* Othello, Coriolanus *and* Timon of Athens. Lanham, MD: University Press of America.

Rudanko, Juhani. 2004. "I wol sterve": Negotiating the issue of a lady's consent in Chaucer's poetry. *Journal of Historical Pragmatics* 5(1). 137–158. https://doi.org/10.1075/jhp.5.1.07rud

Rütten, Tanja. 2012. Forms of early mass communication: The religious domain. In Nevalainen and Traugott (eds.), 295–303. https://doi.org/10.1093/oxfordhb/9780199922765.013.0026

Salmon, Vivian. 1967. Elizabethan colloquial English in Falstaff plays. *Leeds Studies in English* n.s. 1. 37–70. (Reprinted in Salmon and Burgess (eds.), 37–70.)

Salmon, Vivian and Edwina Burgess (eds.). 1987. *A reader in the language of Shakespearean drama: Essays*. Amsterdam: John Benjamins. https://doi.org/10.1075/sihols.35

Schneider, Klaus P. 2005. *No problem, you're welcome, anytime*: Responding to thanks in Ireland, England, and the USA. In Anne Barron and Klaus P. Schneider (eds.), *The Pragmatics of Irish English*, 101–139. Berlin: Mouton de Gruyter. https://doi.org/10.1515/9783110898934.101

Schuelke, Gertrude L. 1958. "Slipping" in indirect discourse. *American Speech* 33(2). 90–98. https://doi.org/10.2307/453177

Searle, John R. 1969. *Speech acts: An essay in the philosophy of language*. Cambridge: Cambridge University Press. https://doi.org/10.1017/CBO9781139173438

Searle, John R. 1975. Indirect speech acts. In Peter Cole and Jerry L. Morgan (eds.), *Syntax and semantics*, vol. 3: *Speech acts*, 59–82. New York: Academic Press. https://doi.org/10.1163/9789004368811_004

Searle, John R. 1976. A classification of illocutionary acts. *Language in Society* 5(1). 1–23. https://doi.org/10.1017/S0047404500006837

Sell, Roger D. (ed.). 1985. Politeness in Chaucer: Suggestions towards a methodology for pragmatic stylistics. *Studia Neophilologica* 57. 175–185. https://doi.org/10.1080/00393278508587918

Sell, Roger D. 1991. *Literary pragmatics*. London: Routledge. https://doi.org/10.4324/978315735849

Sell, Roger D. 1994. Postdisciplinary philology: Culturally relativistic pragmatics. In Francisco Fernández, Miguel Fuster, and Juan José Calvo (eds.), *English historical linguistics 1992*, 29–36. Amsterdam: John Benjamins. https://doi.org/10.1075/cilt.113.05sel

Semino, Elena and Mick Short. 2004. *Corpus stylistics: Speech, writing and thought representation in a corpus of English writing*. New York: Routledge. https://doi.org/10.4324/9780203494073

Skeat, Walter W. 1894. *The complete works of Geoffrey Chaucer*. Oxford: Clarendon Press.

Stein, Dieter. 1985. Perspectives on historical pragmatics. *Folia Linguistica Historica* 6. 347–355. https://doi.org/10.1515/flih.1985.6.2.347

Stein, Dieter. 2003. Pronominal usage in Shakespeare: Between sociolinguistics and conversational analysis. In Taavitsainen and Jucker (eds.), 251–307. https://doi.org/10.1075/pbns.107.12ste

Su, Hang. 2020. Local grammars and diachronic speech act analysis: A case study of apology in the history of American English. *Journal of Historical Pragmatics* 21(1). 109–133. https://doi.org/10.1075/jhp.00038.su

Sylwanowicz, Marta. 2016. *And þan it wole be a good oynement restoratif* . . . Pre- and postnominal adjectives in Middle English medical recipes. *Anglica – An International Journal of English Studies* 2. 57–71.

Sylwanowicz, Marta. 2017. Medieval medical writings and their readers: Communication of knowledge in Middle English medical recipes. *Linguistica Silensiana* 38. 111–124.

Taavitsainen, Irma. 2001. Middle English recipes: Genre characteristics, text type features and underlying traditions of writing. *Journal of Historical Pragmatics* 2. 85–114. https://doi.org/10.1075/jhp.2.1.05taa

Taavitsainen, Irma. 2012. Historical pragmatics. In Bergs and Brinton (eds.), vol. 2, 1457–1474. https://doi.org/10.1515/9783110251609.1457

Taavitsainen, Irma. 2015. Historical pragmatics. In Douglas Biber and Randi Reppen (eds.), *The Cambridge handbook of English corpus linguistics*, 252–268. Cambridge: Cambridge University Press. https://doi.org/10.1017/CBO9781139764377.015

Taavitsainen, Irma and Susan Fitzmaurice. 2007. Historical pragmatics: What it is and how to do it. In Fitzmaurice and Taavitsainen (eds.), 11–36. https://doi.org/10.1515/9783110197822.11

Taavitsainen, Irma and Turo Hiltunen. 2019. *Late Modern English medical texts: Writing medicine in the eighteenth century.* Amsterdam: John Benjamins. CD-ROM. https://doi.org/10.1075/z.221

Taavitsainen, Irma and Andreas H. Jucker (eds.). 2003. *Diachronic perspectives on address term systems.* Amsterdam: John Benjamins. https://doi.org/10.1075/pbns.107

Taavitsainen, Irma and Andreas H. Jucker. 2007. Speech act verbs and speech acts in the history of English. In Fitzmaurice and Taavitsainen (eds.), 107–138. https://doi.org/10.1515/9783110197822.107

Taavitsainen, Irma and Andreas H. Jucker. 2008. "Methinks you seem more beautiful than ever": Compliments and gender in the history of English. In Jucker and Taavitsainen (eds.), 195–228. https://doi.org/10.1075/pbns.176.11taa

Taavitsainen, Irma and Andreas H. Jucker. 2010a. Expressive speech acts and politeness in eighteenth-century English. In Raymond Hickey (ed.), *Eighteenth-century English: Ideology and change*, 159–181. Cambridge: Cambridge University Press. https://doi.org/10.1017/CBO9780511781643.010

Taavitsainen, Irma and Andreas H. Jucker. 2010b. Trends and developments in historical pragmatics. In Jucker and Taavitsainen (eds.), 3–30. https://doi.org/10.1515/97 83110214284.1.3

Taavitsainen, Irma and Andreas H. Jucker. 2015. Twenty years of historical pragmatics: Origins, developments and changing thought styles. *Journal of Historical Pragmatics* 16(1). 1–24. https://doi.org/10.1075/jhp.16.1.01taa

Taavitsainen, Irma and Andreas H. Jucker. 2016. Forms of address. In Carole Hough (ed.), *The Oxford handbook of names and naming*. Oxford: Oxford University Press. https://doi.org/10.1093/oxfordhb/9780199656431.013.54

Taavitsainen, Irma and Andreas H. Jucker. 2020. Digital pragmatics in English. In Svenja Adolphs and Dawn Knight (eds.), *Routledge handbook of English language and digital humanities*, 107–124. Abingdon: Routledge. https://doi.org/10.4324/978 1003031758-7

Taavitsainen, Irma and Päivi Pahta. 2010. *Early Modern English medical texts.* Amsterdam: John Benjamins. CD-ROM. https://doi.org/10.1075/z.160

Taavitsainen, Irma, Päivi Pahta, and Martti Mäkinen (eds.). 2005. *Middle English medical texts*. Amsterdam: John Benjamins.

Taavitsainen, Irma, Andreas H. Jucker, and Jukka Tuominen (eds.). 2014. *Diachronic corpus pragmatics*. Amsterdam: John Benjamins. https://doi.org/10.1075/pbns.243

Thompson, Sandra A. and Anthony Mulac. 1991. A quantitative perspective on the grammaticization of epistemic parentheticals in English. In Traugott and Heine (eds.), vol. 2, 313–329. https://doi.org/10.1075/tsl.19.2.16tho

Toolan, Michael. 2006. Speech and thought: Representation of. In Brown (ed.), 698–710. https://doi.org/10.1016/B0-08-044854-2/00546-0

Traugott, Elizabeth Closs. 1982. From propositional to textual and expressive meanings: Some semantic-pragmatic aspects of grammaticalization. In Winfred P. Lehmann and Yakov Malkiel (eds.), *Perspectives on historical linguistics*, 245–271. Amsterdam: John Benjamins. https://doi.org/10.1075/cilt.24.09clo

Traugott, Elizabeth Closs. 1995/97 (version of 11/97). The role of the development of discourse markers in a theory of grammaticalization. Paper presented at the 12th International Conference on Historical Linguistics, Manchester, UK, August 1995. https://web.stanford.edu/~traugott/papers/discourse.pdf (accessed June 7, 2022).

Traugott, Elizabeth Closs. 1997. Subjectification and the development of epistemic meaning: The case of *promise* and *threaten*. In Toril Swan and Olaf Jansen Westvik (eds.), *Modality in Germanic languages: Historical and comparative perspectives*, 185–210. Berlin: Mouton de Gruyter. https://doi.org/10.1515/9783110889932.185

Traugott, Elizabeth Closs. 2006. Historical pragmatics. In Laurence R. Horn and Gregory Ward (eds.), *The handbook of pragmatics*, 538–561. Oxford: Blackwell. https://doi.org/10.1002/9780470756959.ch24

Traugott, Elizabeth Closs. 2008. The state of English language studies: A linguistic perspective. In Marianne Thormählen (ed.), *English now: Selected papers from the 20th IAUPE Conference in Lund 2007*, 199–225. Lund: Centre for Languages and Literature, Lund University.

Traugott, Elizabeth Closs. 2020. The development of "digressive" discourse-topic shift markers in English. *Journal of Pragmatics* 156. 121–135. https://doi.org/10.1016/j.pragma.2019.02.002

Traugott, Elizabeth Closs. 2022. *Discourse structuring markers in English*. Amsterdam: John Benjamins. https://doi.org/10.1075/cal.33

Traugott, Elizabeth Closs and Richard B. Dasher. 2002. *Regularity in semantic change*. Cambridge: Cambridge University Press. https://doi.org/10.1017/CBO9780511486500

Traugott, Elizabeth Closs and Bernd Heine (eds.). 1991. *Approaches to Grammaticalization*, 2 vols. Amsterdam: John Benjamins. https://doi.org/10.1075/tsl.19.1, https://doi.org/10.1075/tsl.19.2

Valkonen, Petteri. 2008. Showing a little promise: Identifying and retrieving explicit illocutionary acts from a corpus of written prose. In Jucker and Taavitsainen (eds.), 247–272. https://doi.org/10.1075/pbns.176.14val

Vandelanotte, Lieven. 2009. *Speech and thought representation in English: A cognitive-functional approach*. Berlin: Mouton de Gruyter. https://doi.org/10.1515/9783110215373

Vandelanotte, Lieven. 2012. Quotative *go* and *be like*: Grammar and grammaticalization. In Isabelle Buchstaller and Ingrid van Alphen (eds.), *Quotatives: Cross-linguistic and cross-disciplinary perspectives*, 173–202. Amsterdam: John Benjamins. https://doi.org/10.1075/celcr.15.11van

Vandelanotte, Lieven. 2021. Clearer contours: The stylisation of free indirect speech in nineteenth-century fiction. In Grund and Walker (eds.), 131–155. https://doi.org/10.1093/oso/9780190918064.003.0006

Vázquez, Nila (ed.). 2012. *Creation and use of historical English corpora in Spain.* Newcastle upon Tyne: Cambridge Scholars Publishing.

Visser, F. Th. 1972. *An historical syntax of the English language.* Part two: *Syntactical units with one verb.* Leiden: E. J. Brill.

Wales, Kathleen M. 1983. *Thou* and *you* in Early Modern English: Brown and Gilman re-appraised. *Studia Linguistica* 37. 107–125. https://doi.org/10.1111/j.1467-9582.1983.tb00316.x

Walkden, George. 2013. The status of *hwæt* in Old English. *English Language and Linguistics* 17(3). 465–488. https://doi.org/10.1017/S1360674313000129

Walker, Terry. 2007. Thou *and* you *in Early Modern English dialogues.* Amsterdam: John Benjamins. https://doi.org/10.1075/pbns.158

Walker, Terry and Peter J. Grund. 2017. "Speaking base approbious words": Speech representation in Early Modern English witness depositions. *Journal of Historical Pragmatics* 18(1). 1–28. https://doi.org/10.1075/jhp.18.1.01wal

Walker, Terry and Peter J. Grund. 2020. Saying, crying, replying, and pursuing: Speech reporting expressions in Early Modern English. In Ewa Jonsson and Tove Larsson (eds.), *Voices of the past and present – Studies of involved, speech-related and spoken texts. In honor of Merja Kytö,* 64–78. Amsterdam: John Benjamins. https://doi.org/10.1075/scl.97.05wal

Walker, Terry and Peter J. Grund. 2021. Free indirect speech, slipping, or a system in flux? Exploring the continuum between direct and indirect speech in Early Modern English. In Grund and Walker (eds.), 156–182. https://doi.org/10.1093/oso/9780190918064.003.0007

Walker, Terry and Merja Kytö. 2011. Linguistic variation and change in the depositions. In Kytö et al., 215–245. https://doi.org/10.1075/z.162.07ch7

Waltereit, Richard. 2006. The rise of discourse markers in Italian: A specific type of language change. In Fischer (ed.), 61–76. https://doi.org/10.1163/9780080461588_005

Wårvik, Brita. 2013. *Perspectives on narrative discourse markers: Focus on Old English þa.* Turku: Åbo Akademi University.

Weisser, Martin. 2015. Speech act annotation. In Aijmer and Rühlemann (eds.), 84–113. https://doi.org/10.1017/CBO9781139057493.005

Wierzbicka, Anna. 2006. Anglo scripts against "putting pressure" on other people and their linguistic manifestations. In Cliff Goddard (ed.), *Ethnopragmatics: Understanding discourse in cultural context,* 31–63. Berlin: Mouton de Gruyter. https://doi.org/10.1515/9783110911114.31

Wierzbicka, Anna. 2012. The history of English seen as the history of ideas: Cultural change reflected in different translations of the New Testament. In Nevalainen and Traugott (eds.), 434–445. https://doi.org/10.1093/oxfordhb/9780199922765.013.0037

Williams, Graham. 2017. *Wine min Unferð*: Courtly speech and a reconsideration of (supposed) sarcasm in *Beowulf. Journal of Historical Pragmatics* (Special issue on "Historical (socio)pragmatics at present" ed. by Matylda Włodarczyk and Irma Taavitsainen) 18(2). 175–194. https://doi.org/10.1075/jhp.00001.wil

Williams, Graham. 2018. *Sincerity in medieval English language and literature.* London: Palgrave Macmillan. https://doi.org/10.1057/978-1-137-54069-0

Wiltschko, Martina. 2021. *The grammar of interactional language.* Cambridge: Cambridge University Press. https://doi.org/10.1017/9781108693707

Wischer, Ilse. 2000. Grammaticalization versus lexicalization: "Methinks" there is some confusion. In Fischer et al. (eds.), 355–370. https://doi.org/10.1075/slcs .53.17wis

Włodarczyk, Matylda. 2007. *Pragmatic aspects of reported speech: The case of Early Modern English courtroom discourse.* Frankfurt am Main: Peter Lang.

Sources (dictionaries, corpora, primary texts)

ARCHER-3.2 = *A Representative Corpus of Historical English Registers 3.2.* 1990– 1993/2002/2007/2010/2013/2016. Originally compiled under the supervision of Douglas Biber and Edward Finegan at Northern Arizona University and University of Southern California; modified and expanded by subsequent members of a consortium of universities. Current member universities are Bamberg, Freiburg, Heidelberg, Helsinki, Lancaster, Leicester, Manchester, Michigan, Northern Arizona, Santiago de Compostela, Southern California, Trier, Uppsala, Zurich.

Benson, Larry D. 1986. *The Riverside* Chaucer, 3rd ed. Boston: Houghton Mifflin.

Bosworth, Joseph. 2014. *An Anglo-Saxon Dictionary Online* (Bosworth-Toller). Ed. by Thomas Northcote Toller, Christ Sean, and Ondřej Tichy. Prague: Faculty of Arts, Charles University. https://bosworthtoller.com

The Corpus of Contemporary American English (COCA). 2008–. Compiled by Mark Davies. Available online at www.english-corpora.org/coca

Corpus of Early American Literature (CEAL). See Höglund and Syrjänen (2016).

Corpus of Early English Correspondence Sampler (CEECS). 1998. Compiled by Terttu Nevalainen (leader), Jukka Keränen, Minna Nevala (née Aunio), Arja Nurmi, Minna Palander-Collin, and Helena Raumolin-Brunberg. Department of Modern Languages, University of Helsinki. www2.helsinki.fi/en/researchgroups/ varieng/corpus-of-early-english-correspondence

Corpus of Early English Recipes (CoER). 2002–. See Alonso Almeida et al. (2012).

Corpus of Early English Medical Writing (CEEM). 2005–. See Taavitsainen et al. (eds.) (2005), Taavitsainen and Pahta (eds.) (2010), Taavitsainen and Hiltunen (eds.) (2019). https://varieng.helsinki.fi/CoRD/corpora/CEEM/

A Corpus of English Dialogues 1560–1760 (CED). 2006. Compiled under the super-vision of Merja Kytö (Uppsala University) and Jonathan Culpeper (Lancaster University). www.engelska.uu.se/research/english-language/electronic-resources/ english-dialogues/

The Corpus of English Novels (CEN). Compiled by Hendrik De Smet. https://perswww .kuleuven.be/~u0044428/

Corpus of English Religious Prose (COERP). 2015–1800. Compiled by Thomas Kohnen (project leader), Tanja Rütten, Ingvilt Marcoe, Kirsten Gather, Dorothee Groeger, Anne Döring, and Stefanie Leu. http://coerp.uni-koeln.de/

The Corpus of Historical American English (COHA). 2010. Compiled by Mark Davies. Available online at www.english-corpora.org/coha/

A Corpus of Late 18c Prose. 2003–2010. Compiled by David Denison, Linda van Bergen, and Joana Soliva (formerly Proud). University of Manchester. https://personalpages .manchester.ac.uk/staff/david.denison/late18c.html. Available online at www .humanities.manchester.ac.uk/medialibrary/llc/files/david-denison/orford1.htm

The Corpus of Late Modern English (CLMET). Compiled by Hendrik De Smet. https:// perswww.kuleuven.be/~u0044428/clmet.htm

A Corpus of Late Modern English Prose. 1994. Compiled by David Denison with assistance from Graeme Trousdale and Linda van Bergen. University of Manchester. https://personalpages.manchester.ac.uk/staff/david.denison/LModE_Prose.html

The Corpus of Late Modern English Texts, version 3.0 (CLMET3.0). Compiled by Hendrik De Smet, Hans-Jürgen Diller, and Jukka Tyrkkö. https://perswww .kuleuven.be/~u0044428/clmet3_0.htm

The Corpus of Late Modern English Texts (extended version) (CLMETEV). Compiled by Hendrik De Smet. https://perswww.kuleuven.be/~u0044428/clmetev.htm

Corpus of Middle English Prose and Verse (CMEPV). 2006. The Humanities Text Initiative, University of Michigan. Available online at https://quod.lib.umich.edu/c/cme/

Corpus of Scottish Correspondence (CSC). 2007. Compiled by Anneli Meurman-Solin. University of Helsinki. https://varieng.helsinki.fi/CoRD/corpora/CSC/

Darwin, Charles. 1887. *The Life and Letters of Charles Darwin*, vol. 1, ed. by Francis Darwin. London: John Murray. www.gutenberg.org/files/2087/2087-h/2087-h .htm#link2HCH0006.

Davis, Norman (ed.). 2009. *The Paston letters: A selection in modern spelling.* Oxford: Oxford University Press.

Dictionary of American Regional English (DARE). Frederic G. Cassidy and Joan Houston Hall (eds.). 6 vols. Cambridge, MA: Harvard University Press. https://dare .wisc.edu

Dictionary of Old English Web Corpus (DOEC). 2009. Compiled by Antonette diPaolo Healey with John Price Wilkin and Xin Xiang. Toronto: Dictionary of Old English Project. Available by subscription. https://tapor-library-utoronto-ca.ezproxy .library.ubc.ca/doecorpus/index.html

Early English Books Online Corpus (EEBO). 2017. Compiled by Mark Davies. Available online at www.english-corpora.org/eebo/. See https://proquest .libguides.com/eebopqp. Full version available online at https://quod.lib.umich.edu/ e/eebogroup/

Eighteenth Century Collections Online (ECCO). 2003–. Gale Cengage. See www .gale.com/primary-sources/eighteenth-century-collections-online. Available online at https://quod.lib.umich.edu/e/ecco/

Eighteenth-Century Fiction (ECF). 1996–2015. Ed. by Judith Hawley, Tom Keymer, and John Mullan. Chadwyck-Healey. ProQuest LLC. Available by subscription. http://collections.chadwyck.co.uk/marketing/products/about_ilc.jsp?collection=ecf

An Electronic Text Edition of Depositions 1560–1760. See Kytö et al. (2011).

English Drama (ED). 1996–2014. Ed. by John Barnard et al. Chadwyck-Healey Ltd. ProQuest LLC. Available by subscription. http://collections.chadwyck.com/marketing /home_ed.jsp

Early American Imprints, 1639–1800: A Readex microprint of the works listed in Evan's American Bibliography, Evans numbers 1–39162 (Evans). Worcester, MA: American Antiquarian Society, Readex Microprint. See www.readex.com/products/early-american-imprints-series-i-evans-1639-1800. Available online at https://quod.lib.umich.edu/e/evans/

Hamilton, Saskia (ed.). 2005. *The letters of Robert Lowell.* New York: Farrar, Straus and Giroux.

Hanham, Alison (ed.). 1975. *The Cely letters, 1472–1488.* Oxford: Oxford University Press.

Hansard Corpus. 2015. Compiled by Mark Davies. Available online at www.english-corpora.org/hansard/

The Helsinki Corpus of English Texts (HC). 1991. Department of Modern Languages, University of Helsinki. Compiled by Matti Rissanen (Project leader), Merja Kytö (Project secretary); Leena Kahlas-Tarkka, Matti Kilpiö (Old English); Saara Nevanlinna, Irma Taavitsainen (Middle English); Terttu Nevalainen, Helena Raumolin-Brunberg (Early Modern English). Available online at https://helsinki corpus.arts.gla.ac.uk/display.py?what=index

Historical Thesaurus of English. 2020–. 2nd ed. online. Ed. by Michael Samuels, Christian Kay, Marc Alexander et al. University of Glasgow. https://ht.ac.uk

The Lampeter Corpus of Early Modern English Tracts. Compiled by Josef Schmied, Eva Hertal, Claudia Claridge and Rainer Siemund. http://korpus.uib.no/icame/manuals/LAMPETER/LAMPHOME.HTM

Middle English Dictionary (MED). 1952–2001. Hans Kurath and Sherman Kuhn (eds.). Ann Arbor, MI: University of Michigan Press. Part of the *Middle English compendium.* Francis McSparran (chief ed.). Available online at http://quod.lib.umich.edu/m/mec/

The Movie Corpus (Movies). 2019. Compiled by Mark Davies. Available online at www.english-corpora.org/movies/

Newsbooks at Lancaster. Compiled by Tony McEnery. Lancaster University. www.lancaster.ac.uk/fass/projects/newsbooks/

The New York Times. Chadwyck-Healey Historical Newspapers. http://historynews.chadwyck.com

Nicolson, Marjorie Hope (ed.). 1992. *The Conway letters: The correspondence of Anne, Viscountess Conway, Henry More, and their friends, 1642–1684.* Revised by Sarah Hutton. Oxford: Clarendon Press.

Open Source Shakespeare (OSS). 2003. George Mason University. www.opensource shakespeare.org/

The Old Bailey Corpus, 2.0, 1720–1913. 2016. Compiled by Magnus Huber, Magnus Nissel and Karin Puga. hdl:11858/00-246C-0000-0023-8CFB-2

The Old Bailey Proceedings Online, 1674–1913. 2003–2018. Edited by Tim Hitchcock, Robert Showmaker, Clive Emsley, Sharon Hoard, and Jamie McLauglin et al. Version 8.0, March 2018. www.oldbaileyonline.org

Oxford English Dictionary (OED). 2000–. 3rd ed. online. Michael Proffitt (editor). www.oed.com

ProQuest Historical Newspapers™. Available by subscription. https://about.proquest.com/en/products-services/pq-hist-news/

Rosenthal, Bernard (general ed.). 2013. *Records of the Salem witch-hunts*. Cambridge: Cambridge University Press.

The Times Digital Archive. Available by subscription. Gage Cengage. www.gale.com/intl/c/the-times-digital-archive

The TV Corpus (TV). 2019. Compiled by Mark Davies. Available online at www.english-corpora.org/tv/

Zurich English Newspaper Corpus (ZEN). 1993–2003. Compiled by Udo Fries, Hans Martin Lehmann et al. www.es.uzh.ch/en/Subsites/Projects/zencorpus.html

Index

For EU product safety concerns, contact us at Calle de José Abascal, 56–1°,
28003 Madrid, Spain or eugpsr@cambridge.org.

www.ingramcontent.com/pod-product-compliance
Ingram Content Group UK Ltd.
Pitfield, Milton Keynes, MK11 3LW, UK
UKHW020355140625
459647UK00020B/2481